HEAVEN'S INTERPRETERS

HEAVEN'S INTERPRETERS

WOMEN WRITERS AND RELIGIOUS AGENCY IN NINETEENTH-CENTURY AMERICA

ASHLEY REED

CORNELL UNIVERSITY PRESS

Ithaca and London

Publication of this open monograph was the result of
Virginia Tech's participation in TOME (Toward an Open
Monograph Ecosystem), a collaboration of the Association of American Universities, the Association of
University Presses, and the Association of Research
Libraries. TOME aims to expand the reach of long-form
humanities and social science scholarship including digital
scholarship. Additionally, the program looks to ensure the
sustainability of university press monograph publishing
by supporting the highest quality scholarship and
promoting a new ecology of scholarly publishing in
which authors' institutions bear the publication costs.

Funding from Virginia Tech made it possible to open this
publication to the world.

www.openmonographs.org

First published 2020 by Cornell University Press

Library of Congress Cataloging-in-Publication Data

Names: Reed, Ashley, 1975– author.
Title: Heaven's interpreters : women writers and religious
    agency in nineteenth-century America / Ashley Reed.
Description: Ithaca [New York] : Cornell University Press,
    2020. | Includes bibliographical references and index.
Identifiers: LCCN 2019051194 (print) | LCCN 2019051195
    (ebook) | ISBN 9781501751363 (paperback) |
    ISBN 9781501751387 (pdf) | ISBN 9781501751370 (epub)
Subjects: LCSH: American fiction—Women authors—
    History and criticism. | American fiction—
    19th century—History and criticism. | Religion and
    literature—United States—History—19th century. |
    Women and literature—United States—History—
    19th century. | Women and religion—United
    States—History—19th century. | Fiction—Religious
    aspects. | United States—Religion—19th century.
Classification: LCC PS147 .R44 2020 (print) |
    LCC PS147 (ebook) | DDC 813/.3099287—dc23
LC record available at https://lccn.loc.gov/2019051194
LC ebook record available at https://lccn.loc.gov
    /2019051195

Contents

Acknowledgments

This book began during my time at the University of North Carolina at Chapel Hill under the directorship of Jane Thrailkill, who was everything I could wish for in a mentor: caring and rigorous, kind and professional, able to see through messy drafts and vague, hand-waving descriptions to the kernel of the idea beneath. It was my privilege to be her student, as it is now my delight to be her friend. Other scholars at UNC contributed immeasurably to the book: Philip Gura, Laurie Maffly-Kipp, Tim Marr, and Eliza Richards deserve my utmost gratitude, and Joy Kasson, Matthew Taylor, and Joseph Viscomi each contributed in crucial ways to my career. In addition to these mentors, I was blessed with peers who patiently and repeatedly read drafts of this book, and whose intellectual and emotional support made (long) years of work not only bearable but joyful. My long-standing writing group—Kelly Bezio, Ben Bolling, Angie Calcaterra, Harry Thomas, and Jenn Williamson—deserve more thanks than I can possibly express. It's no exaggeration to say that I couldn't have completed this book without them. Other colleagues provided intellectual and personal support; they include Erin Branch, Katie Carlson-Eastvold, Graham Culbertson, Meredith Farmer, Joe Fletcher, Megan Goodwin, Meredith Malburne-Wade, John D. Martin III, Kate Massie, Christin Mulligan, Will and Sarah Shaw, Heath Sledge, Sarah Tolf, and too many others to name.

The English Department at Virginia Tech has been a wonderfully welcoming place to continue this book; here I'm grateful for guidance from many senior colleagues including Tom Ewing, Virginia Fowler, Bernice Hausman, Peter Potter, and Katrina Powell. I have benefited from a grant-supported writing group (for which many thanks go to Rachel Gabriele and the VT Office of the Provost) that includes Katie Carmichael, Tiffany Drape, Estrella Johnson, Christine Labuski, Erika Meitner, Sarah Ovink, Claire Robbins, Sharone Tomer, and Megan Wawro. I am also constantly buoyed by the friendship and collegiality of Silas Moon Cassinelli, Katharine Cleland, Carolyn Commer, Rachel Gross, Shaily Patel, and Abby Walker.

I must acknowledge some specific debts to mentors and fellow scholars. Melissa Homestead provided advice about navigating the Catharine Maria Sedgwick Papers on microfilm and supplied copies of two unpublished conference papers on Catharine Maria Sedgwick that shaped my thinking in chapter 1. Nicole Livengood provided transcriptions of Elizabeth Stoddard's *Daily Alta California* columns, facilitating my work on chapter 5. And Tazeen Ali shared research in progress on the Women's Mosque of America that informs my conclusion. Additionally, Claudia Stokes provided crucial advice on the publishing process; Jared Hickman gave timely critique at the proposal stage; and Justine Murison has been a miraculously kind and generous mentor since the first moment we met. I am grateful to each of them.

Institutional support for this project has come in the form of a Thomas F. Ferdinand Summer Research Fellowship from the UNC Graduate School, a Richardson Fellowship from the UNC Department of English and Comparative Literature, a faculty mentoring grant from the Virginia Tech Office of the Provost, a Niles Research Grant from the VT College of Liberal Arts and Human Sciences, and a publication support grant from the Virginia Tech Center for Humanities. Start-up funding from Virginia Tech enabled me to hire a developmental editor, Heath Sledge, whose thorough critique was crucial to the revision process. Both UNC and Virginia Tech also provided travel funds that allowed me to present portions of this work at numerous conferences and institutes; while I cannot list all of them here, I'm particularly grateful to audiences at the 2010, 2014, and 2017 Catharine Maria Sedgwick Society Symposia and workshop participants at the 2012 and 2016 Futures of American Studies Institutes for their helpful feedback.

I must also thank the incredible libraries and librarians who have lent their resources and expertise to the book. I owe particular thanks to Tommy Nixon of the UNC Libraries and to Virginia Tech's Newman Library staff for their willingness to fulfill endless interlibrary loan requests and for the incalculable gift of campus mail book delivery. I am also grateful to the staff of the Schlesinger and Houghton Libraries in Cambridge, Massachusetts, and to Beth Burgess and Cindy Cormier of the Harriet Beecher Stowe Center, who welcomed me warmly to Hartford and provided insight and assistance with their collections. English Department staff members at both UNC and Virginia Tech have provided cheerful and efficient support. I'm particularly indebted to Linda Horne and Mark Richardson at UNC and to Kristen Cox, Laura Ferguson, Judy Grady, Patty Morse, Sandra Ross, Sally Shupe, Bridget Szerszynski, and Eve Trager at Virginia Tech.

Portions of chapter 5 appeared as "'I Have No Disbelief': Spiritualism and Secular Agency in Elizabeth Stoddard's *The Morgesons*" in *J19: The Journal of*

Nineteenth-Century Americanists 5, no. 1 (2017): 151–77. I am grateful to the editors of *J19* and to the University of Pennsylvania Press for permission to reprint them here. I also thank the Sterling Library at Yale University, the Harry Ransom Center at the University of Texas at Austin, and the Harriet Beecher Stowe Center for permission to reproduce quotations from the letters of Harriet Beecher Stowe that appear in chapters 4 and 5.

My editor at Cornell University Press, Mahinder Kingra, has been a generous reader of this monograph and has shepherded it (and me) through the process of publication with grace and patience. I am grateful to him, to the editorial and production staff at Cornell, and to the two anonymous readers of the manuscript who provided generative responses that, I trust, improved the final product.

Finally, I am grateful to my family for their unwavering support. To my parents, Ralph and Sharon Reed; my sisters, Heather Turner and Shannon Herring; my brothers-in-law, Richard Turner and Daniel Herring; and my nieces, Grace Turner, Abigail Turner, Eden Herring, and Amelia Herring, I offer my thanks and love.

HEAVEN'S INTERPRETERS

Introduction
Writing Women's Religious Agency
in Nineteenth-Century America

This book engages in a deceptively simple task: it reads for religion in antebellum fiction by American women writers. It explores some of the many ways that the imaginative representation of religious doctrine, ritual, and practice offered nineteenth-century women writers a means for imagining new forms of female agency made possible by a rapidly changing religious-secular milieu. Fiction became the medium for exploring these new forms of agency because it provided a space in which women's religious beliefs and ideas might circulate in the public sphere outside of official sectarian outlets. But fiction also offered an imaginative playground where women might picture to themselves and others new ways of being in the world while remaining faithful to what they took to be sacred truths. For the nineteenth-century women writers I discuss in this book, religious fiction was the arena in which the skeleton of doctrine put on the sinews of personal agency and walked forth into the world.

In some ways it seems impossible not to read for religion in nineteenth-century fiction: antebellum writing by both men and women is saturated with Christian religious language and, at a deeper level, with theological assumptions about the order of the universe. Even the most skeptical of nineteenth-century authors felt compelled to pursue the subject; recall Nathaniel Hawthorne's comment that his erstwhile friend Herman Melville could "neither believe, nor be comfortable in his unbelief," but that he was "too honest and courageous not to try to do one or the other."[1] As the religious historian John Modern has asserted, "any viable description of the nineteenth century must account for how one's identity becomes bound up with one's relationship to the religious."[2]

And yet, despite the ubiquity of religious thought and practice in the period, many critical studies of nineteenth-century literature continue to read not *for* religion but around or even against it. Until fairly recently, as Tracy Fessenden notes, religion received "little attention except when it figure[d] as crucial to a progressive, emancipatory politics (Christian antislavery being the readiest example), and often not even then."[3] The recent rise of secularism studies, which treats our modern condition not as a story about the absence of religion but instead about religion's continued but ever-shifting presence in public and private life, has done much to redress this issue. But the study of women's writing has yet to fully benefit from the insights of secularism studies. This is because critics of women's writing have often taken for granted that religion can serve only as an oppressive force in women's lives rather than a matter of personal choice, an aspect of communal belonging, a vehicle for intellection and self-expression, and a sincere apprehension of the nature of the universe and human existence.

This book approaches religious belief and practice as potential sites for imagining and enacting women's agency, and it demonstrates how writing and publishing religious fiction after the Second Great Awakening made it possible for women writers to envision new agentive possibilities that did not rely on political office, clerical ordination, or the franchise. Often, these new agentive options were made possible through the imaginative adaptation of Protestant doctrine. One bedrock assertion of this project is that rather than bringing about the "loss of theology," as Ann Douglas famously asserted, nineteenth-century women writers engaged in what the religious historian Mary Bednarowski calls "theological creativity": the willingness and ability to adapt existing doctrines, or even to invent new ones, in ways that are meaningful for individuals and often for the community as a whole.[4] The authors I study in this book explored their theological ideas in the medium of fiction because fiction provided a space for religious reflection and for imagining alternative ways of being, believing, and acting in the world.

While nineteenth-century women's writing "does not represent a separate, morally superior female world apart from political, theological, economic, and racial tensions," the entanglement of women and religion in the Western imaginary means that nineteenth-century women's religious fiction was neither written nor read in identical terms to religious fiction by men.[5] While male authors also used fiction to engage with religious questions, published fiction provided a particularly welcoming space for women writers whose exclusion from seminaries and sectarian journals left them with few other outlets for public religious discussion. But more than a last resort for religious debate, fictional genres provided frameworks for exploring the contours and consequences of theological positions. When Augusta Jane Evans, whose work is the subject of this book's second chapter, turned to the genre of woman's fiction to explore the implications of free-will theology for white southern women, she both intervened in an ongoing debate between Calvinist and Arminian thinkers and constructed a model of female agency grounded in Wesleyan theological convictions. For Evans and other women writers, the generic space of the historical novel, the sentimental novel, or the escaped-slave narrative provided imaginative scaffolding for exploring possible forms of female agency, spaces where characters—and by extension authors and readers—could "negotiat[e] belonging to a world."[6]

These new forms of agency were made possible and available by the constantly shifting boundary between the religious and the nonreligious and the attendant reshaping of the appropriately public and the normatively private that marked the decades before the Civil War. The American nineteenth century was characterized by the public dominance of Protestant Christianity, but to make this statement is to raise difficulties rather than to settle them, since nineteenth-century American Protestantism was not monolithic but made up of myriad and ever-multiplying denominations—denominations that were, in turn, constantly engaged in transformations of doctrine and practice. These transformations were shaped by internal theological innovation, external efforts toward reform or retrenchment, and the pressure of religious alternatives ranging from Catholicism to Spiritualism to atheism. The proliferation of internal and external differences within and among Protestant sects, this book argues, produced the conditions of possibility for women's religious and literary innovations. The forms of agency this book reveals are those that thrived in these interstitial spaces, claimed by women authors who were willing to imaginatively inhabit such metaphorical gaps.

To recognize the myriad models of religious agency offered in fiction by nineteenth-century women, this book engages in secular reading rather than secularized reading. In making this distinction I am drawing on the recent wave of immensely productive scholarship that has deconstructed the inaccurate and mystifying pronouncements of the secularization thesis and replaced them with a more robust model for studying the complexities of secular modernity. Whereas the secularization thesis once claimed to trace the increasing privatization of religion or even to predict its eventual disappearance, studies of secularity acknowledge the continuing interpenetration of religious and nonreligious modes of belief, action, and understanding in the modern world. To take the example that is closest to home, the current form of American secularity is one in which a public sphere ostensibly cleansed of religious influence or interference actually remains structured by principles and assumptions directly derived from Protestant Christianity, a status that Winnifred Fallers Sullivan calls "small-p protestantism."[7] The misidentification of secularism as the absence of religion *from* society rather than as a particular post-Protestant configuration *of* society allows for the continuing alignment of what is truly "American" with the assumptions of this post-Protestant paradigm and facilitates the othering and exclusion of any religious group that refuses to conform to them.[8] The result is a secular society in which Christian politicians freely quote the Bible in speeches on the Senate floor but Muslim women are harassed for wearing head scarves in public. The American secular public sphere, in other words, is not free from religion but instead tolerates one form of religious display (fundamentalist Christian proof texting) and is openly hostile to another (Muslim sartorial norms). The antebellum secular situation was, of course, different from our own, and engaging in secular reading enables us to see how the religious-secular conditions that marked the antebellum United States enabled certain forms of religious agency to emerge while foreclosing others. This project demonstrates how nineteenth-century women writers used the imaginative space of fiction to negotiate their secular surrounds and to depict new models of religious agency that were grounded in Protestant theological concepts.

In this book I seek to tell an addition story rather than the paradigmatic "subtraction stories" put forward by narratives of secularization, in which "human beings hav[e] lost, or sloughed off, or liberated themselves from certain earlier, confining horizons, or illusions, or limitations of knowledge."[9] Instead of reading for the absence of religion, this project answers Robert Orsi's call "to approach history and culture with the gods fully present to humans" and to "withhold from absence the intellectual, ethical, and spiritual prestige modernity gives it."[10] It offers a capacious and critical approach to women's religious agency under the conditions of nineteenth-century secularity, examining this complex problem in specific literary, doctrinal, communal, racial, gendered, and geographic contexts. In doing so, it reveals how particular sets of secular conditions present in the nineteenth-century United States made it possible for women writers to imagine new models of agency that accorded with their most deeply held beliefs.

This project approaches nineteenth-century fiction as a collection of imaginative worlds in which women's agency became conceivable precisely insofar as such agency was readable and resonant within the terms of antebellum religious discourse—as it represented what William James called a "living option" for a predominantly Protestant Christian people.[11] Recognizing these new forms of agency requires more than simple translation or explication. Cathy Davidson has written that fiction "cannot be simply 'fit into its historical context,' as if context were some Platonic pigeonhole and all that is dark or obscure in the fiction is illuminated when the text is finally slipped into the right slot."[12] The same is true for the role of religious doctrine in fiction: investigating a text's belief system is not simply a matter of researching the details of Calvinist or Unitarian or Spiritualist doctrine and overlaying them onto a text to produce a legible reading of its (or its author's) theological commitments. While this project addresses aspects of authors' religious identifications, often as expressed in their journals and letters, it would be reductive to suggest that Catharine Maria Sedgwick, because she joined a Unitarian congregation, could only write Unitarianly, that Susan Warner could only write Presbyterianly, or that Harriet Beecher Stowe wrote first Congregationally and then Episcopally. Rather, this project examines how nineteenth-century fiction provided not a transparent window into an author's personal beliefs but an imaginative forum for thinking both through and beyond doctrinal and ecclesiastical difference in ways that allowed for new explorations and expressions of personal and communal agency. Since nineteenth-century novels "construct entire fictive worlds in which the validity of a particular set of beliefs is borne out," the details of doctrine are important because they represent cognitive structures through which individuals and communities understood the meaning of their lives.[13]

Literary genres also provide cognitive and imaginative structures for producing knowledge, and one goal of this book is to tease out linkages between doctrinal structures and literary ones. As Gregory Jackson has demonstrated, nineteenth-century religious fiction was grounded in homiletic models that were instantly recognizable to Christian audiences nursed not only on the Bible but on the *Pilgrim's Progress* and other instructive texts. But our "prevailing theories of genre lack a nuanced understanding of the psychology of highly specialized religious readerships" because those theories continue to be guided by secularized reading conventions.[14] Claudia Stokes has urged scholars of antebellum fiction to "recognize narrative form as an agent of religious instruction and evangelism" since "generic conventionality in the nineteenth century also signaled a loyalty to religious conventions and expectations."[15] Taking up the challenge laid down by Jackson, Stokes, and others, this book demonstrates—through studies of the historical novel, woman's fiction, the fugitive slave narrative, the theological romance, and the Spiritualist novel— that the generic conventions of antebellum fiction were particularly well suited to imagining new possibilities for women's religious agency. Generic conventions, it argues, offer conceptual frameworks for imaginative exploration in much the same way that religious doctrines do. Sometimes these frameworks are cages, but sometimes they are jungle gyms.

It has become a truism of American literary scholarship that texts perform "cultural work"—that they are not only products of culture themselves but that they influence culture in particular ways. This is to say that texts themselves have agency—an agency that is influenced but can never be entirely controlled by the agency of their authors. More than what individual authors do, then, this book is about what *texts* do—how fiction participates in and shapes culture by presenting new historically and culturally contingent models of religious agency. Just as individuals and communities experience agency within the forms and structures available to them—most saliently, for the purposes of this study, religious forms and structures—texts exhibit agency within certain generic boundaries. To ask what a text does is to investigate *both* the world from which that text emerged and the reformed world that it makes narratively viable, and to consider what conditions of existence and possibilities for agency it brings into being.

Women's Religious Writing as American Theological Tradition

This project details how U.S. women authors writing between 1820 and 1865 and in various regional, racial, and political circumstances employed powerful combinations of Protestant doctrine and literary genre to imagine fictional worlds full of new agentive possibilities. It approaches the antebellum public sphere as a discourse community in which theological ideas were not simply handed down from clerical authorities to laypeople but instead were socially created. As Gregory Jackson has argued, in nineteenth-century America "elite religious discourse was shadowed—sometimes even overshadowed—by a wealth of popular narrative materials," and the "'formal' doctrine and theology coming out of synods and seminaries . . . were transformed by remarkable men and women on the ground."[16] Such transformations were significant not only for their effect on the American religious landscape but because they enabled individuals and communities to imagine new ways of being and behaving in the public sphere and new ways of acting in the world.

The texts discussed in this book appeared in the wake of the Second Great Awakening, a wave of religious revivals that swept the newly formed United States between 1790 and 1820. With its emphasis on visible and narratable religious feeling and on the primacy of personal experience, the Awakening, along with the liberalization of the culturally dominant New England Congregationalist churches, began to redistribute religious identity and authority in a process that the religious historian Nathan Hatch has called the "democratization" of American Christianity. The Awakening saw the creation of myriad new religious movements and the rapid growth of existing ones, particularly revivalist sects including the Methodists, Baptists, and Disciples of Christ. The result was that "within a few years of Jefferson's election in 1800, it became anachronistic to speak of [religious] dissent in America—as if there were still a commonly recognized center against which new or emerging groups defined themselves."[17] While religious and social historians continue to debate the origins, outline, and effects of the Second Great Awakening, the early nineteenth century undeniably saw "a widening range of spiritual alternatives that turned antebellum America into a unique spiritual hothouse."[18]

As much as the spate of outdoor revivals that most famously characterized the Second Great Awakening (and most unnerved the leaders of settled denominations like the Congregationalists and Episcopalians), the flurry of pamphlets, printed sermons, tracts, and rebuttals produced during and after it solidified the sense that theological debates among people of different beliefs were best conducted in the print public sphere. In the nineteenth century, Protestant doctrine circulated widely and came under continual debate both explicitly, in sectarian journals and printed sermons, and more subtly in the fictional productions that increasingly occupied the popular imagination. As proscriptions against the writing and publication of fiction that had carried over from the colonial era began to fall away, learning to verbalize the "inner condition of true religion" through the medium of published fiction increasingly offered laypeople a means to enter into a culturally dominant Protestant public sphere whose terms of discourse were often explicitly theological.[19]

Nineteenth-century women writers influenced by the Awakening seized on the opportunity to take part in public religious discourse by producing and publishing poems, essays, sketches, stories, and novels. And just as they decried novels while producing thousands of them, they similarly disclaimed any ambition to be writing or debating "theology" even as they produced texts that engaged deeply with theological ideas. Whereas in the former case, of course, critics have recognized the necessary obfuscations at play and treated women authors as novelists, when it comes to theology, they have often accepted these women's demurrals, approaching works of fiction as alternatives to theological thinking rather than vehicles for it. As I discuss in this book's second chapter, studies of women's religious writing continue to be heavily influenced by Ann Douglas's religious-historical reading of nineteenth-century sentimentalism and by her assertion that women writers and the liberal ministers who imitated them initiated the decline and death of American theology. To make this argument, Douglas narrowly defined *theology* to include only a specific strain of Calvinist systematic dogma; all other forms of nineteenth-century religious thought were dismissed as "sentimental heresy" or "feminine heresy."[20] But as E. Brooks Holifield has demonstrated in his magisterial study *Theology in America*, not only did liberal denominations have theologies of their own, but nineteenth-century definitions of theology "were always sufficiently broad to include a variety of genres, such as sermons and popular tracts, and any history of theology in America must consider such sources." Such popular materials as tracts and novels "joined biblical interpretation to a background theory, explicit or implicit, in a way that constituted 'theology.'"[21] Furthermore, systematic theology was never the only form of theology that circulated in the United States. In my fourth chapter I demonstrate how Harriet Beecher Stowe's novels of the late 1850s and early 1860s worked to unite the traditions of speculative and practical theology, thereby satisfying a "demand that theology be practical" that "reflected not only the imperatives of revivalist religion" but "a long history of reflection that had its roots in ancient philosophy."[22]

To recognize the theologically grounded models of agency made available in women's religious fiction, we must dispense with several misapprehensions: that theology, systematic or otherwise, is the sole property of men; that "religion" as a force was in decline in the nineteenth century; and that religion is always experienced by adherents—particularly women—in the same way. By insisting on the theological contexts and investments of literature written by women, my goal is not to return our field to a time before the advent of cultural studies or to insist that race, gender, class, sexuality, and other embodied concerns be subordinated to spiritual ones. The assumption that spiritual and theological concerns are necessarily divorced from issues of identity and embodiment—and that we as scholars must choose between them—is itself a false binary induced by the secularization thesis. It is certainly true that a turn to discourses of secularism can underpin conservative critical moves. But the best work on religion and secularity recognizes that religious identifications are inextricable from and not reducible to other forms of identity.

It is the transformation of theology through the medium of fiction and the consequences of that transformation for women's agency that this book details. It shows how the realm of published fiction provided a conventional space in which women writers might safely explore theological problems and the ramifications of those problems for women's lives. As Lloyd Pratt has noted, the ability to produce superlative examples of conventional forms was much prized in the first half of the nineteenth century: "convention as much as capacity for novelty set expectations for what qualified as literature."[23] But conventionality also provided, in the words of Lauren Berlant, "a profound placeholder that provide[d] an affective confirmation of the idea of a shared confirming imaginary in advance of inhabiting a material world in which that feeling [could] actually be lived."[24] Fictional genres, in other words, with their established conventions, offered a space in which to imagine new ways of acting in the world.

This project takes up Joanna Brooks's charge that scholars of American literature should approach literary texts as "an archive of heterodox marginal, dissenting, and emergent theologies."[25] I begin with a genre that proliferated in the early years of the new republic: the American historical novel. Writing at the end of the Second Great Awakening and at the beginning of an explosion in print publication and circulation, the early national women authors Lydia Maria Child and Catharine Maria Sedgwick initiated a nineteenth-century tradition of women's writing that engaged deeply with theological questions through the medium of popular literary forms. Struggling with dominant liberal discourses that framed women as irrational and unfit for public life and with a tradition of gothic and seduction novels in which female characters existed primarily as objects of political, economic, and sexual exchange, Child and Sedgwick used the emergent genre of the historical novel to argue for women as individuals capable of exercising religious agency. Their new model of agency was premised on women's active participation in a religious culture increasingly identified with the public circulation of theological debate, and it invoked an influential Unitarian Christology that rejected violent sacrifice and located Christ's salvific power in his living language rather than his mutilated body. Applying this theology to tales of colonial North America anchored by devout women, Child and Sedgwick portrayed America's early women settlers as rational actors capable of participating in an increasingly linguistic and literary public sphere. By grounding women's claims to religious agency in their powerful language rather than their perishable bodies and in narratives of America's national origins, Child and Sedgwick made the case for their own authorship and for the generations of religious women writers who would come after them.

In addition to writing historical novels, Catharine Maria Sedgwick also inaugurated the genre of woman's fiction with her 1822 novel *A New-England Tale*. My second chapter explores woman's fiction as a vehicle for practical theology informed by contemporary doctrinal debates. Sentimental fiction in general and woman's fiction in particular have long been approached by critics as a form committed to promoting an undifferentiated and generalized Protestantism. By eschewing doctrinal debate in favor of an emotional and antitheological "evangelicalism," the argument goes, sentimental fiction contributed to the feminization and privatization of religious belief and thus to the ultimate secularization of the American public sphere. My chapter challenges this critical narrative through a careful reading of Susan Warner's *The Wide, Wide World* and Augusta Jane Evans's *Beulah*. While both novels adopt the standard woman's fiction plot identified by Nina Baym, in which an orphaned girl seeks and finds a new family after years of difficult struggle, Warner's novel takes place in a Calvinist universe of predetermined salvational outcomes while Evans's heroine navigates an Arminian cosmos in which eternal damnation is a real and terrifying possibility. My analysis demonstrates how the seemingly simplistic formal elements of woman's fiction enabled Warner, Evans, and other female authors to contribute to the most pressing theological debate of their day—the extent of human and divine agency—in the space of woman's fiction.

By aligning women's life stories with recognizable doctrinal patterns, woman's fiction worked to claim theology for women while strengthening an ideological alignment between Christianity and whiteness. When Harriet Jacobs chose the genre of sentimental woman's fiction as the vehicle for her anonymized autobiography *Incidents in the Life of a Slave Girl*, she both inherited and transformed this dubious tradition. My third chapter reads Jacobs's *Incidents* as a spiritual autobiography that draws on a nascent tradition of black women's religious narrative founded by the itinerant preachers Jarena Lee and Sojourner Truth. Exploring the moments of confession, repentance, and exhortation that structure Jacobs's narrative reveals how Linda Brent's sexual sin becomes the precondition for religious agency rather than the occasion for its destruction. By claiming a prophetic voice that she subtly but repeatedly likens to that of the slave preacher Nat Turner, Jacobs frames Linda's fall from grace as a necessary rebellion against the hypocrisy of white slaveholding Christianity.

Jacobs's *Incidents* engages in both explicit and implicit conversation with Harriet Beecher Stowe's sentimental blockbuster *Uncle Tom's Cabin* (1852). My fourth chapter explores Stowe's post–*Uncle Tom* novels *The Minister's Wooing* and *Agnes of Sorrento*, which I classify as theological romances. I argue that these texts depict forms of communal religious agency rooted in both Protestant millennialism and Catholic Mariology and intended to suture the widening cultural divisions between practical and speculative theology, between public and private religion, and between the "masculine" realms of business and commerce and the "feminine" realm of the home. The women of Stowe's theological romances find their agency in connection with one another and with the communion of saints, living and dead, who populate their lives. Drawing on the work of critics who have studied Stowe's career-spanning interest in Mary the mother of Jesus, I argue that Stowe's fictional Marys, including Mary Scudder and Virginie de Frontignac of *The Minister's Wooing* and the eponymous heroine of *Agnes of Sorrento*, are simultaneously incarnational and iconographic, both representing Mary and reenacting her active role in Christian history. In stories that revise the origins of American Protestantism, Stowe invokes Mary as an incarnation of spiritual and cultural wholeness and an embodiment of women's religious agency.

My final chapter examines another genre of female-authored fiction that reached beyond the boundaries of doctrinal Protestantism to seek agency in an expanded secular milieu: it uncovers the role of Spiritualist doctrine and practice in Elizabeth Oakes Smith's *Bertha and Lily*, Elizabeth Stoddard's *The Morgesons*, and Kate Field's *Planchette's Diary*. As a set of disruptive religious practices that uncoupled agency from accepted hierarchies of authority and placed power in the joined hands of the weak, the poor, the sick, and the politically disenfranchised, Spiritualist mediumship and spirit communication offered opportunities for sympathetic connection and collaborative action among those with the least access to institutionalized religious and political power. In *The Morgesons*, the Morgeson sisters' mediumistic gifts, including clairvoyance and spirit traveling, enable them to circumvent entrenched romantic, domestic, and economic expectations, while *Bertha and Lily* adapts the village tale to address issues of sexual assault and illegitimacy. Field's *Planchette's Diary* enacts a Spiritualist form of collaboration between Field as editor and "Madame Planchette" as author that would facilitate Field's career as a female public intellectual. These and other Spiritualist novels employed and modeled shared forms of agency at both the textual and the metatextual levels, inaugurating a specifically female form of Spiritualist fiction that offered a new kind of authorial agency to women writers.

I end the book with a conclusion that discusses the difficulty of reading for religion today, as persistent and inaccurate narratives of secularization continue to shape our public and political discourse. I then offer a few examples of women's religious agency in our own time—a time that is remarkably similar in some ways to the antebellum period discussed in the rest of this book. Religious women of the twenty-first-century United States, like their nineteenth-century forebears, have seized the opportunities presented by a range of new media platforms to intervene in public discussions about women's role in the religious and political life of the nation. By adapting their words and actions to their own secular situation, they have forged new models of female religious agency that challenge existing structures of authority while remaining recognizable to co-religionists as extensions of shared beliefs.

From Secularized Reading to Secular Reading

That nineteenth-century fiction shows an abiding concern with matters of religious belief and practice is not a new observation. But until recently many treatments of nineteenth-century religious fiction—and particularly religious fiction written by women—have been hampered by inaccurate historical-theological models that remain stubbornly dependent on the premises of the secularization thesis. Arising from Enlightenment-era philosophical ideas and coming to fruition in the early twentieth century in the sociological theories of Emile Durkheim and Max Weber, versions of the secularization thesis posit, among other things, that Western culture is becoming less religious over time, that religion is a private matter that must be held separate from the public arena of politics and commerce, and (in the strongest versions of the theory) that religion will eventually die out entirely as a result of increasing rationalism and scientific discovery.[26] In some formulations, the thesis traces a narrative of progress (or decline, depending on one's point of view) according to which the irrational superstitions of the past are being gradually replaced by rational certainties; Weber called this process *Entzauberung*, a word usually translated as "disenchantment" that has been more literally limned by the religious historian Molly McGarry as "the elimination of magic from the world."[27]

As one critic has rather waggishly noted, "recent interventions into the secularization thesis of classical sociology have resulted in a new consensus: that secularization never happened."[28] And certainly at the most basic demographic level, the thesis is simply historically inaccurate, at least in the United States, where religious adherence has held steady and occasionally risen over the last two hundred years and where religion has never been successfully shunted to the private sphere but instead remains a matter for public debate and political concern.[29] But this pithy overstatement also points to a gap between the secularization thesis's various descriptive functions and its aspirations to predictiveness. While there can be little doubt that Western cultures look radically different now than they did five hundred or even one hundred years ago, changes at the level of civilizations can rarely be explained as "thoroughgoing metaphysical and epistemological totalit[ies]" that can be traced back to a single cause and projected forward to a utopian future.[30]

Beyond its descriptive inadequacies, bigger problems arise when the secularization thesis is applied prescriptively, as a yardstick to separate the enlightened sheep from the primitive goats. In its strongest form, the thesis has been used to justify the othering of groups not considered sufficiently secularized—those for whom magic has demonstrably *not* been eliminated from their worlds. At the global level it serves as a prop to claims of Western cultural superiority: secularized societies are "the province of an Enlightened and white majority, describing and prescribing a transparent world set apart from primitive enchantments, mystery, and things that [go] bump in the night."[31] At the national and regional level it helps to define what is truly (un-)American: religious individuals and groups are tolerated so long as they behave in ways that do not seem particularly "religious"—so long as their beliefs and practices are "rational, word-centered, nonritualistic, middle class, unemotional, [and] compatible with democracy and the liberal state."[32] Groups and individuals who do not fit these categories—who maintain distinctive ritual practices, engage in charismatic forms of worship, reject or defy the norms of the nuclear family (by embracing polygamy or unrestricted childbearing), or show an affinity for nonmainstream political and economic movements—are grouped together under a "nomenclature of marginalization (cults, sects, primitives, and so on)" and subjected to harassment and discrimination.[33]

Responding both to the historical inaccuracy of the secularization thesis and to the way it undergirds critical discourses that obscure and marginalize religious people and their meaning-making processes, anthropologists, religious historians, cultural theorists, and literary critics have posited various theories of modern secularity as correctives to the secularization thesis. Rather than describing a decline in religious adherence or policing the division between a "public" realm of disembodied rationalism and a "private" realm of emotionality, superstition, and belief, studies of secularity describe the state of affairs, present in North American history since the earliest European colonization and always in flux, that creates the conditions of possibility for religious pluralism and cultural change. To study secularity is to describe the "conceptual environment—emergent since at least the Protestant Reformation and early Enlightenment—that has made 'religion' a recognizable and vital thing in the world."[34] Our modern situation—our "secular age," as Charles Taylor has dubbed it—is one in which individuals and religious communities "can no longer maintain religious belief without the simultaneous knowledge that others do not believe, or that others believe differently."[35] This does not imply (or predict) the disappearance of religious adherence, but it does acknowledge that religion in the modern world exists as a salient category for analysis rather than as the accepted background condition of existence.[36]

In the U.S. context, secularity since the early nineteenth century has been the precondition for religious pluralism: the set of circumstances that makes it possible to ask how and in what way one might believe in a particular representation of God as over and against another representation—God as loving father, for instance, rather than God as angry arbiter of punishment. Thus, when Catharine Maria Sedgwick used the historical novel as a medium through which to investigate the doctrine of atonement and the nature of divine forgiveness, she was not "secularizing" the problem of vicarious sacrifice by fictionalizing it. Instead, she was bringing into being a religious-secular configuration in which fiction would become an accepted space for exploring the true nature of God's relation to the world. But secularity is also the set of conditions under which one may question the very nature of religion and its role in modern life. This is the religious-secular configuration at evidence in Elizabeth Stoddard's *The Morgesons*, a novel that is less concerned with the kind of god one believes in than with the way that the rise of spirit communication offered women access to nonhierarchical forms of communal religious experience. It is precisely the descriptive flexibility of secularity studies—its acknowledgment that the religious and the secular are not static categories but are constructed through particular historical events and human identities—that makes it a productive framework for reading for religion in nineteenth-century women's writing.

In a 2018 essay for *Christianity and Literature*, Dawn Coleman argued for the unique contribution of literary studies to the scholarship of secularism. Noting that much major work in the field had been produced by political scientists, anthropologists, philosophers, sociologists, and scholars trained in religious or cultural studies, Coleman insisted that literary texts, including those from the nineteenth century, offer representations of the felt experience of secularity: "By staying close to the weft and warp of experience, literature makes visible the illiberal and non-rational aspects of modern spirituality—the feelings beyond reason, the contingencies that defy theory, the exceptions and specificities of individual lives."[37] But as Peter Coviello and Jared Hickman have demonstrated, bringing the insights of secularism studies to bear on literary texts—and producing new insights of our own—requires that we as critics dislodge the assumptions about religion and secularization that remain embedded in almost every facet of modern scholarship.[38] The forms of criticism valued by twentieth- and twenty-first-century critics have often combined an implicit or explicit characterization of all religious belief as irrational, primitive, and dogmatic with an unexamined belief in criticism itself as a fully and unproblematically secularized project.[39] Beginning from these faulty premises, secularized criticism draws a number of unfounded inferences about religious adherence: that religion is primarily a tool of patriarchy and dominance imposed on believers from above; that gender, race, and class are more authentic sources of personal identity than religion is; that religious language is a code, adopted consciously or unconsciously, behind which "real" concerns are hidden; that religious belief results from ignorance or lack of education; and that nineteenth-century subjects would have been better off without their religious affiliations than with them.

Such misapprehensions are particularly distorting when applied to women writers, and the inaccuracy of secularized criticism is often revealed in the interpretive paradox it produces: the nineteenth-century woman author who values religious adherence and identity appears at one and the same time both shrewd and deluded, both canny and duped. One critic, puzzling over the question of why nineteenth-century women did not leave the Protestant churches in which they were denied leadership positions, posits that perhaps they "needed the consolation of religion more than they wanted to see what it did to them . . . [or] perhaps the lack of education prevented the development of the habit of intellectual analysis."[40] Such readings position religious adherence as self-imposed delusion or simple ignorance and are often offered despite clear accompanying evidence of women authors' education, intelligence, and self-determination. When we as critics read around or through spiritual experience rather than for it, we overlook the complex interleaving of cognition, emotion, memory, and desire that constitutes religious identity; the distinctive intersections of belief, tradition, and ritual that mark particular religious communities; and the norms of affiliation and behavior arising from those intersections.

Responding to the erasures and distortions produced by secularized criticism, over the last several decades scholars have increasingly called for more and better explanations of the role of religion in American literature and culture. As early as 1995, Jenny Franchot complained that scholars of American literature were being trained to ignore "mystery" and "conscience"—primary concerns of early Americans—because "academic orthodoxy ha[d] deemed them deviant." Instead of engaging with the religious beliefs and behaviors of their subjects, literary scholars were expected to perform acts of "translation or 'demystification'" that would "resituate a particular sacred or an individual's interior life into an understanding of culture that denies transcendence."[41] The cultural studies scholar Susan Mizruchi blamed the neglect of religion on the rise of both high theory and a particular brand of Christian fundamentalism.[42] The result was that religion had been "demoted" among scholars to simply "another ideology at play within literature, one that could be taken up, ignored, or seen as a mystification of the economic realities or power relations behind it."[43] This tendency was undergirded by the modern academy's self-conscious positioning as a site for producing "the triumph of empiricism over superstition, reason over faith, and the emancipation of all spheres—science, knowledge, the market, the state—from the oppressive and authoritarian 'yoke of religion.'"[44] This positioning made it difficult to study religion in any manner that did not reduce it to an anomaly to be explained or a disease to be cured.

Fortunately, a recent wave of American literary scholarship has begun to redress secularized critical practices and to demonstrate how careful attention to religion—not as a reified foil but as a vibrant, varied feature of the lives of individuals and communities—can enrich our understanding of the figures and texts we study. Some of this work (including my own) has appeared under the sign of "the secular," which has offered literary critics a set of flexible theoretical terms for discussing the deep imbrication of religion and culture that does not reduce all religious change to decline. Tracy Fessenden's *Culture and Redemption* (2007) launched a wave of scholarship about the role of American literature in producing and obscuring the particular form of post-Protestant secularity in which we live and move and have our being. Soon evidence of a new "turn around" religion in the United States (to borrow the title of a 2011 essay collection celebrating the work of Sacvan Bercovitch) began to appear: in special issues of *Early American Literature*, *American Literature*, and *American Literary History*; in edited collections exploring the "spiritual imagination" of nineteenth-century America and the "lived theologies" of women writers; in monographs by Dawn Coleman, Claudia Stokes, Kevin Pelletier, Jared Hickman, and others; and in the work of emerging scholars, including Toni Wall Jaudon, Molly Robey, Ashley Barnes, and Susanna Compton Underland.[45]

This book joins this recent flowering of scholarship on nineteenth-century religious writing and seeks to further unmask "to what extent our very analytic tools and categories are built to produce the very secularization theses history has since disproven."[46] To do so, it engages in what I am calling secular reading, in contradistinction to the secularized reading that for so long guided our critical projects. I argue that in order to recognize religious agency—and particularly women's religious agency—scholars must engage in secular reading practices. This will seem paradoxical only if we think of the secular (incorrectly, as I have shown) as the space from which religion has been evacuated rather than the space within which religious discourse is constituted. As Nancy Glazener has succinctly stated, critics who wish to illuminate a text must strive to recognize "what assumptions about life and meaning and social relations are the preconditions for its legibility."[47] For nineteenth-century women writers and readers, the preconditions for a text's legibility included the secular conditions under which that text was written and read: the de facto Protestant assumptions that structured the literary milieu into which the text entered, the norms of the religious communities to which the author and reader (almost certainly) belonged, the author or reader's own beliefs and practices, and, crucially, the cradling of all of those interrelated concerns within larger understandings of cosmological truth.

Secular reading acknowledges and works to apprehend such preconditions for legibility. To read secularly is to recognize how religious beliefs, intellections, impulses, and affects shape our subjects' experience of their own agency, their relationships with those around them, and their apprehensions of temporal and eternal good. To read secularly is to enter into partnership with an author and her characters and to acknowledge that the spiritual reality a text inhabits is as much a part of that text as the letters and punctuation on the page. In secular reading, characters, author, and reader navigate "a much more complex world, one in which there are multiple agencies possible," including forms of agency exercised communally, nonrationally, or in collaboration with other realms.[48] The critic who reads secularly must not merely recognize "the power of beliefs over those who hold them" but must also admit "the possibility of the truth of those beliefs."[49] Secular reading, in other words, requires the critic to at least temporarily suspend her own professional disbelief.

Secular reading is not to be confused with Edward Said's model of "secular criticism," which I am inclined to call secularized criticism precisely because of the way Said employs the term *religion* as a shibboleth to mean "an agent of closure, shutting off human investigation, criticism, and effort in deference to the authority of the more-than-human, the supernatural, the other-worldly." The framing of religious adherence as by definition closed, shut off, lazy, and cowardly is a fabulation based on critical presumption rather than on any consideration for the lives of religious persons. But if to engage in "secular criticism" is to attend to "the realities of power and authority—as well as the resistances offered by men, women, and social movements to institutions, authorities, and orthodoxies," then this book engages in secular criticism.[50] But it is a secular criticism that does not simplistically position religion as its opposite and that attends to the ways agency operates within religious structures and communities, not just against them.

Recognizing Women's Religious Agency

The persistence of secularized critical narratives has made it difficult to accurately assess the importance of religion to nineteenth-century literary history and to women writers in particular because these narratives not only discount the importance of religious adherence but also obscure the forms of religious experience most likely to be engaged in by women: informed by theology but also characterized by ritual, emotion, connection, or collective action. One assertion of this book is that in order to recognize religious agency and the new forms it might take in fiction, it is necessary both to understand a variety of nineteenth-century secular situations—the particular doctrinal and denominational contexts of women's religious writing—and to acknowledge modes of agency, individual and collective, that do not appear to be classically willful or self-determined. These modes of agency might include religious rituals, careful ascription to rules, unregulated emotional experiences, or nonnormative (dis)embodiments; there may even be circumstances in which passivity itself becomes an act of agency.

These agentive configurations can seem paradoxical because they do not conform to the assumptions of Western liberal political theory, which constructs agency as a force wielded by autonomous individuals who make rational choices based on enlightened self-interest. Models of agency based on this liberal formulation import the assumption that agency can only be accessed by individual subjects who reject any authority except that to which they have consented—that which they have chosen for themselves.[51] Such models are ill fitted to describe the desires and actions of religious persons and communities, who in many cases attribute ultimate authority to gods or other beings whose will commands the universe. Furthermore, most religious experience—even the "word-centered" Protestant religious experience that has come to serve as a norm for proper religiosity in the United States—is communal, involving the shared beliefs and collective practices of a group that is often (but not always) connected by a common race, region, or nation. Liberal philosophy's emphasis on the rational power of autonomous individuals to select acceptable forms of authority for themselves obscures modes of collective or corporate agency (one reason it is so hard to hold institutions responsible for their crimes) and instances of agency not based in rational choice.

Rather than assuming that agency is dependent on individual autonomy, this project employs instead a model of agency grounded in the philosophies of Michel Foucault and Judith Butler. As Butler has shown, the liberal model of autonomous (or sovereign) agency is a fantasy of the white Western imagination; because subjectivity and agency are enabled by discourse, and because discourse requires, at minimum, both a speaker and a listener, "the address that inaugurates the possibility of agency, in a single stroke, forecloses the possibility of radical autonomy."[52] Subjects are interpellated through discourse, including (and sometimes primarily) religious discourse, and because "the process by which one becomes subjected to relations of power also constitutes the conditions for the exercise of one's agency," no act can be entirely autonomous or liberated.[53] To recognize how historical and literary actors access agency, then, we must "think of agency not as a synonym for resistance to re-

lations of domination but as a capacity for action that historically specific relations of subordination enable and create."[54] Agency, in other words, is better
defined as an ongoing process of adaptation to the power structures within
which one lives than as a series of occasional challenges to those structures.
Agency, including religious agency, is exercised within a matrix of norms, laws,
customs, and geographic and historical conditions and is also expressed in multiple realms—public, private, or somewhere in between. One goal of this
book is to deepen our understanding of women's religious agency by prizing
agency apart from the related but quite different terms with which it has too
often been equated in liberal discourse, including *power, autonomy,* and *self-
determination.*

As with so many of our critical terms, *agency* has its roots in theological
discourses and debates, in this case about the nature of the divine and its relationship to the human. Jonathan Edwards's essay *Freedom of the Will* (1754),
which I discuss in my second chapter, is an extended interrogation of the relationship between "the moral agency of God" and "the moral agency of created thinking beings."[55] As my fifth chapter shows, opponents of Spiritualism
in the nineteenth century were often concerned not with whether supernatural
phenomena were real but with whether the agent at work at the séance table
or in the trance lecture was divine or demonic. In employing *agency* as my operative term, then, I am invoking both recent theoretical formulations and
these earlier meditations and debates.

The interpellation of the subject brings agency into being whether "the address that inaugurates the possibility of agency" is a negative one or a positive
one: negative speech interpellates the subject—discursively calls the subject
into being—just as efficiently as other forms of speech. This insight is key to
understanding how oppressed peoples are able to reinterpret religious doctrines that seem to define them as unworthy or unclean and to transform
those doctrines into vehicles for exploring their own agency. Just as Frederick
Douglass learned that reading and writing were worth pursuing precisely
because Hugh Auld forbade him access to them, nineteenth-century women
told by their ministers to "keep silence in the church" and African Americans
condemned by the curse of Ham intuited how powerful their own religious
agency might be by noting its careful circumscription.[56] Kept out of the pulpit, they found other discursive outlets for their religious ideas.

If we think of agency in these terms, religious adherence "does not in itself deny agency; rather, it creates particular forms of agency"—forms that
are shaped, enabled, or foreclosed by specific social and historical conditions.[57]
Within religious contexts, agency may be shared, circulated, fluid, or collaborative. The will of individuals may be subordinated to the perceived

well-being of the group, or agency may be understood as originating with immaterial beings rather than with individual men and women. For the nineteenth-century women—real and fictional—considered in this book, the expression of their intellectual, emotional, and moral agency was deeply important, and it was exercised *through* their religious identities, not in spite of them. When Ellen Montgomery, the child heroine of Susan Warner's *The Wide, Wide World*, submits herself to the religious teachings of Alice Humphreys rather than the nonreligious commandments of Fortune Emerson, she is exercising agency within the Calvinist doctrinal terms that give her experiences meaning—terms in which subjection to God's and the church's legitimate authority, not the subversion of those authorities, is the highest good.

The assumptions of secular liberalism have made it difficult to recognize religious agency generally but have made it nearly impossible to correctly apprehend women's religious agency. This is because of the fraught position that women hold under Western liberal secularism—a position that scholars of the secular are only beginning to address. Post-Enlightenment rhetorical constructions of the public and private spheres assigned both religion and women to the realm of the normatively "private." By severing reason from religion and consigning the latter to the private sphere, Enlightenment political theorists hoped to both protect politics from unreasoning dogma and protect religion from the meddlesome intervention of the state.[58] At the same time, republican rhetoric assigned women to the private sphere by claiming that their reproductive responsibilities made them "naturally" more attuned to social and familial—namely, private—concerns. The rhetorical, political, and civic separation of the public and private spheres that produced modern liberal secularity relegated both women and religion to the realm of the appropriately private so that, by the nineteenth century, "'public' and 'private' separated the market and politics, instrumental rationality and bureaucratic organization from home and family, spirituality, affective relationality, and sexual intimacy. Men figured on the public side, women on the side of the private."[59] Both religious expression and female identity came to be associated with the private sphere and, crucially, with one another.

Under these conditions, instances of women's public religious expression became the scandal of secularity, an unruly irruption of the properly private into an ostensibly secular, de-sexed, and abstractly rational public sphere. Bryce Traister has argued that women's religious expression poses a problem "on either side of an imagined religious/secular divide" because it instantiates "what the secularization narrative finds troubling about its own religious past: namely that religion is irrational, feminine in its performance and, in its commitment to inner experience, opposed to the political life of public rationality that is an important ideal of modern secularism itself."[60] This entanglement has made gender a central arena of contention in secular modernity, the "flash point" for clashes between "the religious" and "the secular."[61] Whether the question involves contemporary Muslim women wearing hijab or nineteenth-century Quaker women giving abolitionist speeches to mixed audiences, women's public religious expression has long laid bare the gendered underpinnings of Western secular arrangements.

In the eighteenth- and nineteenth-century United States, the carefully maintained demarcation between a rational (male) public sphere and an emotional (female) private sphere was instantiated in an insistent division of religion into two separate realms: theology and piety. Men ostensibly had intellectual minds to think about difficult theological subjects, while women had only passionate hearts to apprehend the more emotional aspects of religion. This was true even for the most religiously liberal denominations: William Ellery Channing, the unofficial head of the Unitarian church in the early nineteenth century, wrote approvingly of "woman's touching expressions of religion, not learned in theological institutions, but in the schools of affection, of sorrow, of experience, of domestic charge."[62] Rancorous theological debate—the masculine form of nineteenth-century religious expression—took place in the public forum of the pulpit, the pamphlet, the newspaper, or the sectarian journal. Personal piety and devotion—nineteenth-century Protestantism's feminine form—took place in the private space of the home and, increasingly, in what Elizabeth Maddock Dillon calls the "intermediary location" of the literary public sphere. Dillon argues that whereas our theoretical models of public and private have tended to assign the print public sphere "to the public side of the public/private divide," the literary public sphere is better understood as "a social space that links public and private and mediates between the two."[63] I demonstrate throughout this book that the intermediary space of the literary public sphere enabled women writers to enter into discussions about the ostensibly masculine subject of theology by bringing it into fictional spaces characterized by feminine piety and devotion. Nineteenth-century women's novels, I suggest, make public theological arguments by means of private domestic subjects, and they do so as a means of establishing women's claims to full religious participation and, therefore, to full humanity.

One of the dominant historical processes of secular modernity, particularly in the United States, has been the series of slow and painful steps by which women have fought their ideological consignment to the realm of the private, the coercive, the embodied, and the irrational and sought to perform themselves as full participants in the public sphere. In describing this precarious process, historians and critics have often assumed that for women, moving into the public sphere required divorcing themselves from the private matter of religion—that feminist progress is and should be accompanied by secularization. Janet Jakobsen and Ann Pellegrini note that "because the discourse of universal secularism equates secularism to progress and claims for itself the mantle of freedom and emancipation, secularism is often promoted as the antidote to women's subordination under conservative religion."[64] The anthropologist and scholar of secularism Saba Mahmood calls this set of assumptions the "progressive-secular imaginary": the "conventional wisdom that secularization, sexual freedom, and women's emancipation run always on parallel tracks."[65] The progressive-secular imaginary is not only inaccurate but potentially dangerous, as it can provide a warrant for particularly virulent strains of white supremacy and Western exceptionalism by reinforcing the idea that non-Christian women in the United States or women in non-Western countries would necessarily be better off—more liberated, more like "us"—if they would only leave behind their primitive religious commitments. Deconstructing it can help Western scholars recognize—in our own culture and others—the important role that religious identification and adherence play in shaping women's agency.

Women and Secular Subjecthood

As scholars of secularism have thoroughly demonstrated over the last several decades, religion and secularism are not opposing forces, not ends of a spectrum. They are sides of a coin or, perhaps more accurately, the coils on a Möbius strip. Long-standing and ever-shifting discourses of secularism have shaped how religion continues to exist in the world: which religious formations are conceived as salutary and which are "destructive," which can be exercised in public and which must be kept private, which are appropriately "personal" and which are dangerously "political." When we talk about secularity, we are talking about religion, and when we talk about religion, we are talking about secularity. Thus, religious agency is not the opposite of secular agency. The forms of religious agency I discuss in this book are, in fact, case studies in secular agency, the special relativity to secular agency's general relativity.

The question of agency is of central concern to scholars of secularism and liberalism because the claim to wield autonomous and sovereign agency, to be enlightened and free from supernatural coercion, stands at the center of modern secular subjecthood. The paradigmatic modern subject, according to Bruno Latour, is one who desires total freedom; for Talal Asad, the idealized secular agent is a person who seeks complete self-knowledge and self-control.[66] But as Emily Ogden has recently demonstrated, enlightenment and enchantment, independence and dependence, are mutually constitutive, and thus total freedom and self-control can never be fully realized. Ogden details how persons seeking to become modern secular agents have constructed the sense of their own freedom from coercion and delusion by endlessly producing the credulity and enchantment of others, as the mesmerist does with his subject. Because the paradigmatic secular agent is a MacGuffin, a phantasm hiding a hole or wound at the center of modernity, the quest for total freedom and autonomy is doomed and "the impossibility of these demands prompts a range of compensatory strategies: attempts to feel like a secular agent if one cannot be one."[67] The primary characteristic separating the modern secular agent from the premodern agent, then, is the capacity for self-deception. To be perfectly modern is to be in denial.

For the modern subject enchanted by the fantasy of total autonomy, the phantasmic character of secular agency will seem like a nightmare. If one is deeply invested in the goal of becoming a paradigmatic secular agent—entirely free, entirely self-controlled—certainly the impossibility of achieving one's goal will prompt the kind of destructive compensatory strategies embodied, as Ogden shows, in Melville's Ahab or, more recently, in Donald Trump. But at every stage of secular modernity there have always been those who lived the impossibility of total autonomy—who have understood what it was to inhabit "the excluded middle," the space between the poles of "enchanter or enchanted, agent or patient."[68] Many, though certainly not all, of these people have been women. I have written a book about women's religious agency in part because examining women's religious agency is the best way to see what cannot be directly observed: the phantasmic character of secular agency. Just as the only way to apprehend the true nature of political liberalism is to look at what—which is to say, whom—it excludes, the only way to see the true nature of secular agency is to look at the forms of religious agency (partial, collaborative, collective, nonautonomous) against which it defines itself. Since we cannot actually observe a nothing, I offer instead the obverse of that nothing, a story of women who exercised their agency through webs of relation instead of seeking an (impossible) route to complete independence and self-determination.

If you are a woman for whom it has always been self-evident that complete autonomy is a mirage, the impossibility of total self-determination is in many ways simply a fact, an everyday occurrence, something you put in your purse and take with you as you move through the carpool line, the morning staff meeting, airport security. In the hands of a Susan Warner, a Harriet Jacobs, an Elizabeth Stoddard (or, more recently, a Toni Morrison, a Marilynne Robinson, or a Barbara Kingsolver), stories of women navigating the everyday compromises and negotiations of a world where total autonomy is never possible become every bit as compelling—perhaps more—than stories of men dashing themselves against the rocks of inevitable dependency. In other words, to understand the workings of secular agency, don't look to men, always enchanted by the chimera of their own self-reliance. Look to women and women's books instead.

CHAPTER 1

"My Resolve Is the Feminine of My Father's Oath"

Ritual Agency and Religious Language
in the Early National Historical Novel

In the late eighteenth century, Pamela Dwight Sedgwick, wife of the Federalist politician Theodore Sedgwick and descendant of the Connecticut Dwights, was frequently ill. She suffered from severe depressions for which she was occasionally institutionalized; these depressions were exacerbated by her husband's long absences from the family's home in Stockbridge, Massachusetts. Theodore, serving in the U.S. House of Representatives or on the Massachusetts Supreme Court, left his wife and children for months at a time while he performed his civic duties in Philadelphia or New York. In a 1791 letter to her husband, Pamela pleaded with him to come home to Stockbridge; she had "lost [her] understanding," and she feared that in her weakened state she would leave their children unprotected.[1] While Theodore was sympathetic to Pamela's trials, he continued his public career, and his wife's illnesses worsened until her death in 1807.[2]

As adults, Pamela's children offered varied interpretations of her difficult life. After her death, her son Henry Sedgwick composed a eulogy in which Pamela's pain worked to the spiritual benefit of her husband, her children, and her country: "It may not be profane or irreverent to suppose that, with some distant resemblance to our Redeemer, she did not suffer solely for herself . . . ; and we may be permitted to hope that her example and her memory . . . will contribute to the eternal welfare of those she most loved."[3] Henry's eulogy invokes the Christian doctrine of atonement: the cosmic mechanism by which

Christ's painful death on the cross effects humankind's redemption from sin. By indicating Pamela's "distant resemblance to our Redeemer" and its potential effect on the "eternal welfare of those she most loved," Henry implies that Pamela shared in Christ's soteriological mission: that as with Christ's crucifixion, Pamela's suffering and death would bring about the eventual salvation of others. Henry's eulogy releases Theodore from culpability: Pamela suffered because she was like Christ—not because Theodore left her alone on the Massachusetts frontier for months at a time—and listeners would do well to learn from her noble self-sacrifice.

Pamela's daughter, Catharine Maria Sedgwick, wrote of her mother's life and death in starkly different terms. In Catharine's memory, Pamela had indeed made Christlike sacrifices for her family and her country: her chief traits were her "character, her wisdom, her conjugal devotion, and self-negation," and she never "expressed one word of remonstrance or dissatisfaction" despite the fact that her "long separations from my father seem to have been almost cruel to her."[4] But in Catharine's telling, Theodore subtly shoulders the blame for Pamela's suffering and death. While he was sorry that Pamela's sequestration exacerbated her physical and mental anguish, his "compunction [was] tempered by the conviction of an overruling duty to his country." Theodore's devotion to public duty, Catharine asserted, "overruled" his consideration for Pamela's private pain. And unlike her brother, Catharine was unwilling to assign atoning power to Pamela's death: in describing the loss of her mother she would say only that Pamela's "sufferings [we]re past, and . . . prepared her to enjoy more keenly the rest and felicities of heaven."[5] For Catharine, Pamela was Christlike, but she was no Christ: her trials brought about no greater good in this world and only speculative benefit in the world beyond.

By the time of their mother's death, Catharine and Henry Sedgwick had heard many sermons about the doctrine of atonement: about Christ's painful death on the cross and the cosmic mechanism by which his unearned suffering secured the salvation of humankind. They had been raised in Stockbridge under the strict orthodox Calvinist regime of the town's Congregationalist clergyman, Pamela's uncle Stephen West, who had assumed the Stockbridge pulpit when it was vacated by Jonathan Edwards. West was an acknowledged authority on the doctrine of atonement: his treatises on the subject explained in precise detail how Christ's agonizing "sufferings and death . . . sensibly and gloriously expressed" God's ostensibly benevolent nature. His sermons, meanwhile, encouraged hearers to emulate Christ's self-abnegation, an instruction Pamela Sedgwick took deeply to heart.[6] As adults, both Catharine and Henry Sedgwick would leave the religion of their childhood to join the Unitarian church, a liberal offshoot of New England Congregationalism that openly rejected the doctrine of atonement. Unitarian theologians of the early nine-teenth century vociferously questioned the meaning and purpose of Christ's death on the cross: as doctrinally liberal Christians who insisted on God's "pa-rental character," they were horrified by the idea that a loving father would require his sinless son to die painfully for the benefit of sinful humankind.[7] And yet, as Henry's eulogy for his mother suggests, the idea that the public good required the sacrifices of women and other already disempowered people continued to structure early national rhetoric even for the most liberal of thinkers.

Many of the Sedgwick siblings would follow in their father's footsteps, be-coming public figures in their own right. Henry would make a career as a lawyer and abolitionist, while Catharine would become the most prominent female author of her generation and one of the earliest American writers to gain a reputation beyond the borders of the young nation. In the first decades of her career, Catharine would take up the problem of atonement in her fic-tion, particularly in her historical novels *Hope Leslie* and *The Linwoods*. While the historical novel is always preoccupied with national sacrifice, Sedgwick and other religiously liberal women authors of the early national period, particu-larly Lydia Maria Child, transformed it into a specifically theological form, one that explores the doctrine of atonement in order to question what—and who— will be sacrificed on the altar of the nation. Sedgwick and her contemporaries adopted the popular genre of the historical novel as a means of interrogating the gendered nature of vicarious sacrifice—the way that models of sacrifice, including the Christian theology of atonement, exacerbate the suffering of the already disempowered in the name of an often dubious higher good.

The problem of vicarious sacrifice was both a religious and a political one in the early United States. Carol Pateman and other feminist scholars of po-litical history have shown how the works of social contract theory that gave rise to the United States' political structures sacrificed women's claims to citi-zenship by constructing and naturalizing a binary opposition between men's freedom and women's dependence. John Locke, Jean-Jacques Rousseau, and other Enlightenment political theorists attributed individuality exclusively to men by constructing men's political freedom as the corollary to women's sup-posedly "natural" subjection. Under liberal political theory, "men possess the capacities required for citizenship"—namely, the ability to "use their reason to sublimate their passions, develop a sense of justice and so uphold the uni-versal, civil law"—while women "cannot transcend their bodily natures and sexual passions" and thus "cannot develop such a political morality."[8] This model of "natural" difference justified the division of social life into public and private spheres, with the public the realm of politics and commerce and the private the realm of domesticity and sexuality. As Elizabeth Maddock Dillon has noted, "the logic of this particularization of women involves not simply pulling rank" but actually "requires defining women as . . . constitutively unable to exercise choice and agency."[9] For the philosophers whose work formed the foundation of the new American republic, the political and public agency of "woman" was sacrificed so that "man" could become the paradigmatic liberal individual.

Thus, even as influential Unitarian clerics were dismantling doctrines of atonement that insisted on vicarious sacrifice as a means to cosmic reconciliation, early American political theory was insisting on the sacrifice of women's self-determination as the price of the new nation's progress. As religiously liberal and politically progressive women authors, Sedgwick and Child stood at the intersection of these discourses, and they composed historical novels that interrogated sacrifice at both of these levels. Child's *Hobomok* and Sedgwick's *Hope Leslie* and *The Linwoods* proliferate scenes of sacrifice and then trace the consequences of those sacrifices for characters living at critical moments in the history of settlement and national formation. In highlighting the similarities between "savage" and "civilized" notions of sacrifice, *Hobomok* and *Hope Leslie* participate in the deconstruction of atonement theology that characterized much Unitarian thought in the early decades of the nineteenth century. Not content with merely questioning atonement, however, Sedgwick would go on to displace sacrifice altogether in her novel *The Linwoods*. Set during the American Revolution, *The Linwoods* replaces atonement doctrine with a model of religious language that enables women to actively participate in history. Isabella Linwood, the novel's heroine, exercises a type of religious agency grounded not in the sacrifice of her body but in her "resolve"—Sedgwick's term for a form of spontaneous and embodied language that expresses the speaker's most sincere beliefs and in doing so transforms the listener's actions. Revising Unitarian theology through the medium of the historical novel made it possible for Child and Sedgwick to imagine a nation united by forces other than violent sacrifice, in which women contributed actively to national advancement instead of being relegated, like Pamela Sedgwick, to seclusion and silence.[10]

Even as they sought to imaginatively rescue white women from the necessity of perpetual self-abnegation, however, Child and Sedgwick raised (but did not settle) the question of where nonwhite Americans fit into national narratives of atonement and sacrifice. Sedgwick's fiction was perpetually haunted by the remembrance of her mother's painful life and death and by the way her suffering was framed as necessary both to her husband's public career and her children's salvation. But there is another figure who reappears throughout Sedgwick's work: Elizabeth Freeman, the African American servant who acted as a "second mother" to the Sedgwick children when Pamela was ill. For Catharine Sedgwick, Freeman provided the model of religious "resolve" offered in *The Linwoods*, one that was not grounded in silent sacrifice but in active self-advocacy. This resolve stirred Sedgwick's literary and political imagination, but it had limited utility for the real-life Freeman and her family. Elizabeth Freeman's persistent presence in Sedgwick's writing—as herself, as an Indian maiden, as a revolutionary-era servant, and elsewhere—indicates the precarious status of people of color in otherwise triumphant early national narratives of women's increasing religious agency.

Sacrifice without Blood: Lydia Maria Child's *Hobomok*

Both Lydia Maria Child and Catharine Maria Sedgwick spent their childhoods in households deeply influenced by a strict New England Calvinism, and both would eventually defect, as adults, to more liberal Christian denominations. Sedgwick took a deep interest in religious and political issues even in childhood: one of her earliest extant letters, written to her father, Theodore, in 1804 when she was fourteen years old, describes a recent election in Stockbridge won by the "Jacobins"—the local Democratic party—who upon their victory had immediately voted to lower Stephen West's clerical salary.[11] As an adult, Catharine would attribute some of the blame for Pamela's mental illness to her mother's severe Calvinist belief system. And yet it would take much urging from her brothers to convince her to leave the "orthodox" Congregationalist church to join a Unitarian congregation. Writing to her friend Susan Channing in March 1821, Sedgwick confessed that she considered the Unitarians to be "nearer the truth, by a very great deal, than the orthodox"; still, she protested, "there are some of your *articles of unbelief* that I am not Protestant enough to subscribe to."[12] Despite these reservations, Sedgwick transferred her membership from the Stockbridge church to a Unitarian congregation later that year.[13]

Child, like her contemporary, spent her childhood in a Massachusetts town thoroughly imbued with Congregationalist Calvinism. Her "gloomy and withdrawn" father imposed his "'fierce theology'" upon her, and her reaction against this early training led to a lifetime of spiritual seeking. After being baptized in her father's Congregational church in 1821, Child did not unite herself with that institution but instead joined a Swedenborgian Society in Boston, despite having assured her family that she was unlikely to be swayed by the sect's "fanaticism."[14] Child's religious beliefs and affiliations would continue to evolve over the course of her lifetime. But when she composed her first novel, *Hobomok*, she was living with her brother, Convers Francis, a Unitarian minister, in Watertown, Massachusetts, and the novel shows evidence of a Unitarian preoccupation with atonement and vicarious sacrifice.[15]

The rise of Unitarian thought was part of a long liberalizing movement among Protestant Christians that stretched back to at least the early eighteenth century. Beginning as a theological insurgency within American Calvinism, by the early nineteenth century the spread of Unitarian ideas had produced a very public and rancorous schism in the Congregational church.[16] New England Unitarianism's three primary tenets were "a commitment to logic and reason in theology, a biblicism that was strict but that demanded critical and historical analysis, and an overriding concern for moral aspiration as the focal point of the Christian religion."[17] Applying critical and historical analysis to the Bible produced Unitarianism's most controversial theological innovation, the one that gave it its name: its rejection of the doctrine of the Trinity, a pillar of Western Christianity since the Council of Nicaea in 325 AD. Finding no clear exposition of this doctrine in the Bible, Unitarians rejected it, insisting instead "that there is one God, even the Father; and that Jesus Christ is not this one God, but his son and messenger."[18] Christ, then, did not partake of God's divine nature but instead was fully human. This conclusion, in turn, unsettled another cornerstone of Christian theology: the doctrine of Christ's atonement.

In its most general terms, atonement is "the satisfying [of] Divine Justice by Jesus Christ giving himself a ransom for us, undergoing the penalty due to our sins, and thereby releasing us from that punishment which God might justly inflict upon us."[19] Most Catholic and Protestant theologians (including Martin Luther and John Calvin) have held to the Anselmian, or satisfaction, theory of the atonement (named for its primary formulator, the eleventh-century archbishop Anselm of Canterbury). The satisfaction theory posits that Christ's sinless death "satisfies" the debt demanded by God for the crime of original sin (committed by Adam but imputed to all humankind): the sinless Christ is sacrificed on the cross and thus bears the punishment earned by humankind. Unsatisfied with the satisfaction theory, Christian liberals of the mid-eighteenth century (including the forerunners of Unitarianism, Jonathan Mayhew and Charles Chauncy) adopted the governmental theory of the atonement. This theory (which was also espoused by the orthodox Congregationalists Samuel Hopkins, Jonathan Edwards Jr., and Sedgwick's great-uncle Stephen West) posits that Christ's crucifixion does not satisfy a debt but instead displays the true majesty of God: it "*exhibit[s] . . .* the righteous displeasure of God against sin, made in some other way than in the punishment of the sinner." Under the governmental theory, Christ's painful death demonstrates God's "divine purity, and hatred of iniquity": God requires Christ to atone for the sins of man because only by allowing his son to die can God display his hatred of sin.[20]

Nineteenth-century Unitarians rejected both the substitutionary and governmental models of atonement because neither of these explanations for Christ's death accorded with the loving, parental, and forgiving God they claimed to find in their reading of scripture. William Ellery Channing, the unofficial leader of the nineteenth-century Unitarian movement (and brother-in-law of Sedgwick's friend Susan Channing), insisted that the God posited by the doctrine of substitutionary atonement, "instead of being plenteous in forgiveness, never forgives; for it is absurd to speak of men as forgiven, when their whole punishment is borne by a substitute."[21] For Channing and other Unitarian theologians, the merchant God of substitutionary atonement was not merciful; he was simply a businessman demanding payment of a debt. The God of the governmental theory was, if possible, even worse; Channing imagined him "erect[ing] a gallows in the center of the universe, and . . . execut[ing] upon it, in room of the offenders, an Infinite Being" while requiring "all beings in heaven and earth . . . to fix their eyes on this fearful sight."[22] Rather than choosing between the satisfaction and governmental theories of atonement, Unitarian theologians of the early nineteenth century objected to the doctrine altogether, for both theological and practical reasons. Not only did the doctrine of atonement make God into a monster who assented to the murder of his own son, they argued, but trying to worship this monstrous God produced gloomy and spiritually stunted Christians incapable of comprehending the Deity's true, kindly, and parental nature.

As works of Unitarian historical fiction, Child's *Hobomok* and Sedgwick's *Hope Leslie* participate in the deconstruction of atonement theology that preoccupied liberal Christian thinkers throughout the early nineteenth century. While Channing and other Unitarian theologians argued against atonement in sermons, sectarian journals, and polemical pamphlets, Child and Sedgwick examined the doctrine not only as an abstract concept but as a concrete, embodied problem with political and social implications. *Hobomok* and *Hope Leslie*, both set in the early years of English settlement in New England, draw parallels between the "primitive" blood sacrifices of their Native American characters and the ostensibly "enlightened" doctrine of atonement embraced by their fictional Puritans. Both structures, they argue, limit women's religious agency by positioning them as perpetual victims in an endlessly repeated cosmic ritual. Together, these novels suggest that the United States' future cannot be secured through the unwilling sacrifices of its female inhabitants.[23]

Hobomok was Lydia Maria Child's debut novel, published in 1824 when she was only twenty-two years old. Set in the 1630s, the story centers on Mary Conant, a gentle maiden who is summoned from England, where she has been living with her grandfather, to the Salem colony to care for her aging mother and father. Mary is in love with the Englishman Charles Brown, but the match is forbidden by her strict Puritan father, who sees Charles's adherence to the Church of England as little better than paganism. When Charles Brown is lost at sea in a shipwreck and Mary's beloved mother dies from the strain of life in the colony, Mary agrees to marry the Native American man Hobomok, who has loved her from afar since her arrival in Salem. Mary bears Hobomok's child, also named Hobomok, but when the couple has been married for three years, Charles Brown reappears in Salem, reports of his death having been greatly exaggerated. Seeing that Mary prefers Charles, Hobomok divorces her and disappears from the colony, leaving his child behind to be raised by Charles and Mary.

Hobomok depicts white women and Native American men as victims of a patriarchal Puritan ideology that demands superhuman sacrifices in the name of filial and conjugal devotion. It tells the early history of the Salem colony as a tale of forced sacrifice imposed on English women by selfish Puritan men. The novel's female protagonists—Mary Conant, her mother (Mrs. Conant), and Lady Arabella Johnson—make devastating sacrifices for the sake of their husbands' religious ideals: they give up comfortable homes and beloved family members in England to follow their husbands to a howling wilderness where starvation and disease blight their lives and take their children. The Salem patriarchs' strict religious proscriptions reflect stubborn defiance as much as theological conviction, but their wives and daughters are nevertheless unwillingly sacrificed to those patriarchs' beliefs. Reflecting Child's increasingly liberal religious attitudes, *Hobomok* decries this demand for sacrifice on the part of white women; at the same time, however, it celebrates the self-elected sacrifice of the novel's titular Native American. *Hobomok* does less to undermine the doctrine of vicarious sacrifice than to reconfigure it, shifting its burdens off the shoulders of white women and onto those of Native men.

The motif of sacrifice appears early in *Hobomok*, when Mary Conant steals out of her father's dreary cabin on the edges of the Salem settlement to perform a forbidden ritual that she hopes will reveal her nuptial future. The novel's unnamed narrator watches from behind a tree while Mary stoops beside a stream and "taking a knife from her pocket . . . open[s] a vein in her little arm, and dipping a feather in the blood, wr[ites] something on a piece of white cloth" (13).[24] Mary then uses a stick to trace a circle on the ground, steps into it, and walks three times backward and forward around its circumference while chanting a rhyme meant to summon her future husband. Mary is expecting Charles Brown to appear, but to her dismay Hobomok jumps into the circle instead. Hobomok, like Mary, has brought a knife to the edge of the stream. But rather than shedding blood, he uses the weapon to cut branches that he will place on his tribe's "sacrifice heap." "'Hobomok much late has been out to watch the deer tracks,'" he explains to Mary, "'and he came through the hollow, that he might make the Manitto Asseinah green as the oak tree'" (14). This early scene links Mary and Hobomok—long before the plot links them in marriage—by revealing their shared investment in sacrificial rituals. But whereas Mary, the supposedly more civilized of the two, has initiated a bloody "pagan" ritual (even Sally Oldham, Salem's resident flirt, is shocked at Mary's having done such "an awful wicked thing"), Hobomok's sacrifice to the Manitto Asseinah involves only the cutting of branches, not skin (20).

By beginning *Hobomok* with sacrifices performed by a white woman and a Native man, Child invokes the central role of sacrifice in the historical novel. Scenes of sacrifice are everywhere in the genre; indeed, sacrifice is at the heart of Georg Lukács's originating theory of it. For Lukács, the historical novel is the product of the revolutionary era and its Enlightenment theory of history, in which "the national idea becomes the property of the broadest masses."[25] In order to represent both "the people" and the best that the new nation has to offer, the hero of the historical novel must be simultaneously "mediocre"— that is, bourgeois or middle class—and the embodiment of a perfect ideal. The feature that marks the hero's simultaneously middling and ideal status is his "capacity for self-sacrifice," which he possesses alongside "a certain, though never outstanding, degree of practical intelligence, a certain moral fortitude and decency."[26] The hero of the historical novel incarnates the best that the nation has to offer, including a willingness to sacrifice everything to bring a country and a people into existence.

But while the hero of the historical novel may possess the *capacity* for self-sacrifice, the actual victims of sacrifice in historical novels are most often women and people of color. Historical fiction relies heavily on scenes of sex and gender violence to consolidate national identity, with the rape, murder, or suicides of female characters providing the impetus for national cohesion. In the works of British historical novelists including Jane Porter, Sydney Owenson, and Walter Scott, Scottish and English national identities are solidified through originary acts of violence against women's bodies.[27] The American historical novel likewise seeks to produce a "usable past, . . . one that democracy can profit by," but as Nina Baym has demonstrated, the most usable objects in American historical fiction are women.[28] James Fenimore Cooper's novels, Baym notes, present women not as individuals or persons but as types; they are objects of exchange among men, for whom they signify the spread of "civilization." Because "they are vital for man's civilizations . . . man has to take them along wherever he goes, and at whatever cost."[29] That cost, however, is usually paid by the woman herself, as with Cora Munro, whose double doom as both female and mixed race necessitates her self-sacrificial suicide in *The Last of the Mohicans*. In both the British and American historical novel tradition, the woman's contested body is the site on which nationhood is built. In the early scene in *Hobomok* in which Mary Conant predicts her future, her bloody arm signifies her status as the woman whose romantic desires will be sacrificed for the ostensible good of the struggling Salem colony.

As a text that embraces a doctrinally liberal, Unitarian-inflected Protestantism, *Hobomok* depicts the Puritan colony of Salem as a backward and primitive settlement guided by violent principles, the effects of which are borne by the women of the colony rather than the men. The things and people women love are sacrificed for principles that the men themselves do not clearly understand and that, Child's narrator repeatedly implies, have more to do with pride than religious conviction. Mrs. Conant follows her husband to the New World and endures there the death of her two sons as well as other scenes of "privation and hardship" (8). Mary Conant, summoned from her home in England to the Salem settlement, must leave behind her beloved grandfather in an act of "'painful sacrifice'" that she nevertheless "'ma[kes] with serenity'" (79). When Mrs. Conant and Lady Arabella Johnson lie dying side by side in the Conants' cabin, Child's narrator pronounces them "both alike victims to what has always been the source of woman's greatest misery—love—deep and unwearied love" (111). In *Hobomok*, the white women of the New England colonies are sacrificed on the altar of love and womanly devotion to men who are more concerned with dry religious questions than with actual relationships and human feelings.

When the Native man Hobomok appears in Mary Conant's enchanted circle with an offering of branches for his "sacrifice heap," he announces himself as the superior of the Puritan men whose notion of religious sacrifice requires the protracted suffering and painful deaths of their wives and children. Hobomok's devotion to a nonviolent form of sacrifice—branches rather than blood—prepares the reader to accept his eventual marriage to the white heroine by symbolically elevating him above the other "savages" that populate the story—including, the novel implies, the savage Puritan men who have ruined their families' lives for the sake of a dubious good. In emphasizing Hobomok's capacity for nonviolent sacrifice, both here and in his later act of peacefully divorcing Mary, Child defies depictions of Native Americans as violent savages and despoilers of white women—the roles they most often played in early national historical novels by Cooper and others. In *Hobomok* it is white men, not Natives, who demand painful sacrifices from the women they have sworn to cherish and protect.

Hobomok's capacity for nonviolent sacrifice repudiates the stadialist ideologies of human progress that had dominated Western historiography since the eighteenth century and that underpinned the historical novel as a genre. According to the "four stages" model of civilizational development, which arranged all cultures on a scale from "savage" to "civilized," one clear mark of indigenous cultures' "savagery" was their supposed engagement in violent, vengeful, and even cannibalistic rites of sacrifice. European explorers in North America had disseminated—often from little evidence—elaborate stories of bloody Indian "sacrifices" meant to establish the primitivism of Native cultures and their need for Christian conversion. Drawing on classical (mis)representations of both the Far West and the Far East and the faulty ethnography of early New World travelers, early modern depictions of native North Americans often conflated torture, cannibalism, human sacrifice, and trophy taking (the collection and display of human body parts collected from the dead in war) and accused all tribes of engaging in these practices.[30] William Robertson's multivolume *History of America* (1777), one of the most influential works of stadialist history, described native North Americans as "characterised by a 'hard, unfeeling temper.' . . . They torture prisoners to death and . . . mak[e] war solely in order to capture prisoners for sacrifice."[31] In stadialist models of history, "civilized" peoples were those who had ostensibly left cultural and religious rituals of violent sacrifice behind.[32]

But as Unitarians and other liberal Christians of the nineteenth century asserted, the Anglo-American West's religio-cultural system was itself grounded in a story of violent sacrifice: the atoning death of Christ on the cross. Protestant theologies of atonement—including those espoused by the New England Puritans who form the subject of *Hobomok*—posit Christ's painful death on the cross as the necessary price exacted by God for the sins of humankind. What stadialist theories did, then, was distinguish the "bad," vengeful sacrifices ostensibly practiced by indigenous peoples from the "good," atoning sacrifice modeled by Christ on the cross. Jean-Luc Nancy, describing the role of sacrifice in Western historiography, labels these the "old" and "new" models of sacrifice. The "old" sacrifice appears as a "pure economy of barter between man and the divine powers. Everything is reduced to the formula of . . . sacrificial 'economism.'"[33] The "old" sacrifice (of grain, lambs, or, as Robertson asserted, men) must be endlessly repeated because the "economy of barter" is circular: offerings are exchanged for good favor, but once favor is granted, sacrifices must once again be offered in thanksgiving and to solicit further blessings. According to Nancy, the "new" sacrifice, exemplified in the death of Christ on the cross, is distinguished from the "old" by four characteristics: it is self-sacrifice, chosen or at least consented to by the victim; it is unique in its occurrence and is "accomplished for all"; its uniqueness "lies in its elevation into the principal or the essence of sacrifice itself"; and it is "itself the transcendence of sacrifice," such that repetitive ritual sacrifices need no longer be performed.[34] In stadialist histories, savages could be recognized by their commitment to an "old" model of pagan sacrifice: imposed, vengeful, and endlessly repeated. Civilized cultures, by contrast, had embraced the "new" model of sacrifice, in which Christ's selfless death on the cross was the single act that made further sacrifice obsolete.

Hobomok defies the stadialist classification of cultures by casting the Englishmen of the Salem settlement as practitioners of the "old" sacrifice: they not only embrace a bloody doctrine of atonement but demand from their wives and children sacrifices unto death. Hobomok, by contrast, practices the "new" sacrifice, best exemplified in his choice to divorce Mary at the end of the novel. His sacrifice is self-chosen, unique, and irrevocable: he divorces Mary without informing her of his decision and disappears by the time she discovers what he has done. He frames his decision to leave as a self-elected offering to a beloved idol: "'She was first his,'" he reflects upon Charles's return to Salem; "'Mary loves him better than she does me. The sacrifice must be made to her'" (139). Both the narrator and Charles Brown reiterate this framing of Hobomok's departure, with the narrator lamenting "the happiness [Hobomok] had so nobly sacrificed" (142) and Brown intoning to Mary that "'the sacrifice that has been made . . . cannot now be remedied'" (148). Hearing of his departure, Mary casts the now-vanished Hobomok in the role of Christ: "'I only have sinned; and yet all the punishment has fallen upon his head,'" a phrase that echoes the description of the coming Messiah in Isaiah 53:5 (147).[35] Charles Brown likewise paints his rival as an Indian Christ: "'I have a story to tell of that savage,'" he announces, "'which might make the best of us blush at our inferiority, Christians as we are'" (145). Indeed, Hobomok not only performs the "new" sacrifice; he perfects it. His sacrifice, unlike Christ's, is innocent of human blood: while he leaves a slain deer and three foxes at Mary's doorstep to signify the dissolution of their marriage, he commits no other harm. In divorcing Mary, Hobomok renounces not his life but his patriarchal prerogative. While he could have dragged Mary from Salem to live among his tribe—as the Puritan husbands in the novel did to their wives and children—

he instead abdicates his conjugal and parental role. He is a one-man glorious revolution.

In accepting Hobomok's gift—his choice to free her from marital obligation—Mary Conant, unlike her dead mother, becomes the beneficiary of sacrifice rather than its victim. The novel praises Hobomok's sacrifice precisely because it is performed for the benefit of white women rather than being demanded of them: Hobomok's selfless act affirms the Indian's status as sacrifice's proper victim and the white woman Mary Conant as the "higher being" to whom sacrifice is owed. Hobomok's act of bloodless self-sacrifice—of his son, of his love for Mary, and of his home—enables Mary's return to white society but eliminates any hope for interracial peace, which is abandoned in favor of silent erasure. While the reformed Mr. Conant treats Hobomok's son, "the little Hobomok," as "a peculiar favorite," Hobomok *père* is quietly effaced from memory: "His father was seldom spoken of; and by degrees [the child's] Indian appellation was silently omitted" (149–50).[36] Once Hobomok has performed his ideal sacrifice, the necessity of sacrifice can be removed from the national narrative, as Unitarians and other liberal Christians wished, through the disappearance of Hobomok himself. *Hobomok* shifts the burden of sacrifice away from white women and onto Native men and then retells violent expulsion as peaceful and self-elected disappearance.

The Limits of Atonement: Sedgwick's *Hope Leslie*

Three years after *Hobomok* appeared, Catharine Maria Sedgwick published *Hope Leslie, or Early Times in the Massachusetts. Hope Leslie* pushes the question of sacrifice further than does Child's *Hobomok*, exploring the structure of sacrifice itself rather than merely shifting the locus of power and oppression. In a story that echoes the history of Pocahontas, the novel depicts the Indian maiden Magawisca's noble act on behalf of her best friend, the young white settler Everell Fletcher. When Magawisca's father, Mononotto, takes Everell to his tribe's "sacrifice-rock," where he plans to avenge the death of his son Samoset in the Pequot Massacre, Magawisca interrupts the ritual by flinging her arm between her father's ax and Everell's neck. Everell escapes and tells the story of Magawisca's brave sacrifice far and wide, but when Magawisca—and her severed arm—reappear in Boston years later, it becomes clear that the memory of her noble act cannot prevent further violence perpetrated by the Massachusetts settlers against her tribe or even against herself. Though celebrated by the Fletcher family and the novel's titular heroine, Magawisca's sacrifice brings about neither racial nor religious reconciliation, not through any fault of Magawisca's but because acts of sacrifice, whether old or new, do not provide sufficient foundation for a new nation.

In the scene in which Magawisca rescues Everell from certain death at the hands of her father, Sedgwick explicitly invokes the doctrine of atonement: like Christ, Magawisca subjects herself to terrible violence sanctioned by her own father to save a beloved friend from a terrible fate. As the Pequot elders prepare to sacrifice Everell, Magawisca scales the side of the rock and arrives at the top just in time to interrupt her father's ritual. When the ax severs her arm, sending the "lopped quivering member" tumbling over the precipice to the ground below, the watching Pequot tribesmen, "uttering horrible yells, rus[h] toward the fatal spot" to recapture Everell (97).[37] Magawisca stops their advance by asserting that she has taken Everell's place, crying, "'I have bought his life with my own!'" The narrator repeats the salvational framing of the scene: before fleeing for his life, Everell "thr[ows] his arms around" Magawisca and "press[es] her to his heart, as he would a sister that had redeemed his life with her own." Accepting the substitute victim, the watching Pequots allow Everell to escape as they pay "involuntary homage to the heroic girl" (97). Magawisca, in substituting her body for Everell's and enduring the (unearned) punishment intended for him, "redeems" his life by imitating on the soil of colonial Massachusetts the ritual of Christ's sacrifice on the cross.

Magawisca's "redemption" of Everell—twice the narrator repeats that Magawisca has "bought" or "redeemed" Everell's life—reverses the terms of the Indian captivity narrative, in which white colonists paid a ransom for the return of a family member kidnapped by Natives. But the scene also narrates an ethical shift from the old sacrifice to the new: from Mononotto's violent and imposed vengeance to Magawisca's self-elected sacrifice on Everell's behalf.[38] Sedgwick casts Magawisca as a redeemer who voluntarily takes Everell's place and pays for the crimes of the white colonists, whose murder of Mononotto's son was the original sin that prompted this act of revenge. *Hope Leslie* fictionalizes the scene of atonement—the crucifixion—with a Native American woman in the role of Christ, the paradigmatic exemplar of the new sacrifice. Magawisca's action is self-elected and unique, and once performed it need never be repeated: for the remainder of the novel, Mononotto will never again attempt to avenge the death of his wife or children by means of violent sacrifice. This moment does indeed, as Christopher Castiglia suggests, juxtapose "the male world of the Old Testament—based on violence, vengeance, and 'artificial codes of law'" with "the feminine world of the New Testament—based on mercy and love, represented by the evoked spirits of the mothers" (173).[39] But according to the Unitarian theology that underlies *Hope Leslie*, there is little to distinguish an Old Testament model of vengeance—exemplified by both the Pequot elders and the Puritan fathers—from the New Testament model of atonement embodied in Magawisca's brave act.

Despite the shift from a model of vengeance to a model of atonement, the scene at the sacrifice-rock remains bound by the terms of a ritual in which there are limited ways to participate. As the anthropologist Maurice Bloch asserts, rituals—religious, political, social, familial—invoke the language of traditional authority, which "reduces the specificity of utterances so that all events are made to appear as though they were all alike."[40] Ritual practices function to maintain a cultural status quo by limiting the forms of language and action that are recognizable within the frame of the ritual. Ritual language "severely restricts the participants' choices of intonation, vocabulary, syntactic forms, and acceptable illustrations (such as scriptural or mythological allusions)" and is thus "coercive: once participants have entered the ritual frame, they are committed to a pre-ordained sequence of events."[41] Human agency, while not obliterated by ritual forms, is restricted to those acts and utterances that are conceivable within the "ritual frame."

When Magawisca interrupts her father's attempt to sacrifice Everell, she performs an act that changes both the signification and the results of the ritual. When she offers her body in exchange for Everell's and cries, "'I have bought his life with my own,'" she both describes and performs the act of redemption. Everell's life is saved, not only by Magawisca's bodily interposition but by her proclamation that the price for Everell's life has been paid in full. This pronouncement demonstrates both the possibilities for and the limits of Magawisca's agency within the terms of Pequot ritual traditions. Magawisca chooses to take Everell's place at the sacrifice-rock, but her brave act does not change the essential terms of the ritual, in which someone's body must be sacrificed to avenge the death of Samoset. Furthermore, insofar as rituals function through the erasure of particularity—"the individuality and historicity of events disappear" because each participant is standing in for something or someone else—Magawisca and Everell represent cultures at the point of violent contact.[42] When the two are read not as individual friends but as stand-ins for their tribes, Magawisca's act ritually performs existing inequalities: the intended sacrifice, eldest son and heir of the white colonizer, escapes unscathed, while Magawisca, doubly disempowered by virtue of her gender and race, is mutilated instead.

At the moment when Magawisca redeems Everell's life at the sacrifice-rock, *Hope Leslie* reaches the point at which Child's *Hobomok* stopped: Sedgwick has successfully shifted the burden of sacrifice away from a white character and onto the shoulders of a noble Native who is now expected to disappear into death or self-exile. In singlehandedly effecting a sudden shift from the old sacrifice to the new, Magawisca's act seems to hold the promise of a more peaceful future. Stadialist history would suggest that Magawisca, at least, if not her father or her tribe, has emerged into the light of "civilization" by rejecting the vengeful, retributive sacrifices of her native culture and embracing the self-elected sacrifice espoused by the Christian colonists. And yet the scene at the sacrifice-rock occurs early in *Hope Leslie*; two-thirds of the novel remains, and Magawisca does not die, as she herself had predicted when "buying" Everell's life. Instead, her maimed body with its missing arm persistently reappears for the duration of the text, complicating attempts by the Puritan fathers to ideologically consign the colony's Native inhabitants to oblivion and suggesting that even noble self-sacrifice cannot bring about either sectarian or racial reconciliation. Because the structure of sacrifice remains intact, Magawisca's noble act of redemption can effect change only on an individual level, not on a social one.

The social inefficacy of sacrifice is a frequent theme in the chapters of *Hope Leslie* that follow Magawisca's redemption of Everell at the sacrifice-rock. Magawisca's act does little to alter relations between the Pequots and the Puritans, which remain marked by the same patterns of war and recrimination that preceded the event. While Everell, his father, and Everell's cousin Hope Leslie feel a lasting debt to Magawisca, the colony as a whole admits no obligation to her. When Magawisca returns to Boston years after the scene at the sacrifice-rock, she is captured by the English authorities and accused of planning an attack on the colony. Conscious of their debt to her, the Fletchers petition the colonial governor John Winthrop to free Magawisca because of her prior service to Everell, but their entreaties do nothing to prevent her imprisonment. When Mr. Fletcher admonishes Winthrop that "'we owe much to this woman,'" Winthrop replies, "'You owe much undoubtedly . . . but it yet remains to be proved, my friend, that your son's redeemed life is to be put in the balance against the public weal.'" Winthrop's statement makes clear that a single act of "redemption" can do little to alter public policies of vengeance, violence, and mistrust: "'private feelings must yield to public good,'" he insists, with the "public good" always defined in political and military terms by Winthrop himself (245).

Magawisca's missing arm marks both the bravery of her sacrifice and the ineffectuality of that sacrifice at a level beyond the personal—it indexes both action and impotence simultaneously. As *Hope Leslie* progresses, Magawisca's severed arm becomes the symbol of both the ritualized violence perpetrated against her and of the limited efficacy of sacrifice at the social and political level. When the colonists place her on trial for her supposed treachery,

Magawisca dramatically reveals the stump of her missing arm, demanding that Winthrop and the Puritan magistrates punish her quickly rather than returning her to prison. Revealing her "mutilated person," she invokes the memory of her dead mother—sacrificed to Puritan vengeance—to demand her own execution: "'I pray you, send me to death now. . . . In her name, I demand of thee death or liberty'" (308–9). Recognizing that the courtroom ritual of the Christian settlers is little different from the sacrifice-rock of her Pequot elders—both are sites at which women and children are sacrificed to the putative needs of the tribe or the state—Magawisca once again invokes the terms of the ritual and offers her body for destruction.[43]

Magawisca, like Hobomok, disappears into the western forests at the end of *Hope Leslie*. But unlike Hobomok, who sacrifices his own happiness for Mary Conant's, Magawisca leaves the Boston colony because she refuses to continue endangering her safety and happiness for her white friends. Having returned to the Boston colony only to fulfill a promise made by an elder of her tribe—and having met there ingratitude and further violence at the hands of Winthrop's government—Magawisca refuses Hope's and Everell's pleas that she remain. These pleas are couched as demands for further self-sacrifice: "'I do not ask you, for your sake, but for ours, to return to us,'" Hope begs. Everell echoes her: "'Yes, Magawisca, . . . come back to us and teach us to be happy, as you are'" (352). In refusing these requests, Magawisca reminds Hope and Everell that the supposed superiority of English culture is a mirage: "'The law of vengeance is written on our hearts—you say you have a written rule of forgiveness—it may be better—if ye would be guided by it'" (349). In the end, the new sacrifice that Magawisca performed in saving Everell is revealed to be little better than the old, and Magawisca rejects both.

Hope Leslie depicts a society in which fathers—both family and founding—are willing to sacrifice their children on the rock of progress. Within systems that valorize sacrifice—including sacrifice refigured as atonement—the responsibility for absorbing and absolving communal guilt falls disproportionately on the backs of those already disempowered: women, people of color, the poor, and children.[44] The ending of the novel suggests that sacrifice must be exploded entirely before the nation can mature—an act Sedgwick symbolically performs when the fallen woman Rosa, who has sacrificed her virtue for a forbidden love, commits suicide by setting a ship ablaze in the final chapters of the text. The title's depressing double entendre—"Hope-lessly," pace Judith Fetterley—reflects the unresolved status of *Hope Leslie*'s central problem: how a culture can form an identity if not through acts of sacrifice, self-elected or otherwise.[45]

From Sacrifice to Self-Representation: Isabella Linwood's Religious Resolve

The problem of vicarious sacrifice was unresolved in official Unitarian theology of the 1820s as well. Having rejected both the substitutionary and governmental models of Christ's atonement, Unitarian theologians had no compelling doctrine with which to replace them. Though they disallowed Christ's divine nature and rejected Trinitarian explications for the meaning of his death, they could agree on no convincing explanation for how human salvation was achieved. William Ellery Channing admitted as much: "We have no desire to conceal the fact, that a difference of opinion exists among us, in regard to an interesting part of Christ's mediation; I mean, in regard to the precise influence of his death on our forgiveness." Some Unitarian theologians saw Christ's death as an example meant to "confir[m] his religion" and "giv[e] it a power over the mind" that would "lea[d] to repentance and virtue." Others thought Christ's death had "a special influence in removing punishment, as a condition or method of pardon," but couldn't explain exactly how that "special influence" functioned.[46] Theologically speaking, Unitarian clerics kicked the can of atonement down the road: Christ suffered and died on the cross for some mysterious but important reason they could not explain.

In her 1835 novel *The Linwoods, or "Sixty Years Since" in America*, Sedgwick picked up the gauntlet where Channing and other Unitarian theologians had thrown it down. Despite the fact that *The Linwoods* is set during the Revolutionary War, the novel eschews scenes of ritualized violence and instead tells the history of the nation's founding as a tale of living language. *The Linwoods* rejects ritual sacrifice, with its inherent violence, its flattening of individual specificity, and its limited opportunities for agency, and instead constructs a theology based on the productive possibilities of religious language. To escape the endlessly iterative ritual conditions in which women's bodies could occupy only the role of sacrificial victim and women's voices could only repeat the story of sacrificial violence, Sedgwick developed a model of spontaneous religious language—one in which women's language gained effective power precisely by freeing itself from ritual forms. By locating the potential for religious agency in women's spontaneous, sincere, and embodied speech—a force that Sedgwick calls "resolve"—*The Linwoods* posits women's active religious agency, rather than their passive participation in ritual forms, as a key driver of American progress.

Though highly original, Sedgwick's theology of spontaneous religious language also has roots in Unitarian thought, since Unitarian Christology held up Christ's words and actions as the true purpose of his ministry. Because Unitarians rejected both the doctrine of the Trinity, according to which Christ is part of the tripartite Godhead and therefore fully divine, and the doctrine of vicarious sacrifice, by which Christ's death on the cross was ordained by God and necessary to effect the salvation of humankind, Unitarians were accused of denigrating Christ himself. They vociferously denied this charge, asserting that in fact Christ was central to their theology and that apprehending Christ as fully human made his actions, his teachings, and his suffering on the cross more—rather than less—meaningful to believers. William Ellery Channing emphasized Christ's role as "son and messenger, who derived all his powers and glories from the Universal Parent" but traced Christ's salutary influence not to his payment of a divine debt but to "his promises of pardon to the penitent, . . . the light which he has thrown on the path of duty, . . . his glorious discoveries of immortality, . . . [and] his continual intercession, which obtains for us spiritual blessings."[47] William Ware, pastor of the First Unitarian Church in New York, where Sedgwick began attending services in 1821, extolled Christ's "prophetical and mediatorial character," insisting "that he is the only true prophet of God, . . . [and] that all the commands, precepts, institutions of Jesus have the force and delegation of divine commands, precepts and institutions."[48] Henry Ware Jr., whom Sedgwick admired (she referred to him in an 1821 letter as "a man wise and skillful . . . full of every gracious affection"[49]) and who would later commission her novel *Home* (1835), described Christ as "the medium through which are communicated all the purposes and revelations of God" and the man who "by his instructions, doctrine, and example . . . did all that was needful to teach men the way of return, and lead them back to God."[50] For these and other Unitarian thinkers, then, Christ was messenger, prophet, mediator, and persuasive example. What he was not was a sacrificial lamb. Indeed, too much emphasis on vicarious sacrifice, Unitarians claimed, had distracted Trinitarian Christians from the true purpose of Christ's life, which was to serve as an example of right behavior. Obsessing about Christ's mediating function in atoning for humankind's sin "leads men to think, that Christ came to change God's mind, rather than their own," with the result that "high sounding praises of Christ's cross seem often to be substituted for obedience to his precepts."[51] For Unitarians, including Sedgwick, it was Christ's life and teachings—his embodied actions and living language—that were to serve as an example to his followers.

The *Linwoods* is the story of the process by which Isabella Linwood's religious language becomes the true religious and political language of the new United States. The *Linwoods* tells the story of Isabella and Herbert Linwood, siblings born in colonial New York to a Loyalist father who regards George Washington and his compatriots as rebellious criminals. When Herbert runs away to join Washington's army, Mr. Linwood vows that Herbert will never reenter the family home. Isabella begs for leniency, but Mr. Linwood strengthens his condemnation of Herbert by swearing an oath against his son: "'You know, Belle, I have sworn no rebel will enter my doors.'" Isabella's reply highlights both her gender and her subordinate position as Mr. Linwood's daughter. But it also lays claim to a specifically feminine "resolve": "'And you know, sir, that I have—not sworn; oh, no! but resolved, and my resolve is the feminine of my father's oath, that you shall hang me on a gallows high as Haman's, before I cease to plead that our doors be open to one rebel at least'" (113).[52] Isabella Linwood's "resolve" is a spontaneous linguistic act—not an oath but a "pleading"—for which her body stands as security: "you shall hang me on a gallows . . . before I cease to plead." The image of the gallows suggests the potential sacrifice of Isabella's body in a public spectacle of ritualized violence. But the reference to Haman invokes the story of Esther, a clever woman who turned the tables on a powerful man and had him hanged on the gallows he built for her people.[53] Isabella's embodied religious language—her resolve—will effect a similar reversal. Mr. Linwood, white, male, wealthy, and with the might of the British Crown behind him, should be the more powerful speaker in the exchange: his masculine "oath" should easily crush Isabella's feminine "resolve." And yet it is Isabella—young, female, politically disenfranchised, and in rebellion against the Crown—who will eventually prevail: Herbert will be readmitted to the Linwood household over his father's unheeded objections.

Isabella's resolve is a form of religious language that is spontaneous, sincere, and embodied and that is explicitly arrayed against the religious and political rituals that guide the behavior of the novel's patriarchs. In using the term *religious language*, I am drawing on a specific set of definitions employed by two contemporary scholars. Webb Keane defines religious language as "linguistic practices that are taken *by practitioners themselves* to be marked as unusual," as distinct from ordinary experience. Though they maintain many of the features of ordinary language, Keane notes, religious language practices have a particular kind of power that ordinary language lacks: they "can assist the construction of forms of agency that are expanded, displaced, distributed or otherwise different from—but clearly related to—what are otherwise available."[54] Bruno Latour defines religious language as speech acts that transform or transport both "the spirit from which they talk" and the spirit (human or divine) to which they are spoken. For Latour, acts of religious language "produce in part personhood"; they generate "new states, 'new beginnings,' as William James would say . . . in the persons thus addressed." "Love-talk," for Latour, is a paradigmatic example of religious language: the couple exchanging "I love yous" for the first time is using religious language just as surely as the priest who pronounces that "the body of Christ is broken for you."[55] Religious language, as I am using it here and as Sedgwick depicts it in *The Linwoods*, makes new forms of agency possible by means of speech acts that transform and transport both speaker and listener.

Religious language can and often does encompass ritual forms; the two are not mutually exclusive. (J. L. Austin's paradigmatic example of illocutionary speech—the wedding ceremony—is also a prime example of religious speech.) But the model of religious language practiced by Isabella Linwood is explicitly opposed to the forms of ritual speech and action displayed in the scene at the sacrifice-rock in *Hope Leslie*. These are also the forms of speech most often embraced by male characters in *The Linwoods*: Mr. Linwood's "oaths," the political "policy" invoked by the British commander Sir Henry Clinton, and the hackneyed language of seduction wielded by Jasper Meredith. Because the romantic, religious, and political rituals that guide the customs of revolutionary-era New York limit women's participation in public matters (and offer them limited choice even in private ones), Isabella Linwood must invent a new form of spontaneous and embodied religious language if she is to effectively advocate for her brother and shape the outcome of the war.

Sedgwick found a model for embodied religious language in her "second mother," Elizabeth Freeman, the African American woman who had tended to the Sedgwick children during Pamela Sedgwick's long illnesses. Freeman, born into slavery around 1742, had joined the family after Theodore Sedgwick successfully sued for her freedom before the Massachusetts Supreme Court in 1781. When Catharine recounted the story of Freeman's emancipation in a sketch in *Bentley's Miscellany*, she emphasized the "resolve" that had convinced her father to take Freeman's case:

> It was soon after the close of the revolutionary war, that she chanced at the village "meeting house," in Sheffield, to hear the Declaration of Independence read. She went the next day to the office of Mr. Theodore Sedgewick [sic]. . . . "Sir," said she, "I heard that paper read yesterday, that says, 'all men are born equal, and that every man has a right to freedom.['] I am not a dumb *critter*; won't the law give me my freedom?" . . . Such a resolve as hers is like God's messengers—wind, snow, and hail—irresistible. . . . Mr. Sedgewick [sic] immediately instituted a suit on behalf of the extraordinary plaintiff; a decree was obtained in her favour.[56]

In Sedgwick's telling, Freeman's embodied and spontaneous response to hearing the Declaration of Independence—her decision to march into Theodore Sedgwick's office and declare her full humanity—overcomes the social and political barriers between the white lawyer and the enslaved black woman.

Though Freeman's goal is political—she wishes to sue for her freedom—her resolve, for Sedgwick, is religious: "like God's messengers," it is "irresistible" and causes the much more powerful Theodore to "immediately" obey her wishes. Because the Sedgwick children credited Freeman's case with ending all forms of slavery in Massachusetts, the story of her emancipation held immense religious and political import for Catharine and her siblings.[57]

It is this model of spontaneous and embodied religious language that provides the pattern for Isabella Linwood's "resolve." In the linguistic-theological system constructed in *The Linwoods*, as in the *Bentley's Miscellany* sketch, it is resolve that brings about individual and social change. This transformative religious language is most effective when it is an expression of one's "natural" self, springing forth spontaneously from a pure heart. For Isabella Linwood, the only truly religious language—the only language that might effect real change—arises outside the confines of even the simplest ritual forms, including her father's oath or the social forms of the English aristocracy. While attending dinner at the home of Sir Henry Clinton, commander of the English forces in New York, Isabella offers a toast to "'*our* native land'" (132, emphasis in original). Rather than following the traditional form of the toast offered by Mr. Linwood, "'the King—God bless him,'" Isabella's toast arises spontaneously and, rather than deferring to a higher authority, includes in its "our" all those at the table who identify themselves as Americans. Isabella also alters the normal ritual of the toast by pledging with water rather than wine. The narrator emphasizes Isabella's refusal to observe the ritual forms of the toast: "Miss Linwood violated the strict rules that governed her contemporaries. She was not a lady of saws and precedents" (132). But her spontaneous speech is transformative, transporting both herself and another attendee at the dinner, Eliot Lee. For Isabella this spontaneous outburst of pro-Yankee sentiment is the first sign of her eventual conversion from Loyalist to revolutionary; for Eliot it is the beginning of his romance with Isabella.

Isabella Linwood's religious language entails a combination of bodily presence and impassioned speech, and it is the most powerful agentive force in *The Linwoods*. In contrast to her father's ineffectual oaths, Isabella's resolve has the power to alter other characters' behavior, both in the moment and retrospectively. When Herbert Linwood considers deserting Washington's army to gain his father's forgiveness and be readmitted to the Linwood family, one sentence from Isabella is enough to end his doubts and cement his loyalty to the rebellion. "'Herbert, is it possible you waver?'" Isabella demands. Her voice "thrill[s]" through Herbert's soul, and his response indicates the power of Isabella's speech: "He started as if he were electrified: his eye met hers, and the evil spirits of doubt and irresolution were overcome. 'Heaven forgive me! . . .

I waver no longer'" (148). Isabella's impassioned resolve overcomes Herbert's "irresolution," and its effects reach well beyond the moment of pronouncement. Months later, when he is starving in an English military prison after being captured and accused of spying for Washington, Herbert recalls that "'there was one moment—but one, thank God! When, tempted by more than all the gold and honour in the king's gift, I swerved. I was saved by a look from Isabella'" (217). The religious terms that infuse these scenes—"evil spirits," "tempted," "Heaven forgive me," "thank God," "saved"—indicate the religious import of Isabella's speech even and perhaps especially when she is discussing political subjects. For Isabella, disenfranchised though she is (and will remain even after the Revolution), her political participation is nevertheless enabled by a spontaneous religious agency brought about through her womanly resolve.

Isabella's religious language is effective, in part, because it demonstrates a high level of what the philosopher Donald Evans calls "self-involvement." Self-involvement is a speaker's degree of personal investment in an utterance; it lies along a spectrum from weak to strong. The statement "I am six feet four inches tall" has a low degree of self-involvement; the statement "I am a follower of the Prophet" likely has a high degree of self-involvement. It implies "a variety of entailments"—moral, behavioral, cultural, perhaps national—each of which reveals something important about the speaker's personhood.[58] Highly self-involved statements are infused with emotional investment; they are "thoughts somehow 'felt' in flushes, pulses, 'movements' of our livers, minds, hearts, stomachs, skin. They are *embodied* thoughts, thoughts seeped with the apprehension that 'I am involved.'"[59] It is Isabella Linwood's embodied self-involvement, rather than any adherence to recognizable ritual forms, that gives her language religious authority and makes it effective in contexts in which she, as a woman and a colonist in rebellion against her king, can claim no other right to be heard.[60]

Writing of Elizabeth Freeman's encounter with Theodore Sedgwick, Catharine Sedgwick emphasized the role of Freeman's physical presence in persuading the lawyer to take her case: "I can imagine her upright form, as she stood [in Theodore's office] dilating with her fresh hope based on the declaration of an intrinsic, inalienable right."[61] Isabella Linwood's resolve also depends on the persuasive medium of her physical presence. Scenes of Isabella transforming others' emotions and actions are always accompanied by descriptions of her "thrilling" and "delicious" voice, her "moistened eye," and "the tears . . . of a young and beautiful woman" (148, 132, 241). When she writes a letter to Sir Henry Clinton begging for news of the imprisoned Herbert's fate, she receives a note expressing Sir Henry's regret that he has "'no absolute power by which he can remit, at pleasure, the offences of disloyal subjects'"—he cannot act spontaneously in response to the dictates of kindness (185). The letter is not from Sir Henry himself but from his secretary; Sir Henry has not even signed it. Sir Henry has thus performed the ritual duty of replying to Isabella's letter, but the letter evinces no real involvement on his part. Isabella responds by increasing her own embodied self-involvement: their next encounter takes place not via letter but via meeting. Seeking a political favor, Isabella offers the language of religious duty: declaring the commander responsible "'to God—so are we all, Sir Henry,'" Isabella promises that long after the war is over, the memory of his own kindness will be "'like the manna of the wilderness'" (241, 242). Once the favor is granted, Isabella promises to "'fall down on my knees, and pray to God to bless you for ever and ever'" (240–43). Isabella leaves the meeting with a letter allowing for Herbert's temporary release—evidence of Sir Henry's transformation through the operation of Isabella's religious language.

Isabella's ability to transform Sir Henry's behavior by means of her spontaneous and self-involved speech points to the inextricability of religious and political concerns in the novel and in the early United States. Writing in the wake of official church disestablishment in the early nineteenth century about the founding of the nation in the late eighteenth, Sedgwick's insistence on placing women and their embodied religious language at the center of American self-fashioning represents a direct response to liberal political theory and nascent separate spheres ideology, which worked together to confine women and their religious agency to the private sphere. As Joan Scott has definitively shown, eighteenth- and nineteenth-century constructions of secularity, including the (imagined but never fully achieved) separation of church and state, insisted that women's dangerous religious passions must be sequestered in the private sphere lest they corrupt the rational workings of the state. Among eighteenth-century liberal philosophers and republican revolutionaries, the "susceptibility of women to priestly influence" was taken as a given, and "feminine religiosity was seen as a force that threatened to disrupt or undermine the rational pursuits that constitute politics [because] like feminine sexuality it was excessive, transgressive, and dangerous."[62] Sedgwick's insistence on placing women at the originary site of American independence repudiates this ideological construction of women's religion as dangerous to the national project. Her depiction of Isabella Linwood's linguistic agency insists that women's participation in the religio-political forces of national development must be driven by their active use of language rather than the sacrifice of their silent, passive bodies.

The Linwoods repeatedly reverses liberal philosophy's insistence that women's natural passions are a danger to the rationally constituted and implicitly masculine state. Instead, in *The Linwoods*, women's spontaneous religious language tempers men's tendency toward impulsivity and violence. In *The Linwoods*, General George Washington and Sir Henry Clinton, like Mononotto and John Winthrop in *Hope Leslie*, serve as figures through whom Sedgwick can interrogate the connection between religious and political authority. Washington and Clinton are political gods with competing expectations for their subjects: Sir Henry Clinton requires deference (punishing revolutionaries for "'the offences of disloyal subjects'" [185]) while Washington commands respect ("'General Washington requires no more than he performs,'" Eliot Lee observes [110]). Clinton, in other words, is the punitive God of orthodox Congregationalism; Washington is the reasonable and parental God of Unitarian Christianity. When Isabella approaches Clinton after Herbert is falsely accused of spying, she asks him to imagine himself this benevolent and loving father-god: "'I commend [Herbert] to your mercy; think of him as if he were your own son, and then mete out to him . . . such measure as a father would allot to such an offence'" (185). Though Clinton knows Herbert is innocent of the crime, he plans to execute him as an example to would-be rebels—the governmental theory of atonement as an act of military policy. In holding to such "artificial codes and traditionary abuses," Sir Henry behaves like the God of orthodox theology—one who places his imagined son in the role of sacrificial lamb (185).

The *Linwoods* does not choose one of these political gods over the other; instead, it positions Isabella as superior to both. Isabella's superiority comes from her command of spontaneous religious language—a uniquely feminine trait that these men cannot safely wield. Male spontaneity, the novel suggests, is dangerous and destructive, even in the best of men. Sedgwick's Washington is "constitutionally subject to gusts of passion"; his well-known "moderation and equanimity" are "effects of the highest principle, not the gifts of nature." While Isabella's spontaneous resolve is always directed to benevolent ends, Washington's passions are a "whirlwind" and a "storm" that he can only control by "a power, almost divine (and doubtless from a divine source)" (203–4). The novel's other model of manly and civic virtue, Eliot Lee, has been similarly "trained in the school of exertion, of self-denial, and self-subjection" (321). *The Linwoods* repeatedly suggests that male spontaneity, unlike feminine resolve, has dangerous consequences; even Herbert Linwood's imprisonment is the result of his congenital habit of putting "'action before thought'" (143).

In portraying women as the natural purveyors of religious resolve and resolve as the most effectual mode of social and political action, *The Linwoods* undermines the ideology expressed by John Winthrop in *Hope Leslie* that "'passiveness . . . , next to godliness, is a woman's best virtue'" (160). Isabella

Linwood's embodied resolve is by definition active—a "performance," as Winthrop would disapprovingly call it. In *The Linwoods*, the United States' transformation from oppressed colony to independent nation is authorized by women's language rather than men's sacrifices. By embedding this doctrine of spontaneous religious language in a story of the American Revolution, Sedgwick transforms the colonial rebellion into a religious-rhetorical struggle that aligns England with a violent masculine past and the United States with a future built on feminine resolve.

Elizabeth Freeman's National Body

As I have discussed, the real-life Elizabeth Freeman provided the model for the fictional Isabella Linwood's religious resolve, but that was not the extent of her influence on Catharine Maria Sedgwick's fiction. In fact, she appears over and over again in Sedgwick's writing as the model for various forms of female religious agency. Most famously, a Sedgwick family legend about Freeman inspired Magawisca's brave act at the sacrifice-rock in *Hope Leslie*. While still enslaved, Freeman had saved a younger sister from a blow with a hot poker by interposing her arm to deflect the weapon, just as the fictional Magawisca interposes her arm between Mononotto's ax and Everell Fletcher's neck. Sedgwick included versions of this event not only in *Hope Leslie* but in an antislavery story she "began and abandoned" in the 1830s, in the already mentioned *Bentley's Miscellany* sketch in 1853, and in an 1865 letter she wrote to James Parton.[63]

Freeman's life story also informs multiple scenes in *The Linwoods*. In one, a woman protects her two blind children from marauding thieves, an event based on Freeman's real-life defense of the Sedgwick household during Shays' Rebellion, while Theodore Sedgwick was away from home on public business.[64] Freeman also appears in *The Linwoods* in the character of Rose, the Linwood family's African American servant who, like Freeman herself, galls under the yoke of slavery. Freeman had once told the young Catharine Sedgwick that "any time, any time while I was a slave, if one minute's freedom had been offered to me, and I had been told I must die at the end of that minute, I would have taken it—just to stand one minute on God's *airth* a free woman—I would."[65] In *The Linwoods*, the fictional Rose makes a similar statement, reminding Isabella Linwood that "'I am a *slave*. . . . I can be bought and sold like the cattle. I would die tomorrow to be free to-day. Oh, free breath is good—free breath is good!'" (136). But whereas the real Freeman's desire for freedom prompted her to take matters into her own hands and resolve to approach The-

odore Sedgwick, in *The Linwoods* it is Isabella, not Rose, who plays the principal role in Rose's emancipation. When Isabella's father offers his eight-year-old
daughter "'any thing you'll ask of me'" if she takes a French prize at school,
Isabella wins the competition and then demands as her reward Rose's manumission (137).

In this novel about the American Revolution, it is fitting that Isabella would
win Rose's freedom by learning the language of the only other democratic
nation in the eighteenth-century world. It is also unsurprising that Isabella wins
Rose's freedom by learning to access a new language, since language formed
the crux of Sedgwick's evolving conception of female agency. But the effective language here is not Rose's own, as it was in the story of Freeman, who
appropriated the words of the Declaration of Independence and the Massachusetts constitution—documents written by white men to guarantee the free-
doms of white men—when she approached Theodore Sedgwick to demand
his legal representation. Instead, the story of Rose's manumission positions
emancipation as a gift granted to slaves by white benefactors—English, French,
or American—rather than a right to be claimed by African Americans themselves.[66] Though Mr. Linwood knows that Rose wishes to be free ("'Rose is a
fool,'" he tells Isabella when she initially requests Rose's manumission, because
"'she *was* free in every thing but the name'" [137]), he gives more weight to
the whims of an eight-year-old child than to the natural rights of an adult black
woman. Sedgwick's narrator grants to Isabella the "resolve" that the real-life
Freeman wielded on her own behalf, while Freeman's fictional counterpart,
Rose, is relegated to the role of grateful servant, attaching herself to the Linwood family and "enjoy[ing] the voluntary service she render[s]" (138). As
Jenny Franchot has explained, historical novels perform their cultural work by
constructing history as a body and then purifying that body of elements foreign to the nation's mythologized self: "To tell the story of America in the historical novel is to recount progressive forgettings of [a] bodily past." But the
"recounting" of a "forgetting" produces its own kind of remembrance, and
"the project of American historical romance is to 'remember' a past otherwise
censored by language, to provide a visible form for otherwise repressed
truths."[67] In Catharine Maria Sedgwick's fictions, the sacrificed body that endlessly reappears as a reminder of America's "repressed truths" is Elizabeth
Freeman's. Though it was Freeman's religious resolve that provided the model
and inspiration for Sedgwick's characters' religious language, Freeman's raced
body—appearing as Magawisca, as Rose—is disappeared or demoted.

What is known about the real Elizabeth Freeman comes almost entirely
from the writings of the Sedgwick siblings; Freeman herself was likely illiter-
ate. She died in 1829, between the publication of *Hope Leslie* and *The Linwoods*,

which perhaps explains why her presence so pervades the latter novel. She was buried not among her own family but in the Sedgwick plot in Stockbridge, Massachusetts. Catharine Sedgwick wrote only briefly and dismissively of Freeman's children: though "absolutely perfect in service" to the Sedgwicks, Catharine claimed, when Freeman "went to her own little home . . . she was the victim of her affections, and was weakly indulgent to her riotous and ruinous descendants."[68] In all of their loving memorials to Freeman, in which they asserted that "in her sphere . . . she had no superior," it seems not to have occurred to the Sedgwick siblings that Freeman's total dedication to them—her status as their "second mother"—might have affected the health and prosperity of her own family or that the hierarchies of racial subordination that continued to structure the economic, political, and social life of Massachusetts even after the abolition of slavery might have facilitated the "ruinous" fates of Freeman's children and of other African American families.[69]

Sedgwick's and Child's historical novels strenuously engaged in making a claim for white women as active participants in a mythic American past that was being rapidly constructed in the national imagination. Sedgwick, in particular, valorized the power of women's religious language over the sacrifice of their bodies. But the authors accomplished this by appropriating the language and traditions of Native Americans and African Americans, both fictional—in the case of Hobomok and Magawisca—and real, as with Elizabeth Freeman. As the tokenized good Indian or faithful black servant, Hobomok, Magawisca, and Rose are neither full members of white communities nor supported by surrounding racial or religious communities of their own. As Joanna Brooks's work on the Brotherton community, black Freemason lodges, the African Methodist Episcopal Church, and other African American and Native American religious groups makes clear, shared religious beliefs and practices provided a source of strength for real communities of color in the early national United States. As with the white women whose self-determination was sacrificed to construct the masculine public sphere, these groups' attempted extermination was justified by Enlightenment narratives that "aimed for the negation of . . . racialized subjects."[70] By removing their fictional characters of color from communal contexts that might have enabled forms of collective agency, Sedgwick and Child sacrificed Native and black Americans, making them into resources for developing white women's religious agency rather than representing their own.

CHAPTER 2

"Unsheathe the Sword of a Strong, Unbending Will"

Sentimental Agency and the Doctrinal Work of Woman's Fiction

In 1822, five years before essaying the historical novel genre with *Hope Leslie*, Catharine Maria Sedgwick published her first novel, *A New-England Tale; or, Sketches of New-England Character and Manners*. Sedgwick's preface modestly set forth her purpose: only "to add something to the scanty stock of native American literature" and to present "some sketches of the character and manners of our own country."[1] After it was published, Sedgwick wrote to her friend Susan Channing that she had "beg[u]n that little story for a tract" but that she had "had no plans, and the story took a turn that seemed to render it quite unsuitable for a tract."[2] The epigraph on the title page of the novel reflects this shift: the stanza from Burns's "Epistle to a Young Friend" reads, "But how the subject theme may gang, / Let time and chance determine; / Perhaps it may turn out a sang, / Perhaps turn out a sermon."[3]

In the early 1820s, Sedgwick produced both a "sang" and a "sermon" for publication. The "sang" was her 1822 religious tract *Mary Hollis*, published under the imprint of the New York Unitarian Book Society. Tracts were expected to be brief so that they could be printed and distributed inexpensively and to present their lessons "in the form of stories of a didactic character, in which the writers assumed the broad principles of Christian theology and ethics which are common to all followers of Christ, without meddling with sectarian prejudice or party views."[4] *Mary Hollis* followed this mandate: the story of a poor widow whose intemperate husband died in a fit of drunkenness, *Mary Hollis* extols the heroine's thriftiness and piety without attributing those virtues to any particular brand of Christianity. The tale's central precept—that correct religion will produce benevolent behavior—is presented as generally "christian" (lowercase *c*) or, even more broadly, as an example of true "morality."[5] The "sermon" that Sedgwick produced alongside *Mary Hollis* was *A New-England Tale*, a novel that, in contrast to its sister tract, meddled quite openly with "sectarian prejudice"—so much so that Sedgwick's orthodox Congregationalist neighbors in Stockbridge, Massachusetts, perceived the novel as an open attack on their revered Calvinist theological tradition. When *A New-England Tale* appeared, Sedgwick's brother Henry noted in a letter that "the orthodox do all they can to put it down . . . and the New Englanders feel miffed."[6] Early readers of the novel recognized its specific doctrinal purpose: to explore Calvinist beliefs and the supposedly deleterious effects of those beliefs on the characters of those who held them. It was precisely the turn from advocating general moral precepts to "meddling with sectarian prejudice" that transformed Sedgwick's text from "sang" to "sermon"—from tract to novel.[7]

A New-England Tale inaugurated one of the nineteenth century's most enduring and popular literary genres: the group of works that Nina Baym famously identified as "woman's fiction," in which "a young girl . . . is deprived of the supports she had rightly or wrongly depended on to sustain her throughout life and is faced with the necessity of winning her own way in the world."[8] Baym unearthed over 130 works published between 1820 and 1870 that fit this broad pattern and traced the genre to its roots in the fairy tale, the comic hero narrative, and even the Miltonic story of the fortunate fall. But woman's fiction, as it grew into a ubiquitous and beloved nineteenth-century literary genre, also adhered to the religious mission modeled by Sedgwick: it remained a vehicle for the transmission of particular Christian doctrines. Born out of the generic distinction between a tract that advocated an unspecified "christian" morality and a novel so obviously sectarian in its theological intentions as to alienate Sedgwick from her orthodox Calvinist neighbors, woman's fiction became a distinctly sectarian literary genre. Women authors adopted woman's fiction's conventions precisely because they offered a model of religious subject formation that was rigid enough to be recognizable as a paradigmatic Christian story but also flexible enough to further specific doctrinal ends. In doing so, these authors imagined into being diverse models of women's religious agency that were both theologically specific and applicable to everyday life.

Woman's fictions present Protestant religiosity as a set of lived religious practices and thus should be read as works of practical theology. They depict their heroines' religious lives as processes of becoming and offer a sophisticated view of the relationship between individual religious commitment, communal belonging, and social and political conditions. The religious practices modeled by heroines of woman's fiction include an intellectual assent to propositions, an emotional attachment to a personalized God, and a cosmological interpretation of daily life. Details of character and plot are driven "by images and ideals of what constitutes goodness—in people, in relationships, and in conditions of life."⁹ For the heroine of a woman's fiction, the highest good is Christian salvation, without which earthly happiness is only a brief delusion. But in the mid-nineteenth century, the mechanism of Christian salvation was still very much up for debate: Did God select a saved few from among his Creation, or was salvation open to all? The former doctrine was held by Calvinist denominations, including, most prominently, Congregationalists and Presbyterians. The latter was embraced by Arminian Christians, including both Episcopalians and members of the rapidly proliferating Methodist church. The debate between Calvinist and Arminian theologies took place not only in the columns of sectarian journals but in the pages of woman's fiction, where it was elaborated through the mechanisms of plot and characterization rather than through abstruse argumentation.

Woman's fiction's theological ambitions have been difficult for critics to recognize because of the scholarly discourse surrounding the nineteenth-century sentimental—the larger cultural mode to which the literary genre of woman's fiction belongs.¹⁰ Critics have recovered and studied sentimental literature since the 1970s and have recognized sentimental texts as offering "an important form of literary agency" because they explore the consequences of unequal power relations for (most often) white middle-class women's lives.¹¹ But critical accounts of sentimental literature have often mischaracterized the crucial ways in which questions of doctrine animated and informed nineteenth-century debates about women's agency—an oversight that can be traced back to two foundational texts in the study of sentimental literature. While Ann Douglas's *The Feminization of American Culture* (1977) characterized sentimental fiction as having little or no doctrinal content—indeed, accused it of bringing about "the loss of theology"—Jane Tompkins's *Sensational Designs: The Cultural Work of American Fiction, 1790–1860* (1985) sought to rehabilitate the religious language of sentimental fiction without engaging very deeply with the particular doctrines held by sentimental writers. Instead, Tompkins characterized all sentimental fiction as vaguely "evangelical" and concerned primarily with the emotional rather than the intellectual aspects of religious adherence.

Douglas's and Tompkins's work gave rise to a wealth of criticism about sentimental literature that has enriched the study of women's writing for the last four decades. Many critics writing in the wake of the Douglas-Tompkins debate accepted its religious-historical terms at face value while turning their attention to the effects of sentimental culture, including the much-debated question of sentimentalism's complicity with racist violence, consumer culture, and imperialist expansion. More recently, however, scholars have begun to interrogate the theological models that operated in Douglas's and Tompkins's work and to refine our understanding of the religious roots of sentimental literature.[12] The goal of this scholarship (as of my own) is not to turn attention away from questions of materialism, embodiment, and territory, but instead to insist that the study of religious belief and practice cannot be productively separated from issues that seem more straightforwardly "political," either in the nineteenth century or in our own. Indeed, the secular reading practice modeled throughout this book requires that we jettison the artificial separation between the religious and the political, which obscures the operations of political theology in the American "small-p protestant" context.[13]

Much of the important and necessary recent work that has addressed the theological sources of sentimental literature has tended to classify the form as theologically monolithic, with Calvinism most often the system under discussion. One of the earliest scholars to treat sentimental theology was Marianne Noble, who tied the form's "masochistic" tendencies to Calvinist doctrines of salutary suffering, arguing that "the mechanisms of sentimentalism . . . yok[e] the Calvinist idealization of affliction to the painful affect that is a central component of all sentimental literature."[14] While Noble's concerns were primarily psychological, other scholars have engaged in the archaeological work of unearthing sentimentalism's specifically Puritan foundations. In *Jonathan Edwards: America's Evangelical* (2005), Philip Gura describes how the works of the influential Calvinist theologian were excerpted and widely circulated by the American Tract Society, so that Edwards's *Life of David Brainerd* and "Personal Narrative" became staple texts of nineteenth-century sentimental Protestantism.[15] Tracing this narrative even further back, Abram van Engen's *Sympathetic Puritans: Calvinist Fellow-Feeling in Early New England* (2015) locates the roots of sentimental discourse—long believed to be an eighteenth- and nineteenth-century phenomenon—in Puritan communities in colonial North America and thus finds in it an underlying Calvinist theological impulse. In contrast to these moves Calvinward, Claudia Stokes's important and influential *The Altar at Home: Sentimental Literature and Nineteenth-Century American Religion* (2014) traces the rise of Arminianism in the nineteenth-century United States and asserts that "the theological contents of sentimental piety derive primarily from Methodism" and from the Arminian "free grace" theology embraced by John Wesley and promulgated by early Methodist missionaries.[16]

Together, these works "challenge [the] notion of a monolithic and culturally bankrupt feminine faith" that has plagued too much criticism of women's
religious writing.[17] They have done much to deepen our understanding of sentimentalism as both a literary and a religious phenomenon, showing, as Van
Engen has noted, that women writers were not mere recipients of religious
ideas but actively "shaped and changed religion" during and after the Second
Great Awakening.[18] But classifying all sentimental literature as reflecting one
theological system or another obscures the sectarian diversity of sentimental
texts—the ways in which sentimental authors, though claiming to rise above
denominational squabbling, nevertheless took part in the doctrinal debates that
continued to animate American Protestantism well into the nineteenth century.
The diverse theologies on offer in sentimental fiction should interest us as
twenty-first-century critics not only because they provide evidence of women's
intellectual engagement with religion—though that is important—but because,
for women adherents, belief enabled agency in ways that were directly tied to
theological questions.

Juxtaposing two major works of woman's fiction—Susan Warner's *The
Wide, Wide World* (1850) and Augusta Jane Evans's *Beulah* (1859)—reveals the
doctrinal diversity on offer in sentimental literature. These two texts, similar
in their basic plot outlines and in their invocation of the central concerns of
woman's fiction—the simultaneous celebration and sundering of family ties
and the concern with how women's choices are curtailed by legal, political,
social, and biological factors—employ different theological models that result
in widely divergent depictions of women's religious agency. As Calvinist and
Arminian works of woman's fiction, respectively, *The Wide, Wide World* and
Beulah explore, by means of both content and form, the same problems that
occupied ordained ministers and professors of theology in the pages of the
Christian Advocate, the *Princeton Review*, and the hundreds of other sectarian
journals that circulated in the mid-nineteenth-century United States. Reading
Beulah and *The Wide, Wide World* in comparative theological perspective uncovers the implicit doctrinal assertions embedded in these two texts and reveals how the heroines of these and other woman's fictions wield *doctrinal
agency*: a mode of belief, behavior, and expression that informs a woman's sense
of self by imaginatively aligning the events of her life with a Christian narrative of salvation.

Closely examining the different theological arguments that inform *The
Wide, Wide World* and *Beulah* can deepen our understanding of how woman's
fiction and the sentimental novel more generally enabled women to imagine
and enact their own agency. To recognize sentimental agency, however, we
must disentangle agency from power. Critics searching for signs of "sentimental

power" have assumed that all power is positive and exercised willfully by conscious actors with particular ideological goals in sight. They have thus sought evidence of sentimental power most often in scenes and acts of resistance—moments when characters subvert or throw off the authority of father, husband, or minister. These critical treatments of sentimental fiction are influenced by the "progressive-secular imaginary" discussed in the introduction to this book: the set of philosophically liberal feminist assumptions that places individual autonomy at the center of discussions about human action and equates agency with self-will, independence, resistance, or subversion.[19] Influenced by such ideas, feminist critics—even those who have displayed a sensitivity to the role of religion in women's lives—have found it nearly impossible to imagine forms of female agency that operate by inhabiting norms of religious obedience and piety rather than by subverting them. And yet in the self-consciously pious, theologically inflected genre of woman's fiction, women's religious agency is more likely to be enacted in scenes of submission, renunciation, and self-mastery than in acts of subversion.

While twenty-first-century critics may find models of religiously motivated agency foreign or unappealing, recognizing them *as* agency is nonetheless crucial to a correct understanding of nineteenth-century women's writing. When viewed through a distorted critical lens, the forms of agency engaged in by the heroines of woman's fiction—agency that often takes the form of passivity or submission—can seem corrupt or damaged. Woman's fiction— and sentimentalism more generally—then becomes dismissible for critics seeking evidence of women's (or of the United States') increasing self-determination. Bringing questions of doctrine and theology to bear on sentimental fiction reveals that there is, in fact, no single model of sentimental power—or, for that matter, of sentimental agency. Different sentimental texts envision the relationship between women's agency and divine agency in different ways—ways that are deeply informed by the novels' theological commitments. The doctrinal structures that undergird woman's fiction must become part of our ongoing discussion of nineteenth-century women's writing if we as critics and readers are to understand the true nature of religious agency in our subjects' time and our own.

Doctrinal Diversity and Religious Agency in Woman's Fiction

As paradigmatic examples of woman's fiction, the plot outlines of Susan Warner's *The Wide, Wide World* and Augusta Jane Evans's *Beulah* are roughly similar: the heroines are separated from their families, thrown into lives of hardship and toil from which they are rescued by kind but demanding benefactors, removed from these chosen families, and then subjected to various challenges to their faith before being reunited with their benefactors in marriage. The model for these and other woman's fictions is the journey taken by Christian, the hero of John Bunyan's *The Pilgrim's Progress from this World to the Next*; it is *The Pilgrim's Progress* that provides the pattern tale for woman's fiction's "overplot."[20] The bookends of the heroine's life—her expulsion from her family at the outset of the novel and her marriage into a new family at the end—correspond to the beginning and end points of Christian's earthly journey: his flight from the City of Destruction and his safe arrival in the land of Beulah. In works of woman's fiction, events in the heroine's life are linked—explicitly or implicitly, depending on the author's preferences—to stops on Christian's journey: his entrance through the Wicket Gate and the loss of his burden of sin; his encounters with the Evangelist and the Interpreter; his sojourn at House Beautiful, followed by his battle with Apollyon and the terrors of the Valley of the Shadow of Death; and the temptations of Vanity Fair and the martyrdom of Faithful. The model of Christian development that *The Pilgrim's Progress* offered to nineteenth-century readers provided the perfect vehicle for woman's fiction's devotional and sectarian ends: widely read, recognized, and loved, the *Progress* was ecumenical enough to serve as a paradigmatic Protestant Christian narrative. At the same time, it was flexible enough to be adapted to divergent sectarian purposes: through the careful selection and explication of plot elements, an author of woman's fiction could imagine a female Christian whose journey toward salvation reflected either a Calvinist or an Arminian cosmology.

Here some capsule definitions may prove helpful. Calvinism and Arminianism are both Protestant theological systems: they insist on God's grace rather than good works or priestly intercession as the true means of human salvation, and they share many basic theological premises. The two systems diverge most sharply in their understanding of who among humankind will be saved and for whom Christ died. The Calvinist doctrine of predestination posits that God has chosen, or predestined, particular human souls to salvation or damnation. Those he has saved are the "elect": Christ died specifically for them (the doctrine of "limited atonement"), and their election is unconditional and irresistible—they cannot choose to be saved or reject their salvation. Arminian theology, by contrast, rejects the doctrines of predestination, irresistible grace, and unconditional election, positing instead that Christ died for all humankind (atonement is unlimited), that grace is offered to all, and that while humans cannot effect their own salvation through good works, they have the option to accept or reject God's offer of salvation. Another crucial difference between the two systems is that Calvinism posits the doctrine of the perseverance of the saints—that those who are among the elect cannot lose that status—but Arminianism asserts that salvation accepted can later be lost: believers can "fall from grace."[21]

While the New England theologians and the Congregationalist and Presbyterian clergy of the seventeenth and eighteenth centuries subscribed almost uniformly to the Calvinist doctrines affirmed at the 1618–1619 Synod of Dort, a nascent Arminianism arose in mid-eighteenth-century New England "as a major, quasi-denominational force in New England Congregationalism under the guidance of particular clergymen," inciting what would eventually become the Unitarian movement. But the most numerous and influential branch of American Arminianism was that propagated by John Wesley, the founder of Methodism. After the American Revolution, Methodism became the fastest-growing sect in the United States: whereas in 1775 only 2 percent of American Christians were Methodist, by 1850 the number had jumped to 34 percent.[22]

Like other woman's fictions, both *The Wide, Wide World* and *Beulah* adhere to the pattern tale of the *Progress*, but the arrangement and interpretation of particular elements reflect each novel's theological assumptions about the course of human salvational history. As a work of Calvinist woman's fiction, *The Wide, Wide World* makes clear that Ellen Montgomery is predestined to salvation; she spends the entirety of the novel seeking—and finding—evidence of her mother's prophecy that she is among the elect. In the Arminian woman's fiction *Beulah*, Beulah Benton begins her eponymous novel with a simple and childlike faith, gifted to her by her devout parents, but early struggles and intellectual searching cause her to fall from grace, and she spends the remainder of the novel seeking the spiritual assurances that will make it possible for her to reclaim God's freely offered gift of salvation. These and other plot differences—Ellen Montgomery's predestination, Beulah Benton's backsliding—mark the novels as reflecting Calvinist and Arminian doctrines, respectively.

Susan Warner's *The Wide, Wide World* is well known to critics of nineteenth-century fiction; it is the story of Ellen Montgomery, a girl of about ten years old who is separated from her ailing, compassionate mother and sent to live with her father's cold and unloving sister in upstate New York. While suffering under her aunt's imperious (and areligious) rule, Ellen is befriended by the kind and pious Alice and John Humphreys, who eventually take her to live with them and who educate her until Alice dies of consumption. When Ellen's mother and father die before returning to claim her, Ellen must leave the Humphreys household and join her mother's relatives in Scotland, the Lindsays, who object to her piety but love her jealously and tyrannically. Through acts of prayer and Christian submission, Ellen manages to maintain her faith while also obeying the Lindsays' wishes until John Humphreys, now a minister, comes to Scotland to rescue and marry her.

Such is the temporal plot of *The Wide, Wide World*. Because the novel is a work of Calvinist woman's fiction, its spiritual plot is the story of Ellen Montgomery finding assurance of her predestined salvation. Events in the novel are arranged in such a way as to reveal to Ellen and to the reader that she is among Christ's elect. When Ellen's mother breaks the news that she and her daughter will soon be parted, she assures Ellen that "'God sends no trouble upon his children but in love; and though we cannot see how, he will no doubt make all this work for our good'" (12).[23] Mrs. Montgomery's assertion that there is "no doubt" about the salutary effects of divinely ordained suffering reflects her belief that Ellen is among the elect and therefore cannot come to eternal grief; it is God's will that Ellen should be saved, and Ellen must arrange her actions and emotions in accordance with that eternal fate. In keeping with this special status, Ellen is soon provided with an opportunity to claim her promised salvation. Separated from her mother, entrusted to the care of two unsympathetic women who will take her by boat to her aunt Fortune's home, Ellen wanders off and befriends a strange man, who comforts her in her sorrows and speaks of Christ's love for her. "'Are you one of his children, Ellen?'" the stranger asks. Ellen replies that she is not (because she loves her mother more than she loves Christ), but the stranger explains that God has taken Mrs. Montgomery away precisely so that Ellen will place her whole confidence in him. Despite Ellen's protestations, the stranger is convinced that Ellen is one of God's children: "'He took your burden of sin upon himself, and suffered that terrible punishment—all to save you, and such as you. And now he asks his children to leave off sinning and come back to him who has bought them with his own blood'" (72). When Ellen promises to "try" to follow Christ, the stranger again insists that God has assured her salvation: "'You can do nothing well without help, but you are sure the help will come; and from this good day you will seek to know and to do the will of God'" (74). The seemingly contradictory logic of the stranger's words to Ellen—you can do nothing to save yourself, and yet you are saved—reflects the novel's Calvinist cosmology: Ellen must seek to do God's will, but this will only be possible if she is already among God's elect.

The stranger on the boat is an embodiment of Bunyan's allegorical Evangelist, the character in *The Pilgrim's Progress* who first points Christian toward the Wicket Gate that will set him on the road to the Celestial City. Ellen will remember her meeting with the stranger as the moment she decided to "become a Christian"; in her first letter to her mother, Ellen describes the man on the boat, writing, "'Oh, mamma, how he talked to me. He read in the Bible to me, and explained it, and he tried to make me a Christian . . . and I resolved I would'" (111). She also brings him up during her first meeting with Alice Humphreys: "'He talked to me a great deal; he wanted me to be a Christian; he wanted me to make up my mind to begin that day to be one; and ma'am, I did'" (151). The stranger even appears in Ellen's dreams, wearing someone else's face, to ask if she has been "pious" (269). While these references to "becoming a Christian" suggest that Ellen's salvation is a matter of choice, in fact it is a foregone conclusion; it is only because Ellen is a child, at the beginning of her Christian journey, that she cannot see this for herself.

Ellen recognizes her election only after her mother's death—fittingly, as a result of encountering The Pilgrim's Progress for the first time. Finding Ellen sunk in grief over the loss of her mother, John Humphreys begins reading to her from Bunyan's work, dwelling on the moment of Christian's conversion, when he "loses his burden at the cross." Ellen is particularly struck by the mark placed on Christian's forehead by the ministering angels—the sign that, as John explains, signifies "'the mark of God's children . . . the change that makes them different from others, and different from their old selves. . . . None can be a Christian without it.'" When he instructs her to search the Bible for the "'signs and descriptions by which Christians may know themselves,'" Ellen spends hours pondering the Bible her mother gave her before their parting at the beginning of the novel (351–52). There she finds the verses her mother inscribed on the flyleaf: "I love them that love me, and they that seek me early shall find me" and "I will be a God to thee and to thy seed after thee."[24] "'That has come true!'" Ellen exclaims, and "'That has come true too! . . . And mamma believed it would'" (352). Praying fervently over the child from whom she would soon be parted, Mrs. Montgomery had hoped and believed her child was among the elect, that she bore the invisible "mark" of God's children. After her mother's death, Ellen comes to realize that Mrs. Montgomery's faith in her daughter's election was correct: "'That has come true!'" The story of The Wide, Wide World is the story of Ellen Montgomery "choosing" to become a Christian while eventually coming to recognize that she never had a choice at all, that her soul was promised salvation from before her birth. Her only true choice was to surrender, in the words of a hymn the stranger reads to her on the boat, her "body, soul, and will" to God (75).

There has been some disagreement among critics of The Wide, Wide World as to whether it is more appropriately classified as Calvinist or Arminian. In

Woman's Fiction Baym refers to the novel as a "Calvinist evangelical fiction" in which "basic morality and Christian faith . . . are distinct discourses."[25] Sharon Kim considers *The Wide, Wide World* to be a work of "Puritan realism" and identifies correlative typology as the narrative device that most clearly indicates Warner's debt to Calvinist orthodoxy.[26] Claudia Stokes, by contrast, classifies *The Wide, Wide World* as theologically Arminian, since in each of her novels "Warner repeatedly stresses that the Christian life is the result of effortful habits, will power, and self-control, and not the effortless divine gift of election."[27] But being among the elect does not release Ellen from the effort of being kind and dutiful or of striving for spiritual perfection. Instead, it makes those responsibilities more imperative, because Ellen's good behavior will provide both evidence of her election and an example of God's grace to those around her. In other words, Ellen's predestined status does not rob her of agency but becomes the condition through which she understands her agency: evidence of election gives Ellen's spiritual striving a specific cosmic meaning.[28]

Augusta Jane Evans's *Beulah* offers a very different model of the Christian's journey: in this Arminian woman's fiction, salvation is not assured, and the heroine struggles to suppress her own doubts and to accept God's offer of free grace. Set in a fictionalized Mobile, Alabama, *Beulah* begins with the eponymous heroine living in an orphan asylum with her sister, Lilly. When Lilly is adopted by a wealthy family and then dies of scarlet fever, Beulah is taken in by Lilly's doctor, Guy Hartwell. They form an arrangement whereby Hartwell will provide Beulah's lodging and education until she is old enough to work as a teacher, when she will repay him for his expense. As she builds a career for herself, Beulah experiences a crisis of faith brought on by her voracious reading in works of philosophy and psychology; when she appeals to the religiously skeptical Hartwell for help, he recommends that she give up teaching and become his wife. Beulah refuses this offer as well, choosing instead to pursue a career as a writer and to continue her philosophical investigations. After many years of loneliness, hard work, and dogged study, Beulah finally reclaims her faith and agrees to marry Hartwell, setting herself the task of quieting his skepticism and converting him to Christianity.

Beulah Benton's process of Christian development is not a story of claiming salvation already granted but of seeking—and possibly losing—a salvation perpetually on offer but also perpetually under threat. As a novel that assumes an Arminian soteriological narrative, *Beulah* operates according to the three most important theological innovations of Wesleyan Arminianism: "free will, falling from grace, and sanctification."[29] Arminian Methodists subscribed to a theology of "prevenient grace," which asserted that while God's grace is "given to each person, empowering that individual to choose between eternal life and eternal damnation," the gift of grace is "resistible": humans may choose to reject God's gift of salvation through the exercise of their own free will. Nineteenth-century Methodists and other Arminians thus took very seriously the apostle Paul's injunction, in Philippians 2:12, to "work out your own salvation with fear and trembling."[30] Since "conversion was a vocation, not a one-time event [and] it was possible for believers to turn from God and lose their salvation," Methodist adherents were encouraged to guard against backsliding by striving for Christian perfection or "entire sanctification" through acts of "self-denial, prayer, scriptural study, and fasting."[31]

Backsliding is precisely the religious experience that the young Beulah Benton undergoes after the death of her parents and sister. Like Ellen Montgomery, Beulah is born to a mother who imparts her sincere Christian faith to her daughter. But the strangers Beulah meets after her parents' deaths are not kind, and these early experiences of cruelty, capped by her sister Lilly's death, set her on a path of religious questioning. Her doubts are only amplified when she gains access to the library of her benefactor, Guy Hartwell, which is full of contemporary scientific and philosophical texts. (Poe's poem "Eureka" is "the portal through which she enter[s] the vast Pantheon of Speculation" [121].) People with whom Beulah discusses her doubts confess similar confusion: her skeptical friend Cornelia Graham is busily trying to fashion a creed out of Emerson's "dim and contradictory" writings—particularly his "Law of Compensation" (230)—and an older mentor, though kindly, warns Beulah that "'I am too unsettled myself to presume to direct others'" (245). Those who are willing to advise Beulah about her faith tell her to go back rather than forward—to suppress both intellect and independence and return to the simple and childlike faith of her youth. When Guy Hartwell warns her not to "read [his] books promiscuously" lest they shake the faith she had "when a little girl," Beulah demands to know whether she should "be satisfied with a creed which I could not bear to have investigated" (129). When her friend Clara Sanders finds Beulah doubting God's plan for salvation ("Why curse a race in order to necessitate a Saviour?" Beulah wonders, echoing precisely those doubts about the atonement that were expressed by Child, Sedgwick, and their Unitarian contemporaries), Clara begs Beulah to give up her dangerous books: "'Throw them into the fire, and come back to trust in Christ'" (208). All of the well-meaning advice from those around Beulah is expressed in binary terms that she refuses to accept: she must be child or adult, brainless or heartless, "panthei[st] or utter skeptic"—all choices that for Beulah are no choices at all (264). Beulah instead struggles to "work out [her] own salvation with fear and trembling."

The character who finally breaks this stalemate, Reginald Lindsay, appears only in the novel's last hundred pages. Narratively, Reginald Lindsay occupies the place held by the stranger on the boat in *The Wide, Wide World* and the Evangelist in the *Pilgrim's Progress*: he quiets Beulah's skepticism and puts her on a Christian path. But he does so not by scolding or shaming her, assuring her that she is already saved, or insisting that she stop studying and return to a simplistic faith; instead he appeals to her mind, explaining why the revelations found in the Bible are the only reasonable solution to the contradictions of philosophy. He gifts her a copy of William Hamilton's *Philosophy of the Conditioned*, which recommends "a 'learned ignorance'" as "the consummation of knowledge" (367). It is this "learned ignorance" that finally enables Beulah's return to grace: she admits her own human frailty and throws herself on God's mercy: "'My God, save me! Give me light: of myself I can know nothing!'" (371). Having finally resolved her doubts and returned to the Christian fold, Beulah can now turn her attention to converting Guy Hartwell.

If we think of agency as a synonym for power or self-determination, it is tempting to claim that Beulah Benton has agency and Ellen Montgomery does not or that one has more agency than the other. But that, I am suggesting, is the wrong way to read woman's fiction—and the wrong way to apprehend women's religious agency more generally. As (fictional) Protestant women whose lives are modeled on a narrative of Christian salvation, Ellen Montgomery and Beulah Benton exercise agency within the terms of their particular belief systems, not in spite of or against them. Ellen Montgomery exercises religious agency by acting in accordance with her predestined election, and Beulah Benton does so by grasping a grace freely offered. Each woman's actions are shaped by her belief in an all-powerful being whose will determines the possible channels through which agency may flow.

Generic Modification as Practical Theology in *The Wide, Wide World* and *Beulah*

While a text's doctrinal work does not necessarily reflect the religious views of its author, Evans and Warner were, in fact, members of Protestant denominations that stood at opposite ends of the Calvinist-Arminian theological divide: Warner was Presbyterian (one of the two major Calvinist denominations in the nineteenth-century United States) and Evans was Methodist (which was Arminian in its approach to salvation). Warner, daughter of a once wealthy New York lawyer and businessman who was eventually bankrupted, began her writing career in 1848 as a way of bolstering her father's meager income. Henry Whiting Warner had bought a pew at the fashionable Mercer Street Presbyterian Church in New York City in 1836, and his daughters frequently attended with him. But it was not until after their father's financial and social downfall that Susan and her younger sister, Anna, decided to join the congregation as well. In her biography of Susan, Anna reported that her sister was inclined toward the doctrinal and intellectual aspects of her new faith; while Anna was relieved that the ceremony by which they were accepted into the church required them to be "put through no strict formula" in describing their conversion experience, Susan remarked afterward "that she could not see how we were admitted, having so little to say."[32] While the Mercer Street Church adhered to New School Presbyterianism—considered less theologically rigorous than Old School Presbyterianism—both sides professed Calvinist principles, and both saw themselves as guardians of an American intellectual inheritance grounded in a proud Puritan history.[33]

Augusta Jane Evans's motivations for writing were similar to Susan Warner's, though she began at a younger age. Evans was born in Columbus, Georgia, in 1835, and her father's financial troubles and the family's frequent relocations led her to begin composing her first novel, *Inez: A Tale of the Alamo* (1855), in her teens. An anti-Catholic narrative full of theological argument, *Inez* was overlooked by critics and the public alike, but Evans's second novel, *Beulah*, which adhered more closely to the established formula of woman's fiction, found both a wide audience and critical approbation, though there were those who objected to its ostentatious intellectualism. Evans was a lifelong Methodist, a strong proponent of free grace who was given to dismissing religious and political enemies with epithets such as "Puritanic locusts."[34] But her personal papers show that, like her character Beulah Benton, she struggled to reconcile her religious faith with the intellectual, scientific, and philosophical advances of the mid-nineteenth century.[35]

Warner's *The Wide, Wide World* and Evans's *Beulah* reflect these distinct religious and regional backgrounds and contribute to contemporary theological debates about predestination and free will that filled the religious press in the 1850s. Vociferous debates about the relative merits of Calvinism and Arminianism—and of the particular doctrines of predestination and free grace—filled the pages of sectarian journals, and these debates were not always conducted calmly or in a spirit of generosity. An 1856 essay in the Presbyterian *Biblical Repertory and Princeton Review* described Methodist preachers as "uneducated and fanatical men" and labeled their Arminian theology "pure rant" that was "disgusting to men of sense, and shocking to men of right feeling."[36] In April of that same year, the *Methodist Quarterly Review* published a reply insisting that "no man, with even a tolerable knowledge of the history of theology, could have honestly written" such a spurious attack on Arminianism.[37] Similarly, in September 1850 the *Puritan Recorder*, commenting on recent changes to the structure of authority in the English Methodist church, complained of "the grosser abuses" of the Arminian system of theology.[38] A month later a commentator in the *Zion's Herald and Wesleyan Journal* replied that, though the *Puritan Recorder* article had been short, a "greater mass of false propositions and dogmatic assumptions, could not well be crowded into so small a compass."[39] When the Presbyterian minister William B. Sprague warned his daughter, in a series of letters later published as a conduct manual, to avoid "the din and clashing of religious combatants," it was this kind of debate to which he alluded.[40]

But nineteenth-century theology was not merely a site for arcane philosophical wrangling and public sniping; it was also assumed to have imminent practical consequences for individuals' lives. Unlike many European theological traditions, "an understanding of theology as practical governed the discipline in America from the outset," and by the mid-nineteenth century, "theologians in America emphasized the close connection between the practical and the moral," with "the ethical side of theology [becoming] increasingly prominent."[41] Ideas about God's plan for salvation were not to be judged solely on their logical merits but on the effects they produced on readers and hearers; a theological system that accurately reflected the truth of God's nature and of his salvational scheme would produce evidence of conversion and sanctification in those who heard and believed it.

Because practical theology was such a crucial component of the American theological tradition, debates between Calvinist and Arminian divines nearly always made reference to the effects that particular doctrines had on believers. The perennial complaint about Calvinists was that the doctrine of predestination produced either hopeless, dispirited melancholics unable to find assurance of their election or, conversely, self-righteous bigots convinced of their salvation and indifferent to the suffering of the non-elect. These are the Calvinist caricatures that appear in Sedgwick's *A New-England Tale*, the inaugural work of woman's fiction that so angered the author's Stockbridge neighbors. Calvinists, in turn, thought Methodists and other Arminians were hopelessly arrogant: they appropriated to themselves, through their belief in free grace, a salvational power that only God could wield. Because of Methodism's association with revivalism and its insistence that salvation, once claimed, could be lost, Arminians were also accused of being spiritually shallow, prone to religious "enthusiasms" that would pass away as quickly as they came.

These debates were ongoing in the sectarian press of the 1850s. In 1856, the *Biblical Repertory and Princeton Review*, edited by the Reverend Charles Hodge, professor at Princeton Theological Seminary and one of the era's most respected Calvinist divines, published a long dissection of Arminian views. Wrapping up his critique of Arminian doctrines of free grace, the author concluded by complaining of the Methodists' "system of revivals and periodical excitements [which] brings within their churches multitudes who profess to be the subjects of divine grace, who are deluded by mere emotional excitement, and who relapse into their former state." These "enthusiasms," far from being incidental or merely a reflection of flawed human nature, were for Hodge the fault of a fundamentally mistaken theology: "It cannot be otherwise. What is false in their system of doctrine and theory of religion, must produce the bitter fruits of evil, just in proportion as it is prominently presented and acted out."[42] In its reply to the *Princeton Review* essay, an article in the *Methodist Quarterly Review*, the foremost Wesleyan journal in the nineteenth-century United States, insisted that not only had the *Princeton Review* author misrepresented Arminianism but that Calvinism "in its *distinguishing* features, is a very mischievous corruption of Christianity" that "destroys at once the moral attributes of God and the free agency of man."[43] Both arguments rested on the assertion that the opposing theology was not only logically incoherent but pernicious in its practical effects, leading potential Christians away from rather than toward salvation.

While avoiding the argumentative intricacies (and the accompanying nastiness) of such explicit theological debate, woman's fiction nevertheless provided a medium for the elaboration and dissemination of practical theology. The aim of practical theology was to impart "knowledge that led to a good beyond itself, specifically to the end of blessedness and union with God."[44] Correct doctrine, nineteenth-century Protestants believed, would produce right living. Woman's fiction, which depicted in detail a young person's transformation from unredeemed child to saved and sanctified adult, offered an extended demonstration of how particular doctrines might produce the outcome of "blessedness and union." It did so not only—or even primarily—through dialogue and explication but through the mechanism of plot. The selection and placement of standard story elements, including adoption and marriage, reflected particular cosmological understandings of the Christian life righteously lived.

Woman's fiction's status as a mode of practical theology elaborated through literary form can be traced through the genre's most fundamental trope: adoption.[45] The heroine's adoption and her response to it reflect a novel's theological assumptions about the nature of salvation and to whom it is distributed.

In the Calvinist cosmos of *The Wide, Wide World*, earthly adoption corresponds typologically to divine election: Ellen's extralegal adoption by the Humphreys siblings parallels her status as a predestined member of the family of God. While Ellen perceives herself as having "chosen" to join the Humphreys family, in fact this choice is made for her by other characters in the novel, as she is selected by Alice, then given to John, and then reclaimed by John after her so-journ in England in a series of "elections" over which she has little control. Furthermore, Ellen's adoption by the Humphreyses is final and irrevocable, as John and Alice's affective claim to her is as "irresistible" as the Calvinist con-vert's unconditional election. When her uncle, who is her legal guardian but a spiritual stranger, insists that Ellen change her last name from Montgomery to Lindsay, Ellen silently reminds herself that she still belongs to God and the Humphreyses: whatever her name, she "'can't be adopted twice'" (490).

In *Beulah*, by contrast, earthly adoption is not the type of God's heavenly election; instead, it is evidence of laziness and dependency, a failure to exer-cise one's God-given free will. When Guy Hartwell retrieves Beulah Benton from the orphan asylum, she agrees to live with him on one condition: "'I am not going to be adopted'" (106). He repeats his offer to adopt her on several occasions: when she graduates high school and takes a teaching job, when she begins a successful career as a writer, and when she rents a home with a friend and lives independently. When Clara Sanders—the novel's Calvinist mouthpiece—advises Beulah to accept Hartwell's repeated offers of adoption, Beulah demands to know whether Clara would be "'willing to change places with me, and indolently wait for others to maintain you?'" Clara replies, "'Gladly, if I had been selected as you were'" (115). Beulah's repeated refusals to be (s)elected by Hartwell index *Beulah*'s commitment to an Arminian world view, according to which the individual believer chooses his or her spiritual fate rather than submitting to a predestined election. Evans makes the con-nection between adoption and spiritual failure explicit when Beulah asserts that her friend Eugene's "'adoption was his ruin'" (296): Beulah tells Eugene that "'in lieu of his gold and influence,'" Eugene's adopted father "'has your will, your conscience. How can you bear to be a mere tool in his hands?'" (187). Instead of "working out his own salvation," as Beulah does, Eugene allows himself to be adopted by the worldly Graham family, an indulgence that leads to alcoholism, a loveless marriage, and a near-fatal accident.

In framing Eugene's downfall as a failure of will, *Beulah* raises another cru-cial distinction between Calvinist and Arminian woman's fictions: their treat-ment of the question of free will. In depicting women's spiritual development and the forms of religious agency available to Christian women, woman's fic-tions reflect divergent theological understandings of human—and particularly female—will. These distinctions were as old as the Reformation but remained central to antebellum sectarian debates.

The Calvinist understanding of free will was thoroughly explicated by the eighteenth-century theologian Jonathan Edwards; his detailed treatment of predestinarian theology appeared in 1754 and depicted an ordered universe in which events are predetermined by God in a long sequence of cause and effect stretching backward to the moment of creation.[46] Edwards insisted that predestination and free will were compatible concepts because individuals are at liberty to act according to their wills, but at the same time, as the "moral cause" of human existence and human history, God determines what all of their choices will be. According to Edwards, human beings are "at liberty to act from their own inclinations. What they cannot control, and what does not enter into the equation of their freedom, is *how* their inclination got to be the way it is and *why* they apprehend as they do."[47] Edwards's nineteenth-century New England successors wrestled with the details of his system but agreed that "God was both the moral governor of responsible creatures and the sovereign efficient cause of every event."[48]

Edwards's treatise on the will was a rebuttal to an anonymous and influential book, published in 1732 in London, called *An Essay on the Freedom of Will in God and in Creatures*, which laid out in some detail the basis of an Arminian view of human will. The author of the *Essay* insisted that human will, so far from being predetermined by God, was self-determining and could choose arbitrarily, even perversely, simply for the pleasure of willing. Any interference from God in determining human will would nullify the very concept of free will and make human existence meaningless: "free will" implied "a Power to chuse or to refuse, to chuse one thing or the contrary among several things which are proposed, without any inward or outward restraint, force or constraining byass or influence."[49] John Wesley, writing in 1798, explained how human will might be exercised in contradiction to divine will: "The Arminians hold, that, altho' there may be some moments wherein the Grace of God acts irresistibly, yet in general, any man may resist, and that to his eternal ruin, the Grace whereby it was the Will of God, he should have been eternally saved."[50] In the Arminian formulation, human will is not predetermined by God's will; indeed, it is so independent that it can defy the desires of an all-powerful God.

For the Calvinist or Arminian believer of the nineteenth century, these distinctions had immense practical implications for human agency. To understand the nature of human free will and its relation to God's will is to recognize the opportunities and limits of one's own agency within a particular cosmological framing of human and divine relation. If God's will is fixed and one's salvational status is predetermined, the human task is one of reconciliation and submission—"to know and to do the will of God," as the stranger says to Ellen on the boat. Attempting to defy God's fixed will can cause only frustration and self-harm. But if salvation is not predetermined but offered to all, the task of human beings is to accept God's gift of grace—to ask, as Beulah Benton does, for God to "'save me!'" In their depictions of Ellen's and Beulah's wills, *The Wide, Wide World* and *Beulah* reflect this very real and consequential distinction and offer divergent models of Protestant religious agency for women in particular. For *The Wide, Wide World*'s Ellen Montgomery, human will is something to be surrendered—her responsibility as a willing subject is to conform her will to divine will. For *Beulah*'s Beulah Benton, human will is something to be exercised—it is the means to salvation rather than a stumbling block to perfect submission.

Throughout the Calvinist fiction *The Wide, Wide World*, women's wills are represented entirely in the negative. Since human will is something to be surrendered, displays of self-will are always punished, while conformity to divine will (as interpreted by godly parents and clergymen) is praised and rewarded. The discipline of conforming to divine will is modeled first by Ellen's mother, then by Alice Humphreys, and then by Mrs. Vawse, until it is finally internalized by Ellen herself. Ellen's mother, mourning the impending separation from her daughter, falls to her knees and prays, "'Not my will, but thine be done'" (30), the same words that Alice uses when informing Ellen that she (Alice) is terminally ill. When Ellen receives no news from her absent father and mother, John advises that she try "'to love [God] more, and to be patient under his will'" (344); when Aunt Fortune's illness keeps Ellen from visiting the Humphreyses, John likewise insists that "'the good Husbandman knows what his plants want . . . so there come clouds and rains, and "stormy wind fulfilling his will"'" (368). John's invocation of the "good Husbandman" recalls Mrs. Montgomery's God, who "'sends no trouble upon his children but in love.'" Similarly, when Alice dies, John comforts himself and Ellen with the assurance that "'dear Alice is well—she is well,—and if *we* are made to suffer, we know and we love the hand that has done it'" (443–44). Late in the novel, Ellen makes a single statement that succinctly encapsulates the novel's Calvinist conception of human will. Asked by the Lindsays to take an action that would violate her conscience, Ellen protests that "'I can't do that . . . and I don't want to'" (563). It is Edwardsean free will theology in a nutshell: since human beings cannot alter God's will, they should train themselves not to want to.

In the Arminian woman's fiction *Beulah*, by contrast, human will is represented not as an unruly obstacle to be wrestled with and surrendered but as a positive force that enables the Christian's eventual salvation. The first thing the reader learns about Beulah Benton is that she has a "warm, hopeful heart," defended by "the sword of a strong, unfaltering will" (14). Beulah's earliest object lessons are not the ones that Ellen learns—that submitting to the will of others will lead to happiness and peace; instead, Beulah's first lessons teach her that surrendering one's will results in moral and even physical death. When the wealthy Graysons adopt her sister, Lilly, from the orphan asylum but refuse to take Beulah (because, the narrator flatly reveals, she is too ugly), Beulah resolves "to bear with fortitude what she could not avert" and convinces Lilly to go with her new parents (19). But Lilly dies within weeks of this separation, and Beulah decides never again to bend her will to others, with the result that when Guy Hartwell takes her into his home, they become embroiled in a decades-long battle of wills. When Hartwell questions Beulah about her origins during their first meeting, her reply to him is, "'No more. You have not the right to question, nor I the will to answer'" (36). Beulah refuses Hartwell's offers to adopt and then to marry her because she recognizes that they are contingent on her complete submission and the suppression of her will: "'He wants to rule me with a rod of iron,'" she infers, "'because I am indebted to him for an education and support for several years'" (174). When Beulah's romantic rival Clara Sanders realizes that Hartwell will never love her, it is "that marvelous bit of mechanism, the human will," that enables her to press on despite this "fierce ordeal, and numbing despair" (205, 206). In *Beulah* a woman's will exists for her protection and self-determination, not as something to be surrendered and suppressed. The repeated lesson offered by *Beulah* is that a woman is better off consulting her own will than conforming to the wills of those around her, however much they love her.

These two treatments of the female will in *The Wide, Wide World* and *Beulah* are not binary; it is not simply that Beulah has a strong will and Ellen a weak one. Both Ellen and Beulah are strong willed, and both are reproved by others for exerting their wills to ends that their advisers see as improper. The difference between the heroines lies in the uses to which Ellen's and Beulah's wills may be properly put under the doctrinal terms of each novel. For Ellen Montgomery, the Christian journey is one of obedience, of conforming her will to God's and to those of her guardians; she follows Christ because her mother wished her to, because all of the kindest people in her life wish it as well, and because, she will eventually come to learn, she was predestined to do so. For Beulah Benton, by contrast, the Christian journey is a struggle to work out her own salvation, to move beyond the dependence to which others would subject her, and to form a robust, mature system of belief to replace the unquestioning faith of her childhood. Beulah can experience her faith as authentic only if it comes as the result of her own intellectual and spiritual effort and uncoerced choice.

In these sectarian woman's fictions, the question of whether and when to exert or control one's will informs every moment of the heroine's life, as it will inform her eventual death. To foreshadow this offstage event, each novel presents the death of one of the heroine's close friends, a sister-mentor who, for better or worse, models mature female existence for the heroine. In *The Wide, Wide World*, the sister-mentor is Alice Humphreys, Ellen's adopted sibling and John's biological one. Alice (who corresponds to the character of Faithful in Bunyan's *Pilgrim's Progress*) dies from that standard disease of woman's fiction: consumption, a wasting away that leaves plenty of time for moral instruction but also for the scenes of loving female care that characterize all works in the genre. Alice's sanctified death affirms a submissive model of human will as she models a calm resignation to her approaching death. Prompted by her unconditional obedience to God, Alice professes herself perfectly happy with her fate and surrenders peacefully to death. Describing John's final embrace of his sister, the narrator details how Alice's arms "fell languidly down; the will and the power that had sustained them were gone. Alice was gone" (441). Alice's will, like Ellen's, exists only in the negative— this act of surrender is the only moment in the novel in which Alice is described as having any will at all.

Compare this beatific death to the harrowing scene in Evans's *Beulah* when Cornelia Graham, friend to Beulah and adopted sister to Eugene, expires from the same wasting illness that takes Alice Humphreys. In this Arminian fiction, Cornelia has the "power to chuse" not to believe, and she exercises that power to the last. When Beulah attempts to comfort her by reminding her that "'they say Jesus of Nazareth slept, and woke again; if so, you will,'" Cornelia replies, "'They say! They say! Yes, but I never believed them before, and I don't want to believe them now. I will not believe it'" (318). In an Arminian universe, Cornelia can resist God's gift of grace through the exercise of her free will, and this is the choice she makes. Though Cornelia does not believe, she nevertheless counsels her friend to seek salvation: "'Don't live as I have, believing nothing. . . . It is because I believe in nothing, that I am so clouded now'" (319). In *Beulah*, belief and unbelief are choices that are made possible through an exertion of will, not its surrender. Because she has chosen not to believe, Cornelia's death is not a gentle letting go but a painful "exit," and she receives no final assurance of salvation, no last vision of loved ones gone before. Unlike Alice Humphreys's peaceful death, Cornelia dies with a "long shudder" and "a deep, heavy sigh" (320).

The differing theologies of the will that guide the plots of *The Wide, Wide World* and *Beulah* also result in divergent attitudes toward authority—particularly ecclesiastical authority. *The Wide, Wide World* contains no fewer than three benevolent minister figures: Mr. Humphreys, John Humphreys, and George Marshman—the stranger on the boat, whose identity and vocation are revealed to Ellen and the reader only after Alice's death. Since Ellen's task is to conform her will to God's, she needs Christian guidance in doing so, and Warner provides her with a plethora of paragons of Christian renunciation, both ordained and unordained. These include her mother, Alice Humphreys, Mrs. Vawse, and the three ministers, as well as negative examples in the godless Aunt Fortune and the flighty Sophia Marshman. *Beulah*, by contrast, includes only one named ministerial figure, the tyrannical Mr. Mortimer, who nearly crushes his young wife's spirit through his demands for total submission. Reginald Lindsay, the man who helps Beulah reclaim her faith, is a politician rather than a pastor; the character who bears the name of American Methodism's first bishop—Dr. Asbury—is a medical doctor and an agnostic one at that.[51] *Beulah*'s dearth of pastoral guides reflects the novel's Arminian stance that individuals must "work out their own salvation" rather than submitting to the wills of others.

Warner's and Evans's divergent attitudes toward the proper role of human will in the Christian life are reflected in both their fictional creations and their personal documents. Like Ellen Montgomery, Susan Warner had a strong will: this is evident in her untiring work to support her family after her father's financial ruin. She and her sister Anna famously rose at four a.m. each day to write by candlelight before turning to the domestic duties of keeping their father's house. This self-discipline reflected the proper use of her will: she was to perform the God-given task of supporting and encouraging others through hard work and devotion to duty. But Susan also struggled with what she called "self-will": a compulsive turning of the mind to things over which it had no control. In a letter that Anna quotes at length in her biography of her sister, Susan excoriated herself thus: "Not long ago my self-will took fast hold of a matter with which it had, lawfully, no manner of concern; inasmuch as it was no more in my power to control it than it was to make one hair white or black. What had self-will to do? But you know mine: it took hold of this matter with so firm a clasp that it has needed a long time to unloose it. . . . You know well enough what my self-will is, to be well convinced that it needs checking." So long as Susan's strong will was submitted to godly purposes, it was a blessing; it was only self-will—the stubborn pursuit of ends other than God's—that was to be avoided.[52]

Augusta Jane Evans showed similar determination in her struggles toward self-mastery, but her primary spiritual goal was discovery rather than submission. In a series of letters to her friend Walter Clopton Harriss, a Methodist minister, Evans described her struggles with spiritual doubt: "My mind was darkened. Questions of vital import, touching on my soul, were folded away in inscrutable mystery. To my anxious cry of 'why are these things?' there came but a mocking echo, that fell back, with a dead crushing weight upon my sickened heart." Evans's own spiritual struggles would provide the model for Beulah Benton's, and while the author assured Harriss that eventually "a green and sunny path led me back to my Father and my God," she also admitted that "whether I shall stay there, is now the question." Later letters show that for Evans, falling from grace remained a real and ever-present possibility, since her Arminian belief system included no provision for the perseverance of the saints. She wrote to Harriss that "even when my soul is serenely, happily basking in the light of an eternal God, and his equally eternal word, a grim guant [sic] spectre stands by me, as my shadow, and makes me doubt the reasonable certainty and absolute proof of the faith that consoles me." Rather than detailing a process of submission or the conquering of "self-will," Evans described an active and perpetual battle that had to be "continually fought over and over" against forces that threatened to rob her of her salvation.[53]

In the overplot of woman's fiction, the spiritual telos is an eternity with God, and the earthly telos is marriage. This final denouement is the heroine's reward for right behavior and the safe haven where she will spend her remaining days on earth. Read against the pattern tale of *The Pilgrim's Progress*, these marriages correspond to the land of Beulah, where Christian and Hopeful rest before making their final passage across the river of death and into the Celestial City. In her original study of the genre, Baym argued that "both the shape of fiction and the shape of reality conspired to suggest marriage as the appropriate ending" to a work of woman's fiction, given that the resolution of romantic complications "is the basic ending of all fiction" and that "marriage and domesticity were still the reality for the overwhelming majority of women" during the antebellum period.[54] Claudia Stokes has explored the theological functions that have been served by the marriage plot at least since the book of Revelation: the "novelistic convention of the marriage plot is in and of itself inherently millenial," Stokes writes, because "it provides reassurances of ongoing improvement and renewal, and it does so by enabling the reproduction of homes and families."[55] In the theologically informed genre of woman's fiction, which envisions female agency exercised according to particular doctrinal patterns, the heroine's choice of mate indexes both her growing self-knowledge—she will choose a reliable and sober partner over an attractive dandy—and the novel's doctrinal work. In *The Wide, Wide World* Ellen is predestined to marry John Humphreys as surely as she is to go to heaven; at their first meeting, Alice pronounces him "'your brother as well as mine,'" to which John responds that Alice is "'giving [them] away to each other at a great rate'" and then demands from Ellen "'a brother's right,'" a kiss on the lips (274). Their informal betrothal in the text's final published chapter is similarly preordained: John tells Ellen that "'if we live we shall spend our lives here together. . . . And what God orders let us quietly submit to'" (565). Though she similarly marries her lifelong mentor, Beulah Benton's engagement is the result of determined choice rather than calm acquiescence; after decades of refusing Guy Hartwell's advances, Beulah accepts his proposals only after she has reclaimed her faith and rejected another worthy suitor. "'Give me your hand, Beulah? . . . Is it mine?'" Hartwell asks, to which she replies, "'Yes, sir, if you want it'" (413). Humphreys and Hartwell enact in their offers of marriage the soteriological schemes of the novels' respective gods.

Feminist readings of woman's fiction often categorize the heroine's marriage as a capitulation, since for women in the antebellum United States marriage almost always entailed the erasure of their legal personhood and an attendant loss of economic power and bodily sovereignty. Even while acknowledging this change in temporal status, however, we can still recognize how these matrimonial endings, read in theological terms, offer their protagonists a greater scope of spiritual action. Both *The Wide, Wide World* and *Beulah* offer small glimpses into their heroines' marriages (though in the case of Warner's novel, this glimpse was withheld from nineteenth-century readers), and these final scenes indicate how the texts envision the duties of a Christian wife.[56] Marriage, in these novels, is not the happily ever after of the fairy tale or the terrifying imprisonment of the gothic romance but the space that unites belief and action—the arena in which the heroine will live out the consequences of her Christian faith and pursue her ongoing spiritual development.

In keeping with *The Wide, Wide World*'s Calvinist cosmology, Ellen Montgomery's postmarriage scene underscores her irresistible and irrevocable election by the holy Humphreys family. Ellen belongs to John Humphreys as she always has, just as she belongs to God as she always has. When the newly wedded Ellen arrives in "one of our pleasantest, though not one of our largest cities," she finds all the same possessions that had stood in the Humphreyses' previous home in the country, "and as near as possible in the same arrangement" (571). The Humphreyses' servant, Margery, transported along with the family's belongings, affirms Ellen's predestined status as a member of the Humphreys household: "'We'll keep you now, won't we? And you're not changed—no . . . you are just the very same! the very same! I see you are Miss Ellen in everything. . . . But will we keep you now?'" The only thing that has changed about Ellen is her name: "'Not Miss Ellen, Margery,'" John points out (573). Mr. Humphreys also pronounces Ellen "'the same child you used to be'" and consents to future visits from Mr. Lindsay only because "'we have you fast now'" (580, 581). These scenes of homecoming enact a temporal repetition that emphasizes the predestined nature of both Ellen's worldly destiny—Alice "gave her" to John when she was only a child—and her spiritual one.

Ellen's nuptial task is to continue subduing her self-will and to be a helpmeet to John, who will watch carefully over her ongoing spiritual development. When she remarks that the beautiful things John has bought her will encourage laziness and luxury, he assures her that "'if you show any symptoms of such a character it will rouse me to a most vigorous opposition.'" Ellen, carefully trained to seek John's approval in all things, finds the thought comforting: "'I am glad of that. . . . I may enjoy myself in perfect security that you will see the beginning of mischief and put a stop to it'" (576). Her only earthly labor is to manage the household, and even that she will do under John's supervision: though he "'shall never ask you how you spend'" the money he sets aside for domestic matters, he nevertheless promises to correct her "'if I see you going very far out of the way in anything'" (582). Though twenty-first-century readers may find this surveillance unnerving (Marianne Noble notes the marriage's similarity to a sadomasochistic relationship), Ellen experiences it as freeing: describing the "puzzles" she gets into while reading, she notes that "'I often launch out upon a sea where I dare not trust my own navigation, and am fain to lower sail and come humbly back to the shore; but now I will take the pilot along . . . and sail every whither'" (577).[57] In her Calvinist universe in which self-will can only lead to self-harm, Ellen accepts John's guidance as a boon—a means of avoiding fruitless spiritual struggle. Like a cat curling up in a box, Ellen finds comfort in the smallness of her surroundings. This particular adaptation to circumstance may frustrate modern readers, but given the blockbuster sales of The Wide, Wide World, millions of nineteenth-century Americans apparently found it a compelling fictional model of female religious agency.

It is decidedly *not* the model of female agency set forth in Evans's *Beulah*. Beulah Benton's marriage to Guy Hartwell is not a refuge, a retreat, or a place of grateful rest; instead, it is a new field of endeavor in which Beulah can fulfill the "'divine decree that all should work'" (310). Instead of recreating the past or positing earthly marriage as a foretaste of heavenly bliss, *Beulah* ends by prescribing its heroine's continuing temporal and spiritual task: "To save her husband from his unbelief is the labor of future years" (417–18). In a rare moment of direct address that echoes Evans's model, Charlotte Brontë's *Jane Eyre*, the narrator asserts, "Reader, marriage is not the end of life; it is but the beginning of a new course of duties" (417). And the novel ends not with static certainty but with an uncertain hope: "May God aid the wife in her holy work of love" (420). *Beulah* concludes with its heroine's long verbal testimony about her own struggles with religious skepticism and her eventual conversion. Praising the advances of science, she nevertheless challenges Hartwell—and the reader—to explain "how matter creates mind," the great question that all her philosophical study has left unanswered. Having worked out her own salvation, Beulah now sets herself the task of effecting Hartwell's.

The fact that much of the context and subtext of *Beulah* and *The Wide, Wide World* is theological does not mean that these novels' concerns were private and restricted to domestic subjects. By involving themselves in theological debates, Warner and Evans engaged in a public discourse about human agency in general and female agency in particular—a discourse that took place both in sectarian journals and in the more popular literary space of sentimental fiction. As June Howard notes, sentimentality always engages with "the development of modern subjectivities in their intricate imbrication with belief systems and social structures."[58] By exploring particular Protestant beliefs through the medium of fiction, Evans and Warner took part in a larger debate about the role of women in the public sphere. In keeping with this larger social question of women's public agency, part of Ellen Montgomery's and Beulah Benton's tasks (as well as the task of their readers) is to reconcile their theological beliefs with their legal and political status as citizens and subjects who cannot elect their own leaders or claim equal protection under the law. As with their spiritual maturation, their political educations are shaped by the theological systems to which they subscribe, and the novels' reflections on women's political lives and duties are inextricable from their theological commitments.

Ellen Montgomery's spiritual and temporal training under the Humphreyses includes lessons in recognizing and conforming to legitimate temporal authority as well as irresistible spiritual authority: in addition to the Bible that Ellen's mother gives her and the copy of *The Pilgrim's Progress* she receives from John, Ellen also receives a copy of Mason Weems's *Life of Washington*, which she absorbs with at least as much attention as she devotes to the other two. When Ellen arrives in Scotland, the name of Washington comes to stand in for the name of John Humphreys: though she "disliked to speak the loved names [of Alice and John] in the hearing of ears to which she knew they would be unlovely" (509), Ellen has no trouble invoking the name of Washington at every turn. When her uncle Lindsay asks whether she is "'one of those that make a saint of George Washington,'" Ellen replies that "'he was a great deal better than some saints'" (506). When Mr. Lindsay brings up the "murder" of John André, Ellen insists that this act must have been right because if it were not, "'Washington would not have done it.'" When Mr. Lindsay accuses Ellen of circular reasoning, she explains herself by insisting that "'when a person always does right, if he happen to do something that I don't know enough to understand, I have good reason to think it is right, even though I cannot understand it'" (515). This is the same reasoning that Alice had earlier applied to John: when Ellen wonders whether John was right in whipping an obstinate horse, Alice replies that "'it is sometimes necessary to do such things. . . . You and I know John, do we not?'" (377). John, like Washington, cannot be guilty of a wrong act—like the Calvinist God that Alice and Ellen worship, John's justice is unquestionable, though his behavior sometimes seems unfathomable. John is both God and Washington to Ellen: he embodies both spiritual and temporal authority, such that Ellen need no longer consult her own will.

The Wide, Wide World, then, would seem to envision both the kingdom of God and the kingdom of this world as representative republics in which women's consent to structures of power can be assumed because those powers are self-evidently benevolent. As I have discussed, Ellen's act of "choosing" John is predetermined by John himself and, presumably, by God. Similarly, Ellen's Americanness, so repugnant to the Lindsays, is also out of her control: when Mr. Lindsay commands Ellen to "'forget that [she was] American,'" Ellen's silent rejoinder that "'there are some things he cannot command. . . . Forget, indeed!'" represents one of the only times in the novel when she does not rebuke herself for pride or rebelliousness (510). Ellen's Americanness, like her Calvinist election and her adoption by the Humphreys family, is irrevocable—"irresistible," in Calvinist parlance; it is not a matter of her own will or choosing, and she could not change it if she wished to.

Beulah sets forth an alternative model of male-female relations in which the narrator and protagonist urge the women of the United States not to submit themselves to godly men but to accept independence and intellectual pursuits as their God-given duty. When Beulah gives the commencement address at the public school where she has been educated, she takes as her theme "female heroism" and sets out to demonstrate "that female intellect was capable of the most exalted attainments, and that the elements of her character would enable woman to cope successfully with difficulties of every class" (140). Beulah concludes her address by encouraging her classmates to make themselves "true women of America" not by submitting to superior men but by proving themselves "angel guardians of the sacred hearthstone, ministering spirits where suffering and want deman[d] succor," and women "qualified to assist in a council of statesmen, if dire necessity ever requir[e] it" (140). American-ness, for "true women" at least, is not a state into which one is born but a dis-tinction to which one aspires.

Evans saw herself as the torchbearer for a new brand of southern litera-ture that would challenge the intellectual and political hegemony of the Bos-ton and New York elite; the Arminian free-will doctrines that Beulah embraces would undergird a new era of southern supremacy based on states' rights and individual (white) self-determination. Evans signals her ambitions in her choice to name her eponymous heroine Beulah. While critics have rightly pointed out that the Hebrew word *Beulah* means "married woman" and that the name thus foreshadows the romantic denouement of the novel,[59] the biblical pas-sage in which the word *Beulah* figures does not refer to an actual woman but to the land of Israel. Predicting a future time of glory for the Hebrew people, the prophet Isaiah asserts, "Thou shalt no more be termed Forsaken; neither shall thy land any more be termed Desolate: but thou shalt be called Hephzi-bah, and thy land Beulah: for the Lord delighteth in thee, and thy land shall be married."[60] In associating her southern heroine with an idealized vision of an agriculturally productive Israel, Evans intimates that the South, not the North, is that region of the country truly chosen and blessed by God. The as-sociation of the southern heroine with bridal imagery also invokes the tradi-tion of the church as the bridegroom of Christ, making southern Arminian churches, rather than New England Calvinists, the true inheritors of the Amer-ican Christian mission.

Sentimental Power and Sentimental Agency, or The Douglas-Tompkins "Debate"

Despite their surface similarities and their shared overplot, *Beulah* and *The Wide, Wide World* describe fictional universes that are shaped by sharply dis-tinct theological premises; their depictions of female moral and spiritual de-velopment directly reflect those differing cosmologies. Protestant doctrine, far from being "epiphenomenal" to woman's fiction, is in fact subphenomenal: it underlies and shades all other aspects of a text.[61] Most importantly, it shapes a text's understanding and portrayal of female agency: the Calvinist Ellen Montgomery's way of being and acting in the world is entirely different from the Arminian Beulah Benton's. This insight is crucial to studies of women's writing because critical treatments of woman's fiction in particular and senti-mentalism more generally have long been concerned with the question of how sentimental texts enable or undermine female agency. Unfortunately, these studies have been driven by reductive debates about whether sentimental power is "good" or "bad"—debates that remain grounded in inaccurate and anachronistic understandings of nineteenth-century American religion.

Discussions of nineteenth-century sentimental fiction have long proceeded under the terms originally laid down by the critics Ann Douglas and Jane Tompkins—terms that were essentially religious-historical, though few later critics approached them as such. Douglas's 1977 tome *The Feminization of American Culture* offered an exhaustive critique of nineteenth-century sentimental writing that supported an openly declensionist argument about American religious history. According to Douglas, nineteenth-century women writers and attention-seeking liberal ministers eviscerated a formerly robust and appropriately masculine Calvinist theological tradition; in doing so, they produced the ostensibly anti-intellectual and "feminized" mass culture of the twentieth century.[62] In response to this argument, Tompkins's 1985 monograph *Sensational Designs: The Cultural Work of American Fiction, 1790–1860* acknowledged sentimentalism's religious underpinnings but rejected the theological declensionism of Douglas's book. Tompkins, reading for cultural effects rather than intellectual history, described how the evangelical revivalism of the Second Great Awakening gave rise to a phenomenon she called "sentimental power": a belief that "those who know how, in the privacy of their closets, to struggle for possession of their souls will one day possess the world through the power given to them by God."[63]

While Douglas told a story of loss and Tompkins one of triumph, the two critics agreed on the undeniable cultural influence of nineteenth-century women's religious writing. Sentimental writers, both posited, fundamentally altered the course of American intellectual and cultural history by writing openly religious fiction about saintly little girls and long-suffering wives. The two critics also agreed on the seemingly self-evident source of this power: evangelical Christianity. But the problem with characterizing sentimental fiction as evangelical is that the term *evangelical* collapses a wide field of nineteenth-century Protestant beliefs under a single heading while at the same time imposing twentieth-century political and religious assumptions onto a nineteenth-century religious context. As such, it obscures the very real doctrinal distinctions between different Protestant sects—distinctions that affect how individual authors envisioned possibilities for women's religious agency. Teasing out these distinctions helps to explain why the terms of the Douglas-Tompkins "debate" remain so frustratingly binding.[64]

The term *evangelical* became a prominent feature of Western European religious identity in the sixteenth and seventeenth centuries, when it was adopted by groups of Christians to signify their allegiance to the nascent Protestant reformation. Denominations, such as the Evangelical Lutheran Church, used the word to mark their dissent from Catholic tradition, their rejection of papal authority, and their embrace of the "good tidings" (Greek: *evangelium*) of salvation by grace rather than by the intercession of priest or saints. The term maintained this relatively straightforward meaning until the nineteenth century, when early religious historians, including Robert Baird and Philip Schaff, began using it to distinguish sects whose doctrines and practices they approved of from those they considered apostate. Baird's *Religion in America* (1844), for instance, placed Christian sects as doctrinally, ecclesiastically, and liturgically diverse as Presbyterians and Quakers under the heading of "evangelical" while including among the "non-evangelical" both self-identified Christians (Unitarians and Universalists) and non-Christians including atheists and Jews.[65] Around the same time, *evangelical* acquired other meanings: in addition to describing identities and beliefs, it came to denote participation in a set of activities particularly important to newly converted American Protestants. To be evangelical was, increasingly, to evangelize: to support Christian reform activities at home and proselytizing missions abroad.[66] It was also, often, to participate in the popular revivals that periodically swept the country. Because these revivals attracted persons of all genders, races, and social classes, and because attendees notoriously experienced ecstatic transports and "inflamed passions," evangelicalism increasingly came to be associated with embodied excess and uncontrolled—perhaps uncontrollable—religious emotion.[67] This set of connotations followed the term into the next century: from the 1930s to the 1970s the term *evangelical* was applied most often to the Pentecostal and charismatic movements, which did not exist before the twentieth century and which emphasized an embodied, mystical, and personal connection to God and Jesus Christ.[68] To confuse matters further, in the 1960s and 1970s the term acquired additional political valences as "one conservative party in almost all the most notable denominations [took] the adjective 'evangelical' to apply to itself."[69] By the late twentieth century, then, when nineteenth-century women's writing was being recovered by feminist scholars, the term *evangelical* had come to indicate a small but vocal group of Christian adherents known primarily for their commitment to emotional and embodied revivalism, to proselytizing activity, and to conservative political causes.

This definition was the one adopted by Ann Douglas: *Feminization* defines "non-evangelical" sects as those that "appreciated distinction and tradition," that "stood for a settled ministry [and] for intellectual elitism," and that either rejected revivals altogether or "wished to see them cautiously conducted in orderly fashion by ministers within their own congregations."[70] The "evangeli-

cals," for Douglas, were everyone else—those who abjured tradition and intellectualism, embraced revivalist "excesses," and wrote sentimental fiction.
Sensational Designs adopted a similarly anachronistic construction of "evangelical" Christianity as its operative religious-historical term: while asserting
that the meaning of a sentimental text "depends upon its audience's beliefs
not just in a gross general way, but intricately and precisely," the term Tompkins used to describe sentimental religiosity, "evangelical," was both gross and
general.[71] The religious-historical assumptions that undergirded the Douglas-
Tompkins debate were thus never up for debate at all. Both *The Feminization
of American Culture* and *Sensational Designs* used a twentieth-century model of
evangelical religion to frame their claims about the nineteenth century: that
Christian evangelicalism was the religious ground of nineteenth-century sentimental fiction, that evangelical religiosity was marked by emotional excess
rather than theological precision, and that this excessive evangelical emotion
was filtered into the culture through the medium of women's crying bodies.

Douglas's and Tompkins's formulations of sentimental power offered a necessary corrective to generations of literary criticism and religious history that
had first aligned the entire intellectual life of the antebellum United States with
Calvinist theological discourse and then (because women could neither attend
universities nor become ordained ministers) assumed that women's influence
on nineteenth-century intellectual culture was negligible. But Douglas and
Tompkins did not respond by looking for signs of women writers' intellectual engagement with theological questions; instead, they located women's
cultural and religious agency in their feeling bodies rather than in their thinking minds. The ahistorical importation of the term *evangelical* thus helped to
undergird a frustrating and persistent critical and historiographic binary: the
assumption that women experience religion emotionally while men experience it intellectually. This binary can be traced through the persistent use of
the ostensibly oppositional terms *evangelical* and *Calvinist*. In *Feminization*,
Douglas accused sentimental authors of using their "evangelical" writing to
introduce "formerly denounced heresy" into a society previously grounded
in a virile Calvinist orthodoxy.[72] Tompkins implicitly maintained the dichot-
omy: when discussing works by Herman Melville and Charles Brockden
Brown, *Sensational Designs* identifies these authors and their writing as "Calvinist"; when analyzing Susan Warner's *The Wide, Wide World* (1850) and Harriet Beecher Stowe's *Uncle Tom's Cabin* (1852)—the blockbusters of the "other
American Renaissance"—it labels these works "evangelical." In both *The Feminization of American Culture* and *Sensational Designs*, male authors have thinking, Calvinist minds while female authors have feeling, evangelical bodies. The

stubborn persistence of this critical binary has often made it difficult to recognize the theological investments of women's writing, including those I trace
in this book.[73]

Recent scholarship on women's writing generally and sentimentalism in
particular has begun to redress the religious-historical problems that attended
the Douglas-Tompkins debate. This work includes Abram Van Engen's exca-
vations of sympathy in Puritan (Old and New) England; Dawn Coleman's discussions of homiletic form in the writing of Harriet Beecher Stowe (and of
the crucial influence of Protestant preaching on antebellum literature more
generally); Susanna Compton Underland's scholarship on the intersection of
secularism and domesticity from the early national period to the Civil War;
Kevin Pelletier's discovery that apocalyptic eschatology fueled nineteenth-
century sentimentalism among authors and activists both black and white;
Tracy Fessenden's work on the intersections of secularism, feminism, and imperialism in the nineteenth century and today; Molly Robey's research on
women writers' literary depictions of the Holy Land; Ashley Barnes's work
on sacramental reading in novels by Harriet Beecher Stowe and Elizabeth Stuart Phelps; Randi Tanglen's studies of the intersections of race, class, and religion among women authors across a range of denominations; Claudia
Stokes's extensive exposition of the theology of sentimentalism in *The Altar
at Home* and her subsequent work on religion and disability in *The Lamplighter*,
and the essential essays collected in Mary McCartin Wearn's *Nineteenth-Century
American Women Write Religion: Lived Theologies and Literature*. These and other
works of literary history and criticism have offered detailed examinations of
women's religious writing that take into account both the enormous sectarian diversity of the antebellum United States and the myriad ways that women
experience religion: intellectually and emotionally, individually and communally, publicly and privately.[74]

More work needs to be done, however, if we are to understand the nature
of women's religious agency in the nineteenth century and in our own time.
It is crucial to accurately apprehend the religious-historical and theological
commitments of woman's fiction and of sentimental writing more generally
because these novels' depictions of female agency are inseparable from their
conceptions of divine power. Critics of sentimental fiction have often read sentimental religiosity as a cunning strategy for accruing worldly power; as
Tracy Fessenden has noted, the religiosity on display in sentimental fiction has
frequently been approached not for its own sake but as "simply the cultural
camouflage under which female power moves into public discourse."[75] This
critical preoccupation with power—usually conceived solely as a question of
a text's "politics"—limits discussions of sentimental fiction to analyses of

whether these power plays worked and, if they did, whether their cultural consequences were positive or negative according to the critic's own lights. Hence the reductiveness of the Douglas-Tompkins debate: *women's power bad* vs. *women's power good*, with religion considered primarily as a metonym for power.

The models of religious agency offered by woman's fiction and the sentimental novel have been difficult to apprehend because they do not always conform to the "progressive-secular imaginary"—the Western feminist narrative that assumes that women's flourishing requires their emancipation from religious adherence. This narrative rests on a foundation of presentist and secularist arrogance, "a deep self-assurance . . . that the life forms [secularization] offers are the best way out for . . . unenlightened souls, mired as they are in the spectral hopes that gods and prophets hold out to them."[76] Under these terms, in which religion can function only as a delusion from which the subjects of critical discourse must be freed, it is difficult for scholars to recognize and acknowledge forms of agency enabled by religious belief and practice.

The progressive-secular imaginary thus hampers serious critique of nineteenth-century women writers: religious women authors of the nineteenth century take on the anthropological role of Other in the writings of some twenty-first-century critics, their religion representing a primitive residue of nineteenth-century culture to be left behind on the journey toward feminist enlightenment. But as the anthropologist and legal theorist Leti Volpp notes, when "culture and feminism are believed to be opponents in a zero-sum game, women will be presumed to be emancipated when they have abandoned their cultures."[77] Since the authors of nineteenth-century sentimental fiction, now long since dead, can no longer abandon their religious cultures but have left evidence of them in their novels, critics have too often done the abandoning for them, writing around the question of religion or assuming that it exists only to mask other concerns—gender, race, class—more interesting to latter-day scholars.

Paradoxically, the persistence of the progressive-secular imaginary has made it easiest to identify female power in sentimental texts that embrace religious beliefs that seem especially foreign to a secularized critical stance, like the strict Calvinism of Susan Warner. Often the perceived strangeness of the texts' religiosity makes it easier to dismiss that religiosity as a cultural accretion. If women like Susan Warner and her protagonist Ellen Montgomery are able to wield agency and develop subjectivity (as critics of the sentimental novel insist, quite correctly, that they do) even while embracing a religion that ostensibly demonizes individual self-determination, that religion must not be effective and can be dismissed as an historical artifact with little bearing on the "real" problem of power. Baffled by the possibility that female agency might be exercised *through* religious adherence rather than in spite of it, critics have sought ways to write around women's religion rather than about it. Thus, even those critical formulations of sentimental power that have claimed to treat the religiosity of nineteenth-century women's literature with respect have often furthered secularized critical narratives that dismiss religion from serious discussion.

Novels like Evans's *Beulah* fit uneasily into this secularized understanding of women's social and political power because the model of religious agency that they offer aligns with liberal assumptions about autonomy and self-determination while simultaneously rejecting an attendant narrative of personal or communal secularization. *Beulah* short-circuits the progressive-secular narrative that celebrates the supposedly inevitable—but contested and ideologically naturalized—conjunction between secularization and women's intellectual and social liberation. Beulah Benton's quest for scientific and philosophical knowledge leads her *toward* rather than away from religious devotion, and her religious beliefs, in turn, bolster rather than undermine her feminist agency. She finds in her Arminian Christianity a warrant for statements like this one, which she makes to her friend Clara:

> You are opening your lips to repeat that senseless simile of [male] oaks and [female] vines; I don't want to hear it; there are no creeping tendencies about me. You can wind, and lean, and hang on somebody else if you like; but I feel more like one of those old pine trees yonder. I can stand up. Very slim, if you will, but straight and high. Stand by myself; battle with wind and rain and tempest roar; be swayed and bent, perhaps, in the storm, but stand unaided, nevertheless. I feel humbled when I hear a woman bemoaning the weakness of her sex, instead of showing that she has a soul and mind of her own inferior to none. (116)

Because the progressive-secular imaginary assumes that feminist enlightenment and religious adherence are incompatible, critics of nineteenth-century woman's fiction have found no place in their narratives for a text like *Beulah* that combines fierce religiosity with feminist sentiment. Evans has been overlooked, in part, because her religious feminism is unrecognizable according to a progressive-secular narrative that assumes that women can achieve agency only by rejecting religion.

To take women's religious adherence seriously is not the same as uncritically celebrating it. We should not simply replace one critical monolith with another: *women's power good* with *women's religious agency good*. Evans was unapologetically proslavery and pro-secession; she maintained friendships with prominent southern politicians and military leaders, including P. G. T. Beauregard and J. L. M. Curry, and during the Civil War her novel *Macaria, or Altars of Sacrifice* became a best-selling work of Southern apologetics. In *Beulah*, Beulah Benton's ostentatious performances of theological and philosophical learning are intended, in part, to display her intellectual immunity to the "superstitious" beliefs and behaviors of the novel's black characters, particularly Guy Hartwell's enslaved housekeeper, Harriet, whose folk wisdom Beulah repeatedly rejects. Evans's Arminian Christianity is a crucial component of her white feminism, and ignoring it means missing an opportunity to explore how white women's religious agency has often functioned to bolster white supremacy.

Recognizing entanglements between theology and politics in the nineteenth century can, in turn, make us better and more astute observers of our own time. It is easy to see in Beulah Benton the precursor of wealthy suburbanites who attend televised megachurches and vote for conservative political candidates. If Beulah Benton's God is the God of white slaveowners, women—and indeed, everyone—would be better off without him. But the skepticism and secularization celebrated by proponents of the progressive-secular imaginary also forms a key component of what Sara Farris calls "femonationalism." Femonationalism is the political-military-religious alliance that justifies Western imperialism by insisting that the true aim of the United States' global military conquests is the liberation of women—particularly Muslim women—from their self-evidently oppressive religions.[78]

Under femonationalism, religious and nonreligious ideologies conspire to become complementary tools of patriarchy and empire. Femonationalism objectifies nonwhite women (both within and outside the United States) by refusing to recognize their religious beliefs and practices as evidence of agency and as crucial and consequential aspects of their identities. This refusal can be justified in the name of either religion (usually a Protestant Christianity ostensibly cleansed of its patriarchal elements) or skepticism (there is a reason that the New Atheists almost uniformly embrace a rabid anti-Muslim ideology).[79] Combating femonationalism requires, at minimum, that we acknowledge women as conscious agents capable of making their own choices about their religious and political lives. We must take women's religious agency seriously, in other words, precisely because that agency is multivalent and has sometimes unpredictable effects.

Attending to the wide array of religious positions on display in women's writing helps to complicate critical narratives that presume that for women to exercise agency, they must resist repressive religion in favor of an ostensibly liberating skepticism. What woman's fiction, in all its doctrinal diversity, demonstrates is that women authors engaged deeply with nineteenth-century theological questions—that they approached religion both intellectually and emotionally rather than eschewing one approach in favor of another. Just as importantly, recognizing the theological arguments at work in woman's fiction helps us to see that women's agency is not an either-or proposition, even and perhaps especially when that agency grows out of religious principles. If critics are to continue to assert the important role of nineteenth-century women authors in literary history and to understand the complex models of agency at work in their texts, we must adjust our approach to these texts to include all possible avenues to female agency, religious and nonreligious.

CHAPTER 3

"I Have Sinned against God and Myself"

Bearing Witness to Enslaved Women's Agency
in *Incidents in the Life of a Slave Girl*

As every reader of sentimental literature knows,
deathbed scenes are crucial to the form, as they provide narrative circumstances for enacting the mode's affective purposes. As a novel's characters
gather around the deathbed of a beloved mother, friend, sister, or child, they
form a tableau vivant that emblematizes the sympathetic relations binding
born and created families together. In woman's fiction, the deathbed scene is
also a crucial indicator of a novel's theological positioning; it provides a central character with a final opportunity to engage in an act of doctrinal agency.
When *The Wide, Wide World*'s Calvinist Alice Humphreys declares herself
"'perfectly happy'" before surrendering the "will and the power that had sustained [her]" and succumbing to death, she makes a final gesture of renunciation that crowns a lifetime spent suppressing self-will and acting in accordance
with her divine election.[1] When *Beulah*'s skeptical Cornelia Graham insists in
her final moments that she "'do[esn't] want to believe'" in Christ's resurrection (or her own), she is exercising the Arminian option to "chuse or to refuse" salvation.[2]

Harriet Jacobs's *Incidents in the Life of a Slave Girl*, like these and other sentimental novels, includes a number of deathbed scenes. In one that appears
early in the text, two adult women hover by the bedside of a dying girl to hear
her final words. The girl is not surrounded by loving friends; nor is she dying
peacefully of consumption. Instead she is in agony and, like the protagonist

of many a seduction novel, is dying from the effects of childbirth. Because she has mothered "a child nearly white," her mistress stands over her, cursing her for the supposed seduction of her husband. "'You suffer, do you?'" the mistress demands sadistically. "'I am glad of it. You deserve it all, and more too.'" When the girl's mother predicts that the fading girl will soon follow her dead child to heaven, the mistress pronounces that "'there is no such place for the like of her and her bastard'" (16).[3]

This scene sets up in five paragraphs the legal and moral impasse at the heart of *Incidents*, which thematizes the contradictory standards to which enslaved women were held: a Christian moral law that judged women according to their sexual purity—their ability to resist seduction—and the slave laws that defined any act of resistance as insubordination or crime.[4] Mangled in the gears of these interlocking systems, the dying girl, like her white "sisters" in sentimental fiction, makes a final assertion of religious faith: she appeals directly to a higher power. "'Don't grieve so, mother,'" she says to the weeping woman at her side; "'God knows all about it; and HE will have mercy upon me'" (16). In the presence of the white mistress who condemns her, and in the absence of the white master who raped her, the girl does not plead innocence or beg forgiveness; to do so would be to accept the mistress's—or the law's—right to pass judgment. Instead, the unnamed girl rhetorically circumvents both of these standards—legal and moral—by insisting that her innocence or guilt can be adjudicated by no one but God himself.

While the girl's final words betray no particular doctrinal commitment— Jacobs does not even name her, much less reveal a denominational affiliation— her statement is a very clear declaration of theodicy: an assertion about the nature of divine justice and the meaning of evil and human suffering. Indeed, the scene stages a contest of interpretation in which, in Jacobs's telling, the dying black girl has the final word. For the white mistress, the girl's suffering is evidence of God's righteous anger: she suffers because this is the deserved punishment for the sin of "seducing" her master. In contrast to this cruel and punishing deity, the girl invokes a God who sees and knows and who judges with compassion rather than condemnation. Aware that she suffers not as the result of her own sin but of her master's, the girl declares that she is known to God and that he will treat her mercifully. The unnamed girl's last agentive act on earth is not to proclaim her innocence but to invite divine judgment for her deeds.[5]

This scene appears early in *Incidents in the Life of a Slave Girl*, and it introduces the book's primary motifs: the ubiquity and sadistic variety of sexual crimes against enslaved women and the hypocrisy of a "benevolent" and "Christian" slave system designed to shield the perpetrators of those crimes while punishing and shaming their victims. But the scene also presents the primary theological argument of *Incidents*: that the "sins" of enslaved women cannot be judged by their corrupt enslavers or those enslavers' "virtuous" wives and instead can and will be judged by no one but God himself. Inserted into the story at a point where the narrating Linda Brent is still a child, the scene foreshadows the fate that Linda herself will narrowly avoid by entering into a relationship with a white man who is unmarried (and thus has no wife to accuse her) and not her master. The confession of this crime—the sin of allowing herself to be "seduced" by Mr. Sands—provides both the narrative impetus for the writing of *Incidents* and the spiritual warrant for Jacobs's antislavery appeal. Like the dying girl's final words, "God knows all about it," *Incidents* is a confession that doubles as a claim to cosmic recognition. But unlike the ill-fated and unnamed girl, whose confession is also her last testimonial act on earth, the death of Jacobs's sexual virtue enables the resurrection of her narrative voice. *Incidents in the Life of a Slave Girl* takes the form of a spiritual autobiography in which Jacobs's confession of her sexual sin is not the end of her religious authority but the necessary precondition for it.

Much of the critical literature devoted to *Incidents in the Life of a Slave Girl* has explored its generic hybridity and traced its narrative relations. The text's most obvious frame is the escaped-slave narrative, which by 1861 was a firmly established but male-dominated genre. As critics have noted, *Incidents* is formally distinct from most male slave narratives, as Linda's escape is long and protracted, more a string of varied imprisonments than a clean break with slavery.[6] Even at the end of the story, after her legal manumission, Linda declares herself not completely free but only more free: "as free from the power of slaveholders as are the white people of the north," which, because of the Federal Fugitive Slave Law, is "not saying a great deal" (225). Like William Wells Brown's *Clotel*, *Incidents* also follows a pattern similar to woman's fiction: it traces Linda's development from a sheltered child to a mature woman as she encounters trials and difficulties, experiences physical and spiritual growth, and is shuffled from one "home" to another. That Linda self-consciously ends her story "with freedom; not in the usual way, with marriage" suggests that Jacobs intentionally invoked this popular genre and deliberately deviated from its narrative line (224).[7] With its appeals to readers' pity and compassion, *Incidents* is also clearly in conversation with the larger sentimental mode to which woman's fiction belongs. But that conversation is often staged as argument or ironic commentary: as narrator, Linda Brent frequently denies the sympathetic identification on which sentimentalism depends, admonishing her readers, for instance, that "if you have never been a slave, you cannot imagine the acute sensation of suffering" occasioned by the potential loss of her children (219).

Finally, as Saidiya Hartman has thoroughly demonstrated, *Incidents* must also be read in the tradition of the seduction novel, a genre that policed women's potential emergence as liberal individuals by reinforcing their status as sexual property.

Surprisingly, however, critics have rarely situated *Incidents* in relation to what would seem the obvious generic tradition of the spiritual autobiography. As William Andrews and others have shown, the earliest examples of black autobiography took the form of spiritual narratives, closely following the existing conventions of conversion and captivity tales; when James Gronniosaw (1770), John Marrant (1785), and George White (1810) published their life stories, they adopted these familiar popular genres, and the escaped-slave narratives of the antebellum period, even when less explicitly devout, maintained the "pervasive use of journey or quest motifs that symbolize[d] multiple layers of spiritual evolution."[8] Despite this well-established history, studies of Jacobs's slave narrative have tended either to downplay the text's spiritual elements or to divorce them from its political aspirations as a work of antislavery writing.[9] Margaret Lindgren, following Elizabeth Fox-Genovese, has suggested that when writing their autobiographies, the "political/cultural realities which dominated the lives of Black women denied them the 'luxury' of confessional or spiritual motives."[10] In these readings, "politics" is essential and "spirituality" is a luxury, a secularized framing that anachronistically puts asunder what, for many nineteenth-century African Americans, God had joined together. Studies of *Incidents* that do examine the text's religious rhetoric have often focused on the disciplinary force imposed by nineteenth-century Protestantism's cult of female sexual purity. Nell Irvin Painter laments the effect that Molly Horniblow's "attachment to the feminine ideal of chastity" had on Jacobs's "emotional life," and Ann Taves, noting Jacobs's adherence to a Christian standard that equated "sexual purity and spirituality," asserts that in the conflict with Dr. Flint, Jacobs's "ideas about purity allowed [Linda] to fight, but they did not allow her to win."[11] These readings apprehend Jacobs's (and Linda's) attachment to Christian moral standards primarily as oppression—as another form of enslavement, one that Jacobs apparently never managed to escape.

Many readings of *Incidents*, in other words, frame Linda Brent's religious and moral commitments as constraints on her agency because they seem to prevent her from achieving full autonomy. But as Saidiya Hartman has definitively demonstrated, the agency of enslaved persons cannot be discussed in terms of autonomy and self-determination—the concepts with which agency is usually conflated. "The notion of the autonomous self endowed with free will is inadequate and, more important, inappropriate to thinking through the issue of slave agency," Hartman asserts, since "the self-possessed subject with his inalienable attributes is quite unthinkable or unimaginable in this case." Because slave agency could exist only under conditions of coercion and legal nonpersonhood, historians and critics seeking evidence of slave agency must "endeavor to scrutinize and investigate the forms, dispositions, and constraints of action and the disfigured and liminal status of the agents of such acts."[12] Acknowledging the agency of the enslaved in no way mitigates the guilt of the slaveowner or the evil of slavery, but it can assist us in recognizing the humanity of the enslaved. Reading *Incidents in the Life of a Slave Girl* as a spiritual autobiography reveals the disfigured, liminal, but no less real ways Jacobs envisioned and enacted her own agency and that of her protagonist, Linda Brent.

This agency took shape according to the terms offered by a black Christian autobiographical tradition that Jacobs inherited, adapted, and integrated with the white sentimental mode to which her northern readers were accustomed. Adopting a form that undergirded spiritual autobiographies by the nineteenth-century black women preachers Jarena Lee and Sojourner Truth but also the black revolutionary Nat Turner, Jacobs relates the "incidents" of Linda's life according to a Christian narrative pattern of sin, confession, and redemption that positions Linda's sin as the necessary precursor to both her spiritual salvation and Jacobs's own literary authority. By presenting her narrative as a spiritual autobiography, Jacobs is able to confess her sexual sin to her audience while maintaining her singular narrative voice and developing a unique hortatory style—something impossible for the sentimental heroines to whom Linda Brent has most often been compared. In a political, legal, and moral system in which enslaved women's agency was assumed to be nonexistent or was acknowledged only when it appeared in the form of sexual "crime," Harriet Jacobs found a small but no less real space for religious agency and literary authority—a loophole—by confessing her sexual sin and making a direct appeal to divine judgment. That appeal, in turn, became the ground on which the redeemed Linda Brent could stand and exhort the women of the United States, black and white, to work for the abolition of slavery.

Confronting "the Demon Slavery": *Incidents* as Spiritual Autobiography

When Linda Brent decides, after months of persecution by her lecherous master, Dr. Flint, to engage in an affair with another white man in her North Carolina town, she frames this decision as a suicide. Learning that Dr. Flint is building "a small house . . . in a secluded place, four miles away from the town," in which he plans to "make a lady of" her, Linda vows to "do any thing, every thing, for the sake of defeating him" (59). Imagining her existence as Flint's concubine as a kind of "living death," Linda chooses a different kind of death instead: like Clotel Jefferson throwing herself from the Long Bridge in Washington, DC, Linda becomes "reckless in [her] despair" and makes "a plunge into the abyss" (60, 59). Detailing the impossible choice offered to her—be raped by Dr. Flint or "give [her]self" to Mr. Sands—Linda reiterates the figure of flight through suicide: "Seeing no other way of escaping the doom I so much dreaded, I made a headlong plunge" (61). She describes this decision in terms of the sense of temporal—and temporary—power that it afforded her: "It seems less degrading to give one's self, than to submit to compulsion. There is something akin to freedom in having a lover who has no control over you, except that which he gains by kindness and attachment" (61).

Jean Fagan Yellin has suggested that by engaging in an affair with a white man who was not her master, Jacobs "abandoned her attempt to avoid sexual involvements in an effort to assert her autonomy as a human being."[13] "Autonomy," as Geoff Hamilton discusses, is best translated as "self-law" (and not simply as "individualism"): the ability to rule oneself rather than be ruled by others.[14] But complete autonomy was not possible for Jacobs, or indeed for almost any nineteenth-century woman, and Linda quickly learns that she cannot achieve "self-law" by transgressing the legal codes that define her entirely by her reproductive value to Dr. Flint. In the event, Linda's sexual transgression defines more precisely her lack of power under slave law; it "intensifies the constraints of slavery and reinscribes her status as property . . . at the very moment in which she tries to undo and transform her status."[15] Learning of Linda's pregnancy, Dr. Flint, rather than selling her or her (yet unborn) child to her lover as she had hoped, reiterates his claim to her: "'You are my slave, and shall always be my slave. I will never sell you, that you may depend upon'" (67). What Linda finds in her affair with Mr. Sands is "something akin to freedom" but not freedom itself.

What Linda's sexual transgression *does* allow her to do is define her actions according to a different moral code than that set forth by Dr. Flint. Though Flint continues to claim legal ownership of Linda's body and of her future children, he cannot lay claim to her soul. When Flint accuses Linda of being "criminal towards" him, Linda's rejoinder is that "I have sinned against God and myself . . . but not against you" (65). For Linda, submitting to a Christian sexual standard rather than to slave law allows her to choose whom she will sin against, if not whom she will serve.[16] If, as Saidiya Hartman has shown, any display of independent will on the part of the slave represented transgression under slave codes that defined slaves as entirely subject to masters, then choosing the authority against whom one would transgress was itself an act of agency. Antebellum slave codes insisted that enslaved persons "[could] not be governed by the same common system of laws" as free persons, "so different [were] their positions, rights, and duties."[17] Linda insists on being judged by a Christian moral standard rather than the standards set by slave law because only under God's law can she be understood to have any moral agency at all.

In writing and publishing *Incidents*, Jacobs grounded Linda Brent's right to speak on the fact of this sexual fall—and of her resurrection from it. This seemingly paradoxical agentive configuration accords with both the convoluted legal, social, and moral restrictions surrounding chattel slavery and the correspondingly complex formal and narrative conventions of Jacobs's text, in which the most obvious place (Aunt Marthy's house) is the most hidden and the most public place (the town of Edenton) is the most protected. The shape of Linda's story becomes more legible when we read *Incidents* in the light of another generic tradition of which Jacobs would likely have been aware: black women's spiritual autobiographies. Reading *Incidents* as a spiritual autobiography helps to clarify how Linda's sexual sin, rather than robbing her of agency, becomes the ground on which she bases her right to speak.

In the spiritual autobiography tradition to which *Incidents* rightly belongs, conviction and confession of sin are the first steps in a spiritual journey toward redemption, conversion, testimony, and, in some cases, exhortation. The spiritual autobiography was a ubiquitous form in America from the seventeenth through the nineteenth centuries, and its roots can be traced to the writings of St. Augustine and, even further, to the apostle Paul, whose conversion on the road to Damascus set the pattern for the spiritual narrative's tale of conviction, conversion, and public witness.[18] The spiritual autobiography was "highly formulaic, composed according to the requirements of a strictly defined convention."[19] Whether narrated by a colonial Congregationalist, an eighteenth-century Quaker, or an antebellum Methodist, the spiritual narrative was likely to follow a conventional pattern: the speaker would describe a childhood full of "thoughtlessness, frivolity, or willfullness" meant to "signify an early state of spiritual lostness and hopelessness" but also marked by "profound religious impressions." After encountering some form of Christian preaching or proselytizing, the speaker would become convinced of his or her sinful nature and experience "distress, guilt, and anxiety about their spiritual welfare." This "sense of guilt and occasionally paralyzing anxiety trouble[d] the prospective Christian" until he or she experienced, usually as a teenager or young adult, a realizing sense of God's grace: the certainty that his or her sins had been forgiven through Christ's atoning death on the cross.[20] For the Protestant Christian, this event marked the moment of conversion, though not necessarily the end of doubt or striving.[21] Many speakers recounted experiencing "period[s] when delight and assurance yielded to doubt, as converts discovered that some of the old 'corruption' persisted in their hearts"; these times of doubt would often alternate with "period[s] of renewed consecration, accompanied by a return of peace and joy." Spiritual narratives often concluded by offering justifications for their own existence: the convert, having reached a place of spiritual assurance, felt called to share his or her experience with others and to give "an account of the 'fruits' of the experience—usually zealous conduct of evangelical activity."[22] More even than conversion itself, this call to share with others a common experience of spiritual change and growth provided a warrant for the work of self-definition and self-expression enacted in the spiritual autobiography.

This narrative pattern can be found in the spiritual autobiographies of Jarena Lee and Sojourner Truth, antebellum African American women exhorters whose narratives Jacobs may have encountered during the year when she attended to the daily operations of the Rochester Anti-Slavery Office and Reading Room.[23] Lee's *Life and Religious Experience of Jarena Lee* (1836) describes the author's early conversion to Christianity, her experience of sanctification, and her call to become a Christian exhorter. Despite being born to parents who were "wholly ignorant of the knowledge of God," in early life "the spirit of God moved in power through [her] conscience, and told [her she] was a wretched sinner" (27).[24] Lee received further conviction of sin while listening to the preaching of a Presbyterian missionary. After four years of anxiety about the state of her soul, Lee was "gloriously converted to God" during a Methodist service led by the African American preacher Richard Allen, the first bishop of the African Methodist Episcopal Church (29). Crying to God for forgiveness, Lee felt "as if a garment, which had entirely enveloped my whole person, even to my fingers ends, split at the crown of my head, and was stripped away from me, passing like a shadow, from my sight—when the glory of God seemed to cover me in its stead" (29). Released from the "shadow" of her sins, Lee went on to achieve sanctification, an experience described by John Wesley in which the believer "gradually dies to sin, and grows in grace."[25] In her narrative, Lee's experience of sanctification secures her place in a Christian history stretching all the way back to the early apostles: "So great was the joy, that it is past description. There is no language that can describe it, except that which was heard by St. Paul, when he was caught up to the third heaven, and heard words which it was not lawful to utter" (34). After receiving assurance of her salvation and sanctification, Lee found herself called to preach the gospel and spent much of her life as a traveling exhorter.

The Narrative of Sojourner Truth, though longer than Lee's narrative and containing more personal details, conforms to a similar pattern. It is difficult to know how much of the shape of Truth's narrative originated with Sojourner herself and how much was imposed by her amanuensis and editor Olive Gilbert, but Truth, too, depicts herself as a rebellious young person given to early religious impressions and an increasing awareness of her own sinfulness. As a child the young Isabella Baumfree's mother tells her of "a god, who hears and sees you" and who "lives in the sky" (17).[26] With only this rudimentary religious education, Isabella "go[es] to God in all her trials, and every affliction," speaking her prayers aloud and asking for whatever she desires (27). After successfully suing for the return of her youngest child, Peter, who was illegally sold into slavery in the South, Isabella receives a vision of God "revealed . . . to her, with all the suddenness of a flash of lightning" and, subsequently, a vision of Jesus (65–67). Convinced of her own "vileness" and shamed by the contrast between her sin and "God's holiness and all-pervading presence" (69), Isabella begs for intercession from Jesus and finally receives assurance of her reconciliation to God. Years later, living in New York City, Isabella feels "called in spirit to leave it, and to travel east and lecture" and takes the name of Sojourner, embarking on a career as a traveling exhorter and activist (99).

Jacobs's narrative of sin, redemption, and witness follows this narrative structure, but the fact of slavery subverts her spiritual autobiography's form. Whereas Jarena Lee describes a childhood fraught with "distress, guilt, and anxiety about [her] spiritual welfare," Jacobs recalls a bucolic childhood in which she was not yet aware of her slave status and the consequences it would have for her life. I was "born a slave," the narrating Linda asserts as she begins her narrative, but "never knew it until six years of happy childhood had passed away" (7). Like Lee and Truth, Linda receives some rudimentary religious training, in her case by a kind mistress who teaches her to "read and spell" (10), but she also absorbs the "blasphemous doctrine" that, though a slave, she is also a human being (12). Whereas Lee was "converted . . . in rather spectacular fashion" in adolescence, Jacobs's teen years bring her to a realizing sense of Dr. Flint's disgusting desires, and it is to thwart his unholy power over her that she engages in an affair with Sands.[27] Jacobs's narrative reaches its spiritual crisis point in a scene in which Aunt Marthy orders Linda out of her house after hearing the confession of her affair, and it is only after she relents, placing her hand upon Linda's head and murmuring, "'Poor child! Poor child!'" that Linda is able to continue her story (64). To complete her journey to salvation, Linda must flee not only her own sin but Dr. Flint's—she must escape the slaveholding South altogether. After surviving "alternat[ing] patterns of spiritual light and darkness" during her years in hiding, Linda achieves true spiritual peace during a trip to England with her first northern employer.[28] There, beyond the reach of slavery, she "receive[s] strong religious impressions" as grace "enter[s] [her] heart," and she kneels "at the communion table . . . in true humility of soul" (206).

To do justice to the purpose of *Incidents* as both spiritual autobiography and antislavery polemic, Jacobs must be explicit about the nature of her sin. In most spiritual autobiographies, the exact nature of the convert's sin is unclear; to describe one's sins in too much detail would corrupt listeners and surrender narrative space to the works of Satan. Jarena Lee describes her transgressions in conventional terms, without dwelling on their particularities: she told a lie as a child; she was tempted to destroy herself; she was, in the words of a hymn she quotes, generally "vile, conceived in sin / Born unholy and unclean" (27). The details of her sin are irrelevant because the telos of her narrative is her conversion and calling to an itinerant ministry; the only fact readers need to know about her sins is that they have been washed clean. Jacobs, because she is writing a spiritual autobiography that is also an exposé of slavery, indicates the precise nature of her sin: driven to despair by the persecutions of her master, she had sexual relations and bore children with a man who was not her husband. "I was struggling alone in the powerful grasp of the demon Slavery," Jacobs writes, couching her battle with Flint in the language of cosmic struggle, "and the monster proved too strong for me. I felt as if I was forsaken by God and man; as if all my efforts must be frustrated; and I became reckless in my despair" (60). Because the conviction and confession of sin is always the first event in a spiritual testimony, Jacobs's confession lays the groundwork for the remainder of her story, in which she will assume a hortatory voice similar to that of Jarena Lee and other itinerant preachers. But because she will exhort her readers to join the abolitionist cause, she must first expose the enabling and perpetuating condition of slavery: the sexual exploitation of female slaves.

The presence of "the demon Slavery" also marks the relationship between *Incidents* as spiritual narrative and as antislavery text. The devil was a primary and very real character in the black spiritual autobiography tradition, whose practitioners were apt to employ "biblical tropes . . . literally rather than metaphorically."[29] Lee describes hearing the devil's voice in her ear and even seeing him crouched in her room "in the form of a monstrous dog" (30). When she is called to preach the gospel, the devil attempts to undermine her vocation by convincing her that she is too bad to be saved—so sinful that even God's grace cannot redeem her. Even after her conversion, Satan continues to torment her: when she prays for sanctification, the devil's voice audibly replies,

"'No, it is too great a work to be done'" (34). In Lee's and other black spiritual autobiographies, Satan is the cosmic antagonist who uses spiritual, psychological, and sometimes material means to prevent the would-be Christian from fulfilling his or her spiritual and temporal mission.

Dr. Flint's machinations against Linda and her family mark him as the devil's earthly avatar, determined to prevent Linda from maintaining her virtue and, later, from escaping his domain. He seems omnipresent, meeting Linda "at every turn" and seeming to appear out of nowhere (31). He invades her thoughts, "whisper[ing] foul words in [her] ear" in an effort to "corrupt the pure principles [her] grandmother had instilled" (30). When she refuses to accept his notes, he insists on reading them aloud, requiring Linda "to stand and listen to such language" (35). His "dark shadow . . . follows her to even her most private of moments" and "achieves a kind of omnipresence by invading [her] psychological world"; he seems to "multiply his presence exponentially, even when he might be physically absent."[30] Flint's diabolical actions drive Linda into the arms of Mr. Sands, an event that affirms his infernal character since the devil's role in the cosmic play is to tempt human beings to sin and then curse them with despair at the thought that their sins are unforgivable.[31] After confessing her affair with Mr. Sands to her grandmother, Linda, like Jarena Lee, contemplates her fallen nature and considers destroying herself: she "pray[s] to die; but the prayer [is] not answered" (63). "Truly," Linda assures her readers, "Satan had no difficulty in distinguishing the color of [Dr. Flint's] soul!" (38).

It is tempting to read Dr. Flint's diabolical nature as metaphorical, especially given his infernal pseudonym; James Norcom was, of course, a historical person with total legal power over Harriet Jacobs and her children. But as historians have detailed, slavery itself functioned as not only a legal system but also a theological one, insofar as slaveholders could claim complete temporal and spiritual authority over their chattel. In the early centuries of the slave trade, the Christianization of "heathen" races by means of their enslavement was seen by many religious leaders as the providential purpose of colonization, and the laws that detached slave status from baptism in early Virginia protected slaveholders' right to own human chattel while promoting the "propagation of christianity by permitting children, though slaves, . . . to be admitted to that sacrament."[32] Because he controlled both the daily lives of his slaves and their access to spiritual goods, the slaveholder's total and unquestionable power approached that of an omnipotent deity.[33]

Given slaveholders' aspirations to godlike status, a crucial part of Linda's personal and theological challenge to Dr. Flint is her refusal to address him as the god he claims to be. "'If you deceive me,'" Flint threatens, "'you shall feel the fires of hell'" (65). But while describing him as practically omnipresent, Linda attributes Flint's powers not to his divine nature but to his diabolical one: his "restless, craving, vicious nature rove[s] about day and night, seeking whom to devour" (20).[34] Just as a personal devil was a very real source of torment and temptation to Jarena Lee and Sojourner Truth, Linda Brent is stalked by a demonic presence whose danger to her is only heightened by the temporal authority he also wields.

To defy the theological and temporal power of the slaveholder-god, abolitionists invoked the doctrine of Christian universalism, a staple of Christian theology from the earliest years of the church. Christian universalism asserts that all human beings, regardless of nation or race, are children of God and eligible for salvation. It is grounded in three crucial verses from the New Testament and linked to the great commission, Christ's instruction to his disciples in Matthew 28:19: "Go ye therefore, and teach all nations, baptizing them in the name of the Father, and of the Son, and of the Holy Ghost."[35] From the earliest centuries of Christianity, Christian missionary and conversion activities were grounded in "the doctrine that the Crucifixion offered grace to all willing to receive it and made all Christian believers equal before God."[36] The book of Acts recounts the working out of the great commission among Christ's apostles as they went forth in the wake of the resurrection to "teach all nations"; early Christians "celebrated the conversion of Africans as evidence for their faith in the spiritual equality of all human beings"; and medieval Christian missionaries "honored black converts as living evidence of the universality of their faith."[37] While the late classical and medieval periods were rife with prejudice and violence directed at various ethnic and religious groups— particularly Jews—the official doctrinal position of the Catholic church remained that all people were eligible for salvation and that sincere conversion was always possible.[38]

The two major theological systems of the Protestant Reformation, despite their deep divisions regarding matters of soteriology, retained the doctrine of Christian universalism. From a Calvinist point of view, the doctrine of predestination is perfectly compatible with Christian universalism; though only a small number of the human family might be among the elect, there is nothing in the New Testament to suggest that election entails a racial component. Indeed, Paul's assertion in his letter to the churches in Galatia that "there is neither Jew nor Greek, there is neither bond nor free, there is neither male nor female: for ye are all one in Christ Jesus" suggests that the elect will be found among all nations.[39] While in practice the elect of New England were most likely to be middle class and of English descent, in theory "neither slave nor free" were excluded from salvation. Arminian free-grace theology is even more amenable to Christian universalism, since according to its proponents, Christ's atonement has been accomplished for all humankind and salvation is offered freely to everyone rather than reserved for a select few. Early Methodist missionaries to North America often preached indiscriminately to racially mixed congregations made up of young and old, male and female, rich and poor, slave and free, and their emphasis on the universal availability of salvation contributed to the denomination's explosive growth during and after the Second Great Awakening.

According to historians of race and racism, the invention of racial categories that began in the fourteenth and fifteenth centuries was necessitated in part by the persistence of Christian universalism. To justify slavery and colonialism and to obviate the theological imperative to convert the indigenous peoples they encountered, slaveholders, colonial legislatures, and church leaders took a multipronged approach to defusing the doctrine. Theologically, they pointed to the curse of Ham as biblical justification for the enslavement of African peoples. This curse ostensibly exempted the "children of Canaan" (Ham's son) from the promise of Christian salvation because they had been condemned to be the "servants of servants."[40] Juridically, defenders of chattel slavery passed slave codes that made slave status dependent on "heathen ancestry" as transmitted through the mother.[41] Later, the scientific revolution of the seventeenth and eighteenth centuries would give rise to another set of tools for defining Africans and other non-Europeans as fundamentally inferior to white Christians: proponents of race science used dubiously compiled evidence of physical differences to construct a theory of polygenesis that could undermine the biblical assertion of monogenesis. Only after the ostensible inferiority of blacks had been theologically, juridically, and scientifically established and baptism's threat to the legality of slavery had been dismantled were serious Christian missionary efforts directed to the enslaved peoples of North America.[42]

Even as these racial discourses were being formulated, however, the doctrine of Christian universalism—with its assertion that all human beings are children of God and therefore eligible to experience salvation—remained a powerful theological and political force. The earliest abolitionists, white and black, seized on the doctrine as justification for their antislavery efforts and emphasized again and again the primal heresies of slavery: that it denied enslaved people's status as children of God, that it withheld from them the means of salvation, and that its hierarchies replaced an immortal God with a mortal man as the source of highest authority.[43] David Walker challenged southern slaveholders to refute the assertion "that God made man to serve Him *alone*, and that man should have no other Lord or Lords but Himself—that God

Almighty is the *sole proprietor* or *master* of the WHOLE human family."[44] Henry "Box" Brown described the confusing theology of slave life: while his mother taught him not to steal or lie, the young Brown "really believed my old master was Almighty God, and that his son, my young master, was Jesus Christ."[45] William Wells Brown played this confusion for comedy in *Clotel*: when a northern visitor asks an enslaved woman if she serves the Lord, she replies, "'No, sir, I don't serve anybody but Mr. Jones; I neber belong to anybody else.'" Another man, when asked if he has ever heard of John the Baptist, replies, "'Oh yes, marser, John de Baptist. . . . [H]e libs in Old Kentuck, where I come from.'"[46] And in *Uncle Tom's Cabin*, Topsy famously answers Miss Ophelia's question as to whether the Lord made her with the speculation that "'I spect I grow'd. Don't think nobody never made me.'"[47] According to antislavery authors and speakers, slavery's original sin was that it denied slaves' status as God's children and mandated idolatry. The catechism's most basic tenets, that "God created man, male and female, after his own image" and that God's creatures owed "total obedience" only to their Creator, was undermined by the legal stipulation that slaves owed total obedience not to God but to their earthly masters.[48]

In the context of Jacobs's spiritual autobiography, the doctrine of Christian universalism is the warrant for Jacobs's confession of her sexual sin and her insistence that she be judged by the same Christian higher law that her readers are held to. Christopher Z. Hobson has described how the shared conviction of sin became a crux of black Christians' claims to equality with whites: "If 'great and small, bond and free,' are all prisoners of sin, then differences between them must be derivative and trivial; the governing classes and the whites cannot differ in kind from Africans and laborers."[49] In confessing her sexual sin to her readers, Linda acknowledges their right to offer or withhold compassion—"Pity me, and pardon me, O virtuous reader!" she exclaims—but also emphasizes their fundamental inability to comprehend her actions (61). Since her white readers have been "shielded by the laws" from the ravages of slavery, they cannot know "what it is to be a slave; to be entirely unprotected by law or custom; to have the laws reduce you to the condition of a chattel" (60, 62). If her readers have not seemed to be "prisoners of sin," it is happenstance rather than innate virtue that has shielded them from the knowledge of their own unworthiness, since "all have sinned, and come short of the glory of God."[50] Given these differential circumstances, Jacobs's readers "ought not" to judge her "by the same standard as others"; indeed, only God can justly weigh Linda's sins and her repentance (62).

Adopting the conventions of the spiritual autobiography enabled Jacobs to present the undeniable fact of slavery's sexual abuses as, in her case, the precursor to agency rather than the occasion for its destruction, as abolitionist rhetoric and the seduction and sentimental novel traditions would have it. Acting as a spiritual warrior engaged in a battle for her soul gives Linda Brent space for agency even under the terrible conditions of enslavement to Dr. Flint. It is a role that does not reduce her to one of the "helpless victims or whores" who populated both proslavery and antislavery writing—the very position to which Dr. Flint wishes to reduce her.[51] Though Jacobs invests "the demon Slavery" (62) with a diabolical will, forever fearing that it will "succeed in snatching [her] children from [her]" (168), her response is to pit her own divinely vested agency against the will of the slave system and its demonic representative, Dr. Flint. Even after her affair with Mr. Sands, Linda continues to assert that she is superior in Christian virtue to her lecherous master. When he renews his harassment on the day after his confirmation in the church, she rebuffs his advances with the rejoinder that "'if I could be allowed to live like a Christian, I should be glad'" (83). Flint takes it upon himself to instruct Linda in the ways of Christian virtue: "'You can do what I require; and if you are faithful to me, you will be as virtuous as my wife'" (83). When Linda replies that "'the Bible [doesn't] say so,'" Flint's angry reaction reveals how unprecedented her accession of scriptural authority is: "'How dare you preach to me about your infernal Bible!'" he exclaims. "'What right have you, who are my negro, to talk to me about what you would like, and what you wouldn't like? I am your master, and you shall obey me'" (83). Linda's independent act of interpretation challenges Flint's reading of the Bible and, in doing so, forces him to once again reveal his diabolical nature when in his fit of temper he curses the name of the holy scriptures ("your infernal Bible").

By answering Dr. Flint's definition of virtue with a biblical one—Flint explicitly calls it "preaching"—Linda declares herself the servant of another master, one whose commands she is perfectly capable of reading and interpreting on her own. Linda's insubordination is an act of biblical exegesis couched as revelation: Linda knows the real truth about the Bible—"the Bible doesn't say so"—just as she knows the real truth about the children that the "respectable" Dr. Flint has fathered. And she is willing to share this knowledge with other enslaved people, even at the risk of whipping and imprisonment. When an older enslaved man, Uncle Fred, asks Linda to teach him to read, she finds "a quiet nook, where no intruder was likely to penetrate," and teaches him to read through the New Testament in a few months (81). Learning to read the Bible on his own—a task that must be performed in secret because of proscriptions against educating slaves—will enable Uncle Fred to see through the disguises and concealments of proslavery doctrine just as Linda can: the way it silences, for instance, the story of the Israelites' escape from slavery in Egypt while proclaiming the curse of Ham. Since "slave narratives are almost always founded upon a fundamental lack of knowledge," to know the truth—and to know the truth about God, the most powerful being in the universe—is among the most seditious acts of revelation possible to a slave.[52]

Harriet Jacobs as Christian Exhorter, or The Confessions of Linda Brent

In her spiritual autobiography, Jarena Lee presented her experiences of conversion and sanctification as first steps in a journey toward Christian vocation that culminated in her divine call to become a traveling exhorter. This calling provided the warrant for every act of apparent insubordination, every deviation from race and gender norms. In eighteenth- and nineteenth-century spiritual autobiographies written by women, including Lee and Truth, the experience of conversion and salvation prompts a change in behavior: "Converts fe[el] obligated by the very fact of this momentous experience to tell their stories and persuade others," but to do so they must "overcome their shyness and timidity enough to exhort relatives, enter strange homes, address groups of strangers, inspire and organize other women, and, of course, publish their stories."[53] Here, too, *Incidents* follows the pattern of spiritual autobiography, as Linda increasingly adopts a hortatory style that condemns both southern slaveholders and their northern collaborators.

Incidents offers some of the most scathing critique to be found in antebellum abolitionist writing, a fact sometimes overlooked by scholars preoccupied with the more sentimental aspects of Linda's narration. In a thundering dismissal of white Protestant churches' evangelizing efforts on behalf of faraway "savages," for instance, Linda calls for Christian missions to white enslavers: "Talk to American slaveholders as you talk to savages in Africa. Tell them it is wrong to traffic in men. Tell them it is sinful to sell their own children, and atrocious to violate their own daughters. Tell them that all men are brethren, and that man has no right to shut out the light of knowledge from his brother. . . . Are doctors of divinity blind, or are they hypocrites?" (82) Jacobs contrasts her firsthand knowledge of slavery's horrors with the blindness of the "doctor of divinity" who applauds slavery as a "beautiful 'patriarchal institution'" because he has seen it only through the slaveholder's eyes (83). Claiming the moral authority of one who has read the Bible and taught others to do so as well, Linda adopts the position of Christian exhorter, admonishing her readers to acknowledge slavery as a demonic institution and to join the fight against it—a fight full of both earthly and cosmic importance.

The role of exhorter was a specific position of religious authority that was occupied in the nineteenth century by Jarena Lee, Sojourner Truth, William Apess, and Nat Turner, among many others. Though "the terms preacher, minister, and exhorter" were sometimes "used interchangeably for black religious leaders" in the nineteenth century, the term *exhorter* had a somewhat different meaning than *minister* or *preacher*.[54] While a minister or preacher was usually officially ordained by a denomination, the title *exhorter* could be an honorary one bestowed by one's community or an official one granted by an established religious body. Nat Turner was an unofficial exhorter, one who was not regularly ordained but who, "being admired and respected by his fellow slaves, . . . often spoke to them on the Sabbath get-togethers."[55] Jarena Lee, by contrast, was a licensed exhorter; she preached with the official sanction of the African Methodist Episcopal (AME) Church, the first independent black Protestant denomination in the United States. The license to exhort (which was not exclusive to the AME Church but was offered by other Methodist denominations and some Baptist congregations) was one of the few official clerical designations available to women of any denomination in the nineteenth-century United States. While it carried the official imprimatur of church leaders—Lee received her license directly from Richard Allen, the founder and first bishop of the AME Church—it was "the lowest position in the church's preaching hierarchy," and even licensed exhorters "had to have permission before addressing individual congregations."[56] Exhorters could give testimony, witness to their own conversion experiences, and hold prayer meetings in homes, but they could not choose texts from which to speak—only an ordained minister could do so—or preach from the pulpit.

The position of exhorter, while superior to that of a mere congregant, was subordinate to the position of preacher and often served as a consolation prize for those deemed unsuitable for full ordained ministry. The Pequot convert William Apess, who joined a Methodist community in 1818, spent ten years seeking an official exhorter's license from the majority-white Methodist Episcopal Church; while he did finally obtain his license, he was forced to change denominations—to the less rigid and more racially diverse Methodist Society— before he was allowed to preach independently.[57] Such exclusions frequently characterized black churches as well as white: Lee, though she convinced the African Methodist Episcopal Church to grant her an exhorter's license in 1819, never received official permission to preach despite decades of advocacy for her own and other women's vocation as ministers.[58] And even as a licensed exhorter, Lee encountered "repeated instances over many years of male ministers resisting her right to [exhort] or congregations challenging a woman's ability."[59] Nevertheless, for licensed exhorters like Lee and Apess, who fought race and gender prejudice to reach even this lowest rung of the ecclesiastical ladder, the position could become a space for critique and even for prophecy.

Harriet Jacobs grants to her protagonist-narrator Linda Brent the authoritative voice of the Christian exhorter. Adopting the rhetorical position of the convert called to witness to others, Linda speaks as one who has experienced both the terrors of slavery and the depths of sin to which it drove her, and who has emerged from the experience with a vision and a voice both unique and representative. Linda's status as redeemed sinner enables her to critique the Christians and Christianities she encounters both north and south. She contrasts the quotidian kindness of her first mistress with that mistress's decision to bequeath Aunt Marthy's children, including Linda, to relatives rather than leaving them all free. Though grateful that her mistress at least taught her to read and write, Linda notes the contradiction between the content of these lessons and the import of her teacher's actions: "My mistress had taught me the precepts of God's Word: 'Thou shalt love thy neighbor as thyself.' 'Whatsoever ye would that men should do unto you, do ye even so unto them.' But I was her slave, and I suppose she did not recognize me as her neighbor" (10). Like the Episcopal priest Reverend Pike, who defines the slave's duty to God as identical to his submission to the master, Linda's "kind" mistress preaches a golden rule that binds only Linda and not herself. Linda recognizes this as "blasphemous doctrine," even when it is preached by her own grandmother. When Aunt Marthy "strive[s]" to convince her children and grandchildren that their enslavement is "the will of God: that He had seen fit to place us under such circumstances," Linda and Benjamin "condem[n] it," reasoning that "it was more the will of God that we should be situated as she was," free and with homes of their own (19). Painter asserts that Molly Horniblow's "grandchildren admired, but could not share, her heartfelt Christian piety."[60] But while Linda and Benjamin "condemn" Aunt Marthy's particular interpretation of her faith—that morality consists in remaining patient even under unjust authority—they do not reject Christian piety altogether. Instead, they weigh the faith Aunt Marthy recommends against other religious positions, applying reason to experience to craft an adaptation of Christianity that honors both Aunt Marthy's living example and their own understanding of the "will of God."

To see how Linda Brent's religious identification offers a route to agency and an outlet for her hortatory voice, we need only compare her text with the framing of women's religion that appears in the most widely read escaped-slave narrative of the nineteenth century, Frederick Douglass's *Narrative of the Life of Frederick Douglass, an American Slave, Written by Himself* (1845). In a famous passage in the *Narrative*, Douglass deconstructs the biblical curse against Ham that was used to justify slavery: "A very different-looking class of people

are springing up at the south, and are now held in slavery, from those originally brought to this country from Africa. . . . If the linear descendants of Ham
are alone to be scripturally enslaved, it is certain that slavery at the south must
soon become unscriptural; for thousands are ushered into the world, annu-
ally, who, like myself, owe their existence to white fathers, and those fathers
most frequently their own masters."[61] In this passage, Douglass associates slavery with scripture and scripture, implicitly, with black mothers. To be "scripturally enslaved" is to be descended from Ham, but these mixed-race slaves,
including Douglass himself, are descended from Ham only on their mothers'
sides. Even as they are invoked, however, these black mothers are deftly removed from the procreative process as mixed-race slaves are spontaneously
generated by white slaveholders, "springing up at the south" and being "ushered into the world" while owing "their existence to white fathers," with
mothers nowhere to be found. In this crucial passage, scripture—particularly
the curse of Ham—is associated with black mothers, and then both are made
to disappear, rendering both black women and their religious agency invisible or impossible.

When religious women do appear in Douglass's *Narrative* it is only in the
aggregate and as the victims of religious white men. The women who appear
in Douglass's *Narrative* are not the myriad women, white and black, who participated in Christian antislavery societies—not the Angelina Grimkés and
Sarah Louisa Fortens—but oppressed women whose abused state serves as a
signifier of evil slaveholding practices. "We have men-stealers for ministers,
women-whippers for missionaries, and cradle-plunderers for church members," Douglass avers. "He who sells my sister, for purposes of prostitution,
stands forth as the pious advocate of purity."[62] Like Jacobs, Douglass points to
the hypocrisy of a slave system perpetuated by white men's sexual crimes and
excused by a white Christianity that blesses such actions. But for the male author, the bound and whipped woman is not an agent in her own right but an
emblem of essentialized victimhood.[63] Even Sophia Auld, the kind white
woman who is chastised by her husband for teaching young Frederick to read,
is initially presented in terms that echo Christ's commendation to the "good
and faithful servant" in Matthew 25:35–36 but is robbed of her religious agency
by the power of slavery: "Slavery soon proved its ability to divest her of these
heavenly qualities. Under its influence, the tender heart became stone, and the
lamblike disposition gave way to one of tiger-like fierceness."[64] Slavery, not Sophia Auld, is granted all of the agency in this passage; for her, Christianity is
little more than a dangerous trap she fails to avoid, leading her in the "simplicity of her soul . . . to treat [Douglass] as she supposed one human being
ought to treat another" until she is disabused of this notion.[65] The *Narrative's*

semantic framing of women as the victims of religion rather than its practitioners suggests Douglass's doubtful opinion of the possibilities for black or white women's religious agency.[66]

As John Ernest has noted, over the last forty years Jacobs's *Incidents* has joined Douglass's *Narrative* as the most anthologized escaped-slave narrative, with the two texts frequently paired by literary historians and classroom instructors in a kind of "his and hers" representation of slavery.[67] Yet despite the fact that by 1861 Douglass's was the most widely read escaped-slave narrative and Douglass himself the most well-known black American, *Incidents* makes no mention of Jacobs's famous contemporary or his work, even as it offers oblique or explicit allusions to other abolitionists and public figures, including Harriet Beecher Stowe, Amy Post, and Jeremiah Durham. The black political and religious figure whom Jacobs *does* explicitly invoke is Nat Turner, whose 1831 rebellion shook the South, including Jacobs's native town of Edenton, North Carolina. By referring more than once to Turner's revolt, *Incidents* implicitly aligns Linda Brent's act of sexual insubordination with the revolutionary events of the Northampton rebellion and, more specifically, with the resurrected narrative voice that circulated in the *Confessions of Nat Turner*.

In *Incidents*, the details of Nat Turner's rebellion and its aftermath are sandwiched between the chapters that announce the births of Linda's two children. The arrangement of these chapters, while chronologically accurate (Joseph Jacobs was born in 1829 and Louisa Jacobs in 1833), also places Linda's affair and her new maternal identity in implicit dialogue with Turner's particular brand of insurgent religious agency. Turner, like Jacobs, learned to read and write at an early age, and like Jacobs he attributed his strong religious impressions to the influence of his grandmother. His *Confessions*, like Jacobs's *Incidents*, can be read as a spiritual autobiography in which Christian conviction prompts radical antislavery action. Dictated to Thomas Gray on the eve of his execution, Turner's *Confessions* devotes five pages (of an eleven-page document) to describing the series of signs and wonders that convinced Turner that he was a prophet called to do a great work that would hasten the arrival of the judgment day.[68] While Gray sought to frame Turner's religious convictions and his prophetic visions as perversions of Christianity—the word "fanatic" appears three times in Gray's introductory material and once in the court's pronouncement sentencing Turner to death—Turner describes his religious history as a combination of intellectual engagement (reading the Bible and preaching), ritual participation (fasting, baptism), and direct revelation (he hears the voice of "the Spirit that spoke to the prophets in former days").[69] Though Turner's experiences were more mystical than those of typical white converts, they closely followed the pattern of the black spiritual autobiography.

The focus on Turner in *Incidents* may in some respects be attributable to the influence of Jacobs's editor, Lydia Maria Child, who while working with the manuscript requested further details about the aftermath of the insurrection. "You say the reader would not believe what you saw 'inflicted on men, women, and children, without the slightest ground of suspicion against them,'" Child wrote to Jacobs. "What were those inflictions? Were any tortured to make them confess? . . . Please write down some of the most striking particulars, and let me have them to insert."[70] *Incidents* accordingly includes accounts of the invasive searches to which Jacobs and her neighbors were subjected after the revolt was put down, as well as descriptions of innocent black residents "whipped till the blood stood in puddles at their feet," "tortured with a bucking paddle," and "cruelly scourged" (71). But while Child had requested—and Jacobs apparently provided—more information about the physical violence visited on Edenton's black population after Turner's revolt, Linda as narrator dwells at even greater length on the destruction of the slaves' religious communities and on the agentive possibilities those communities represented.

As the social historian Walter Johnson has noted, "neither African nor African-American cultural forms," including African American Christianity, "were *inherently* resistant to the *system* of slavery. And yet it was through employing shared cultural forms . . . that enslaved people flourished even in their slavery, and set about forming the alliances through which they helped one another resist it."[71] Recognizing the opportunities for collusion that black Christian connection could enable, in the wake of Turner's rebellion Edenton's white authorities begin by demolishing the black believers' "little church in the woods, with their burying ground around it," which was "built by the colored people," and where "they had no higher happiness than to meet . . . and sing hymns together, and pour out their hearts in spontaneous prayer" (75). In place of this independent religious practice, the slaveholders substitute supervised worship: Edenton's black population is "permitted to attend the white churches" on Sunday mornings, where they are relegated to seats in the gallery and served communion only after the service is over (75). The white community also institutes separate evening services in which they determine to "give the slaves enough of religious instruction to keep them from murdering their masters" (57). At the first of these segregated services, the minister, Reverend Pike, takes as his text Ephesians 6:5: "Servants, be obedient to them that are your masters according to the flesh, with fear and trembling, in singleness of your heart, as unto Christ."

Having seen in Turner's rebellion how unsupervised biblical interpretation could lead to violent collective action among slaves, Pike and the slaveholders who employ him decide that the best way to head off the most revolutionary results of religious agency is to control which parts of the Bible are made available to slaves. But his strategies backfire as the slaves make their exclusion the ground of their critique, interpellating themselves as observers rather than objects of proslavery preaching and treating Pike's sermons as performances staged for their entertainment. "Highly amused" with Pike's preaching, his audience returns a few more times to hear "pretty much a repetition of the last discourse" and then, tiring of these harangues, opts to attend a "Methodist shout" instead (58). At the "shout" and at Methodist class meetings (small group gatherings led by whites), the slaves note the hypocrisy of the white Christians (one white class leader snickers at a bereaved black woman whose last child has been sold) even as they recognize the liberatory potential of Christian teaching and their own capacity to practice a piety superior to that of white Christians. Linda reflects on the sincerity of the enslaved and asserts that "many of them [are] nearer to the gate of heaven than sanctimonious Mr. Pike, and other long-faced Christians, who see wounded Samaritans, and pass by on the other side" (78). Jacobs's free and enslaved blacks voice their awareness of white Christian hypocrisy through slyly coded songs: "Ole Satan's church is here below. / Up to God's free church I hope to go. / Cry Amen, cry Amen, cry Amen to God!" (79). In these and other scenes, Linda and her fellow black believers appropriate the white teachings intended to pacify them and adapt them instead to their own liberatory purposes, just as Nat Turner and his fellow insurgents had done.

By enfolding the history of Turner's revolt and its consequences into the story of her sexual rebellion, Jacobs implies that Linda's moral suicide—her "plunge into the abyss"—has set free a resurrected narrative voice that is akin to the prophetic voice that circulated in *The Confessions of Nat Turner*. From its first publication, the *Confessions* seemed to defy the purposes for which its white editor intended it, raising as much sympathy for the slaves' cause as it did condemnation. In the pages of the *Liberator*, William Lloyd Garrison satirically suggested that "a large reward" be offered "for the arrest of Gray and his printers," since the *Confessions* was as likely to foment antislavery sentiment as to quash it.[72] If abolitionism was the Lord's work, as black and white abolitionists so frequently claimed, the voice of Nat Turner, as it circulated in the *Confessions*, had become the voice of God.

In *Incidents*, Linda reminds readers of Turner's rebellion not only in the chapters between the birth of her children but again when she begins her long escape from Dr. Flint. Just before fleeing the Flint plantation to seek shelter in the attic room of a white friend, Linda passes by "the wreck of the old meeting house, where, before Nat Turner's time, the slaves had been allowed to meet for worship." There she seems to hear her father's voice emanating from it, "bidding me not to tarry till I reached freedom or the grave" (101). When describing each of her desperate plunges—into sin and into hiding—Linda invokes the name of Nat Turner. And just as Turner's story rose from the ashes of his revolt, the Linda Brent who emerges from the "living grave" of her grandmother's attic claims a hortatory voice that rages against slavery and its abuses (164).

Mastering the authoritative voice of the Christian exhorter enables Linda to unleash thundering condemnations of both southern slaveholders and their complacent northern enablers. After praising abolitionists, Linda wonders why more do not join their ranks: "Why are ye silent, ye free men and women of the north?" she apostrophizes (33). Living in New York City after the passage of the Fugitive Slave Act, Linda calls it the "City of Iniquity," lamenting that "while fashionables were listening to the thrilling voice of Jenny Lind in Metropolitan Hall, the thrilling voices of poor hunted colored people went up, in an agony of supplication, to the Lord, from Zion's church" (213). The reference to "Zion's church" ties a specific northern black congregation—Zion Church in New York City, which had split from the white-dominated Methodist Episcopal Church in 1821 to become the founding church of the AME Zion denomination—to the "sincere" southern black worshippers who had prayed to be taken "up to God's free church" (79), and also to the Old Testament Israelites set free by the hand of God and led to their Promised Land. Just as adopting the conventions of the spiritual autobiography enabled Jacobs to narrate her sin and redemption as a story with cosmic importance, assuming the voice of Christian exhortation allows Linda to condemn corrupt white Christians while celebrating the faith of black believers.

Eavesdropping on *Incidents*

The formulaic nature of the spiritual autobiography—its tendency to draw on a well of generic images and phrases to describe a process of personal transformation—has sometimes led critics to overlook or undervalue the processes of self-making and self-expression it both describes and enables. For the black spiritual autobiographer in particular, however, the genre enables the accession of selfhood so strenuously denied by the slave system. The narrator of the spiritual autobiography describes "a spiritual journey through the trials of life, growing in strength and wisdom as he or she grapples with these trials, gradually becoming worthy of his or her ultimate destination of everlasting life with God."[73] To be known by God—not the false slaveholder-god but the all-powerful deity embraced by Christian believers—was to be recognized as worthy of divine notice and consideration, even in the worst of circumstances. As Saidiya Hartman has asserted in her study of slave humanity and agency, "serving God was a crucial site of struggle" because "the exchange of blacks as commodities and their violent domination were often described in terms of being treated as if one did not have a soul."[74] When Linda, at sixteen years old, repudiates Dr. Flint's "clai[m] . . . to rule me, body and soul," she is engaging in the most fundamental act of agency available to a slave, and one that forms the basis for all of her later actions (43).

Recognizing how the established genre of the spiritual autobiography structures *Incidents* helps to reveal how Linda Brent's agency operates through her religious and moral commitments—including the shame engendered by her sexual sin—and not solely or primarily in spite of them. Decoupling Jacobs's agency from a secularized notion of total autonomy helps us as readers and critics to see the full range of Jacobs's agency and, thus, of her humanity. As I have demonstrated in earlier chapters of this book, conflating agency with autonomy obfuscates our understanding of the religious experiences of free white women. But when applied to enslaved women, this practice results in much more serious and damaging forms of misapprehension that are tantamount to epistemic violence. Acts of epistemic violence "violat[e] the most fundamental way that a person or people know themselves" by denying, destroying, or erasing their experience, cosmology, or world view.[75] Harriet Jacobs knew herself as a Christian woman, and she apprehended her agentive options in the light of that knowledge.

As Carla Kaplan has discussed in her reading of *Incidents*, critics of the text have often appointed themselves the judges of Linda Brent and of her author, Harriet Jacobs. Seeking to recuperate Jacobs's agency, critics have identified her acts of literacy and literary production as subversive by definition, holding up *Incidents* itself as evidence of her "triumph" over James Norcom and the slave system. Kaplan, like Hartman, exposes how such readings do violence to slaves' stories and obscure the workings of slavery by imposing ideals of autonomy onto their subjects. While such recuperative criticism "restores important texts, helps us to reshape the canon, [and] maps the lines of ideological struggle along which canons have been laid out," Kaplan writes, by "substitut[ing] the critic's own agency for the textual agency supposedly being restored," the recuperative critic also "places him- or herself in a juridical position," claiming the right to pass judgment on a text and its author.[76] Beyond the single case of Harriet Jacobs, judging enslaved people by their capacity for rebellion or subversion reinscribes the very terms that justified their enslavement, since liberal notions of autonomous agency, Walter Johnson reminds us, "were themselves worked out in self-conscious philosophical opposition to the condition of slavery." Lauding Jacobs for achieving autonomy through publication not only elides the many forms of oppression she continued to endure after her manumission but also erases "a[ny] consideration of human-ness lived outside the conventions of liberal agency, a consideration, that is, of the condition of enslaved humanity."[77]

Though *Incidents* is explicitly directed to white women—the epigraphs on the book's title page, the prefaces by Jacobs and Child, and the many apostrophized variations on "you happy free women" make this direction clear (18)—these readers are exhorted not to pass judgment but to listen: to bear witness to Linda Brent's testimony of sin and redemption. The first of the text's epigraphs decries northerners' continued ignorance of slavery: despite a tradition of escaped-slave narratives that was by then decades old, northern readers continue to naively believe that slavery is "perpetual bondage only." To repair these faulty northern beliefs, Jacobs's second epigraph counsels attention and rapt listening: "Rise up, ye women that are at ease! Hear my voice, ye careless daughters! Give ear unto my speech!" (1). The epigraphs, taken together, imply that Jacobs, as author of the text and expert on the horrors of slavery, is not the subject of judgment but the practitioner of it. In ignoring "the depth of *degradation* involved in that word, slavery," and allowing the slave system to remain in place for hundreds of years, Jacobs's northern readers have given ample evidence of their own sinful natures. The extract from Isaiah, read in context, offers both an admonishment ("Hear my voice") and an accusation:

> For the vile person will speak villany, and his heart will work iniquity, to practise hypocrisy, and to utter error against the Lord . . .
>
> Rise up, ye women that are at ease; hear my voice, ye careless daughters; give ear unto my speech.
>
> Many days and years shall ye be troubled, ye careless women: for the vintage shall fail, the gathering shall not come.
>
> Tremble, ye women that are at ease; be troubled, ye careless ones: strip you, and make you bare, and gird sackcloth upon your loins . . .
>
> Upon the land of my people shall come up thorns and briers; yea, upon all the houses of joy in the joyous city.[78]

Writing from the City of Iniquity to her northern white neighbors and speaking in the passionate voice of the Christian exhorter who invokes an ancient prophet, the Jacobs of the epigraph pronounces judgment not on the "slave girl" of the narrative's title but on the northern readers, "careless" and "at ease," who have allowed "villany" and "hypocrisy" to run rampant in the land. It is the "careless daughters" of the North who should cower before the Lord's righteousness, not the pitiable victims of slavery's degradations.

Those among Jacobs's readers who would usurp the right to pass judgment on her occupy the place of the sadistic mistress in the deathbed scene with which I began this chapter. In the scene, the dying girl never speaks to or even acknowledges the white mistress hovering over her; instead, all of her words are addressed to God and to her mourning mother. "'Oh Lord, come and take me!'" the girl begs. She then commands her mother not to grieve and expresses faith in God's righteous judgment. Though the white mistress obtrudes herself on the scene, the dying girl takes no notice. Her statement of theodicy—"God knows all about it"—is directed to her mother and not to the white woman who has appropriated to herself the right to accuse (16).

If *Incidents in the Life of a Slave Girl* is a spiritual autobiography akin to the narratives of Jarena Lee, Sojourner Truth, and even Nat Turner, we as readers and critics are called less to pass judgment than to bear witness. Caleb Smith has argued that Jacobs's narrative is best read as testimony, the mode through which Garrisonian abolitionism sought to bring about its antislavery ends by constructing the abolitionist press as "an arena of justice that was both more democratic and more capable of honoring the higher truths of divine law" than were the earthly courts that merely exacerbated brutality against enslaved people.[79] *Incidents* makes a direct appeal to the higher law by enacting the ritual of personal confession that begins the spiritual autobiography, in which conversion requires first the conviction of sin. But whereas court testimony is offered to facilitate earthly judgment, the testimony offered in the spiritual narrative asserts that judgment has already been rendered. God "knows all about" the convicted sinner, and we as readers are summoned to hear a confession and a testimony whose primary audience is God. Just as Jarena Lee testified before Bethel Church while Richard Allen remained silent, and just as Nat Turner spoke past Thomas Gray and offered his testimony before the congregation of enslaved people, Jacobs offered a confession that we, as readers, are called to witness but not to adjudicate.

CHAPTER 4

"The Human Soul . . . Makes All Things Sacred"

Communal Agency in the Theological Romances of Harriet Beecher Stowe

In the introduction to her brother Charles's 1849 book *The Incarnation; or, Pictures of the Virgin and Her Son*, Harriet Beecher Stowe made a plea for romance as a vehicle for religious truth. *The Incarnation* is a narrativization of the gospels, and Stowe acknowledges that some readers might find the fictionalization of scripture objectionable: "There may be some who at first would feel a prejudice against this species of composition, as so blending together the outlines of truth and fiction as to spread a doubtful hue of romance over the whole" (iv–v).[1] Having linked romance and truth as opposites in the imagined minds of her readers, Stowe goes on to throw a "doubtful hue" not over romance but over truth. Since pictures of historical events are constructed in the mind, no textual rendering of those events can ever be really true, which is to say both satisfyingly thorough and factually accurate: "The blank, cold, vague, misty images of an uninstructed mind are no *more* like the truth, than the conceptions of a vivid imagination chastened and guided by accurate knowledge" (v). Stowe offers an example of the problem of erroneous conception by outlining her readers' probable attitudes toward the Virgin Mary:

> No one ever heard of the Virgin Mary without forming some kind of an image or conception of her, it may be, borrowed from some antiquated engraving or old church painting . . . ; or it may be that there is

only a kind of formless mist connected with the sound of that name. But neither the formless mist nor the antique effigy are a whit nearer to the reality than the conception of one who, . . . gathering all the intimations of Scripture touching her descent, character, and external position, should embody to himself, as nearly as possible, the *probable* truth of the case. (v–vi)

Dealing in probabilities rather than certainties, Stowe makes a case for the author of romance as the creator of truth. Her repeated use of the word *conception* to describe her brother's depiction of Mary suggests the act of incarnation engaged in by the author of romance. The romancer gives flesh to the "formless mist" or "antique effigy" that exists in the reader's mind, bringing into being true "conceptions" that are "guided by accurate knowledge." For Stowe, romance comes closest to "truth" because it places facts, which are always obscured by the mists of history, in service to the higher powers of human imagination.

Stowe elaborated her defense of romance a decade later in her 1859 novel *The Minister's Wooing*. In it, her narrator offers a gently facetious "plea" to those serious readers who have come to the novel expecting a "history" of the eighteenth-century New England clergyman Samuel Hopkins and have instead discovered "a love-story, after all" (73).[2] Unlike the biographer or historian, Stowe claims, the author of romance has eyes "anointed to see what poems, what romances, what sublime tragedies lie around us in the daily walk of life" (73). To the complaints of "all prosaic, and all bitter, disenchanted people [who] talk as if poets and novelists made romance," Stowe's narrator counters that "GOD is the great maker of romance. HE, from whose hand came man and woman,—HE, who strung the great harp of Existence . . . HE is the great Poet of life" (72). Since romance is God's own creation, the "scoffing spirit that laughs at romance is an apple of the Devil's own handing from the bitter tree of knowledge;—it opens the eyes only to see eternal nakedness" (72). The narrator of *The Minister's Wooing* associates this original sin—the denial of romance—with capitalist accumulation and consumption: "When Mr. Smith or Mr. Stubbs has brought every wheel of life into such range and order that it is one steady, daily grind," he throws "all but this dead grind, and the dollars that come through the mill, . . . into one waste 'catch-all' and label[s] it *romance*" (70). The female corollary to Mr. Smith and Mr. Stubbs is "the fascinating Mrs. T., whose life is a whirl between ball and opera, point-lace, [and] diamonds" (71). The spoils of industrial capitalism—mindless labor, pointless acquisitiveness, and conspicuous consumption—are the temptations offered by "the devil's own handing"; it is the task of the romancer to rebuke these temptations through the incarnation of higher truths.

In the late 1850s and early 1860s, Stowe would counter what she saw as a growing antiromantic strain in American culture by composing what I am calling theological romances, a term that, for Stowe, is fundamentally redundant since, if God is the "great maker of romance," the writing of romance *is* theological. Romance, the realm of imagination and emotional connection, is where God's—which is to say, reality's—ultimate expression is to be found, and it is the representation of that reality not in the "blank, cold, vague" outlines of material fact but in all its spiritual, physical, and conceptual fullness that is the romancer's lot. To write romance is to push back against the allied forces of religious disenchantment and capitalist accumulation that together conspire to rob the world of mystery and replace it with acquired goods whose empty materiality amounts to only a pale echo of a higher truth. Rather than a childish retreat from the facts of life, the "smiles . . . tears . . . [and] intense excitement" of romance are "the reality . . . of which the romancer is the second-hand recorder" (MW 73).[3]

For Stowe, the writing of romance is as much a religious vocation as an artistic and literary choice, and both *The Minister's Wooing* and her 1862 novel, *Agnes of Sorrento*, can be read as theological romances that rewrite religious history to envision how women's religious agency—and particularly their romantic agency—might provide a source of resistance to the encroaching forces of liberal capitalist modernity. Set in the late-eighteenth century, *The Minister's Wooing* critiques the increasing specialization of nineteenth-century social, economic, and religious life and decries the culturally enforced distance between the "speculative" and "practical" domains of endeavor. In it, the women of postrevolutionary Newport, Rhode Island, practice a form of communal agency that circulates by means of the material objects they create together: dresses, cuffs, blankets, tablecloths, ribbons. Rather than feeding the "dead grind, and the dollars that come through the mill" or fading shabbily before Mrs. T's point lace, these created objects embody an enchanted materiality that, because of its association with lost loved ones, cannot be reduced solely to its economic value.

Agnes of Sorrento—published shortly after *The Minister's Wooing* and, like its predecessor, in the *Atlantic Monthly*—likewise depicts a form of female communal agency that, as Jenny Franchot has argued, "eases the Protestant (and particularly Calvinist) burdens of isolation": the titular Agnes finds her agency, not in autonomous action, but in collaboration with the community of saints, the Christians living and dead whom she claims as her companions and guides.[4]

The enchanted materials that circulate through this theological romance are works of religious art: paintings, drawings, frescoes, and sculptures that turn lifeless materials into representations of a living faith. Set in a time and space that precedes both the Protestant Reformation and the rise of Enlightenment liberalism, *Agnes of Sorrento* denaturalizes disenchantment, revealing not only its imbrication with capitalism—the way secular modernity disenchants objects to better suit them for capitalist exchange—but its conspiracy with patriarchy. Agnes herself is the novel's prime example of enchanted materiality: like the Virgin Mary she prays to, she is both fully human woman and the vessel for divine revelation. And yet whether she is under the control of the Catholic priest Father Francesco or the proto-Protestant cavalier Agostino Sarelli, Agnes finds herself the victim of a patriarch who would deny her agency and reduce her to an object for possession.

Theological romance offered a counterweight to the nineteenth-century literary movement that Gregory Jackson has recently identified as homiletic realism. As Jackson has discussed, Stowe and her post-Calvinist peers did not subscribe to "the dialectical relationship between realism and idealism" that structures our modern secular world view; rather, in nineteenth-century Protestantism's "fundamentally Augustinian moral order . . . fact and fiction [were] two sides of the coin of representation; both offer[ed] insight only as they directly mediate[d] an invisible, spiritual reality." The homiletic realism practiced by such authors as William T. Stead and Charles Sheldon, Jackson argues, offered lurid and shocking portraits of poverty and degradation that audiences were meant to read *through* if they were to apprehend human suffering correctly, as an opportunity for spiritual volition.[5] Stowe's work shared this same Augustinian genealogy, and she was surrounded throughout her life by ordained ministers whose preaching prowess was often attributed to their ability to paint realistic and terrifying portraits of brothels, wine sinks, and other dens of iniquity.[6] Critics of Stowe's work from her own time to ours have rightly identified her novels as homiletic and her authorial career as a lay ministry that challenged and even exceeded her father's and brothers' successes. Dawn Coleman's recent work on Stowe has identified the thundering sermonic voice that develops in *Uncle Tom's Cabin* and highlighted the "democratization of preaching" that takes place in that text.[7] And yet Stowe's later novels, including *The Minister's Wooing* and *Agnes of Sorrento*, increasingly repudiate the implicit voyeurism of homiletic realism, with its tight focus on material conditions, and insist instead that theological romance is the best mode for representing the substance of invisible things and the reality of unseen and enchanted forces.

Since her recovery by feminist scholars in the 1970s and 1980s, Stowe has been one of only two nineteenth-century women writers—alongside Emily Dickinson—whose religious ideas have received sustained and serious attention from critics. Because of her explicit engagement with Calvinist intellectual traditions and with the sermonic form through which they were passed down, Stowe has largely escaped the accusation that her works are devoid of theology. Charles Foster, Stowe's mid-twentieth-century critic and biographer, gave careful attention to her Calvinist inheritance, while Lawrence Buell investigated Stowe's post-Puritan writings in his *New England Literary Culture* (1986) and elsewhere, comparing her favorably with her contemporary Nathaniel Hawthorne and labeling them both "maverick children of . . . colonial Puritanism."[8] These and other critics have most often focused on the influence of Jonathan Edwards's millennialism on Stowe's own theology. Helen Petter Westra has limned the similarities and differences between Edwards's millennial vision and Stowe's, highlighting Stowe's belief that slavery (rather than the persistence of non-Christian religions) was the great sin preventing the return of Christ.[9] Mason I. Lowance Jr. has elaborated the rhetorical techniques that Stowe derived from exegetical traditions, including her use of "biblical types, Platonic and allegorical figures, [and] millennial and prophetic language," and Carla Rineer has argued that the works of explicit biblical exegesis that Stowe produced in her later career, *Woman in Sacred History* (1872) and *Footsteps of the Master* (1877), represent "a collection of religious documents [intended] to codify the precepts of her matriarchal millennialism into a tangible gospel."[10] While most treatments of Stowe's theological writing emphasize her turn to a nurturing, maternal God, a few critics, including Karen Halttunen, Jeffrey Cass, and, most thoroughly, Kevin Pelletier have argued for the persistence of an "apocalyptic terror" that was fundamental to Calvinist theology and that animated Stowe's sentimental fiction in previously unrecognized ways.[11]

Given this attention to Stowe's theology and its social effects, one critic has registered concern that readings of Stowe's work might in fact be *too* doctrinal, that critics may have distorted her texts by producing interpretations that are "schematic and strictly theological" (558).[12] Yet even as they acknowledge her capacity for theological engagement, many critical treatments of Stowe continue to fall prey to the intellect/emotion binary I have discussed elsewhere in this book—the persistent misconception that women experience religion emotionally while men approach it intellectually, a mistake that can be traced back to Enlightenment liberalism's yoking of femininity with irrationality and religion.[13] Other critics position Stowe's religious ideas as reactionary or consolatory rather than generative: she is represented as a rebellious daughter engaged in an interpersonal struggle with her overbearing father, a popularizer of doctrines initiated and promulgated by male clerics (whether living or dead), or a mourning mother sanding off Calvinism's hard edges to make it more amenable to grief.[14] While these pictures carry some truth, they are themselves "vague, misty images" that underestimate both Stowe's intellectual and theological creativity and her concrete contributions to nineteenth-century Protestant thought.

To understand Stowe's theology and its implications, we must employ the technique of secular reading that I have been advocating throughout this book. As Mary McCartin Wearn has recently argued, "Stowe's writing is no renunciation of theology and is not the reactionary anti-intellectualism" of which she has sometimes been accused; instead, her work must be read as "a call to an intellectually honest theology that is translated to Christian practice in the real world."[15] We can begin by acknowledging Stowe as a creative producer of theology rather than as someone who waters down complex Calvinist doctrine for a lazy reading public. Just as importantly, reading Stowe secularly means recognizing the ways in which her texts are themselves interrogations of nineteenth-century secularity. By depicting women's religious agency as simultaneously distributed and powerful, *The Minister's Wooing* and *Agnes of Sorrento* challenge the atomizing and disenchanting impulses of secular modernity. By appearing as both icons of idealized womanhood and incarnated daughters, granddaughters, and wives, Mary Scudder and Agnes repair the increasing fragmentation of modern life by uniting in their persons the spiritual and the material, the temporal and the eternal, and the holy and the profane. As works of one of the nineteenth century's most astute cultural and religious critics, Stowe's novels offer sophisticated critiques of her secular situation—which is, of course, the prehistory of our own.

The Minister's Wooing: From Disinterested Benevolence to Infinite Kindness

In a February 1858 article in the *Atlantic Monthly* titled "New England Ministers," Stowe took issue with William Buell Sprague's recently published *Annals of the American Pulpit*, the first volume in a new history of notable American clerics. Recalling her own experience of having grown up among the New England clergy at the beginning of the nineteenth century, Stowe complained about what she considered Sprague's inaccurate portraits of eighteenth-century New England clerical life.[16] Where Sprague portrayed stuffed shirts poring over ancient tomes, the real forefathers of the current New England clerical class, Stowe asserted, had possessed "a rare fund of humor, shrewdness, genius, and originality" (221). Rather than locking themselves in cells to pursue their intellectual callings, learned divines including Jonathan Edwards and Samuel Hopkins had farmed, gardened, and taken in scholars to supplement their meager incomes and had often served as doctors and lawyers to their congregants. According to Stowe, Sprague's *Annals* imposed on its eighteenth-century subjects a distinctly "modern" understanding of how a minister should behave in the world; she diagnosed this modern malady as "the doctrine that a minister is to maintain some ethereal, unearthly station, where, wrapt in divine contemplation, he is to regard with indifference the actual struggles and realities of life" (228). The revered clergy of the eighteenth century, Stowe asserted, had drawn no such artificial distinctions between the intellectual work of theologizing and the practical work of ministering to parishioners and maintaining a household. Rather, Hopkins, Edwards, and their contemporaries had embodied "a rare union of the speculative and the practical" (221), a felicitous combination of intellectual rigor, personal piety, domestic faculty, and pastoral concern. Sprague had misrepresented his subjects by overspecializing the role of the clergy, exalting the "ethereal" and "unearthly" over the practical and the "real"—a failing Stowe attributes to Sprague and his "modern" colleagues but not to Sprague's subjects.[17]

As I have noted elsewhere, *speculative* and *practical* are theological terms that can be traced back at least as far as the thirteenth century, to the work of Thomas Aquinas. Speculative theology had as its aim "the beholding of God as an end in itself"; practical theology "led to a good beyond itself"—to tangible and salutary effects in the world.[18] Historically these two theological modes had been conceived as complementary, particularly in the American Protestant tradition. But *speculative* and *practical* were also the terms that John Locke adopted to describe the proper distribution of religious and civil powers in a liberal state. "Articles of religion," Locke asserted, "are some of them practical and some speculative," and though "both sorts consist in the knowledge of truth, yet [the speculative] terminate simply in the understanding, [the practical] influence the will and manners." On "speculative opinions" and "articles of faith," Locke insisted, the state should have nothing to say; but as to practical matters, "moral actions belong . . . to the jurisdiction of both the outward and inward court; both of the civil and domestic governor; I mean both of the magistrate and conscience."[19] From the state's perspective, in other words, speculative religion was a private matter, while the effects of practical religion could be publicly regulated.

In its critique of the "modern" clergy, "New England Ministers" invokes all of these theological and political valences. By dividing speculative theological work from practical ministerial work, the essay implies, the new generation of New England ministers was both betraying a long-standing Christian integrative tradition and capitulating to a political ideology that diminished the church's worldly influence by divorcing matters of "private" belief from matters of "public" concern. Not only were Stowe's contemporaries neglecting an important part of their religious duty by elevating speculative theology over practical matters, but in doing so they were contributing to a liberal privatization of religion that removed matters of theology from the public square and robbed the church of what Stowe regarded as its proper moral mission.

Ten months after Stowe published "New England Ministers" in the *Atlantic*, the first installment of her novel *The Minister's Wooing* appeared in the same journal, with the eighteenth-century clergyman Samuel Hopkins as a central character. Stowe's novel seemed to contradict her earlier critique of Sprague's biographies, since the Hopkins of *The Minister's Wooing* is almost literally a stuffed shirt: he has neither humor, shrewdness, genius, nor originality, and he cannot so much as darn a sock, much less manage a garden or farm. *The Minister's Wooing* willfully misrepresents the historical Hopkins in precisely the way that Stowe had accused Sprague of misrecognizing him: the fictional Hopkins dwells entirely in the realm of the speculative while his practical needs are ministered to by the women around him. Even when engaged in the most material of activities, the eating of meals, the fictional Hopkins is immersed in ruminations about the future fate of humankind: he sits at his landlady's supper table, oblivious as always to the domestic preparations happening around him, and "calmly expand[s] and soliloquize[s] on his favorite topic, the last golden age of Time, the Marriage-Supper of the Lamb, when the purified earth, like a repentant Psyche, shall be restored to the long-lost favor of a celestial Bridegroom, and glorified saints and angels shall walk familiarly as wedding-guests among men" (119). Rather than enjoying—and expressing gratitude for—the meal placed before him, Hopkins transforms all material things into metaphors for life in the world to come. This fictional Hopkins becomes the vehicle for the extended critique of "modern" New England Protestantism that Stowe had begun in her earlier essay—a critique that, in keeping with an integrative theological tradition, is both speculative and practical.

As a work of theological romance, *The Minister's Wooing* attacks what Stowe called the "arithmetical theology" formulated by the real-life Hopkins and promulgated by his nineteenth-century biographer Edwards Park: the doctrine of disinterested benevolence that, according to Stowe, turned millions of human souls into the universe's useless waste. In its stead the novel offers what I will call—in a borrowing from Stowe's mother, Roxana Foote—the doctrine of infinite kindness, a soteriological scheme that locates salvation in the relations between God and the human community rather than in God's predestined and inflexible will. While the narrator of *The Minister's Wooing* occasionally argues explicitly with the long-dead Hopkins, the doctrine of infinite kindness is less debated than incarnated by the community of women who perform domestic and theological work side by side. The women of *The Minister's Wooing* unite the speculative and the practical in their daily lives as Stowe's "New England ministers" of old had done and in the process enact a form of collaborative communal agency. The incarnated theology offered by this community adheres to no systematic formula that might compete with Hopkins's work, but for Stowe the romancer, it comes much closer to the "probable truth" of the kingdom of God.

The hub of the novel's female community is *The Minister's Wooing*'s romantic protagonist, Mary Scudder, a beautiful, modest, and devout maiden living in Newport, Rhode Island, in the wake of the American Revolution. Mary has fallen in love with her longtime friend James Marvyn, but when James is reported lost at sea before having made any provision for the fate of his immortal soul, Mary is plunged into grief. When she emerges from her mourning, she agrees to marry Doctor Hopkins, who boards in her mother's home and whose feelings for her have grown from paternal to romantic. Mary is warned against this decision by her friend Virginie de Frontignac, a Catholic immigrant who is married to an older man she does not love and who has become romantically entangled with New England's most notorious rake, the genteel and godless Aaron Burr. When James returns from sea alive and well, Mary feels it her duty to fulfill her promise to marry Hopkins, but through the intervention of the Marvyns' servant Candace and the town seamstress, Miss Prissy Diamond, Hopkins is informed of the young couple's love for one another and graciously relinquishes his claim to Mary.

The real Samuel Hopkins, like Stowe's fictional minister, was an outspoken and sincere opponent of slavery. Unlike Stowe's forty-something bachelor boarder, however, the real Hopkins was married by age twenty-seven and fathered eight children. By the 1850s, he was best remembered as a strict Calvinist theologian and an elaborator of Jonathan Edwards's "New Divinity" theology. His most controversial theological innovation—and the one that preoccupied Stowe—was the doctrine of disinterested benevolence. Whereas Edwards had asserted that true human virtue was defined by "benevolence to Being in general," Hopkins took this position further, asserting that "the genuine expression of disinterested benevolence . . . always gives up a less good for a greater, and the private good of individuals for the sake of the public good, or the salvation of many." This elevation of the public good over the "private good of individuals" meant, for Hopkins, that a Christian's true virtue consisted in a "willingness to be damned for the glory of God."[20] With this extension of Edwardsian thought, Hopkins had "aroused a furor" because his system "allowed no middle ground between sinners and saints. One either loved God above self or one loved self above God."[21] If, as Hopkins insisted, the only true evidence of salvation was an almost superhuman unselfishness—the willingness to be damned for God's glory—then almost no one was saved.

In *The Minister's Wooing*, Stowe's narrator describes how Hopkins's theology made Christian salvation not a process but a product: "There is a ladder to heaven, whose base God has placed in human affections, tender instincts, symbolic feelings, sacraments of love, through which the soul rises higher and higher, refining as she goes, till she outgrows the human, and changes, as she rises, into the image of the divine. . . . This Ultima Thule of virtue had been seized upon by our sage as the *all* of religion. He knocked out every round of the ladder but the highest, and then, pointing to its hopeless splendor, said to the world, 'Go up thither and be saved!'" (53–54) In letters to family and friends, Stowe would use less gentle language to describe Hopkins's straightforward assertion that the ultimate expression of God's glory could be found in the damnation of millions of souls. In a letter to her brother Henry Ward Beecher, Stowe complained of "the Hopkinsian arithmetical method of disposing of the great majority of the human race up to our day and on to the millennium as damned without benefit of clergy."[22] In another letter to family friend Martha Wetherill, who, like Stowe herself, had recently lost a child, she again decried a theology that "by very simple arithmetical calculation" would insist that "the whole human race with some small exceptions is made for everlasting misery—for the number who have been true saints is certainly in comparison to the human race only the proportion of one in a million."[23] For Stowe, a God who could "dispose of" millions of souls without a thought was not worth glorifying at all.

When Stowe wrote "New England Ministers" and *The Minister's Wooing*, Hopkins had been dead for decades. But she was not idly quibbling with a moribund patriarch; she was wrangling with a living one. In 1859, Hopkins's theology was being vociferously championed by Edwards Amasa Park, the Abbot Professor of Christian Theology at Andover Seminary during Calvin Stowe's tenure there from 1852 to 1864 and the biographer and staunch admirer of Hopkins.[24] Stowe, who had a front-row seat to theological politics at Andover in the 1850s, complained to Henry that Park not only required Andover's clergy in training to subscribe to the belief "that by using up three million in this way thirty three million times more happiness can be made to exist in the end" but that he also insisted they praise such a God as "both just and generous."[25] The "arithmetical theology," Stowe thought, was dangerous both to the church and to individual human souls, because believers like Martha Wetherill were close to forming the heretical conclusion "that instead of Christ's having brought a glorious gospel of salvation—he has only brought the news of damnation."[26] The doctrine of disinterested benevolence was demonstrably false because it denied the holiness of human relations, which—as Christ repeatedly demonstrated in his parables—were the type of relations between God and humankind. As Stowe saw it, Hopkins and his follower Park, in trying to imagine the perfectly unselfish person, had created a monstrously selfish God.

In *The Minister's Wooing* the details of human relationships, rather than abstract doctrinal principles, impart a right understanding of God's benevolence. When Mary Scudder considers the possibility of James Marvyn's unredeemed death, she wonders, "If he were among the lost, in what age of eternity could she ever be blessed? Could Christ be happy, if those who were one with him were sinful and accursed?" Extrapolating from her own feelings to Christ's, Mary reasons that a God who would die for his children would not gladly see those children damned; nor would he break in eternity the bonds of "self-devoting love" that had formed on earth (205). When Hopkins warns Mary that "a mere selfish love" for God might "take the place of that disinterested complacency which regards Him for what He is in Himself, apart from what He is to us," Mary's response is to wonder how it would even be possible to love God "apart" from oneself. Asked whether she has never felt her heart "rising up against" God, Mary replies, "Against *Him*? against my Heavenly Father?" (168, 169). Repeating the prepositional "against," Mary emphasizes the relationship *between* herself and God; to rebel would be to rebel not abstractly but *against* a particular being, a member of her family, her Heavenly Father. Mary's reply foregrounds God as a partner in relationship rather than a source of terrifying cosmic power; to rise up against him would be to break her own heart.

Mary follows this conversation with a letter to Hopkins that is modeled on a letter Stowe's mother, Roxana Foote, had written to Lyman Beecher during their courtship in the late eighteenth century.[27] In the letter, Roxana-Mary challenges Beecher-Hopkins's understanding of divine goodness. Hopkins defines divine goodness as individual blessing: he feels gratitude and love for God "'because God has done me good'" (168). Mary instead insists that divine love arises in the relation between and among God and his creatures: "'God is a benefactor to me and my friends . . . and when I think of God, every creature is my friend'" (171). This God does not choose to do good to some creatures and not others, as Hopkins's cosmology implies; Mary's God cannot help but do good to all creatures: "'From a Being infinite in goodness everything must be good, though we do not always comprehend how it is so.'" Rather than expecting individual blessings from a capricious deity, Mary "'bless[es] the hand that, with infinite kindness, wounds only to heal'" (170). As Roxana's words flow from Stowe's—and her fictional character Mary's—pen, the three women (dead, alive, and invented) collaborate outside of time to transform Hopkins's (and, not incidentally, Edwards Park's) lifeless theology into a living doctrine of relational salvation. After reading the letter, Hopkins feels "as if he could have kissed the hem of her garment who wrote it" (171), a phrasing that positions Mary as a queen and Hopkins as her subject but also, far more radically, Mary as Christ and Hopkins as the woman with the flow of blood who touched Christ's garment to be healed.[28]

What Mary offers in response to Hopkins's elaboration of disinterested benevolence is not a watered-down version of Calvinist theology but a counter-doctrine grounded in Calvinism itself and fleshed out—incarnated—with the details of lived experience. Hopkins's theology positions salvation as atomizing and competitive: believers approach the throne of God as isolated individuals who in order to demonstrate their true election must cheerfully accept the potential damnation of themselves and everyone they love. Mary's doctrine of infinite kindness assumes a community of believers that includes God and Christ, who as members of the community themselves must wish only for its collective and eternal good. In *The Minister's Wooing*, bringing the practical (the emotional reality of believers) into conversation with the speculative (meditation on the nature of God) produces a relational theology grounded in an idea of communal agency. The network of believers caring for one another can bring about the collective salvation of all.

While Mary enunciates the doctrine of infinite kindness in her letter to Hopkins, it is most consistently embodied in the character of Candace, an African American woman who is enslaved at the novel's opening but later freed. Like the real-life Elizabeth Freeman, Candace has heard the Declaration of Independence proclaimed and, since she "'a'n't a critter,'" knows she must be included among its "'all men'" (104). She also subscribes to the doctrine of Christian universalism, a stance she shares with Doctor Hopkins, who regards the slaves who pass through Newport, in her words, "'as ef he felt o' one blood wid 'em'" (164). But Candace traces slavery's immorality less to slaves' ontological status as human than to the way slavery removes its victims from a communal economy of loving servanthood: "'Dem dat isn't free has nuffin to gib to nobody;—dey can't show what dey would do'" (104). Slavery, in other words, doesn't just steal the slave's labor; it steals the *meaning* of that labor, the love that domestic tasks like cooking, sewing, and childcare would otherwise convey, by placing enslaved people outside the network of communal agency. Once Candace is freed, she, too, can participate in the spiritual economy of Christian relation formed by the women of Newport. One of her first acts in this new state is to prevent Mrs. Marvyn from driving herself mad at the thought that her son has died unredeemed. Candace's love is the milk that feeds Mrs. Marvyn's soul when Reverend Hopkins's theology would choke her: "'Now honey, I knows our Doctor's a mighty good man, an' larned,—an' in fair weather I ha'nt' no 'bjection to yer hearin' all about dese yer great an' mighty tings he's got to say. But honey, dey won't do for you now; sick folks mus'n't hab strong meat'" (202). Now that she is free, Candace can "show what [she] would do" and assumes at once the role of friend, nurse, and spiritual teacher.

For Stowe, finding the true relation between the speculative and the practical had implications not only for the salvation of souls in the next world but for the improvement of lives in this one. The privatization of religion that characterizes secular modernity has often facilitated the progress of market capitalism by removing religion's ethical functions from discussions surrounding politics and economics. While many American Protestants—individually and denominationally—have accommodated themselves to capitalism's worst abuses by embracing theological adaptations like proslavery doctrine and the prosperity gospel, many of the most successful reform and social justice initiatives of the nineteenth century were both religiously motivated and "antithetical to emerging capitalism (and imperialism)." These movements "needed to be swept out of the way" to make room for further capitalist and imperialist domination.[29] Insisting that religiously motivated morality had no place in the public sphere was one way of doing so, since "representing religious practices and ideas as otherworldly and apolitical is a useful means of truncating their political meanings and social functions."[30] Part of the secularization thesis's obfuscatory power arises from its ability to mystify the workings of capitalism by claiming that the values of the marketplace are rational and inevitable markers of progress rather than intentionally orchestrated processes that favor the goals of capital. Separate-spheres ideology worked hand in hand with this process: the public dominance of secular market capitalism—and its control by men—was facilitated by relegating women to the home and making them the primary keepers of "private" matters like religious values and moral teaching. *The Minister's Wooing* illuminates how an increasing differentiation between speculative and practical matters could perpetuate horrors like the slave trade by privatizing and spiritualizing questions of doctrine and morality and rendering them inapplicable to economic concerns.

Thus, while "arithmetical theology" might cause terrible pain for individual Christians like Martha Wetherill, Stowe foresaw grave social and political consequences as well. In *The Minister's Wooing*, Reverend Hopkins's inability to tie his theological system to practical application undermines his effectiveness as a moral teacher. It is because he cannot be bothered with the business of day-to-day life that his parishioners find it easy to ignore his ethical pronouncements, particularly his opposition to slavery. The "heartless" Simeon Brown, for instance, imitates Hopkins by approaching "the great question of the salvation and damnation of myriads as a problem of theological algebra" (36). But he uses Hopkins's speculations as an excuse to disregard his ethical commands: "'You are not a practical man, Doctor. . . . Your theology is clear;— nobody can argue better. But come to practical matters, why, business has its laws'" (96). Hopkins's unwillingness to involve himself in matters of business and housekeeping leaves him unequipped to engage with the practical matter of the abolition of slavery.

By rewriting the doctrine of disinterested benevolence in *The Minister's Wooing*, Stowe offered an urgent intervention into both economic and spiritual questions—or rather, she refused to concede that economic and spiritual matters could or should be divorced from one another. Critics of the novel have recognized how the fictional Hopkins's theological pronouncements affect the emotional lives of individual women in his congregation: Joan Hedrick, for instance, observes that "in *The Minister's Wooing*, men make theological systems—abstractly—but women . . . must deal with the emotional reality behind them."[31] But Stowe's doctrinal critique is also intimately tied to her economic and social project. Stowe objects to the doctrine of disinterested benevolence not only because it makes mothers miserable but because the God it imagines is a monstrous robber baron, the preferred deity of slaveowners and sweatshop foremen, "using up" millions of souls for the benefit of a lucky few. Stowe counters this theology with the doctrine of infinite kindness, a theology of plenitude incarnated in Candace the mother-minister, for whom each soul, like each child, is precious: "'Jesus didn't die for nothin,'" she insists; "'all dat love a'n't gwine to be wasted'" (202).

In the critique she began in "New England Ministers" and continued in *The Minister's Wooing*, Stowe contrasted modern clergy with their (superior) ministerial predecessors; in other words, she constructed a declension narrative of American Protestantism. Like the twentieth-century religious and literary historians who came after her, Stowe described nineteenth-century American Protestantism as falling from a previous state of grace. But for Stowe that decline was not marked by the diminution or loss of theology, as twentieth-century critics would claim, but by its hyperspecialization: speculative theology had been differentiated from practical work, and the clergy had begun to see themselves not as ministers to entire communities but as producers of theological products. Stowe's declension narrative is not a secularization narrative: "modern," "moonshiny" nineteenth-century clergy were not losing their religion. What they *were* doing was reshaping American Protestantism from a system of home or village production, in which the minister worked with and beside his parishioners to produce carnal and spiritual goods—whether food, solace, or doctrine—into a factory system in which upper management (the clergy) did the thought work of producing speculative theology and left the practical work of ministering and pastoral care to laypeople on the ground. *The Minister's Wooing*, with its incarnated doctrine of infinite kindness, offers an alternative, integrated theological and economic vision for nineteenth-century American Protestantism.

Stowe's Enchanted Materialities

As myriad critics have noted, Stowe's New England upbringing and her commitment to sentimental domesticity combined, in both fictional tales like *Uncle Tom's Cabin* and nonfiction manuals including *The American Woman's Home*, to align moral uprightness with domestic order. Indeed, the discourse of salvational domesticity was a crucial part of Stowe's theological project, as Jane Tompkins definitively demonstrated in *Sensational Designs*. *Uncle Tom's Cabin*, Tompkins argued, was "the *summa theologica* of nineteenth-century America's religion of domesticity, . . . the story of salvation through motherly love."[32] This story of salvation depended on a specifically matriarchal idea of the Deity; as Joan Hedrick argues, Stowe's "image of God was based on her own understanding of a mother's love."[33] The doctrine of domesticity imbued women's work with a sense of purpose, making the home the site of national redemption, but as Amy Kaplan has influentially argued, it also bolstered U.S. imperialism by "unit[ing] men and women in a national domain . . . to generate notions of the foreign against which the nation [could] be imagined as home."[34] Indeed, when viewed from the perspective not of the white women who stand at the center of many sentimental depictions of domesticity but of the raced and classed others relegated to its periphery, the theology of domesticity takes on a much more complex cast. Allison S. Curseen has argued that "Stowe's domestic theology" centers "a graceful whiteness moving in corrective opposition to an ungraceful blackness, which . . . shows up as both a heathen disruption and a hauntingly hard-to-see nothing."[35] And Rosemarie Garland Thomson has demonstrated how the benevolent maternalism constructed by Stowe and other sentimental authors, including Elizabeth Stuart Phelps and Rebecca Harding Davis, depended on the rhetorical othering and diegetic destruction of disabled female bodies and highlighted, by comparison, a perfectly able and abundantly reproductive maternal female body.[36]

The Minister's Wooing is central to Stowe's doctrine of domesticity not only because the novel's primary plot lines are domestic but because domestic duties are the vehicles for an incarnated theology that is lived in community by Newport's women. In the novel, right relations between the doctrinal and the ministerial, the speculative and the practical, are realized in the communal agency that enables orderly and optimal domestic arrangements. This communal agency is instantiated in the many scenes of sewing that punctuate the story. Clothing—produced by women working in community, imbued with the personality of both maker and wearer, and freighted with biblical symbolism—unites the practical and the speculative in a single garment, making women and women's work not just necessary but holy. Both The Minister's Wooing and, as I will show, Agnes of Sorrento insist on an enchanted materiality: on the inextricability of matter and spirit.

Enchanted materiality is difficult to grasp because discussions of materiality in nineteenth-century women's writing have tended to treat a concern with material objects as evidence of corruption, of capitulation to a capitalist scheme. In these readings, the religious/theological is opposed to the secular/aesthetic, with the two epistemologies assumed to be in competition. Lori Merish has argued influentially that in sentimental narratives "desire for control over, and psychic investment in, domestic possessions is an index of a psychic sense of futility in the larger social realm"; thus, a concern with possessive ownership "operate[s] to articulate the distribution of economic resources in *personal* and *moral*, rather than *collective* and *political*, terms."[37] In this reading, the "domestic" is opposed to the "larger social realm," and between the "personal and moral" and the "collective and political" there is a great (italicized) gulf fixed. Christopher Wilson, writing specifically of The Minister's Wooing, associates Miss Prissy with the material and therefore with the secular or the "fallen" and asserts that her character "signifies the unresolved status in Stowe's epistemology between art and artifice, . . . [between] woman's role as artist (influence) or artifact (ornament)."[38] Both of these readings assume a critical position in which Stowe and other sentimental authors, faced with a series of binary choices—material *or* spiritual, artist *or* artifact, personal *or* collective, moral *or* political—always choose the "wrong" one.

Lynn Wardley's work on the fetishistic resonance of sentimental materiality provides a counterpoint to these binarized readings. Wardley, taking note of the hair, shoes, ribbons, paper, ink, books, and other treasured objects endlessly enumerated and exchanged in sentimental texts, reads them for their tal-ismanic resonances and traces this reliquary tradition not only to Roman Catholicism but to pan-African survivals; in her reading, the materiality of sen-timentalism is a means for expressing nonrational and nonlinguistic religious affects within a hyperlinguistic literary mode.[39] Gillian Brown's study of *Uncle Tom's Cabin* also offers a more nuanced discussion of materiality in Stowe's writing: rather than seeking to make the home complicit in maintaining mar-ket capitalism, Brown argues, Stowe depicted "an economy of abundant mother-love built on an excess of supply rather than the excess of demand and desire upon which both the slave economy and Northern capitalism oper-ated."[40] But Wardley and Brown label Stowe's materialism "fetishistic," a term implying that the viewer of an object projects onto it a spiritual pres-ence or soul that isn't actually there. Treating sentimental materiality as fe-tishization assumes an excarnated world in which spirit and agency can inhere only in minds, not in objects; in such a universe, any spirit or agency objects may seem to have is the product of human delusion or false consciousness.

What Wardley and Brown share with Wilson, Merish, and other critics of sentimental materiality is the assumption of disenchantment. This assump-tion is produced by the secularization of criticism that I have been discussing throughout this book. Our current secular situation, Charles Taylor notes, is one in which "a naturalistic materialism is not only on offer, but presents it-self as the only view compatible with the most prestigious institution of the modern world, viz. science."[41] In the secular paradigm that structures con-temporary Western societies, belief in nonmaterial realities is one of the fea-tures that seems to most clearly distinguish religious people from nonreligious ones or "bad" religions from "good" ones. An excarnated materiality is the cor-nerstone of the secularization thesis: it anchors the supposed "disenchant-ment" of existence—the "elimination of magic from the world."[42]

This is emphatically not the model of materiality operative in *The Minis-ter's Wooing*, which is theologically invested in the unity of the material and the spiritual worlds and in women's privileged knowledge of this unified real-ity. In the novel, material objects created in community are infused with the spirit of their makers and wearers, such that souls living and dead are incar-nated in them:

So we go, dear reader,—so long as we have a body and a soul. Two worlds must mingle,—the great and the little, the solemn and the trivial, wreath-ing in and out, like the grotesque carvings on a Gothic shrine;—only, did we know it rightly, nothing is trivial; since the human soul, with its awful shadow, makes all things sacred. . . . For so sacred and individual is a human being, that, of all the million-peopled earth, no one form ever restores another. . . . You are living your daily life among trifles that one death-stroke may make relics. (120–21)

Invoking the "Gothic shrine," Stowe gestures toward Catholicism's commingling of the earthly and the divine. But in place of bodily relics, Stowe's narrator offers instead the stuff and detritus of everyday life: "the penknife, the pen, the papers, the trivial articles of dress and clothing" (121). Items used and worn by the beloved become infused with the spirit of the lost loved one, linking heaven and earth. That Stowe should juxtapose the items used and created by the author with those of the milliner and the seamstress suggests the heavenly vocation she claims for both professions, both implicitly positioned as "women's work." Sewing and writing infuse inanimate objects—cloth, paper—with soul and spirit that outlast the life of the wearer or the writer.[43] By writing theological romance, Stowe performs an act of incarnation that unites the speculative and the practical by investing everyday language with eternal import and insisting on the materiality of enchantment.

The "Gothic shrine" passage appears in the middle of an oft-quoted scene in which Miss Prissy, Newport's local dressmaker, prepares Mary Scudder for an important party. Miss Prissy's status as comic relief has sometimes obscured the fact that she, along with Candace, is one of the characters who best exemplifies the doctrine of infinite kindness, as she serves as both the hub of human and divine relations in Newport and the mistress of enchanted materials.[44] "I should like to hemstitch the Doctor's ruffles," she asserts; "he is *so* spiritually-minded, it really makes me love him" (120). That the Doctor's spiritual mind should require the most carefully wrought and lovingly stitched ruffles seems comical to the reader but self-evident not only to Miss Prissy but to the narrator, who extols the "gauze, lace, artificial flowers, linings" that are Miss Prissy's domain (119). While trimming Mary's dress, Miss Prissy interrupts a hymn about the "New Jerusalem" to prevent Katy Scudder from ruining a piece of silk; to head off the disaster, she falls "down at once from the Millennium into a discourse on her own particular way of covering piping-cord" (120). The imagery of "falling down" might suggest a separation between the spiritual and the material, the celestial and the temporal; but the fact that Miss Prissy delivers a "discourse" on piping cord belies this separation. For Miss Prissy, the Millennium and the covering of piping cord are intimately related, and her seamless shift from singing about "The New Jerusalem . . . / Adorned with shining grace" to "discoursing" on piping cord unites the "speculative" and the "practical" as the best New England ministers, Stowe told us, do.[45]

When Miss Prissy presents Mary to Doctor Hopkins and demands to know if he "ever saw anything prettier" than Mary in this remade wedding gown, the reader is reminded of Hopkins's "soliloquy"—not, significantly, a discourse—at that day's supper table, in which he offered a vision of "his favorite topic . . . the Marriage-Supper of the Lamb" (119). Unlike Miss Prissy's ministerial work, which unites the spiritual and the material, Hopkins's systematic theology takes the real work done by women like Miss Prissy, Katy Scudder, and Mary Scudder and empties it of its practical import; his "soliloquy" renders the practical speculative instead of uniting the two. Mary, on the other hand, unites the practical and the speculative in her person: the dress she wears is not a symbol of her worldliness, her vanity, her materialism, or her fallen earthly nature but instead "seem[s] to represent a being who [is] in the world, yet not of it" (124).[46] Mary's embodiedness—her beauty, as enhanced by the dress—is a type of a particular Protestant value: the ability to be both in and out of a sinful, fallen world or, in Stowe's terminology, to unite the speculative with the practical. Mary's repurposed wedding dress invokes the "Marriage-Supper of the Lamb," as the fictional Hopkins's soliloquy would have it, and unites that theological concept with the actual labor of the dress's original maker and of Miss Prissy, who so lovingly "adapted" it. In *The Minister's Wooing*, it is women's labor, incarnated in women's clothing, that unites the speculative with the practical and creates an enchanted world in which material objects exist in intimate relation to both the physical and spiritual realms.

The enchanted materials produced by the everyday labor of devout women instantiate the agency of the Newport community in physical, tangible ways that reach backward through time. The "ancient wedding-dress" that Mary wears links her not only to the biblical trope of the "bride of Christ" but to the many brides and would-be brides from whom she is descended. The dress has been retrieved from Mary's "boudoir," a nook she has constructed in the garret using the family's ancestral linens. These treasures, the narrator reminds readers, are "not *common* blankets or bed-spreads, either,—bought, as you buy yours, out of a shop,—spun or woven by machinery,—without individuality or history. Every one of these curtains had its story" (146). Handicraft gives a piece of cloth its "story," raising again the association between clothing and authorship. Katy Scudder's aunt Eunice has infused the unused wedding clothes she left behind; a gentle pun—Eunice is reunited with her dead lover "beyond the veil," that is, in death, but also after she has finished sewing her bridal outfit—plays on the biblical associations between veiling and revelation that Claudia Stokes discusses as key tropes of both scriptural apocalypticism and Stowe's domestic fiction.[47] A blanket used at Valley Forge and a quilt made from "pieces of the gowns of all [Mary's] grandmothers, aunts, cousins, and female relatives for years back" are "mated" for eternity in Katy's garret (147).

The narrator's dismissive reference to linens bought "out of a shop" points to the hierarchization and specialization of skilled labor that was occurring in Stowe's own time and parallels her critique of the modern clergy who would separate practical ministry from speculative theologizing. The dressmaking trade had boomed between 1820 and 1860; while men could buy ready-to-wear clothing as early as the 1840s, "the elaborate design, tight fit, and rapidly changing vogues that characterized much feminine apparel thwarted the ambitions of would-be manufacturers."[48] But while an eighteenth-century dressmaker might have employed an assistant or taken on a live-in apprentice, by the 1840s "new divisions of labor . . . emerged in both the millinery and dressmaking trades": stitching a dress paid less than cutting and fitting it, and the women who constructed hats earned less than the ones who trimmed and decorated them, with the dressmaker or milliner managing the whole process.[49] Like other antebellum industries, dressmaking had succumbed to a specializing tendency that hierarchized what had previously been a holistic process and then exploited that hierarchy to concentrate power, wealth, or both in the hands of a single individual at the top. The warm, intimate relationship between Miss Prissy and the Scudders and the domestic scenes of sewing and spinning that recur throughout *The Minister's Wooing* represent a mode of imaginative resistance to the increasing specialization and hierarchization of labor in the nineteenth century—a process that, as the novel elaborately illustrates, had infected not only sectors like textile manufacturing but the clerical classes as well.[50]

Stowe's enchanted objects transcend individual possession—too easily perverted into conspicuous consumption and the commodification of persons—by embodying a communal subjectivity that is greater than the sum of its parts. For the correctly apprehending viewer (and reader), they point not to themselves or to their market value but to a reality beyond the immediately tangible: the "human soul, with its awful shadow." *The Minister's Wooing* and Stowe's subsequent novel *Agnes of Sorrento* work to construct an incarnational theology that might reveal the truth of an enchanted materiality. In *The Minister's Wooing* this enchanted materiality is signified by the quotidian objects sewn by Newport's women—tablecloths, quilts, wrist ruffles, wedding dresses—that become inspirited with the souls of maker and wearer. In *Agnes of Sorrento* enchanted materiality is signified in works of sacred art and in Agnes herself as inspiration for that art.

The Great Cloud of Witnesses: Intercessory Agency in *Agnes of Sorrento*

As theorists of secular modernity have demonstrated, secularism has appropriated to itself religion's claim to explain "how the world [is] in essence."[51] The seemingly commonsense assertion that the material is real and the nonmaterial is unreal (or at least unmeasurable) is a relatively recent development in human history, and yet this universalist claim purports to describe not only our current situation but all of time, space, and history. Secularism, like the lifeworlds that are now lumped together under the term *religion*, is a tool for engaging in what Talal Asad calls "the mechanics of reality maintenance."[52] As a discourse, it draws a set of boundaries around "the real," and these boundaries, like those of any territory mapped by human hands, have changed over time. Our current secular state of affairs, in which the real and the material are assumed—at least in official and scientific discourses—to be coextensive, can be traced, at the earliest, to the late nineteenth century, and, as Charles Taylor notes, "it is wildly anachronistic . . . to project this very familiar scenario" onto earlier eras.[53]

Writing in the late 1850s and early 1860s, when the Industrial Revolution was well underway but the paradigm shift of Darwinian science was yet on the horizon, Stowe experienced a milieu in which immaterial realities were yet possible but under threat. Writing to her husband Calvin Stowe in January 1860, Harriet complained of "the intense materialism of the present age," which had lost sight of even Martin Luther's "personal devil." Though she was suspicious of the recent rise of séance Spiritualism, to which Calvin seemed susceptible, Stowe pointed to "a real scriptural spiritualism which has fallen into disuse."[54] In her novel *Agnes of Sorrento*, she would describe a prior age not yet plagued by such "intense materialism": "To the mind of the really spiritual Christian of those ages the air of this lower world was not as it is to us, in spite of our nominal faith in the Bible, a blank, empty space from which all spiritual sympathy and life have fled." In place of the "blank, empty space" Stowe apprehended in her own time, the "really spiritual Christian" of pre-Reformation Italy had moved in a world that, "like the atmosphere with which Raphael has surrounded the Sistine Madonna, . . . was full of sympathizing faces, a great 'cloud of witnesses'" (71).[55] Setting *Agnes of Sorrento* at a point just before the Protestant Reformation offered Stowe a vantage point from which to explore the question of women's religious agency outside the frame of the Enlightenment, an intellectual movement that reconstructed reality according to its own assumptions about materiality and gender.

With its tale of a bottomlessly corrupt papacy and a priest who lusts after his virginal congregant, *Agnes of Sorrento* capitulates to many of the anti-Catholic tropes detailed in studies of the nineteenth century by Susan Griffin, Elizabeth Fenton, and Marie Pagliarini.[56] The titular Agnes begins the novel at fifteen years old, already a spiritual savant. Living with her grandmother Elsie on an isolated mountainside near the village of Sorrento in fifteenth-century Italy, Agnes pines to join the nearby convent of Saint Agnes and live out her days in holy worship. Elsie guards her granddaughter's purity jealously but is less accepting of her piety: she wishes to marry Agnes to a local trades-man rather than surrender her to the sisters. Though oblivious to the charms of romance, Agnes is pursued by two men: Agostino Sarelli, a cavalier who has been excommunicated by the pope for crossing the powerful Borgia family, and Father Francesco, a Capuchin monk who approves of Agnes's plan to join the convent because it will enable him to keep her under constant surveillance. When Francesco forbids Agnes even to speak to Sarelli, Agnes adopts a regime of painful penances that culminates in a pilgrimage to Rome. There she un-dergoes a series of revelations: that the pope she had adored as Christ's emis-sary on earth is instead a corrupt and venal despot and that she herself is not an obscure peasant but the secret daughter of a now-dead prince. When Ag-nes is abducted by the Borgias and rescued by Sarelli, she abandons her plan to enter the convent and agrees to marry her valiant suitor.

As Jenny Franchot, Michael Gilmore, Ashley Barnes, and other scholars have demonstrated, Stowe's relationship to nineteenth-century Catholicism was a complex one, "oscillat[ing] between identification and cautious cri-tique."[57] *Agnes of Sorrento*, though set in Catholic Italy rather than Protestant New England, engages in a project similar to that of *The Minister's Wooing*: it depicts a form of communal religious agency apprehended and exercised through the incarnation of a correctly integrated theology. The novel's guid-ing theological principle is the Catholic doctrine of saintly intercession: in the novel the church visible and invisible, the saints living and dead, cooperate in a form of communal agency that transcends not only earthly difference but death as well.[58] Agnes's religious agency is exercised through her saint-like communion with this invisible but very real "cloud of witnesses." Speaking to her uncle, a monk and artist, of her aspirations for the salvation of way-ward souls, Agnes declares, "'Oh, my uncle . . . I feel ready to die for this cause! What is one little life? Ah, if I had a thousand to give, I could melt them all into it, like little drops of rain in the sea! . . . Let us think what legions of bright angels and holy men and women are caring for us'" (220). Like the commu-nity of Newport, busily at work repairing souls, bodies, and britches, the com-munion of saints weaves a tapestry of protecting prayer that binds together the church militant and the church triumphant without regard to time or geographic distance. And like Newport's mutual servanthood, this form of agency enlists all, high and low: "the softest supplication of the most ignorant and unworthy would be taken up by so many sympathetic voices in the invisible world, and borne on in so many waves of brightness to the heavenly throne, that the most timid must have hope in prayer" (143). Agnes's religious agency is situated in the devotional, penitential, and intercessory practices that link her to this transtemporal communion of saints.[59]

Agnes's intercessory agency is semivolitional but no less empowering for that. When Father Francesco commands her to "'detest . . . as a vile enemy'" anyone who would dare to question the pope's authority, including her suitor Agostino Sarelli, Agnes replies, "'My Lord will keep me, . . . [and] my heart prays within me for this poor sinner, whether I will or no; something within me continually intercedes for him'" (130). Agnes recognizes this inward compulsion to intercessory prayer as a part of her self: God's spirit moving within her as the infant Christ moved within the Holy Mother. The novel figures Agnes's intercessory agency as a form of "intense sympathy" that sweeps away personal will: "Agnes was pouring out her soul in that kind of yearning, passionate prayer possible to intensely sympathetic people, in which the interests and wants of another seem to annihilate for a time personal consciousness, and make the whole of one's being seem to dissolve in an intense solicitude for something beyond one's self. In such hours prayer ceases to be an act of the will, and resembles some overpowering influence which floods the soul from without, bearing all its faculties away on its resistless tide" (123). Agnes does not experience this annihilation of personal consciousness as a loss of agency but as a form of collaborative agency engaged in with Christ and with the entire communion of saints: she "receive[s] this wave of intense feeling as an impulse inspired and breathed into her by some celestial spirit" and perceives herself to be participating "in an infinite struggle of intercession in which all the Church Visible and Invisible were together engaged" (124). One hears in this description a mobilization of the doctrine of infinite kindness: Agnes's sympathy reaches out along the webs of relation that link her to the saints living and dead, and she experiences her religious agency in the form of this embodied, self-aware, but not necessarily willful mode of intercession.

Agnes is aware of the communion of saints—she can sense the presence of "all the dear saints and angels . . . busy all around us"—because she possesses a pure vision that can rightly apprehend the spiritual substance of material things, a vision that is the gift of both the saint and the Christian artist (220). When her uncle, the traveling monk Father Antonio, seeks a block of marble for a shrine he is planning, the stonecutter tells him that there is "'a spot, a little below here on the coast, where was a heathen temple in the old days; and one can dig therefrom long pieces of fair white marble, all covered with heathen images." Instead of rejecting this "heathen" marble, Antonio fairly applauds with enthusiasm: "'So much the better, boy! . . . A few strokes of the chisel will soon demolish their naked nymphs and other such rubbish, and we can carve holy virgins, robed from head to foot in all modesty, as becometh saints'" (153). Those who are neither artists nor saints must learn to read with the holy eyes of romance—to look through the corruptions of the visible world and toward the purities of the invisible one. The task of the novel's hero, Agostino Sarelli, is to see past the "adulterous, incestuous, filthy, false-swearing, perjured, murderous" deeds of the current Borgia pope, Alexander (80), and recognize the "true Church" that stands behind this "false usurper" (159). This is a difficult task for the wealthy Agostino, but like Augustine St. Clare he has the advantage of a romantic upbringing and a saintly mother. When his servant accuses him of infidelity because he has spoken ill of the pope, Agostino retorts, "'Did you never hear in Dante of the Popes that are burning in hell? Wasn't Dante a Christian, I beg to know?'" (81). The servant, who thinks Christians faced with evidence of papal crimes have a duty only to "shut our eyes and obey," warns, "'Oh, my Lord, my Lord! a religion got out of poetry, books, and romances won't do to die by'" (80). For Stowe the author of theological romance, a religion "got out of" romances is in fact the *only* religion to die by, since the author of romance captures "the *probable truth*" of eternal things.

As author of *Agnes of Sorrento*, Stowe herself is of course the creator of romance, the artist who presents purified visions of material and spiritual things to a correctly apprehending readership. And like the novel's Father Antonio with his "heathen marble" or the nun Jocunda who transforms the story of Ulysses and the sirens into a Catholic legend by weaving in relics like "a piece of the true cross" and "holy wax" (64), Stowe takes a "heathen" genre—the convent captivity or convent escape narrative—and transforms it into a "pure" tale of ecumenical Christian triumph fit for the middle-class Protestant readers of the *Atlantic Monthly*. By rewriting the convent captivity narrative as a chaste theological romance, Stowe revealed the patriarchal structures that continued to undergird secular modernity despite Protestant ideologies of progress. In juxtaposing the sympathetic Catholic villain Father Francesco with the fallible proto-Protestant hero Agostino Sarelli, *Agnes of Sorrento* demonstrates how secular modernity's aspirations to disenchantment function by rhetorically positioning women as modernity's—and men's—enchanted others and shows how acts of enlightened disenchantment are as likely to subject women to epistemic violence as did any enchanted past.

Convent captivity narratives, which reached their heyday between 1830 and 1860 when a wave of Catholic immigrants was reaching American shores, traded in fears of "Romanism" and "popery" by proliferating tales of innocent Protestant women tricked into joining Catholic sisterhoods. These narratives "proceed[ed] as tales of seduction (often initiated in the confessional) of a girl by a lecherous priest"; in them, the victimized young woman was subjected to rape, forced childbirth, spiritual suppression, and a lifetime of "morbid confinement" unless she was lucky enough to be offered "escape and succor by the Protestant church."[60] Convent captivity narratives fall into a well-established line of Western sensational texts that center on the travails of imperiled women, including "the older, more established genres of the gothic, Indian captivity narratives, and a long European tradition of anti-Catholic literature."[61] In each of these genres, it is not solely the woman's survival that is at stake but her sexual purity; the convent captivity narrative in particular centers on "the symbol of the pure American woman debauched and ruined by the Catholic priest through the transgression of normative sexual and gender codes."[62] Like tales of gothic imprisonment or Indian captivity, the convent captivity narrative drew dramatic force from the spectacle of a woman's endangerment and her potential sexual corruption.[63]

Agnes of Sorrento contains many of the elements of the convent captivity narrative: a young and impressionable virgin, a licentious priest, an ostensibly welcoming but possibly sinister sisterhood, and scenes of both sensual indulgence and painful physical penance. But instead of countering the anti-Catholic convent exposé with a factual rendering of cloistered life—answering sensationalism with realism—Stowe uses romance to interrogate the discourse of ignorance and revelation on which the convent captivity narrative depended. In this discourse, women figured as the deluded victims of Machiavellian priests or the grateful beneficiaries of benevolent rescue but rarely as religious agents in their own right.[64] Like Antonio the artist-monk, Stowe chisels off the genre's sensationalist "rubbish"—its "naked nymphs"—to produce a portrait of women's religious agency that might counter the voyeuristic impulse of the convent captivity narrative, which reveled in its protagonist's helplessness at the hands of overwhelming (and foreign) religious forces.

In Stowe's redeemed convent captivity narrative, Father Francesco fills the role of the lustful priest who usurps holy prerogative, taking advantage of the private space of the confessional to substitute his earthly authority for God's heavenly one. Having discovered Agnes's attraction to Agostino Sarelli and, with it, his own attraction to her, Francesco plans to "dive into the recesses of her secret heart, and, following with subtle analysis all the fine courses of those fibres which were feeling their blind way towards an earthly love, . . . tear them remorselessly away" (227). Knowing that Agnes wishes to join the convent of Saint Agnes, Father Francesco decides to hasten the process of her holy confinement: "If she could not be his, he might at least prevent her from belonging to any other,—he might at least keep her always within the sphere of his spiritual authority" (180). Father Francesco wishes to "cherish [Agnes's] evident vocation" to the life of a nun—to twist her enchantment to his own purposes (180). To do so, he will seal her in marriage to the church, where he can have constant access to her.

Agnes escapes this fate not by fleeing into the arms of a Protestant rescuer like the victimized protagonists of convent escape narratives but by turning to the community of saints through whom she has come to experience her agency. After refusing an offer of marriage from a local tradesman, thereby proving to her grandmother the "force and decision of her young will" (218), Agnes conceives her plan to "'walk on foot to the Holy City, praying in every shrine and holy place'" (245). She expects to be guided in this journey by her namesake saint, who will accompany her along with her grandmother and "'save us from all wicked and brutal men who would do us harm'" (247). Here Stowe's narrator interjects to describe the saint's special role as "the ministering agency through which [God's] mediatorial government on earth was conducted" (248). While Elsie wishes to provide "'a protector'" for Agnes by marrying her to "'a good strong man,'" Agnes places her trust in the "ministering agency" of the communion of saints and angels (215).

Agnes does indeed meet with "wicked and brutal men" on the road to Rome, and it is in her encounter with them that *Agnes of Sorrento* most thoroughly revises the convent captivity narrative. While Father Francesco does not finally succeed in imprisoning Agnes in a convent, the novel does contain a captivity subplot—one that is effected by its proto-Protestant hero and suggests that, for women at least, the terrors of disenchantment might far outstrip the dangers of enchantment. As Agnes and Elsie make their pilgrimage to Rome, a troop of men accosts them and conveys them to a "damp, mouldering" castle, in the middle of which stands an apartment, "which to [Agnes's] simplicity seemed furnished with an unheard-of luxury" (307). Agnes is separated from her grandmother and placed under the care of Guilietta, a peasant woman who appears wearing "great, solid ear-rings of gold" and "a row of gold coins displayed around her neck" (308). When Agnes demands to see Elsie, Guilietta replies that "'there is one that's master of us both, and he says none must speak with you'" (309). This "master" is not God but Agostino Sarelli, and Agnes is fortunate, Giulietta pronounces, that he is such a "'holy and religious knight,'" for he is "'born to command, and when princes stoop to us peasant-girls, it isn't for us to say nay.'" Sarelli must be "'as good as Saint

Michael himself,'" Giulietta opines, "'or he would do as others do when they have the power'" (312).[65]

As Guilietta seeks to soothe Agnes with the assurance that the only thing preventing her imminent rape is the virtue of an excommunicated bandit who has kidnapped and forcibly separated her from her only guardian, Sarelli himself is riding toward the fortress. As he approaches, he fantasizes about the spiritual deflowering he plans to perform by revealing to Agnes the crimes of the corrupt pope whom she still venerates:

> Now the time was come, Agostino thought, to break the spell under which Agnes was held. . . . All the way home from Florence he had urged his horse onward, burning to meet her, to tell her all that he knew and felt, to claim her as his own, and to take her into the sphere of light and liberty in which he himself moved. He did not doubt his power, when she should once be where he could speak with her freely, without fear of interruption. Hers was a soul too good and pure, he said, to be kept in chains of slavish ignorance any longer. (318)

Sarelli has imprisoned Agnes for the purpose of disenchanting her: he hopes to clear the "mist of veneration" through which she beholds the pope and his cardinals (318). But the voluptuous bedchamber, Guilietta's necklace of coins, and Agnes's separation from Elsie all suggest another motive for his actions: he wishes to possess Agnes and to control her movements, just as Father Francesco did. Like the priest in the confessional, Sarelli plans to make himself Agnes's god, and he does not "doubt his power" to do so. The language of the passage—"break the spell," "burning to meet her," "claim her," "take her"—frames Agnes's coming disenchantment as an act of spiritual (and likely physical) ravishment. The markers of indirect discourse—"Agostino thought," "he said"—distance the narrator from Sarelli's perspective, suggesting that he is as deluded about the "sphere of light and liberty" in which he ostensibly moves as Agnes herself is about the virtues of the sitting pope.

While the Catholic Father Francesco *wants* to imprison Agnes in a convent, the excommunicated Sarelli actually *does* imprison her in a fortress, and these attempted captivities demonstrate that both enchantment and disenchantment can facilitate physical and epistemic violence against women, since both can be wielded as tools of patriarchy. Fantasizing about Agnes's future life in the convent, Father Francesco savors the thought that "yet through life he should be the guardian and director of her soul, the one being to whom she should render an obedience as unlimited as that which belongs to Christ alone" (41). Guilietta, acting as Sarelli's mouthpiece while tending to Agnes in her gilded prison, treats her charge like the heroine of a fairy tale, addressing her as "my little princess" and offering her resplendent clothing and sumptuous food (309). In both situations, however, Agnes's spiritual vision cannot be clouded. She interprets the comforts of the castle as temptations intended to distract her from her holy pilgrimage, as the devil tempted Christ in the wilderness.[66] When Giulietta offers her food, she answers, "'How can you speak of such things in the holy time of Lent?'"; when Giulietta promises her "'gowns . . . all of silk, and stiff with gold and pearls,'" Agnes refuses even to undress (310). Agnes regards this "strange interruption of her pilgrimage" as a "special assault on her faith, instigated by those evil spirits that are ever setting themselves in conflict with the just" (314). When Sarelli arrives to "break the spell," she identifies him as the evil spirit behind these temptations and refuses even to listen to his entreaties.

Agnes's response to her imprisonment is to pray for delivery for both herself and her captor Sarelli, whose soul she perceives to be in mortal danger. As she does so, the narrator pauses to contemplate the idea of disenchantment itself: "We of the present day may look on her distress as unreal, as the result of a misguided sense of religious obligation; but the great Hearer of Prayer regards each heart in its own scope of vision, and helps not less the mistaken than the enlightened distress. And for that matter, who is enlightened? who carries to God's throne a trouble or a temptation in which there is not somewhere a misconception or a mistake?" (315) Instead of ruling on the "correct" interpretation of Agnes's dilemma—the worldly or the heavenly one—the narrator declines to usurp Agnes's interpretive powers in the manner that both Father Francesco and Agostino Sarelli wish to. Since God is the only arbiter of reality—the only being with an entirely unclouded spiritual vision—it is not for Stowe's narrator to presume to pass judgment on Agnes's experience, despite the fact that Stowe herself is, in the most literal sense possible, Agnes's Creator.

Agnes of Sorrento suggests that female believers, young and impressionable though they may be, are best equipped to determine their own spiritual and temporal destinies. When Agnes finally does come to acknowledge the crimes of the pope and his political allies the Borgias, it is not because she has been enlightened by Sarelli but because she has seen their sins for herself. When she arrives in Rome, the pope's nephew notices her beauty and summons her to what Stowe's narrator suggests is an orgiastic revel. The novel, however, depicts nothing of Agnes's sojourn among the Borgias: she simply disappears from the narrative, which recenters on Elsie and on Agnes's newfound aunt, Princess Paulina, as they wait in agony for news of the girl's whereabouts. When Sarelli appears at Paulina's villa with a fainting Agnes in his arms, he explains, "'I tried all I could to prevent her coming to Rome, and to convince her of the vileness that ruled here; but the poor little one could not believe me, and thought me a heretic only for saying what she now knows from her own senses'" (359). Agnes's firsthand experience of Rome's corruptions—the evidence of "her own senses"—is the only form of enlightenment the novel will endorse: describing the recovered Agnes, Stowe's narrator remarks, "The veil had been rudely torn from her eyes; she had seen with horror the defilement and impurity of what she had ignorantly adored in holy places, and the revelation seemed to have wrought a change in her whole nature" (363). The "revelation" of sin's horrors can come only through human sense apprehension, not through lurid descriptions, since "pictures of eternal torture" only "exert a morbid demoralizing influence which hurrie[s] on the growth of iniquity" (36). Once again, Stowe refuses the sensationalism of the convent captivity narrative, with its sexualized depictions of female victimization.

For many critics, Agnes's religious agency has been unrecognizable precisely because it is exercised through the dissolution of her individuality—the melting of her "one little life" into a larger communal consciousness. Models of agency dependent on ideals of self-determination and autonomous action cannot apprehend self-lessness as a form of agency. Jenny Franchot, for instance, finds in Agnes's acts of intercession only a form of self-soothing that exacts a high psychological cost: "The potent communalism of Catholic piety can only emerge from Agnes's radical separation from herself," Franchot argues; indeed, Agnes ostensibly "knows nothing of herself."[67] And yet Stowe's heroine would seem to exercise considerable agency over the course of the novel: she rejects a marriage arranged for her by her overbearing grandmother; convinces that same grandmother to accompany her on a long and arduous pilgrimage to Rome; rebuffs the advances of Agostino Sarelli and, when he forcibly kidnaps her and locks her in a fortress, persuades him to release her; and finally, makes an informed choice between a religious vocation and marriage to an honest suitor. Agnes would seem, based on her diegetic actions, to know herself and her wishes quite well, and yet because of the assumption that all agency—including religious agency—must be exercised individually, strategically, and toward conscious ideological ends, it has been difficult for critics to recognize Agnes's actions as agentive performances.

Agnes of Sorrento is a novel about women's religious agency and about the ways that enchantment and disenchantment, while positioned as opposites or as the before-and-after images in a narrative of enlightened Protestant progress, at best depend on a shared denial of women's agency and at worst facilitate physical and epistemic violence against them. Stowe's theological romances insist on the fact of women's religious agency—the fact of religion as a potential means to agency—even when that agency is exercised communally or semivolitionally. In doing so, they contest two of contemporary secularism's most cherished beliefs: that those who practice religion are the victims of delusion and that the oppressed can obtain greater access to agency only if they are willing to abandon their religions. By rewriting the convent captivity narrative as a tale of Agnes's spiritual triumph over multiple forms of patriarchy, Stowe argues for women's religious agency as an active force and a means of resisting oppression, whether that oppression is perpetrated in the name of enchantment or enlightenment.

Pondering Stowe's Marys: Iconicization and Incarnation in Liberal Modernity

As suggested by her preface to Charles's *The Incarnation*, Stowe's primary figure for thinking through the issue of women's religious agency was Mary the mother of Jesus. As numerous critics have noted, Stowe showed a career-long interest in Mary as a figure for religious womanhood, not only in her novels (Evangeline St. Clare, Mary Scudder, Virginie de Frontignac, Agnes of Sorrento, and Mara Lincoln can all be read as variations on the Holy Virgin) but in her poetry ("Mary at the Cross," "The Sorrows of Mary"), her devotional nonfiction (*Woman in Sacred History, Footsteps of the Master*), and even her choice of home decor.[68] Kimberly VanEsveld Adams has traced the increasing importance of Mary and her shifting significance in Stowe's writing, arguing that the Marys of *The Minister's Wooing* and *Agnes of Sorrento* function "as prophets, as saints, and as contemplative virgins"—resembling the Mary of the Annunciation—and that Mary as mother appears much later in Stowe's career, where she comes to embody "the prophetic mother [who] brings forth the Word in her own image."[69] John Gatta treats Stowe's interest in Mary as a curiosity, something "one might not have predicted in a woman of her era, place, and religious background."[70] But as Elizabeth Hayes Alvarez has demonstrated, Stowe's attention to the Virgin Mary was not exceptional but commonplace. While anti-Catholicism was a very real and dangerous phenomenon in the nineteenth-century United States, "because of her role as exemplar of Christian womanhood, Mary was a shared, culturally constructed figure that linked together various Christian groups and helped shape the period's gender ideology."[71] It was precisely as "exemplar of Christian womanhood" that Stowe employed the figure of Mary. Her Marys are not merely icons suitable for worship—though they are sometimes that—but also active agents in their own salvation and in the salvation of others.

Stowe used the figure of Mary to negotiate the tension between the iconi-cization and incarnation of women in nineteenth-century Protestant culture—between *woman's* cultural role as icon of idealized Christian piety and *women's* domestic roles as incarnators of the family: mothers and makers of homes. Gregory Jackson has described the nineteenth-century United States as increas-ingly driven by pictorial impulses: homiletic narratives like *The Pilgrim's Pro-gress* trained a Protestant readership to correctly view and interpret both descriptions and visual images of human life as figures for eternal truths and calls to greater spiritual engagement.[72] David Morgan has described the pro-cess by which nineteenth-century Americans, raised in rich oral and sermonic traditions, gradually learned to accept the viewing of religious imagery as "an act imbued with the power of belief or to make one believe."[73] For women readers, however, this training was complicated by a long history, both Cath-olic and Protestant, of transforming women into images—of making women not the viewers but the viewed. Though the iconicization of women in Cath-olic tradition is obvious, this impulse persisted into the Protestant era, with women serving as holy exemplars or demonic terrors in a dominant male re-ligious imaginary, as when Thomas Weld propagated tales of the "monstrous births" produced by Anne Hutchinson and Mary Dyer as warnings to other religious dissenters or when Jonathan Edwards used the experiences of his wife, Sarah Pierrepont, as a salutary example for those who were inclined to doubt the sincerity of revivals in his church.[74] Even *The Pilgrim's Progress*, that staple of Protestant devotionalism and the pattern tale for the wildly popular woman's fiction genre, presents the monstrous females Queen Mab and the Whore of Babylon to the horrified eyes of Christian and Hopeful; when women become Bunyan's protagonists in the *Second Part of the Pilgrim*, which tells the story of Christian's wife, Christiana, and her children, these women are treated to a vision of themselves as spiders "whose Venom is far more de-structive than that which is in her."[75] In both the Catholic hagiographic tradi-tion and the Christian homiletic tradition that Jackson traces, women, good or bad, were apt to appear only as static icons—flat pictures rather than living flesh.

The rise of secular modernity did not undo the iconicization of women but in fact made it a constitutive feature of a politics supposedly cleansed of religious influence. During the French Revolution, with its secularization of public space, "signs of religious devotion—statues of saints, crucifixes, and church bells—were replaced by allegorical embodiments of secular concepts (liberty, fraternity, equality, the social contract, philosophy, reason, virtue) in idealized classical forms"; these idealized forms were characterized by a "desperate insistence on the repetition of . . . sexual dimorphism," particularly women's naked breasts, that reified women's "foreignness to republican culture."[76] Early U.S. political expression also employed idealized female bodies as icons of the new nation—particularly Columbia but sometimes Lady Liberty—even as actual women were systematically excluded from political participation. The democratic revolutions that advanced secular modernity left women in a position largely analogous to the one they had held in the premodern West: hypervisible as static icons of religion or politics, nearly invisible as agentive individuals.

The persistence of Mary the mother of Jesus into Protestant modernity and her increasing relevance in the diversifying antebellum United States offered Stowe a vehicle for thinking through women's status as perpetual icons. *The Minister's Wooing* and *Agnes of Sorrento* counter Western culture's iconicizing impulse not by repudiating the representational burden borne by women but by presenting iconic Marys and then "fleshing them out"—incarnating them—by emphasizing their indivisible wholeness: the inseparability of body, mind, and spirit. Importantly, Stowe did not advocate for women as either icons or incarnations; rather, her Marys syncretize these roles: they are both objects of adoration and contemplation for the men and women around them and creators who grow and tend the fruits of the spirit. They find their religious agency in the space created by the juxtaposition of icon and incarnation.

The Minister's Wooing offers two Mary figures, one Protestant and one Catholic: Mary Scudder and Virginie de Frontignac. As always with Stowe, this pairing does not represent a simple binary but instead offers different models for women's religious agency as Mary and Virginie embody various qualities of the Virgin turned Holy Mother. Virginie, raised in a convent, provokes from other characters the standard Protestant assumption that Catholic identification entails thralldom: "I suppose she is a Roman Catholic, and worships pictures and stone images," the staunchly orthodox Miss Prissy assumes (258). But Mary Scudder sees in the beautiful Virginie an active embodiment of the Madonna: rather than worshipping material objects, Virginie herself is a living incarnation of the Holy Mother, with "pomegranate cheeks" that "glo[w] with the rich shaded radiance of one of Rembrandt's pictures" (173). Apprehending Virginie's beauty, Mary's face begins to "reflec[t] the glowing loveliness of her visitor, just as the virgin snows of the Alps become incarnadine as they stand opposite the glorious radiance of a sunset sky" (174). *Incarnadine*, "flesh-colored," arises from the root *incarnato*, "clothed or invested with flesh." The effect of Virginie's glowing Madonna-like beauty is to incarnate the "virginal" Mary Scudder, a process that consists in awakening "all the slumbering poetry within" the "delicate" New England maiden. Mary's adoration, in turn, awakens Virginie's "warm nature," and the two are transformed from romantic rivals to bosom friends (174).

This incarnated response to Virginie's beauty is contrasted with that of the novel's villain, Aaron Burr, who apprehends Virginie not as an embodiment of her namesake but as an empty image, an object for cold speculation. Observing Mary and Virginie's first meeting, Burr categorizes Virginie as a voluptuous "sultana" and Mary as her "faded, cold" obverse: "In Antwerp one sees a picture in which Rubens . . . has embodied his conception of the Madonna, in opposition to the faded, cold ideals of the Middle Ages, from which he revolted with such a bound. His Mary is a superb Oriental sultana, with lustrous dark eyes, redundant form, jewelled turban. . . . As Burr sat looking from one to the other, he felt, for a moment, as one would who should put a sketch of Overbeck's beside a splendid painting of Titian's" (174). Rather than responding with "slumbering poetry" to the womanly excellence before him, Burr imagines himself the curator of a gallery, arranging items for display. When Virginie is finally disabused of her idealizing love for Burr, it is precisely this flat and calculating observation that repels her: "'He was admiring me like a picture; he was considering what he should do with me. . . . But he does not know me'" (226). For Burr, Virginie is a disenchanted icon, a soulless object designed not for pious contemplation but for patriarchal consumption.

The titular heroine of *Agnes of Sorrento* is Stowe's most literal embodiment of the Virgin Mary, a woman who exists simultaneously as an icon to be worshipped and an incarnation of divine love. Gail K. Smith has argued that *Agnes of Sorrento* represents "an extended study of how a patriarchy uses and misuses a woman's body as metonymy for art" and that Stowe produced the novel as a means to "meditat[e] on art's mission and construc[t] her own artistic self."[77] Accordingly, characters in *Agnes of Sorrento* can be judged by whether they apprehend Agnes as an empty object or a living incarnation of the Madonna, with the "correct" reading the one set forth by her uncle, the artist-monk Father Antonio. Beholding Agnes's adolescent beauty and pure spirit, he chooses her as the model for the Virgin Mary in the breviary he is preparing: "'Dear child,'" he tells her, "'there be women whom the Lord crowns with beauty when they know it not, and our dear Mother sheds so much of her spirit into their hearts that it shines out in their faces. . . . Dear little child, be not ignorant that our Lord hath shed this great grace on thee.'" Agnes replies, "'I am Christ's child. If it be as you say,—which I did not know,—give me some days to pray and prepare my soul, that I may offer myself in all humility'" (91). This scene invokes the angel's Annunciation to Mary that she is pregnant with the Christ child: Gabriel proclaims, "'The Holy Ghost shall come upon thee'"; Mary replies, "'Behold the handmaid of the Lord; be it unto me according to thy word.'"[78] In *Agnes of Sorrento*, the message to be conveyed is not that Agnes is with child but that she is beautiful and that, rather than becoming the vessel for the incarnation of Christ, she herself is the embodiment of Mary's holiness. Agnes is simultaneously both icon and incarnation of Mary. When she meets her future lover, Sarelli, he will proclaim that her "'dear face has been more to me than prayer or hymn; it has been even as a sacrament to me, and through it I know not what of holy and heavenly influences have come to me'" (160). Mary's beauty is not for mere consumption—which Sarelli will learn after she escapes his gilded cage—but for a contemplation that, properly welcomed, results in religious transformation.

The moments when women's iconographic power combines with their incarnational agency are often marked by the word *pondering*, Stowe's signal term for a kind of holy cognition that brings together mind, body, and spirit to form a complete being. As Mary the mother of Jesus, after the birth of her son, the visit of the shepherds, and the adoration of the Magi, "kept all these things, and pondered them in her heart," so Stowe's Marys contemplate the environment around them, the texts and images they encounter, their own intellectual and emotional processes, and their relations with others and transform these raw materials into religious agency: into women's work in the world.[79] The work of pondering can be described in June Howard's phrase "embodied thought that animates cognition with the recognition of the self's engagement."[80] Stowe herself invokes John Donne: "her pure and eloquent blood / Spoke in her cheeks, and so distinctly wrought / That you might almost say her body thought" (*MW* 309).[81] Pondering is the agentive action of this thinking body: the process by which the speculative and the practical, the spiritual and the material, the intellectual and the emotional, and the iconographic and the incarnational are knit together in a single person, that "sacred and individual" thing.

In *The Minister's Wooing*, pondering is the process by which women bring their active minds to bear on the artistic and intellectual materials of this earth and transform them into enchanted icons: objects for sacred contemplation. Mrs. Marvyn "ponders" the unseen cathedrals and unheard symphonies of Europe and in so doing transfigures the "uncouth old pulpit" and "faw-sol-la-ing" of Newport's Congregational choir into objects suitable for accompanying Christian worship (62). Mary Scudder spends hours "pondering" an engraving of a da Vinci Madonna that has washed up on the shores of Newport "after a furious storm"; the "seaworn picture" provides "a constant vague inspiration" for her thoughts on "that wonderful man" da Vinci (147) but also on Jonathan Edwards's "treatises on the Will" (15).[82] Had she been born in Italy, the narrator notes, she would have turned out an Agnes of Sorrento rather than a Mary Scudder of Newport and "might, like fair St. Catherine of Siena, have seen beatific visions in the sunset skies, and a silver dove descending upon her as she prayed" (15). She might have been, in fact, not only a saint but the mother of Christ herself: after the "death" of James Marvyn, as Mrs. Marvyn describes the peace that Candace's Christology has given her—"'There is but just one thing remaining, and that is, as Candace said, the cross of Christ'"—Mary Scudder "ke[eps] all things and ponder[s] them in her heart" (207).

In *Agnes of Sorrento*, the term *pondering* marks moments when Agnes encounters new forces and new information that will infuse her spiritual being and incarnate her as a complete woman with earthly desires as well as celestial ones. Agnes ponders a poem that Agostino Sarelli has written for her in which he compares his love for her to the veneration of the Virgin (98); that night she dreams of an angel with the face of Sarelli and awakes the next day to "pond[er] over and over the strange events of the day before, and the dreams of the night" (114). After Sarelli rescues her from the Borgia dens at Rome, Agnes ponders "the dark warnings of Father Francesco" about Sarelli's ill intentions and compares them to the cavalier's valiant efforts on her behalf; she likewise ponders the change in station effected by the revelation of her nobility: "She was, in birth and blood, the equal of her lover" (364). In both *The Minister's Wooing* and *Agnes of Sorrento*, women who ponder as Mary did engage in acts of religious agency that bring body, mind, and soul into alignment with the will of God and the communion of saints both living and dead.

By being both fully embodied and paradigmatically spiritual, Stowe's Marys resist the liberal political and social discourses that create "woman" as a flat image and project onto her irrationality, irresolution, and lack of agency. Rather than divorcing women from spirituality in an effort to facilitate individual (white) women's entrance into the public sphere—a move that would reinforce the larger cultural forces tending toward disenchantment, rationalization, and unrestrained capitalism—*The Minister's Wooing* and *Agnes of Sorrento* insist on enchantment, vesting it both in individual women and in the communities that cohere around them. Though capable of performing rationality by engaging with doctrine, Stowe's women more often enact religious agency by incarnating theology. In *The Minister's Wooing* and *Agnes of Sorrento*, true theologizing is daily action performed in relation with others. Romance is the literary form in which these enchanted women are incarnated, and theological romance becomes the means of conveying cosmic truths and resisting the fragmentation, differentiation, and disenchantment of modern life.

CHAPTER 5

"I Have No Disbelief"

Women's Spiritualist Novels and Nonliberal Agencies

In a November 1860 letter to Elizabeth Barrett Browning written as she was composing *Agnes of Sorrento*, Harriet Beecher Stowe described a Spiritualist medium who had channeled her dead son Henry very exactly. Though maintaining a polite distance from most Spiritualist activities, Stowe confessed to Barrett Browning that "when such things come," she did "what Mary did—'Keep and ponder them in my heart.'"[1] Stowe had written to her husband Calvin earlier that year that "circles and spiritual jugglery" were nothing but "lying signs and wonders, with all deceivableness of unrighteousness." But after repeated private encounters with spiritually gifted people whose presence brought her "very strong impressions from the spiritual world, so that I feel often sustained and comforted, as if I had been near to my Henry and other departed friends," Stowe was willing to admit that there were "doubtless, people who, from some constitutional formation, can more readily receive the impressions of the surrounding spiritual world."[2] By 1860, Stowe might well have found herself wavering on the question of Spiritualism, since "circles and spiritual jugglery" were everywhere in the United States. In the years since two young girls, Margaret and Kate Fox, had heard ghostly rappings in their home in Hydesville, New York, in 1848, spirit communication had spread rapidly across the country, growing from "a children's ghost story, [to] an after-dinner entertainment, [to] a popular national phenomenon and a powerful new religion" in little more than a decade.[3]

Though emerging from European religious ideas that had circulated for centuries, American Spiritualism began in earnest in the United States with the "spirit rappings" in Hydesville. When the Fox sisters heard knockings and other mysterious noises in their upstate New York home, they attributed the noises to the spirit of a dead peddler who, they claimed, had been murdered in the house years before and now sought to communicate with its living inhabitants. The girls devised a way to exchange messages with their spirit companion through a system of alphabetic knockings; when they did so in front of curious visitors, local papers reported the events. The story was picked up by other publications through the network of the nineteenth century's extensive newspaper exchange system, and readers in other towns soon began forming small circles of curious participants who wished to try the spirits for themselves. As the movement spread, it emerged from the parlor and into the public sphere, as the most gifted mediums began performing publicly in "trance lectures" in which they displayed their Spiritualist gifts for the entertainment and edification of believers and skeptics alike.[4] The most powerful mediums were often women, as their supposedly "natural" passivity ostensibly made it easier for them to suppress their own individuality and to surrender their bodies and voices to inhabiting spirits, who could range from William Shakespeare to Benjamin Franklin to an attendee's mother.

Since traditional Protestant doctrines either denied the possibility of communing with the dead or classed such activities as witchcraft, participants in the Spiritualist movement quickly developed their own doctrinal frameworks to explain the sudden lifting of the veil between the living and the dead and its implications for those on both sides of this newly porous barrier. Self-appointed Spiritualist leaders, including Andrew Jackson Davis and Emma Hardinge Britten, drew from the European phenomena of Swedenborgian religion and mesmeric practice to craft cosmologies that diverged considerably from a dualistic Protestant universe. Besides refusing to assign the dead to heaven or hell for all eternity (Spiritualists, like Swedenborgians, came to believe that the dead ascended through "spheres" of enlightenment), Spiritualist teaching differed most starkly from traditional Protestant beliefs about death in its insistence that human souls retain the unique characteristics they once displayed on earth—including an attachment to family and friends and a concern about ongoing political and social events—and that the dead are capable of communicating with the living. Spiritualism's characteristic practices included communication with the spirits of dead loved ones or famous figures (conducted either by a medium during public or private séances or individually using an automatic writing apparatus like the planchette), spirit traveling (in which a medium viewed events or vistas at great distances from her own physical location), and clairvoyant communication. Dismissed or decried by mainstream religious and cultural authorities, Spiritualism nevertheless continued to spread rapidly through Europe and the United States, resulting in "the democratization of the otherworld" as "millions, from the urban working classes to royal families . . . experiment[ed] on each other through spiritualist séances, mesmeric waves, telepathic transmissions and out-of-body travelling."[5]

As a widespread and rapidly growing religious and social movement, Spiritualism quickly made its way into American fiction, most famously in Nathaniel Hawthorne's *The Blithedale Romance*. According to the literary critic Howard Kerr, Hawthorne's tale of the economic (and likely sexual) manipulation of the female medium Priscilla by the Svengaliesque magician Westervelt established a literary template for all Spiritualist fiction of the American nineteenth century. Kerr's *Mediums, and Spirit-Rappers, and Roaring Radicals: Spiritualism and American Literature, 1850–1900* asserted that "the spiritualistic movement exercised a distinct and fairly unified influence on the American literary imagination" by providing nineteenth-century authors with an easy target for humorous attacks or a storehouse of vague occult symbols.[6] And yet Kerr's stable of nineteenth-century American authors included only white men; while providing dismissive accounts of the activities of female Spiritualist mediums, including the Fox sisters, Cora Hatch, and Britten, Kerr's monograph overlooked Spiritualist fiction by women except for an occasional footnoted reference to Stowe or Elizabeth Stuart Phelps.[7] As a result, the "unified" (male) literary approach he traced mostly registered a conservative fear of Spiritualism, which was a dangerous and frightening phenomenon not only because it contradicted traditional Protestant doctrines but because it was closely associated with abolitionism and the nascent movement for women's rights.[8]

Addressing the work of women writers who engaged with the Spiritualist movement paints a very different picture of the cultural work performed by Spiritualist fiction. Authors including Elizabeth Stoddard, Elizabeth Oakes Smith, and Kate Field often fictionalized the beliefs and practices associated with Spiritualism in ways that critiqued not the Spiritualists but the patriarchal underpinnings of orthodox Protestantism and the antebellum public sphere. Much of this fiction by women writers is Spiritualist not only in its subject matter but in its form. Women authors, in other words, invoked Spiritualist practice as literary practice in ways that enabled them to depict new and socially disruptive forms of female agency.

The forms of female agency constructed in and through women's Spiritualist fiction do not conform to secularized ideals of autonomous and self-willed action, and thus, like the other forms of religious agency I have discussed in this book, they can be difficult for modern critics to comprehend. The rapid proliferation of religious options that characterized the nineteenth century—what Charles Taylor has called the "nova effect" of Western secularity—resulted in a nineteenth-century American public sphere that was not denuded of gods but practically overrun by them.[9] Given these changes and the disconcerting advances in technology that obliterated distance and distorted time, nineteenth-century Americans often found themselves living in a haunted state "in which one's actions [were] acted upon by others from a distance—people, to be sure, but also and perhaps more importantly, concepts, representations, and words."[10] The flowering of Spiritualist practice after 1848 was both effect and sign of this haunted modernity, and the phenomenon of the trance troubled rational liberal models of human agency that framed agency as unitary, proprietary, and voluntary—something owned and wielded by individuals acting consciously and independently. In a society in which ontological and epistemological boundaries may shift at any moment, agency may inhere in objects and organizations as much as in individuals and may circulate between secular subjects. It is the circuitous functioning of religious agency—the unpredictable movement of motive forces between sympathetic persons—that women's Spiritualist fiction dramatizes.

To recognize the forms of agency at work in Spiritualist fiction, we must amend our reading practices to do justice to the mysteries of a secular world rather than the certainties of a secularized one. Secular reading is particularly essential for understanding Spiritualist fiction by women writers, since the agencies enabled by Spiritualist religiosity have the potential to disrupt and defy entrenched structures of power. In her now-canonical bildungsroman *The Morgesons*—most often read by critics as a novel of secularization and religious decline—Elizabeth Stoddard employs Spiritualist phenomena to endow Cassandra and Veronica Morgeson with unexpected agentive options. While Stoddard hints obliquely at her characters' Spiritualist gifts, Elizabeth Oakes Smith's *Bertha and Lily* and Kate Field's *Planchette's Diary* explicitly engage with Spiritualist practices and supernatural phenomena. In each of these texts, characters allow spiritual agencies to circulate between them rather than ceding agency to those who would dominate them. By doing so they maintain a unique but precarious in(ter)dependence, temporarily circumventing social narratives that enforce women's economic, romantic, and spiritual dependence on men (fathers, lovers, clergy). Adopting Spiritualist forms of connection allows these characters to forge relationships in which dominance and subordination are ever shifting and always at play—in which power does not flow downward from God to men and from men to women but instead moves unpredictably between the spiritual realm and the material and between members of both sexes.

Spiritualist configurations of agency are short-lived and unstable: while Spiritualist practices enable women to intermittently suspend or temporarily inhabit the interstices of the power relations that structure their lives, they do not permanently overturn those relations. Hence the moments of religious agency in Spiritualist novels are often also moments of pain and frustration. But to ignore them because they are not sustainable is to misunderstand—or miss entirely—the power of female religious agency in a secular society. If, as I have argued throughout this book, agency is a capacity for action enabled by particular conditions—not the ability to transcend or ignore those conditions, as it is often framed—then all agency is contingent, temporary, and unstable, constructed on the fly, so to speak, from conditions on the ground. But our secularized critical practices have effaced the forms of agency at play in women's Spiritualist fiction and distorted our understanding of women's spiritual power both historically and in our own time.

Spiritualism and Circulating Agency in *The Morgesons*

Elizabeth Stoddard's *The Morgesons* is the story of Cassandra and Veronica Morgeson, two sisters living in a New England shipping village in the 1830s. Raised by a religiously devoted mother and an agnostic father—named Mary and Locke, to solidify the associations—Cassandra and Veronica must find their moral and spiritual bearings in a rapidly industrializing antebellum milieu. Cassy is the more skeptical of the two; while adoring her devout mother, she seeks personal and sexual self-determination, and her rocky path to adulthood includes an emotional affair with a married man. Veronica, by contrast, is a New England saint, given to strange visions and mysterious bouts of illness and frequently compared to the Virgin Mary. Quiet and domestic, Veronica marries Ben Somers, one of Cassy's friends from boarding school, but his unchecked alcoholism poisons their union and leads to his early death. Cassy, after recovering from the death of her lover, marries Ben's brother Desmond and lives with him in the home she has inherited from her parents.

An early scene in *The Morgesons* finds the sixteen-year-old Cassandra standing on the sofa in her Massachusetts home giving a mock sermon "after the manner of Mr. Boold, of Barmouth, taking . . . for my text, 'Like David's Harp of solemn sound'" (67).[11] Cassandra's parody of the local clergyman brings several members of the household to sympathetic laughter as she mimics his expressive gestures and pompous tone. When her father enters the room with a strange man, Cassy is neither abashed nor ashamed: she "wave[s her] hand . . . a la Boold" and descends from her perch to greet the newcomer who will one day become her lover (67).

Cassy's Boold-ness—her willingness to ridicule and disregard the pronouncements of New England's orthodox clergy—has led to the critical consensus that *The Morgesons* depicts, or even celebrates, secularization and religious decline. Reading "religion" as primarily the domain of ordained Protestant clergy, critics have asserted that because the clerics who appear in *The Morgesons* are ridiculed or relegated to diegetic obscurity, religion is not a central concern of the text.[12] This critical tendency indicates the persistence of a particularly American version of the secularization narrative, one in which "the public influence of the Protestant clergy is [considered] the most important measure of the role of religion in American society."[13] The continuing identification of "religion" with "New England Protestantism" is not so much a historical fact as an ideological superstructure that assumes that attitudes, values, and institutions that do not align with mainstream Protestant assumptions are alien not only to Protestant Christianity but to the United States itself.[14] If "religion" and "Protestant clerical authority" are believed to be the same, any text that questions the cultural centrality of Protestant ministers—as *The Morgesons* does—will seem to be attacking religion as an aspect of human experience and reflecting or even contributing to the secularization of American culture.

But, in fact, explorations of religion in *The Morgesons* go beyond the occasional jab at a pompous village preacher, and they are revealed not by examining the static pronouncements of the clergy at the margins of the story but by attending to the fluid spiritual power of the women at its center. There is another religious discourse at work in the scene in which Cassandra mocks Mr. Boold: the discourse of Spiritualism, in which minds separated by death and distance are nevertheless sympathetically connected and past and future are legible texts to those with the gifts to read them. When Charles Morgeson enters the room where Cassandra is "preaching," Veronica solemnly predicts his approaching death: "'There are six Charles Morgesons buried in our grave yard'" (67). Her clairvoyant powers invoke the ambient discourse of Spiritualism that by the time of the book's publication permeated every corner of American culture, and they suggest that *The Morgesons* is best read not as a story of Protestant decline but as a Spiritualist novel that reflects the rapidly changing secular conditions of mid-nineteenth-century New England.[15]

The Morgesons is a novel *about* Spiritualism, in which characters engage in acts of clairvoyance, trance speaking, and spirit traveling. But it is also a novel that enacts a literary form of Spiritualist practice at the level of the text.[16] It steers a course between overt supernaturalism and sterile scientism by invoking the conditions of secularism that characterized antebellum New England, conditions in which religious authority and its attendant agentive possibilities were not in decline but rather set free to circulate in new and less hierarchical ways. In *The Morgesons*, the practices associated with Spiritualism help to highlight forms of female agency that might operate outside the bounds of commerce, competition, conversion, and domination that hem in the Morgeson sisters' lives. These Spiritualist practices are premised on the acceptance of certain doctrines: the persistence of individual human personalities beyond death, the ability of the living to speak with the dead, the "magnetic" or mesmeric influence of certain spiritually gifted persons, and the possibility of clairvoyant communication between people of great emotional sensibility.

Even as it implicitly embraces these premises and practices, however, *The Morgesons* avoids the ritualized (and often commercialized) trappings of the séance and the trance lecture. Among the New York literati with whom Stoddard socialized, Spiritualism was often ridiculed because, like other insurgent religious and social movements, it attracted large numbers of the poor and working classes. Dismissive depictions of Spiritualism often emphasized the vulgarity of its participants and practitioners. The Fox sisters were rumored to crunch peanuts during their public séances, and Lydia Maria Child referred to public demonstrations of spirit communication as "the merest mass of old rags, saw-dust, and clam-shells."[17] In the early 1860s as *The Morgesons* was going to press, Stoddard's close friend Bayard Taylor, to whom the novel is dedicated, was in the midst of publishing three short stories in the *Atlantic Monthly* that lampooned Spiritualism and other religious and social reform movements.[18]

For these reasons, I suggest, Stoddard might have invoked Spiritualist practices in her novel without depicting the trance lecture or the séance, since including such scenes would subject Veronica's and Cassandra's mysterious powers to similar public scrutiny by the novel's readers and critics. These authorities could then pronounce judgment upon the sisters' spirituality in the same way that the novel's various fictional patriarchs pronounce judgment on their beauty, piety, and intelligence. *The Morgesons*, accordingly, employs Spiritualism not as a simple plot device but as a symbolic force and a set of discursive practices that together enable new visions of agency at the level of plot and character and new generic possibilities for female authorship. In doing so, it models a style of secular reasoning by way of a literary form that elevates indeterminacy above certainty and locates possibilities for agency in mysterious interactions between persons.

The Morgesons opens in Mary Morgeson's "winter room," where the reading materials chosen by the Morgeson women signify the welter of religious modalities that circulate through the novel. Cassandra, ten years old and outspoken, climbs a piece of furniture to reach a shelf full of books, among them *Northern Regions* (1827) and *The Saints' Everlasting Rest* (1658).[19] The two books seemingly could not have less in common: Richard Baxter's *Saints' Everlasting Rest* is a Protestant devotional manual and meditation on death; *Northern Regions* is an adventure book for children that tells the sensational stories of the Arctic explorers Richard Parry and John Franklin. But both books have connections to the Spiritualist movement: Baxter's manual described the afterlife in symbolic terms that would later be adopted by proponents of Spiritualism, and Sir John Franklin, subject of *Northern Regions*, was a frequent otherworldly attendant at trance lectures of the 1850s and 1860s.[20] Cassandra's expedition to the top of the bookshelf also yields a copy of Laurence Sterne's *Sentimental Journey* (1768), the font of much nineteenth-century sentimental literature.[21] By invoking Sterne alongside *The Saints' Everlasting Rest* and *Northern Regions*, Stoddard both situates her novel within an ongoing sentimental literary tradition and indicates the centrality of Spiritualist relations to her tale. At the same time, she connects these literary and religious movements to ongoing theological debates: as Cassandra is climbing shelves, her mother and aunt are reading aloud from the *Boston Recorder* an article describing a doctrinal feud between ministers of the Congregational church. The juxtaposition of these many texts allows the scene to face, Januslike, both backward and forward, invoking traditional Puritan devotionalism, contemporary sectarian controversies, popular literary trends, and a progressive scientific spirit as they met on the common ground of Spiritualist belief and practice.

Cassandra's memory of Mary Morgeson's winter room takes on a ghostly quality, with past, present, and future collapsing into one as the narrating Cassandra notes that "the hands of [the house's] builders have crumbled to dust" (8). Describing the middle-class Victorian comforts of the room—its chintz chair covers, serge curtains, "chocolate-colored" carpet, and cheerful Franklin stove—Cassandra describes a warm domestic scene in which the comingling of different literary and religious forms (the devotional manual, the Spiritualist memoir, the sectarian journal, the sentimental novel) facilitates female community and authorial agency (8–9). When Aunt Mercy declares the adventuresome Cassandra "possessed," she identifies Cassandra as the focal point for these secular circulations of belief. As reader and auditor, Cassandra is possessed by the spirits of Franklin and Parry, by Sterne, by Baxter, and by the memory of those whose "hands have crumbled to dust"; as Mary's daughter and Mercy's niece, she is possessed by their theological concerns even when she does not share them; and as narrator of the scene, she is possessed by Stoddard's authorial voice. Rather than indicating a narrative of religious decay from the doctrinal concerns of Mary and Mercy's generation to the Spiritualist interests of Cassandra's, this scene offers a depiction of female religious identification not bound by narratives of progress, decline, or even chronological time: Protestant devotionalism, Spiritualist explorations, sentimental fiction, and sectarian debate coexist within the loose temporal frame of Cassandra's memory and the book's opening pages, offering a depiction of female community and agency enabled by the novel's transtemporal secular milieu.

Cassandra's "possession" is an ongoing motif of *The Morgesons*, a moniker applied to her when she performs actions deemed willful or unladylike—in other words, when she asserts unclassifiable or ostensibly inappropriate forms of female agency. To be possessed by another is to transgress boundaries of individual identity—to deny apparent separations between unique minds and bodies and even between this world and the next—and thereby to defy notions of individual agency and self-determination. In *The Morgesons*, episodes of trance speaking, clairvoyance, spirit traveling, and other Spiritualist practice both indicate and simultaneously construct unique sympathetic connections between characters, while the fluid and unpredictable nature of Spiritualist agency enables new configurations of interpersonal power. As Veronica and Cassandra mature from "possessed" children to self-possessed women, Spiritualist practice enables kinds of sympathetic connection among the sisters and their friends that need not conform to the narratives of romantic love, sibling rivalry, sudden conversion, and economic dominance that their New England neighbors would impose on them.

Cassandra and her future brother-in-law Ben Somers, for instance, refuse to fall into the romantic rituals prescribed by their school companions at Rosville. At their first meeting Ben describes, accurately and without ever having seen her, Cassandra's sister Veronica: "'[I] fancy that the person to whom the name belongs has a narrow face, with eyes near together, and a quantity of light hair, which falls straight; that she has long hands; is fond of Gothic architecture, and has a will of her own'" (96). Their non sequitur conversation and immediate rapport (Ben: "'Are your family from Troy?'" Cassandra: "'Do you dislike my name?'") suggest an ongoing acquaintance, though they have never met, and when Cassandra's eyes wander, Ben asks, "'Are you looking for your sister?'" as though Cassandra and Veronica could communicate across the distance between Surrey and Rosville as Ben and Veronica apparently can (96). Ben's inexplicable clairvoyance—his ability to accurately describe a woman he has never met and whom he will someday marry—and the immediate psychic connections between Veronica, Cassandra, and Ben signal both the novel's resistance to predictable romantic narratives (why talk to a beautiful woman about her distant and less attractive sister?) and a model of shared agency that can cross boundaries of time and space. Rather than imagining herself as the recipient (or victim) of Ben's romantic attentions and placing herself in a position of dependence on him, Cassandra forms a friendship with Ben in which the dominant role shifts with circumstance and need.

Ben and Cassandra's emotional interdependence is premised on their Spiritualist forms of communication and enables them to maintain their platonic friendship in the face of social conventions that would cast them in standard romantic roles. Ben, described by other characters as "visionary" (179, 256), foresees the bad end to which Cassandra's romance with Charles Morgeson will lead (he twice predicts the other man's death), but rather than imposing his will on Cassandra, he expresses his opinions only telepathically: "We looked at each other without speaking, but divined each other's thoughts. 'You *are* as true and noble, as I think you are lovely. I must have it so. You *shall not* thwart me.' 'Faithful and good Ben,—do you pass a sufficiently strict examination upon yourself? Are you not disposed to carry through your own ideas without considering *me*?' Whatever our internal comments were, we smiled upon each other with the sincerity of friendship" (204). Cassandra's access to Ben's thoughts gives her the authority to resist his moralizing even as their clairvoyant connections allow them to defy the romantic expectations of others. Cassandra's friendship with Ben circumvents the well-worn romantic plot—two wealthy and attractive young people related distantly by blood or marriage fall in love and unite their fortunes—and their unconventional friendship is literalized in their ability to communicate outside the bounds of spoken conversation. The uniqueness of their relationship is brought into sharp relief by the reactions of those around them, who interpret their behavior according to the expected terms of nineteenth-century sexual politics. Observing the strong but unspoken connections between them, Ben's friends assume the end of a predictable romance that never took place: "'It is all over with them'" (204). Ben's mother, too, offers a conventional explanation for Cassandra and Ben's closeness: Cassandra wants Ben for his money. But Cassandra and Ben refuse these categorizations—the jilted man, the gold-digging woman—which assume fixed power relations between men and women (women control sex, men control money). Instead, their sympathetic Spiritualist communion enables them to form temporary affective havens where they are momentarily sheltered from romantic expectations, or at least able to defer them.

The Spiritualist abilities demonstrated by characters in *The Morgesons*, including the clairvoyant connections between them, offer explorations of shared agency and demonstrate how unpredictable agentive formulations can disrupt expected interpersonal narratives—not only those involving romance and marriage but those that depend on hierarchical family dynamics. Though Cassandra finds it difficult to communicate with her mother in this life, after Mary Morgeson dies, Cassandra, like an effective medium, can recall Mary's spirit from beyond the grave: "When my thoughts turned from her, it seemed as if she were newly lost in the vast and wandering Universe of the Dead, whence I had brought her" (235). Such inversions are disruptive precisely because they undermine the traditions of inheritance and economic possession that structure Cassandra's and Veronica's lives: as daughters the girls are worth less than sons. When their younger brother, Arthur, is born, Cassandra and Veronica are quickly made aware of their relative value. One servant, Hepsey, declares, "'Locke Morgeson should have a son . . . to leave his money to,'" while another, Temperance, points out that this tradition is grounded in local Congregationalist customs: "'Girls are thought nothing of in this 'ligious [religious] section; they may go to the poor house, as long as the sons have plenty.'" Mrs. Morgeson herself confirms the primacy of sons when she tells Cassandra after Arthur's birth, "'I am glad it is not a woman'" (29). After Mrs. Morgeson's death, Cassandra reverses the terms of this unequal relationship with her mother, performing a Spiritualist inversion of childbirth by bringing Mary back into a world in which, like a newborn babe, she finds herself "scared and troubled by the pressure of mortal life around her" (240). Though she mourns her mother, Cassandra inherits her parents' home and comes to feel "an absolute self-possession, and a sense of occupation I had long been a stranger to" (255). "Possession" here, as elsewhere in the novel, takes on a double meaning: Cassandra comes into possession of her home and herself by way of her gift of Spiritualist possession, as the fluid agencies enabled by Spiritualist mediumship invert the power relations inherent in a mother-child relationship founded on patriarchal structures of inheritance and female worth.

Under nineteenth-century gender conventions, to possess one's home as a woman is both to fulfill and to defy domestic expectations; Cassandra's inheritance could be legitimately categorized as either progressive or conservative, since it confines her to domestic space even as it makes her master and mistress of that space.[22] But plotting Cassandra's possession along a political spectrum would reduce the complexities of her Spiritualist self-negotiation. Histories of the nineteenth-century Spiritualist movement often display such an instrumental understanding of religious agency as they attempt to pin down Spiritualism's effects by categorizing the content of spirit communications as either positive or negative, either progressive or conservative. Ann Braude's *Radical Spirits*, one of the first works of religious history to treat nineteenth-century Spiritualism as an important historical movement, describes how the inverted assumptions that undergirded Spiritualist practice—that the weak and sensitive could most easily access the powers of the spirit world—enabled female trance mediums to make progressive political and social assertions, including feminist and antislavery declarations, before mixed audiences of men and women. Robert S. Cox has complicated Braude's argument by noting that nineteenth-century spirits "spoke in voices that spanned nearly the entire political spectrum of midcentury America . . . from immediate abolition to gradualism to pro-slavery, from egalitarianism to antiegalitarianism, capitalism to socialism."[23] More important than the content of spirit communications, however, was their form: Spiritualism's radical potential lay not only in what the spirits said but in the transformations of agency and authority embodied in the phenomena of spirit channeling and clairvoyance. By invoking the spirits as their guides and interlocutors, women, the working classes, and people of color gained a voice—a voice not entirely their own, but not entirely not their own either—in the most crucial political, social, and religious discussions of their day. Whether the voices' pronouncements were progressive or conservative, the very act of speaking was for these mediums a radical intervention into the nineteenth-century public sphere.

Among literary critics, the tendency to read Spiritualist mediumship as either progressive or conservative while overlooking its agentive potential has prompted misreadings of the Morgeson sisters' spiritual agency. One critic, classifying the sisters' Spiritualist gifts as "antinomian," reads a friendly conversation between Cassandra, Ben, and Helen Perkins about Helen's tattoo as a sign of Cassandra's "secret evil" and Ben's supposedly "Svengali-like power" over her.[24] Removing the declensionist assumption behind this understanding of Spiritualism, however, results in a different reading: one in which three strangers quickly overcome the constraints imposed by New England propriety and achieve a swift and lasting intimacy. The conversation provides Cassandra with a new way to understand herself and her attraction to Charles Morgeson: during the conversation, Cassandra is "possessed" to speak of her home in Surrey; Helen is "moved" to reveal a secret tattoo of her lover's initials; and Ben, divining Cassandra's feelings for Charles Morgeson, hints that "'we shall all be tattooed,'" foretelling the carriage accident that will kill Charles and leave Cassandra "tattooed" with scars (103, 163).[25] Resisting the urge to classify Spiritualist practice or Spiritualist gifts as inherently good or evil makes it possible to recognize the unusual and empowering nature of the platonic cross-gender friendships enabled by the novel's secular spiritualities.

One key to secular reading, then, is attending to form as well as content: looking not only to what Spiritualists said or did but also to what Spiritualism, as a social and literary force, could do. Spiritualism did not progress from a single sensationalist ghost story to a nationwide religious movement with stunning social and political valences by virtue of its content alone. Rather, Spiritualism became a transformative religious discourse not only by changing what could be said but by altering the dynamics of who was allowed to speak and how—by blurring the boundaries between the spiritual and the material and between individual minds. Spiritualist belief and practice posited the agency that flowed through Spiritualist circles as an unpredictable and fluid force wielded collectively and adroitly by those with the least access to sources of temporal power, whether extrinsic (wealth and education) or intrinsic (maleness and whiteness). Many of the most successful Spiritualist mediums were female, working class, people of color, or some combination of the three. Spiritualism thus gave those traditionally positioned as meaning's repositories unprecedented access to channels of communication through which meaning might travel and be changed in the process.

Veronica Morgeson, like her sister, is possessed of Spiritualist talents, but her particular gift most resembles the Spiritualist practice of trance speaking: the power to channel the words and feelings of others as though she herself were speaking or experiencing them. This is simultaneously the most explicit and the most paradoxical way in which Spiritualist mediumship undermines individual and hierarchical models of agency: Veronica can channel and ventriloquize those who should have authority over her. Veronica's first words in the novel are in the third person, as though something or someone were speaking through her: as a clumsy child she overturns a milk pan on her head and begs her mother, "'Help Verry, she is sorry,'" perhaps divining the very words that are in her mother's mind (16). Later, when she is ill, the third person recurs: "'It is the winter that kills little Verry'" (153). This time it may be Cassandra or the family servant Temperance, watching by her bedside, whose voice she has borrowed. Veronica's clairvoyance also allows her to divine and express hidden emotions that defy ordinary speech. Shortly after Charles Morgeson dies, Veronica expresses her sympathy for the heartbroken Cassandra (who has confessed her affair to no one) through the kind of strange and ghostly melodies associated with the Spiritualist séance: she "went to the piano, and played music so full of wild lamentation, that I again fathomed my desires, and my despair. . . . She stopped, and touched her eyelids, as if she were weeping, but there were no tears in her eyes. They were in mine" (147). On the night before her wedding, Veronica dreams not of her own future husband but of Cassy's: when dream-Desmond pricks dream-Veronica with a dagger, Veronica awakes to find a red mark on her arm, and years later, when she meets Desmond for the first time, she identifies him as "'the man I saw in my dream'" (258). In each of these cases, Veronica, though sick or frightened, is able to assume the thoughts and feelings of those around her either to enlist their sympathy or to enter more deeply into their emotional lives. This ability gives her a claim to recognition in a household in which, as the younger, less attractive, and less engaging sister—their mother "did not love her as she loved me," the narrating Cassandra observes (16)—she has little to command attention.

Where Cassandra's Spiritualist gifts help her defy romantic conventions and disrupt patriarchal family narratives, Veronica's sympathetic clairvoyance embeds her more deeply within the family while simultaneously enabling her to repudiate the pieties of class that structure Surrey society and to form meaningful relationships across social divides. When the girls' strictly religious grandfather dies, Veronica refuses to attend his funeral, correctly intuiting that "'grand'ther Warren nearly crushed'" Mary and Mercy "'when [they] were girls of our age'" (70). Instead, she sends her custom-sewn mourning bonnet to a local widow's daughter, who turns up at church wearing the expensive object in the "Poor Seats"—an act that highlights the arbitrariness of class distinctions artificially naturalized in the details of church seating and mourning rituals.[26] While the wealthy Morgesons condescendingly allow the local poor to warm themselves at the kitchen fire, only Veronica befriends them, and on a trip to Boston she uses her shopping allowance to buy presents for the "cadaverous" children of a missionary on his way to India. Veronica's willingness and ability to empathize with others across boundaries of class is both sign and effect of her Spiritualist gifts—she channels others' thoughts and feelings—and it widens the circle of emotional connection within which she lives. Rather than restricting herself to friends from finishing school, as Cassandra does, Veronica is able to seek out relationships with women like the seamstress Lois Randall, whose working-class origins should place her beneath the Morgesons' notice. Veronica's Spiritualist agency, then, finds its expression in sympathetic relationships in which agency is shared even between persons of different social classes.

Veronica's unique and socially unsettling ability to empathize with those outside of her class is exemplified in her relationship with the family servant Fanny, whose ambiguous class status is a constant source of unrest in the Morgeson household. The Morgeson family "adopts" Fanny as a putative kindness to the girl's dead mother and uses her as kitchen help. Veronica and Fanny share an unspoken sympathetic connection that expresses itself in mutual understanding that nevertheless does not conform to the patterns (or platitudes) of simple friendship: Veronica sees through Fanny's attempts to spite Cassandra, uncovering the girl's true motivations ("'*I* admire her; you do too'"), while Fanny predicts Veronica's approaching illnesses ("'you are going to be sick; I feel so in my bones'") (151). When Mrs. Morgeson complains that she has "'never seen a spark of gratitude'" from Fanny, Veronica remarks that she "'never thought of gratitude, it is true; but why must people be grateful?'" (135). Veronica channels Fanny's anger—"I never thought of gratitude" could be Fanny's own words—and recognizes it as a legitimate response to events outside of her control. Mary Morgeson, lacking Veronica's sympathy or her clairvoyance, attributes Fanny's anger to a bad character—"'her disposition is hateful. She is angry with those who are better off than herself'" (135)—while ignoring the economic and class privilege that make it possible for the Morgesons to appropriate an orphaned child and install her as household staff. Veronica's willingness and ability to empathize with others across boundaries of class is both sign and effect of her Spiritualist gifts—she can *feel with* others, even when they are not her social equals—and it widens the circle of emotional connection within which she lives.

These forms of agency are unstable and temporary and as such have been largely overlooked by critics, particularly in light of the novel's tragic ending, in which Ben dies in delirium tremens after Veronica gives birth to their disabled child. The kinds of religious agency enabled by Spiritualist practice are difficult to sustain precisely because they exist in opposition to a liberal ideal that emphasizes self-determination, individual achievement, and the rejection of religious authority—an ideal often reserved for men. But it does not follow that because these forms of agency are available only intermittently and often as a result of struggle and difficulty, they are therefore invalid or unworthy of study. It is by stringing together such moments of collective agency that Veronica and Cassandra—and many women—create a life.

Critics have overlooked the Spiritualist elements of *The Morgesons* in part because Stoddard's own biography does not reflect sustained engagement with Spiritualism. But her letters reveal that she crossed paths with its practitioners and may have turned to its comforts late in life. In New York in the 1850s Stoddard was attended by the physician John Franklin Gray, a homeopathist and Spiritualist with an interest in animal magnetism (now called hypnosis); in 1865 she worried that her estranged friend Edwin Booth might have married the trance medium Laura Edmonds. And in 1901, after the death of her son Lorimer, Stoddard wrote her friend Lilian Whiting to ask whether Whiting had ever "believed in" the Spiritualist medium Leonora Piper or whether Whiting might be in touch with Kate Field: "Sometimes I so long to touch Lorry's beautiful hand," she wrote, "that I would . . . stretch myself towards what I can never see."[27]

Around that same time, in the preface to the 1901 reissue of her three novels *The Morgesons*, *Two Men*, and *Temple House*, Stoddard told the origin story of her writing career: "One day when my husband was sitting at the receipt of customs . . . I sat by a little desk, where my portfolio lay open. A pen was near, which I took up, and it began to write, wildly like 'Planchette' upon her board."[28] Describing the process of composition that had led to each of her novels, Stoddard recalled how "the shadow of a man passed before me, and I built a visionary fabric round him"; her literary productions now seemed to her "as if they were written by a ghost of their time."[29] Stoddard's gestures to "planchette" and to the "visionary" origins and "ghost"-like qualities of her novels retrospectively framed the composition of her longer works as a tale of Spiritualist mediumship harnessed for literary purposes. Like Harriet Beecher Stowe describing the inspiration for *Uncle Tom's Cabin*, Stoddard obscured the agencies that brought her novels into being. But in place of the singular liberal Calvinist deity acknowledged in Stowe's "God wrote it," Stoddard pointed to a host of ghostwriters named and unnamed.[30]

The Cultural Work of Women's Spiritualist Fiction

It was precisely the unstable and unpredictable nature of Spiritualist agency and its consequent potential for social disruption that made Spiritualism such a controversial movement in its own time. The perceived dangers of circulating agency were made apparent by the vehemence with which Spiritualism's claims were repudiated, most often through attempts to determine the "true" source of the power that lay behind Spiritualist practice. Scientists, clergymen, and other cultural representatives performed investigations or logical exercises whose purpose, irrespective of their methodologies, was to deny the fluidity of agency and locate a stable source for Spiritualist power, whether that source was the machinations of a fraudulent medium, the overactive imagination of an impressionable teenager, or the connivings of the devil himself. The most famous of these was the so-called "Cambridge Investigations," in which the Harvard professors Benjamin Peirce, Louis Agassiz, and Eben Horsford were invited to view a demonstration and pass judgment on the Spiritualist gifts displayed by the Fox sisters and other famous mediums. The investigations, according to the well-known medium and Spiritualist spokeswoman Emma Hardinge Britten, were disappointing to all involved: the professors considered the demonstration a failure because the mediums were unable to provide proof of their gifts under experimental conditions; the Spiritualists considered it a failure because the presence of too many skeptics made it impossible for them to make contact with other realms.[31]

The work of dissecting and denigrating the circulating agencies of Spiritualism took place in the popular press as well, with newspapers and magazines publishing dismissals of spiritual phenomena side by side with reports of the most recent Spiritualist wonders. An essay in the August 1854 issue of *Putnam's Monthly* provides a representative illustration of the problematics of agency that informed nineteenth-century debates over Spiritualist practice and the argumentative lengths to which its detractors would go to pin down the source of the power at work in Spiritualist activity. Titled "Spiritual Materialism," the anonymous essay insists that the dangers of Spiritualist belief and practice lay not in the movement's physical phenomena but in its practitioners' refusal to locate agency in stable and predictable places.[32] The essay draws a fixed line of demarcation between the spiritual world and the material, insisting that the twain will never meet, "that it is impossible that a spirit should manifest itself physically."[33] Faced, however, with the fact that thousands of Americans claimed to have seen spinning tables and heard mysterious knockings and ghostly music apparently brought about by spiritual means, the essay goes on to explain that, if such things *are* possible, they must be achieved by the suppression of participants' wills to those of their spiritual accomplices: "There remains, so far as we can see, but the one way in which physical phenomena can be the action of spirits. If the spirits can obtain the complete control of a human agent; if the persons in a 'circle,' beneath whose fingers a table takes to its legs and perambulates, are really and truly acting without any volition of their own, under the immediate *possession* of spirits, then, and not otherwise, may these manifestations be in a certain sense spiritual."[34] According to the author of "Spiritual Materialism," agency must be located *either* in the doings of spirits *or* in those of the séance's participants: there can be no cooperation between the spiritual and the material realms. Seeking to deny the possibility of collective forms of agency, "Spiritual Materialism" insists that agency is competitive rather than collaborative: for one person to have agency, another's "must have been destroyed."[35]

These and other attempts to debunk Spiritualist claims to religious and social authority sought to undermine accounts of the phenomenon by appealing to the liberal model of "sovereign agency" according to which agency is held and wielded individually and in competition with other sovereign subjects. Spiritualist practitioners, by denying the absolute separation of the material and spiritual worlds and positing that men and women might act collaboratively with the dead, were upending not only traditional Protestant doctrines about the afterlife but patriarchal agentive formulations that located authority and power first in a male-identified God and then in his earthly (male) anointed. Both Spiritualist practice and women's Spiritualist fiction offered an embodied and discursive critique of this model of agency; by "untethering the speech act from the sovereign"—lending their voices to the dead in the space of the séance, the trance lecture, or the Spiritualist novel—Spiritualist mediums and the women authors who adapted their practices to literary form foregrounded new models of unconscious, circulating, and collective agency.[36]

While authors including Stoddard may have sought to avoid ridicule or mask the agentive implications of their texts by referring to Spiritualist practice only obliquely, others incorporated Spiritualist practice more explicitly in their novels, with broader consequences at the level of both plot and form. The popular poet Elizabeth Oakes Smith composed at least two long works that invoked Spiritualist practices and tenets.[37] One, *Shadow Land* (1852), is an extended account of Smith's dream life, including her ruminations on the Bible, astrology, and other assorted topics. In the text, the narrating voice shifts frequently between the waking Smith, her dreaming self, and other unnamed presences.[38] But it is Oakes Smith's 1854 novel *Bertha and Lily* that best exemplifies how women's Spiritualist fiction enabled both thematic and formal innovation, extending the range of subject matter "appropriate" to women's novels and the ways in which the author might experience sympathetic and spiritual connections with the reader.

Bertha and Lily is the story of the eponymous Bertha, a beautiful but sad woman who arrives in a small town in rural New York to live with a former family servant.[39] The town is in the midst of a spiritual drought simultaneously caused and lamented by the local minister Ernest Helfenstein, who is baffled as to why his weekly theological ruminations aren't moving his parishioners to enthusiastic revival. Bertha's appearance in town turns Helfenstein's personal life upside down: she convinces him to adopt two local orphans, Lily and Willy, despised because of their unknown parentage, and her myriad graces undermine his more conventional attachment to his beautiful but shallow cousin Julia. Meanwhile, Bertha's powerful mediumistic gifts begin reconfiguring the town's religious loyalties: she gathers a spiritual following that soon overwhelms Helfenstein's congregation in number and devotion, until even Helfenstein professes himself not only her lover but her spiritual student.

Like *The Morgesons*, *Bertha and Lily* locates religious power in the words and actions of spiritually gifted women while sidelining ordained religious leaders. Though lacking Stoddard's satirical edge, Oakes Smith similarly casts the Congregational clergy as supporting characters in a tale about the uncanny but undeniable power of women's spirituality. (Helfenstein means "rock of help," and Ernest's narrative purpose is to assist Bertha in her quest to transform the town.) But this power does not exist in a linear relationship with agency. Bertha's Spiritualist gifts appear to be largely involuntary; after attending church one Sunday, she finds herself assaulted by "so many shadowy images crowding upon my mind, that I shrank from revelations, which, at another time, would have been hailed with joy. 'Not now, not now,' I cried, 'I am too weak to bear more'" (35–36). Both she and Ernest's adopted daughter, Lily—a "sinless child" in the mode of Oakes Smith's famous poem—have the power to summon a "child-angel," but this spirit appears unbidden and does not speak; her presence is her only revelation. Bertha, likewise, does not set out to "found" a new congregation in opposition to Helfenstein's; as the towns-people come to recognize her spiritual power, they begin following her without her invitation and with only her tacit consent. At the level of plot, *Bertha and Lily* demonstrates the superiority of Spiritualist religiosity without openly claiming it.

But *Bertha and Lily*'s real commentary on circulating forms of Spiritualist agency can be better observed at the level of form than of plot: the novel employs a shifting narrative perspective that mimics for the reader the unstable agency in evidence in the Spiritualist séance. The first five chapters of the novel are narrated in Bertha's first-person voice, which intersperses descriptions of events with long ruminations on social issues (including gender equality in marriage and church reform), contemplation of her own virtues, and devotional poems. But at the start of chapter 6 a new and unnamed first-person narrator intervenes in the text to proclaim, "We must now lay aside the journal of Bertha"—a journal "we" did not know "we" were reading—and summarize events to this point in the text while further praising Bertha's virtues (47). After a few paragraphs, and once again without any narrative marking to predict a shift in voice, Ernest Helfenstein's diary enters the text. The remainder of the novel continues this pattern, with the narrating voice shifting—often midchapter and almost always without warning—between Bertha's journal, Ernest's diary, and an unnamed third-person narrator who may or may not be the voice of the "child-angel."

Because of these shifts in narrative voice and perspective, reading *Bertha and Lily* can be a frustrating and disconcerting activity. Stoddard herself acknowledged this when she reviewed Oakes Smith's novel for the *Daily Alta California* and proclaimed herself "[un]able to divine its meaning" but attracted to its "sketches of character."[40] The novel's "meaning," however, lies precisely in its confusing form: the unstable narrative voice mimics the circulating agency of the séance circle, in which the voice of the medium could abruptly change from a playwright to a president to a personal friend, and the content of the spirits' messages could be poetic, polemical, romantic, or conversational.

Bertha and Lily, even more than *The Morgesons*, is Spiritualist in its form as much as its plot, as the alterations in perspective draw the reader into new and uncanny relation with narrator(s) and characters.

And like *The Morgesons*, *Bertha and Lily*'s unusual form enables new narrative figurations of female agency, particularly regarding women's sexuality. The Lily of the novel's title is revealed late in the story to be Bertha's own daughter, the product of a rape perpetrated against Bertha as an adolescent. (The lengthy passages in which various narrators extol Bertha's virtues are thus in part prophylactic: they prepare the reader for the then-damning revelation that Bertha is an unwed mother.) Lily has inherited her mother's Spiritualist gifts; both have the innate power to summon the child-angel whose presence indicates God's blessing. Bertha and Helfenstein's marriage at the novel's end thus results in the creation of a nontraditional or "blended" family—one that now includes the child-angel, since by purifying Ernest's spiritual vision Bertha has allowed him to see their heavenly visitor as well. This ending simultaneously fulfills the generic requirements of the domestic sentimental novel and depicts a radical union: an ordained Congregational minister marries a fallen woman and adopts her illegitimate child. As women authors took up the topic of Spiritualism, then, this religious discourse affected not only the subject matter of their fiction but, increasingly, its form. Women's Spiritualist writing came more and more to reflect the conventions of the séance and the trance lecture, with fictional circulations of voice and agency enabling women authors to tell new stories and enter discussions generally considered outside of woman's sphere.

This trend may have reached its apotheosis in 1868. This was, of course, the year when Elizabeth Stuart Phelps's blockbuster novel *The Gates Ajar* was published. *The Gates Ajar* has long held a (not always positive) reputation as the most famous Spiritualist novel of the nineteenth century. But *The Gates Ajar* is less a meditation on Spiritualist agency than an extended apologia on the compatibility of Spiritualist beliefs with liberal Christian religion.[41] In fact, the 1868 publication that made far more radical use of the literary possibilities of Spiritualist activity was Kate Field's *Planchette's Diary*.[42]

Published by J. S. Redfield of New York, *Planchette's Diary* records Field's experiments with the automatic writing apparatus, sometimes in company with her (living) friends and sometimes while alone with only the spirits for companionship. During her sessions at the planchette, the spirits comment on family matters (Field's late father, Joseph, is a frequent interlocutor and guide), on politics (including the machinations of the Copperheads in Congress), and on the act of spirit communication itself (Planchette complains about the "terrible war that is waged by conservatives against the new religion" of Spiritualism [25]). No topic is off limits either to Field or her spirit communicants, and sessions with "Madame Planchette" and "Her Boardship" (Field's charm is everywhere evident) are interspersed with anecdotes from Field's social and intellectual life, including a visit to a haunted house inhabited by friends and a glowing review of Elizabeth Stuart Phelps's October 1868 *Harper's* story "The Day of My Death."

The result is a text that is part fiction, part travelogue, part gossip column (barely masked public figures like H.G.—Horace Greeley—appear throughout), part religious and political polemic, and part tribute to Field's loved ones living and dead. Though similar perhaps to the eclectic newspaper columns Field had been publishing since the early 1860s, it otherwise defies all attempts at classification. Field is listed in the text not as its author but its "editor," and in her editorial preface she insists that the text's contents are not fiction but that they should nevertheless be taken with caution: "That which I relate, I have seen in the presence of intelligent men and women of acknowledged standing in society . . . [but] the human mind is prone to doubt, and it is wise to treat even one's own senses with incredulity" (iii). Field's preface also baldly acknowledges the crisis of attribution and agency instantiated in her text: speaking as the text's editor, Field "apologiz[es] for the unavoidable prominence of the personal pronoun *I*" (iv). This apology is both a feint at expectations of feminine modesty and an honest expression of perplexity: who is the narrating *I* of *Planchette's Diary*? Planchette "herself" has no volition: "My common sense denied the possibility of any intelligence whatever in a piece of wood," Field sensibly intones (6). The spirits speak through Planchette at Field's behest, and yet Field declines to claim credit for Planchette's agency or theirs—this is, after all, Planchette's diary and she may choose to converse with whom she will.

Rather than seeking to root out and classify the source of the spirits' communications, Field welcomes their opinions, shaping her expectations and her text to Planchette's whims. At a dinner party, the narrating Field meets a Professor H with whom she discusses Planchette. Professor H "totally denie[s] the possibility of spiritual agency" and tells Field "to watch the manifestations closely, for the purpose of getting at the truth," a piece of advice Field blithely ignores (43). In Field's text, Planchette's various voices appear in conversation with Field's own inner monologue—itself often indistinguishable from the voice of Planchette—and with the opinions of those in her familial, social, and professional circles, both reflecting and facilitating Field's famous gregariousness and her commitment to women's independence. Rather than mere delusion (as Professor H implies) or evidence of a demonic agent "controlling" Field's will (pace the author of "Spiritual Materialism"), Planchette is Field's social and literary collaborator, the author to Field's editor—a literary arrangement that would foreshadow Field's later career as the editor of her own national review, *Kate Field's Washington* (1890–1895).

Unlike the male-authored texts that Kerr identifies, *The Morgesons*, *Bertha and Lily*, *Planchette's Diary*, and other female-authored explorations of Spiritualist belief and practice do not seek to debunk or ridicule the "trans-identic experiences" (as Eliza Richards terms them) associated with Spiritualism but instead explore them through forms of narrative experimentation that unsettle the subject positions of characters, narrators, and audience.[43] The confusions of narratorial identity found in *Bertha and Lily*, *Planchette's Diary*, and other Spiritualist texts written by women represent textually what the Spiritualist medium embodied in her presence and voice: the fluidity of subjectivity and agency made possible by the sympathetic environment of Spiritualist practice.

Secularized Reading and the Misdiagnosis of Women's Spiritualist Fiction

Nineteenth-century Spiritualist practice famously foregrounded the medium's bodily experience as central to communication between mortals and spirits, the human and the divine. Whether in public trance lectures before a crowded hall of people, small séances in suburban parlors, or private hours between an individual and her planchette, "mediumship and the physical body became inseparable."[44] Spiritualist religion was controversial not only because it defied doctrinal tradition and obscured the source of the medium's agency, but because its manifestations were so frustratingly *this-worldly*: performances that purported to include communications from the spirit world seemed ridiculously grounded in this one. The Spiritualist insistence on the centrality of the medium's body—often poor, sick, female, black, or all of the above—only heightened this impression. Spiritualist practice, instead of denying or denigrating the body, placed it at the center of religious experience, positing the body, rather than a particular building or book, as a holy space through which spirits and their attendant agencies might circulate.

Women's Spiritualist fiction adopted this concern with embodied experience, interrogating cultural ideologies surrounding women's "delicacy" and "frailty" to explore new possibilities for women's embodied religious agency. But modern critics, operating from a sovereign model of agency that requires fully formed human subjects to be independent, self-determined, and "strong," have misunderstood or overlooked the explorations of agency at the heart of these texts. Here it is helpful to return to *The Morgesons*, since as the nineteenth-century Spiritualist novel that has received the most attention from recent critics, its recovery and reception offer a prime example of the way secularized reading has distorted critical understandings of women's Spiritualist fiction.

The Morgesons is a text that embodies mystery in its form and its plot, seeking to channel the ineffable rather than unmask it or explain it away; like the saint from whom Veronica takes her name, its guiding symbol is the veil. Steeped in New England orthodox traditions that define the body in general and the female body in particular as "the temporary prison of the soul" and the seat of temptation, Cassandra and Veronica Morgeson seek out other ways of understanding their bodies as sites of both material experience and spiritual transcendence.[45] In The Morgesons Veronica's illnesses, standing on the line between two interpretive regimes—the medical and the spiritual—are the embodied expression of these fluid and unpredictable forms of agency. Cassandra sits up with her sister during one of her terrifying episodes, in which Veronica

> could not speak, but shook her head at me to go away. Her will seemed to be concentrated against losing consciousness; it slipped from her occasionally, and she made a rotary motion with her arms, which I attempted to stop; but her features contracted so terribly, I let her alone. "Mustn't touch her," said Temperance. . . . Her breath scarcely stirred her breast. I thought more than once that she did not breathe at all. Its delicate, virgin beauty touched me with a holy pity. We sat by her bed a long time. . . . Suddenly she turned her head, and closed her eyes. . . . In a few minutes, she asked, "What time is it?" "It must be about eleven," Temperance replied; but it was almost four. (153)

This sickroom scene is shot through with religious language and imagery: the "virgin beauty" of Veronica's body recalls the incorruptibility of the Virgin Mary (an association that recurs throughout The Morgesons), while the misrecognition of time suggests a scene of worship removed from the temporalities of everyday life. Temperance, the Morgesons' family servant, has participated in the ritual many times and knows its patterns: "'Mustn't touch her.'" Instead, it is Cassandra who is "touched" with holy pity. The unclear impersonal pronoun "its" that Cassandra employs—"its delicate virgin beauty"—reiterates the mysteriousness of these attacks and Veronica's otherworldliness: Is the "it" Veronica's breath? Her illness? Veronica herself? The narrating Cassandra, like the reader, stands outside of the scene, puzzling through its possible interpretations. Veronica's "will" is present but intermittent: Is she imprisoned in this unruly body or acting through it? Is she physically ill or spiritually inspired? Is Veronica the agent or object of these attacks—a "she" or an "it"? Does Veronica, Cassandra, or Stoddard herself even know?

The multiple valences of the scene reflect the hermeneutic indeterminacy of nineteenth-century Spiritualist practice: the same symptoms welcomed by Spiritualist mediums and their followers as signs of divine anointment were diagnosed by medical professionals as debilitation—evidence of women's inherent delusion and disorderliness (or, in the case of male mediums, of the unnatural feminization of men). Veronica's malady is not the wasting-but-beautiful consumption of Alice Humphreys or Little Eva, but neither is it the mean-spirited malingering of Marie St. Clare. Indeed, Veronica's illnesses seem almost a parody of the death scenes that mark sentimental fiction: rather than gathering her family and servants around her, she tries to lock them out of her room, and though she does cut off her hair, the act is more compulsive than comforting—she bestows no locks on her family and continues cutting for so long that by the time she has recovered she is nearly bald.

What Veronica's inexplicable illness does resemble is the Spiritualist trance: "There were two main variations . . . : falling into a fainting trance, sometimes called catalepsy, and uncontrolled thrashing, jerking, or trembling. . . . The sufferer alternately sobbed and laughed violently, complained of palpitations of the heart, clawed her throat as if strangling, and at times abruptly lost the power of hearing or speech. A deathlike trance might follow, lasting hours, even days."[46] The uncontrollable "rotary motion" of Veronica's arms, her prolonged breathless unconsciousness, and her voiceless protests against Cassandra's nursing mark her seizure-like attacks as similar to Spiritualist trances. But rather than come down on one side of the question or the other—the only diagnosis the novel will make is "delicacy of constitution" (30)—*The Morgesons* leaves the mystery of Veronica's embodiment unsolved.

Twentieth- and twenty-first-century critics, by contrast, have diagnosed Veronica's illnesses as selfishness and psychosomatic delusion, "the hysterical reaction of a young woman who does not want to grow up and face her anger at her severely restricted life."[47] Rather than consider the possibility that Veronica's religiously inflected illnesses might point to the centrality of the body to her Spiritualistic construction of the self, critics have sought other explanations for her behavior, most often diagnosing it as anorexia nervosa.[48] Such diagnoses accord with Jenny Franchot's observation that literary critics employing Marxist, psychoanalytic, or poststructuralist theoretical principles have tended to approach religion as though it were disease: "About those who 'had it' in the past, scholars often write either 'around' the belief . . . or isolate it as a deviant element to be extracted for diagnostic analysis."[49] The critical discourses Franchot invokes are all subject to the larger (a)historical narrative of secularization, in which the scientific processes of rationalization and disenchantment promise emancipation from superstition and "solutions" to all the spiritual mysteries a text might hold.

These readings of *The Morgesons* have obscured how Veronica's spirituality—signaled, in part, by her frequent illnesses—enables her to experience her body not as an opaque signifier of a binary identity (male or female, beautiful or ugly, rich or poor, sick or well) or the source of temptation to men (she will have nothing to do with the local clergyman, who shows a more than spiritual interest in her) but as a fluid medium for accessing the possibilities of the mysterious and the divine. Like her Spiritualist gifts and acts of cross-class charity, Veronica's illnesses are multivalent: while it is possible to read them as transparent bids for attention or attempts to make herself the center of family life, they also provide opportunities for those around her to act on their best impulses (as when Fanny claims that Veronica's illnesses give Fanny the chance to "'be somebody'" [154]) while helping Veronica herself to make sense of her existence. Cassandra as narrator notes, "We did not perceive the process, but Verry was educated by sickness; her mind fed and grew on pain, and at last mastered it. The darkness in her nature broke; by slow degrees she gained health, though never much strength. Upon each recovery a change was visible; a spiritual dawn had risen in her soul: moral activity blending with her ideality made her life beautiful, even in the humblest sense" (65). It is the creativity of Veronica's life—the way that Spiritualist agency enables her to imagine ways of being in the world that are not defined by patriarchy and privation—that critics who ignore her spiritual aspirations or diagnose them as delusion or selfishness simply cannot see.

The rush to diagnose Veronica is a symptom of a secularized critical tradition in which "the real problem is that women, persons of color, and other members of historically oppressed groups are not generally allowed to be both subject and object at once." Like the nineteenth-century author of "Spiritual Materialism," modern critics have been anxious to assign agency and hold it fast, so that "the moment [fictional figures] display characteristics not conforming to absolute rationality and dignity, they seem inexorably reduced to pure objects, sheer victims of determining forces beyond their individual control."[50] Such assumptions make it impossible to understand religious phenomena, including Spiritualist mediumship, that offer a "psychic double play of . . . subjectivities that blu[r] the boundaries between active, speaking subject and passive object."[51] Since women operating within the regime of Western secularity have often constructed opportunities for agency in the psychic and physical spaces opened by these blurred boundaries, the critical inability to see these spaces has too often left religious women's authorial and personal in-novations unremarked.

The secularized critical regime of the twentieth and twenty-first centuries has ironically recapitulated the "monopoli[zation] of all knowledge" that nineteenth-century Spiritualists complained of: the mania among lawyers, phy-sicians, clergy, scientists, and educators to pass judgment on and dismiss the embodied experiences of Spiritualist mediums and their fellow seekers.[52] One outgrowth of this monopolization of knowledge was a phenomenon that Wil-liam James called "medical materialism"—the rage to reduce all strong spiri-tual feeling to a product or symptom of disease: "Medical materialism finishes up Saint Paul by calling his vision on the road to Damascus a discharging le-sion of the occipital cortex, he being an epileptic. It snuffs out Saint Theresa as an hysteric, Saint Francis of Assisi as an hereditary degenerate. George Fox's discontent with the shams of his age, and his pining for spiritual veracity, it treats as a symptom of a disordered colon. Carlyle's organ-tones of misery it accounts for by a gastro-duodenal catarrh. . . . And medical materialism then thinks that the spiritual authority of all such personages is successfully under-mined."[53] As a cultural discourse emphasizing firsthand knowledge of the uni-verse gained through collective, shared seeking, Spiritualism offered a vociferous challenge to "the incipient professionalism of science [and] medi-cine," whose practitioners claimed the authority to assign meaning to existence by appealing to scientific principles "which to most people [were] as invisible as ghosts."[54] As such, Spiritualism provided opportunities for personal and col-lective self-definition that were not bound by the binaries of professional dis-course.

Though those opportunities were often short-lived, unstable, and subject to ridicule, they nevertheless formed an important arena for female and sub-altern agency—both in fiction and in everyday life. Restricting readings of nineteenth-century religious women, real or fictional, to diagnoses that treat embodied religiosity and nonliberal agency as mental or physical illness rein-scribes the same limiting cultural discourses that, even in the 1860s, already sought to narrow the ways in which women's minds, bodies, and voices might exist in the world. By invoking the embedded indeterminacies of Spiritualist practice and refusing to resolve them at the level of narrative, women's Spiri-tualist fiction challenged totalizing discourses that would seek to reduce human experience and human agency to singular and mutually exclusive explanations.

In *The Morgesons*, Veronica and Cassandra complain about the monopoli-zation of knowledge—the foreclosing of mystery that total comprehension entails. When Locke Morgeson quizzes Veronica about her impending marriage to Ben with the question, "'Do you know each other?'" Veronica replies, "'We do not know each other at all. What is the use of making *that* futile attempt?'" (169). Cassandra, facing the prospect of life as the mediator of Ben and Veronica's marriage, muses that her sister and soon-to-be brother-in-law "would have annihilated my personality, if possible, for the sake of comprehending me" (163). Complete and total knowledge—the kind provided by the professional discourse of doctors and many modern literary critics—is framed within the novel as an annihilation that must prove fruitless precisely because of its thoroughness. When Ben Somers probes Cassandra's feelings for his brother, Desmond, he dismembers a book in his agitation: "taking up a book, which he leaned his head over, and whose covers he bent back till they cracked," Ben performs the action that later critics would perform on the book of Veronica and Cassandra. "'You would read me that way,'" Cassandra avers, and she could be speaking to twenty-first-century critics as much as to Ben (232). Like Cassandra's mythical namesake, who foresaw the future but was unable to change it, Elizabeth Stoddard predicted the dissection to which her text and others' would be subjected—a future in which critics, like surgeons, would probe Spiritualist novels for signs of disease.

Conclusion
Women's Religious Agency Today

In this book I have emphasized the importance of leaving behind secularized reading practices and adopting what I have termed secular reading. When we approach nineteenth-century women authors, secular reading requires that we devote careful attention to the particular religious conditions in which these writers found themselves and consider how they negotiated their agency and their authorship with respect to those conditions. Secular reading requires attention to religion because secularism as a cultural discourse sets the terms by which religion can be practiced and even apprehended and thus shapes how religious affiliations, acts, and expressions are received and remediated in the public sphere. American secularity is protean, however; the line between acceptable public and private expressions of religion has shifted over time, as has the role of religious belief and practice in public life. So what would it mean to read our current situation secularly?

For one thing, it means recognizing both the differences and the continuities between our current secular situation and earlier eras of American religious history. While each generation believes it is living at a time of unprecedented rupture and change, the fact is that in its broad outlines, the twenty-first-century United States is not all that different from the nineteenth-century United States. Our era is marked by an explosion of communication and new media technologies that have altered how we communicate with one another and the world; by debates about race, immigration, and citizenship whose participants seek to adjudicate who and what is properly American; by military actions that extend the colonial and imperial reach of the state; by white supremacist nationalism and the incarceration and destruction of black and brown bodies; and by patriarchal systems that, despite advancements in women's equality, continue to police women's personal, professional, social, and embodied experiences.

Among these continuities, the religious situation in the United States remains similar in outline, though different in its details, to the early nineteenth century. Just as the period following the Second Great Awakening showed a rise in religious affiliation, a proliferation of Christian sects, and the flowering of theological innovations that arose not only from the clergy but from devout laypeople, including the authors in this book, we are currently living through a period of immense religious ferment. Our current form of secularity can be difficult to discern, however, because persistent ideas about secularization continue to distort our public discussions of religion. I conclude this book by thinking through our secular situation and pointing to some of the ways that secular agency operates in the political and religious lives of women in our own time.

Seeing Religion Clearly

In 2012 the Pew Research Center's Religion and Public Life project produced a new report on religious affiliation in the United States. Titled *"Nones" on the Rise*, the report began by proclaiming that the "number of Americans who do not identify with any religion continues to grow at a rapid pace." According to Pew, the religiously unaffiliated had increased in number, from roughly 15 percent to 20 percent of all U.S. adults, between 2007 and 2012, and 6 percent of the U.S. adult population had come to describe themselves as "agnostic" or "atheist."[1] The story of the country's increasing religious apostasy was picked up immediately by major news outlets. The *Washington Post* ran the headline "Losing Our Religion: One in Five Americans Are Now 'Nones'" and focused primarily on the political implications of the survey, particularly for Republicans.[2] NPR likewise landed on both the REM reference and the political possibilities: "Losing Our Religion: The Growth of the 'Nones,'" it reported, as well as "Religious Nones Are Growing Quickly: Should Republicans Worry?"[3] *USA Today* also invoked the political angle: "The Emerging Social, Political Force: 'Nones,'" it proclaimed.[4]

The Pew Center's findings received considerable media attention because they seemed to confirm an assumption that has animated American public discourse at least since the 1960s: that American religion is in decline, except perhaps among the "religious right." But buried somewhere deep in each of these articles was a caveat: the Pew Center's report had shown that while religious *affiliation* was declining among U.S. adults, other measures of religious adherence or identification, such as belief in God, frequency of prayer, or self-identification as "religious" or "spiritual," had largely remained steady. Indeed, despite Pew's own attention-grabbing headline, the report provided ample evidence of continuing religiosity; 80 percent of Americans still described themselves as affiliated with a religion.[5] The percentage of Americans who attended religious services had hardly changed. And even among the 20 percent of Americans who declared themselves religiously unaffiliated, the "nones," 68 percent said they believed in God, and 41 percent said they prayed at least once a week. Lack of religious *affiliation*, in other words, does not equate to lack of religious *attachments*. Indeed, between 2007 and 2012 the number of self-identified atheists in the United States grew by only 0.8 percent, a number that was statistically significant but did not evidence a drastic decline in American religiosity.[6]

Four years after the nones findings appeared to much media attention, the Pew Center issued another report, this time on the relative participation of women and men in religious activities. Titled *The Gender Gap in Religion around the World*, the report aggregated survey data from 192 countries and six different religious groups: Christians, Muslims, Buddhists, Hindus, Jews, and the religiously unaffiliated. Researchers measured multiple indicators of religious commitment, including religious affiliation, attendance at worship services, frequency of prayer, and the self-reported importance of religion in a person's life. They found that "globally, women are more devout than men by several standard measures of religious commitment." These measures differ among regions and religious groups, of course, but the gender gap was significant and observable across most traditions and measures of religious commitment: women, on average, are 3.5 percent more likely than men to claim a religious affiliation and 8 percent more likely to report that they pray daily. Among Christians, the differences are stark: around the world, Christian women's religious commitment exceeds men's on all measures, by as much as 10 percent. In the United States, the differences are particularly pronounced, with Christian women, for instance, up to 14 percent more likely to engage in daily prayer than men.[7]

In contrast to the 2012 report on the nones, however, the 2016 report received little media attention; most responses to it came from scholars of religion and Christian denominational publications. Mainstream outlets that covered it were most likely to express befuddlement. The *Washington Post* ran the story but was more interested in puzzling out the why than reporting the what: their article "Why Women Are More Religious Than Men" skipped to the (short) portion of the report that posited potential explanations for the gender gap.[8] The UK *Guardian* accompanied their article "Women More Religiously Devout Than Men, New Study Finds"[9] with a stock photograph of a niqab-clad woman and a link to an editorial titled "It's Not Surprising That Women Are More Religious Than Men: What Else Do They Have to Believe In?"[10]

These expressions of befuddlement expose the gendered ground on which our fantasies of an increasingly secularized society rest. If religion is destined to die out, these headlines imply, why haven't women gotten the memo? The progressive-secular imaginary insists that women must shed their religion in order to become properly secularized subjects and thus worthy participants in the rational public sphere. When they don't—when they display consistently higher rates of religious belief and behavior than men—they defy the progressive-secular narrative that insists that to be fully self-actualized, women must disentangle themselves from their religious attachments.[11] When those higher rates of religious affiliation persist across national, regional, and ethnic borders—when women remain religious in both Western, "developed" nations and Eastern or Southern "undeveloped" ones, and when they remain religious in Hindu, Buddhist, Christian, and even Muslim countries—they undermine Western secular chauvinism, which prides itself on "freeing" oppressed and deluded people, particularly women, from their "backward" religions.

Reading our secular situation correctly, then, means attending to the continued importance of religion in the life of the nation generally but specifically in the lives of women, who are its most numerous and ardent adherents. Despite evidence that women make up the majority of participants in nearly all American religious movements, however, U.S. popular and political discourse consistently identifies "religion" with "fundamentalist Christianity" and both with white men. In some ways, this association seems self-evident: the male leaders of the Christian right regularly insert themselves into political discourse and particularly into debates surrounding gender and sexuality, as they inveigh against gay marriage, contraception, and abortion. And yet their voices are not only loud but likely to be amplified: their authority, as always in the American public sphere, is conditioned on whiteness, maleness, and inherited privilege. And as self-appointed spokesmen for a fundamentalist religious movement, men like Jerry Falwell Jr. and Franklin Graham attract attention in a public sphere that prefers to think of itself as fully secularized and as having efficiently done away with public expressions of religion.

Consider, for instance, the amount of media attention directed toward the Westboro Baptist Church, an extremist congregation that has made a name for itself by staging hate-filled demonstrations at Pride parades and service members' funerals. The Westboro church is a tiny organization—it claims about seventy members total—and yet the media coverage it receives suggests a large and widespread movement. While white evangelicals do much damage in the United States, the mainstream media's obsessive focus on them is an artifact of our post-Protestant version of secularity, in which "good" religious people (Episcopalians, for instance, who vote largely Democratic, don't take the Bible literally, and are less likely to proselytize or speak in public about their faith) fly under the radar while "bad" religious people (white Southern Baptists, who vote Republican, insist on the Bible as the literal word of God and use it as a warrant for conservative political positions, and insist on placing religion at the center of political discourse) receive outsized attention in the putatively secularized public sphere.[12]

Our national tendency to recognize religion only when it is loudly performed by white men distorts our political discourse and makes it difficult to effect meaningful change around policy or social issues. The aftermath of the 2016 presidential election provides a particularly salient example. One of the most circulated headlines to come out of the election (again from Pew) proclaimed that "81% of Evangelical Christians Voted for Trump." It is indeed a sobering statistic, one that paints evangelical Christians as both brainwashed (in an election in which certain states were decided by less than 1 percent of the total vote, a group with 81 percent agreement on a candidate seems monolithic) and hypocritical: how could four out of five so-called values voters choose a candidate with three ex-wives, numerous ongoing lawsuits, and a leaked video in which he bragged about grabbing women by their pussies?

Again, however, the public discussions surrounding the Pew Center's findings (and, in many ways, the findings themselves) obscure more than they reveal. "Born-again/evangelical" is a self-reported category that cuts across many Christian sects and denominations and includes some Protestants, Catholics, and Mormons.[13] White evangelicals made up 26 percent of the 2016 electorate, a striking fact in its own right, but as I discussed in my second chapter, the term *evangelical*, which was once a simple synonym for *Protestant*, has been appropriated in the last thirty years by "one conservative party in almost all the most notable denominations."[14] For many born-again Christians, in other words, *evangelical* is a political designation as much as a religious one: it is synonymous with *conservative* or *Republican*. And to report that conservatives voted overwhelmingly for a Republican candidate is a truism rather than a revelation.

The conflation of "white" with "born-again/evangelical" in the Pew report also functioned to erase nonwhite evangelicals and evangelical women from discussions about the 2016 election. A quarter of American evangelicals are nonwhite, but their voting behavior was not mentioned in Pew's exit poll reports.[15] The voting behavior of other religious groups, however, suggests that race was a more determining factor in the 2016 election than religion: white Catholic voters, for instance, supported Trump by a 23-percentage-point margin (60 percent to 37 percent), while Hispanic Catholics supported Clinton by a 41-percentage-point margin (67 percent to 26 percent).[16] White evangelical voters, in other words, likely voted for Trump as much because they were white as because they were evangelical. And neither of the Pew Center's reports about the white evangelical vote examined the gender distribution of religious voters, leading most commentators who reported the 81 percent statistic to either ignore gender altogether or to assume that male and female evangelicals voted for Trump in equal numbers. But while Pew's exit poll reports erased female evangelicals, preelection polling of likely voters conducted in September and October 2016 by the Public Religion Research Institute showed a gender gap in every white Christian group. While 71 percent of white evangelical Protestant men supported Trump before the election, 60 percent of white evangelical Protestant women did (a number that is still high but noticeably lower). Mainline Protestant men supported Trump at 54 percent, while mainline Protestant women supported him at 45 percent (a number identical to their support for Clinton). White Catholic men, meanwhile, supported Trump at 58 percent, while white Catholic women supported him at 38 percent (and Clinton at 49 percent).[17]

Attending to race and gender differences in religious and political affiliation, it turns out, reveals significant and sometimes stark distinctions between religiously affiliated whites and nonwhites and between men and women, both within and outside of Protestant Christianity. But just as it was easier to blame working-class Americans for Trump's victory than to admit that wealthy white suburbanites voted for him because of racial resentment, it has been more convenient to blame a poorly differentiated "evangelical" voting block for our current political morass than to admit that the primary motivating factor behind many Americans' voting behavior is white supremacy.[18] I am not suggesting, of course, that our discussions of politics should ignore religion and focus solely on race or gender or that race and gender identity will always overrule religious identity in political decision making. White heteropatriarchy's long history of wielding Christianity as a weapon against racial and sexual minorities is a theopolitical arrangement that is dangerous to excluded individuals and to the nation as a whole. But conflating religion, Christianity, whiteness, and conservatism serves the purposes of white Christian heteropatriarchy by doing its dirty work: effacing the agency or the very existence of women and racial minorities.

This erasure can be seen in the predictable recurrence of calls for a "religious left," which are repeated ad nauseum during every election cycle, always as if the "religious left" were a new and unthought idea. Most recently, as of this writing, Pete Buttigieg, a gay, Episcopal military veteran running for the presidency in 2020, has chided the Democratic Party for "los[ing] touch with a religious tradition that I think can help explain and relate our values. . . . It helps to root [in religion] a lot of what it is we do believe in, when it comes to protecting the sick and the stranger and the poor, as well as skepticism of the wealthy and the powerful and the established."[19] The coming rise of the religious left is an evergreen trope in American politics, but the "religious tradition" at issue is, of course, never Islam or Buddhism or Judaism but a more progressive form of Christianity. And as the statistics above suggest, the United States has and has long had a Christian left—it's simply made up of African Americans, Hispanic Americans, and women.[20] Members of historically black Christian congregations, for instance, already vote overwhelmingly Democratic. Furthermore, the conflation of religion with Christianity in such calls reinforces the notion that American politics is Christian by definition, thus reifying the outsider status of non-Christian politicians, including but certainly not limited to Ilhan Omar and Rashida Tlaib (Muslim members of the House of Representatives), Jared Huffman (atheist member of the House of Representatives), and Ravi Bhalla (Sikh mayor of Hoboken, New Jersey).[21]

When it comes to triangulating religion and politics with race and gender, in other words, our public discourse is stubbornly inaccurate. "Religious" means "Christian," "evangelical" means "conservative," and all three mean "white and male"; non-Christians, women, and people of color are either erased or treated as monolithic. Given the obfuscating tendencies of our popular political discourse, reading our current moment secularly requires that we as scholars devote careful attention to the interpenetration of religion with politics and with other forms of identity, including gender, race, and class.

Women's Religious Agency in our Secular Age

Precisely because the religious agency of women, people of color, and non-Christians is so apt to be erased, reading our current situation secularly also means working to recognize the myriad ways that religious agency continues to operate in our contemporary world. As I have emphasized throughout this book, discussions about modern religion and secularity are always discussions about gender. Because secular modernity constructs women (real and imagined), with their ostensibly passionate, unruly, reproductive bodies, as outsiders to a public sphere defined as rational, deliberative, and disembodied, any attempt to define appropriate forms of secular subjecthood invokes the problem of gender, if only implicitly. As definitional outsiders to secular modernity, women have struggled for centuries to imagine forms of secular subjecthood that would allow them to achieve agency in a public sphere premised on their passivity and objectification.

Because both women and religion were constructed as secular modernity's Others, the struggle for agency has sometimes prompted women to reject religion altogether—to sever ties with a tradition or set of practices that seemed to shackle them to an unenlightened past. But just as often, women have found ways to enact forms of agency that operated *through* their religious beliefs, behaviors, and affiliations. This book has examined some of the many ways women of the antebellum period used the novel to imagine new forms of religious agency within the secular situation of the early to mid-nineteenth century. I will close with a few examples of contemporary religious women who are negotiating their agency within the terms of our current secular situation—with all the complexity that entails.

As I noted above, popular discussion of American Christianity tends to focus on its fundamentalist wing, conservative evangelicalism, and within that on its most vocal white male members. And yet even within the openly patriarchal white evangelical movement, women have found ways to exercise both religious and political agency. Emily Johnson's *This Is Our Message: Women's Leadership in the New Christian Right* traces the crucial role played by white women in the evangelical movement of the 1970s and 1980s. Conservative Christian women including Beverly LaHaye, Tammy Faye Bakker, Dale Evans Rogers, Anita Bryant, and Marabel Morgan adapted many of the strategies used by nineteenth-century women writers to justify their involvement in public and political matters. They professed that their unwillingness to engage in public action had been overcome only by God's call to witness; they claimed that their special status as Christian wives and mothers required them to weigh in on matters of family policy, including abortion and marriage equality; and they insisted that women's voices were necessary to counter the rise of a godless feminism. Through denominational and ecumenical organizations and conferences, through authorship and publication, and through the new media genre of the television talk show, these women claimed central roles for themselves within a movement that most often expressly forbade women's ordination and looked askance at all forms of leadership that placed women above the authority of men. To dismiss late twentieth-century evangelical Christianity "as simply patriarchal or anti-woman," Johnson writes, "is to ignore the millions of women who attend conservative Christian churches, who support conservative Christian organizations, and who vote for conservative Christian candidates."[22] Doing so also ignores a potent form of women's religious agency that has far-reaching effects in the world—effects that those with progressive political commitments would do well to understand, if only to better counter them.

While women's religious agency is easy to overlook when it occurs within such patriarchal structures as the modern evangelical movement, it is also often ignored or erased in contexts where religion is perceived as inappropriate or embarrassing. Azza Karam has remarked on "the relative amnesia Western feminists have of their own trajectory," forgetting as they do the explicitly religious origins of the women's rights movements in England and the United States.[23] Ann Braude's studies of the National Organization for Women reveal the critical role that Catholic nuns, Methodist lay leaders, and other religious feminists played in the group's founding in the 1960s, as they established "an Ecumenical Task Force on Women and Religion that organized worship services as well as supporting women's rights in religious contexts." Histories of second-wave feminism that appeared during the 1980s and 1990s, however, erased these religious origins, "portraying religion exclusively as an enemy of feminism" and emphasizing the success of the "secular feminist" movement.[24] Because histories of second-wave feminism have often deemphasized the movement's religious roots in order to claim its proper place in a secularized public sphere, acknowledging women's religious agency may mean retelling our own story to include the myriad opportunities for affiliation and commitment that religious belief and behavior have enabled.

Even within contemporary American evangelicalism, however, the inheritors of first- and second-wave feminism are exercising a new form of religious agency—one that counters the seemingly commonsense alignment of evangelical Christianity with conservative political causes. The progressive evangelical movement that has arisen in the last fifteen to twenty years has been contemporaneous, not coincidentally, with the global reach of social media, and though it has popular male spokespersons (Rob Bell, Shane Claiborne), it is being led by politically engaged women with massive social media followings. These women include Jen Hatmaker, Glennon Doyle, and Jamie Wright, each of whom maintains a multimedia presence that includes Facebook, Twitter, and Instagram accounts, long-form works of autobiography and devotional writing, conference and public speaking appearances, and podcast and talk show interviews. Together and individually, these women have been criticized by conservative male religious leaders for their unorthodox and ostensibly "unbiblical" teachings about religious patriarchy and abuse, LGBTQ equality (Doyle is gay and married to the soccer star Abby Wambach), white supremacy, Christian imperialism (Wright nicknamed herself "the Very Worst Missionary" for her critique of evangelical missions), and women's bodily autonomy.

Among the most successful and controversial of these progressive evangelical women was Rachel Held Evans, who died suddenly at the age of thirty-seven in May 2019. Once labeled by the *Washington Post* as "the most polarizing woman in evangelicalism," Evans had a huge and devoted social media following.[25] She was a perpetual thorn in the side of conservative evangelical men, particularly when she published an article in *Vox* in August 2016 encouraging fellow evangelicals to vote for Hillary Clinton.[26] Though not an ordained member of the clergy, she was frequently invited to preach in progressive churches, where she administered the sacraments to members who had fled or been expelled from other congregations. And while she hadn't attended seminary, she published four books of popular theology that earned the distinction of being labeled "unbiblical and theologically dangerous" by a leader of the Southern Baptist Convention.[27] A Christian author and colleague tweeted that "What @rachelheldevans did for American Christian theology cannot be overstated. She democratized it. She insisted that a woman from small-town Tennessee without a theological degree could engage the sacred cows of Christian doctrine with common sense" (@MAGuyton, May 4, 2019). In doing so, many of her mourners claimed, she had changed not only her readers' personal beliefs but the course of American Christianity.

While she was accused by Christian conservatives of embracing a "toxic theology" (@travis_vanmeter, May 4, 2019), Evans insisted that her arguments for feminism, LGBTQ equality, and racial justice were consistently biblical. Refusing to surrender the practice of exegesis to fundamentalist leaders, she aligned herself with a progressive Christian tradition that had been in place since at least the antebellum period. In a 2013 blog post titled "Is Abolition 'Biblical'?" Evans noted that the Bible verses used in the nineteenth century to argue in favor of slavery are the same now used to justify gender inequality and LGBTQ exclusion in evangelical churches. Reiterating her own pro-LGBTQ stance, Evans wrote that "sometimes it's not about the number of proof texts we can line up or about the most simplistic reading of the text, but rather some deep, intrinsic sense of right and wrong."[28] In another post inspired by *Huckleberry Finn*, Evans wrote that when conservative Christians told her "the Bible is clear" about the sin of homosexuality, she often thought of Huck's decision to "go to hell" rather than perform the supposedly righteous act of returning Jim to slavery. "The Bible has been 'clear' before, after all," she wrote, "in support of wiping out entire people groups, in support of manifest destiny, in support of Indian removal, in support of anti-Semitism, in support of slavery, in support of 'separate but equal,' in support of constitutional amendments banning interracial marriage." Like Huck, Evans wrote, she had decided that "sometimes true faithfulness requires something of a betrayal."[29]

Abandoning biblical literalism and proof texting in favor of a holistic reading of the Bible as a text that supports inclusion and social justice placed Evans in a long line of liberal Christian writers and thinkers, many of them women. Evans invoked one of these women in the "Is Abolition 'Biblical'?" post: Harriet Beecher Stowe. In a brief discussion of *Uncle Tom's Cabin*, Evans quoted the famous scene in which Senator Bird offers this patronizing response to his wife's critique of the Fugitive Slave Act: "'Your feelings are all quite right, dear, and interesting, and I love you for them; but, then, dear, we mustn't suffer our feelings to run away with our judgment.'" Evans's reaction, she wrote, was to "laugh out loud. . . . Reminds me of a few book reviews I've received." Writing in a progressive Christian tradition that chose to err on the side of inclusion and welcome rather than exclusion and condemnation, Evans was subjected to the familiar gendered critique that she was writing from her "feelings" rather than from her "judgment."[30]

News of Evans's death broke around the same time that the president of the United States was publicly attacking a Muslim member of Congress, Ilhan Omar, by retweeting a video that intercut a speech she made before the Council on American-Islamic Relations (CAIR) with footage of the 9/11 attacks.[31] Omar makes an attractive target for anti-Muslim bigotry because she is an outspoken Muslim woman and an immigrant born in Somalia who wears a headscarf in public.[32] Her religious agency is literally inseparable from her political agency: as a U.S. congresswoman, she wears the visible evidence of her Muslim identity on her body at all times, including on the floor of the House of Representatives. Conservative attacks on Omar rhetorically align her with 9/11 (as the president's retweet did) by drawing tenuous links between CAIR and Hamas while also accusing Omar of conspiring with authoritarian governments. Commentators on both the Right and the Left, meanwhile, have accused her of anti-Semitism because she vocally objects to pro-Israel lobbying groups' influence in Washington. While U.S. involvement with Israel is a long-standing source of disagreement in American politics, Omar's statements receive outsized attention because of the visible intersection of her race, her gender, and her religion. A *New Yorker* profile of Omar noted that she "refuses to assume the posture of the good immigrant" and "performs neither humility nor gratitude."[33] A white male columnist for the conservative online magazine *The Federalist* called Omar "an avatar for the intersectionalist, America-loathing, progressive-Islamic supremacist set" who hides behind "an identity politics veil."[34] The reference to Omar's supposed commitment to "Islamic supremac[y]" alongside the gesture to the notorious "veiling" of Muslim women suggests how Omar's Muslim identity functions in multivalent ways in the American media landscape. She is accused of overperforming a Muslim political identity associated with fundamentalism and violence while simultaneously failing to embody a Muslim female identity, signified by the veil, that should require her to be modest and submissive to authority. At the same time, her explicit religious and racial otherness to white American Protestantism makes her symbolically valuable to a white supremacist political faction that equates Protestant Christianity with whiteness and both with true Americanness.

The double bind in which Omar finds herself is shared by many American Muslim women, who appear most often in public discourse as abused victims of fundamentalist ideology or sinister agents of foreign power—sometimes simultaneously. Like anti-Catholic discourses of the nineteenth century that prompted not only the convent captivity narratives I discussed in chapter 4 but the burning of Catholic churches and violent attacks on Catholic immigrants, these depictions emphasize the supposed foreignness of Muslim women, even when those women were born in the United States and display myriad political and cultural markers of American identity. While hundreds of American Muslim women have raised their voices to dispute popular misconceptions about Islam and the role of women in it (Linda Sarsour and Mona Eltahawy are prominent examples), I would like to focus here on a particular expression of Muslim women's religious agency: the Women's Mosque of America (WMA).

The Women's Mosque was founded by M. Hasna Maznavi in 2015 "to provide a platform for brilliant Muslim women to speak in a religious capacity for the benefit of the entire Muslim Ummah."[35] Headquartered in Los Angeles, the organization holds monthly woman-led Friday prayers; because it has no building of its own, it first offered services in an interfaith center and now meets in a Unitarian church. The Friday service is open to women and children only; while some co-ed events are held on other days, the Friday prayer services are (and, the organizers assert, always will be) restricted to women. The organizers compare the mosque to a women's college where they seek to create "an atmosphere in which Muslim women are surrounded by their peers and feel comfortable exploring more active leadership roles in a safe space."[36] The mosque's website describes it as a "middle ground space that welcomes all Muslims from every sect, background, school of thought, and level of religious practice" while also accommodating particular traditions. (Shi'a worshippers, for instance, are provided with rose petals and clay *turbahs* for use during prayer). And the mosque has a "come as you are" dress code policy, "meaning everyone is welcome to come dressed as they normally do outside of the mosque."[37] Attendees, in other words, need not wear a specific head covering to be welcome. Monthly prayer services and other offerings are meant to complement traditional mosque attendance, where services are sex segregated and leadership roles are filled by men; participants are encouraged to take what they have learned back to the mosques they regularly attend.

At each Friday meeting, a woman invited by the community delivers a *khutbah*, or discourse; these women are usually Muslim, but the Women's Mosque "invite[s] our interfaith sisters from all religious backgrounds to join us as observers, participators, and supporters," and thus *khateebas* (women delivering the khutbah) sometimes represent non-Muslim faiths. According to the mosque's website, each khateeba "brings her own unique first-hand perspective and insights to topics that have either previously gone unaddressed in mosques or that have rarely been spoken about from the female perspective."[38] These topics include domestic violence and sexual abuse, and the mosque has also held discussions that address social justice movements, including Black Lives Matter. Khateebas often preach from English translations of the Qur'an, a stance that challenges the long-standing alignment between the scriptural authority of the Qur'an and its original Arabic language. Since women have not always had opportunities to study the Qur'an in Arabic, preaching from English translations challenges patriarchal clerical prerogative. Khateebas engage in exegesis of the Qur'an while bringing to it a specifically female perspective—one the founders of the WMA claim has been excluded from Islamic tradition and that, they insist, can benefit every Muslim, not just the women who attend the mosque.

In keeping with their calling to benefit "the entire Muslim Ummah," the Women's Mosque of America maintains a robust internet presence. While attendance at Friday prayer services rarely crests 50 people (a drop from the 75–100 who attended services when the mosque first opened in 2015),[39] the WMA YouTube channel has 724 subscribers and its archived videos of khutbahs and co-ed events at the mosque have received over 60,000 views. The mosque also maintains iTunes and SoundCloud accounts where users can listen to khutbahs or to episodes of the WMA podcast. This savvy use of social media extends the mosque's reach well beyond its local Los Angeles community and makes its ideas available to women who are prevented—by geography or other constraints—from attending the mosque themselves.

The creation of a specifically female space in which Muslim women from various sects and communities can meet to engage in prayer and discussion represents a liberalization of Muslim religious practices that the mosque's founders insist is consistent with Islamic tradition. Their "aim [is] to increase community access to female Muslim scholars and female perspectives on Islamic knowledge and spirituality"—not a deconstruction (as Rachel Held Evans's followers sometimes claimed to be doing with evangelical Christianity) but a restoration.[40] While the mosque's website insists that the WMA is neither a progressive nor a conservative organization, the act of choosing women as imams and khateebahs extends religious authority to women in previously unprecedented ways. But by framing the mosque as a supplement to existing worship spaces rather than a replacement for them and by offering khutbahs that engage in direct exegesis of specific passages from the Qur'an, attendees and organizers of the Women's Mosque present this immense accession of religious agency as the fulfillment of Islamic tradition, not a rebellion against it. The founders of the mosque insist that "a major part of uplifting the Muslim community is to harness the potential of the whole Ummah, including Muslim women, who make up more than half of our community."[41] In this nonsectarian Muslim space, women access greater religious agency by adopting, adapting, and reinterpreting Islamic tradition.

Like the nineteenth-century Christian women writers I have discussed in this book, the organizers and attendees of the Women's Mosque are carving out space for agency in a tradition that might seem ill fitted or even hostile to their efforts. Unsatisfied with secularized discourses that insist that agency can only be found outside the bounds of organized religion or that self-actualization is synonymous with rebellion, these twenty-first-century religious women are adapting their communities' sacred texts and traditions in ways that facilitate their agency while keeping them connected to a shared past. Women writers of the nineteenth century took advantage of increased literacy and cheaper print technologies to spread theological ideas by means of the popular novel. The Women's Mosque's organizers are embracing digital media—Instagram, YouTube, podcasts, and apps—to spread new visions of what religion can be in our secular age.

Like the subjects of this book, we are living through a time of immense social, economic, and technological upheaval. And though shifts in religious identification—including rising numbers of religiously unaffiliated people—might suggest that the long-promised secularization of American society is finally coming to fruition, a closer look tells us that while religious beliefs and practices are changing, they are hardly on the decline. Though the loudest voices in American religion may be those of fundamentalist men, women are changing the face of American religion by finding new spaces for and modes of agency. In social media, in popular publishing, in conferences and workshops, and in houses of worship, women are shaping American religion by applying their minds to the social and intellectual needs of their communities. And they are doing so in ways that will have profound implications for the future. Just as nineteenth-century women writers changed the world—for better and for worse—by wresting theology from the hands of clerical leaders and wielding it in the public sphere, religious women of the present are shaping their families, communities, and the nation by making religious matters their own.

NOTES

Introduction

1. Quoted in Laurie Robertson-Lorant, "Mr. Omoo and the Hawthornes: The Biographical Background," in *Hawthorne and Melville: Writing a Relationship*, ed. Jana L. Argersinger and Leland S. Person (Athens: University of Georgia Press, 2008), 46.

2. John Lardas Modern, *Secularism in Antebellum America* (Chicago: University of Chicago Press, 2011), 3.

3. Tracy Fessenden, *Culture and Redemption: Religion, the Secular, and American Literature* (Princeton, NJ: Princeton University Press, 2007), 2.

4. Ann Douglas, *The Feminization of American Culture* (New York: Knopf, 1977), 121; Mary Farrell Bednarowski, *The Religious Imagination of American Women* (Bloomington: Indiana University Press, 1999), 15.

5. Susan M. Griffin, "Women, Anti-Catholicism, and Narrative in Nineteenth-Century America," in *The Cambridge Companion to Nineteenth-Century American Women's Writing*, ed. Dale M. Bauer and Philip Gould (Cambridge: Cambridge University Press, 2001), 158.

6. Lauren Berlant, *The Female Complaint: The Unfinished Business of Sentimentality in American Culture* (Durham, NC: Duke University Press, 2008), 3.

7. Winnifred Fallers Sullivan, *The Impossibility of Religious Freedom* (Princeton, NJ: Princeton University Press, 2005), 7.

8. For a detailed explanation of the post-Protestant secular, see Fessenden, *Culture and Redemption*, 1–12.

9. Charles Taylor, *A Secular Age* (Cambridge, MA: Belknap Press of Harvard University Press, 2007), 22.

10. Robert A. Orsi, *History and Presence* (Cambridge, MA: Harvard University Press, 2016), 8.

11. William James, "The Will to Believe," in *The Will to Believe and Other Essays in Popular Philosophy* (Cambridge, MA: Harvard University Press, 1979), 14.

12. Cathy N. Davidson, *Revolution and the Word: The Rise of the Novel in America* (Oxford: Oxford University Press, 2004), 70.

13. Susan M. Ryan, "Charity Begins at Home: Stowe's Antislavery Novels and the Forms of Benevolent Citizenship," *American Literature* 72, no. 4 (2000): 765, http://doi.org/10.1215/00029831-72-4-751.

14. Gregory S. Jackson, *The Word and Its Witness: The Spiritualization of American Realism* (Chicago: University of Chicago Press, 2009), 161.

15. Claudia Stokes, *The Altar at Home: Sentimental Literature and Nineteenth-Century American Religion* (Philadelphia: University of Pennsylvania Press, 2014), 139–40.

16. Jackson, *Word and Its Witness*, 4.

17. Nathan O. Hatch, *The Democratization of American Christianity* (New Haven, CT: Yale University Press, 1989), 7.

18. Jon Butler, *Awash in a Sea of Faith: Christianizing the American People* (Cambridge, MA: Harvard University Press, 1990), 2.

19. For a detailed discussion of the increasing respectability of fiction writing in the early national United States, see David S. Reynolds, "From Doctrine to Narrative: The Rise of Pulpit Storytelling in America," *American Quarterly* 32, no. 5 (1980): 479–98, http://doi.org/10.2307/2712409. Talal Asad, *Genealogies of Religion: Discipline and Reasons of Power in Islam and Christianity* (Baltimore: Johns Hopkins University Press, 1993), 48.

20. Douglas, *Feminization*, 11, 234.

21. E. Brooks Holifield, *Theology in America: Christian Thought from the Age of the Puritans to the Civil War* (New Haven, CT: Yale University Press, 2003), 4.

22. Ibid., 8.

23. Lloyd Pratt, *Archives of American Time* (Philadelphia: University of Pennsylvania Press, 2010), 17.

24. Berlant, *Female Complaint*, 3.

25. Joanna Brooks, "From Edwards to Baldwin: Heterodoxy, Discontinuity, and New Narratives of American Religious-Literary History," *American Literary History* 22, no. 2 (2010): 449, http://doi.org/10.1093/alh/ajq001.

26. Detailed discussions of the thesis helpfully tease out its entangled assumptions. Janet Jakobsen and Ann Pellegrini identify seven strains of thought that usually structure discussions of secularization: rationalization, enlightenment, social-structural differentiation, freedom, privatization, universalism, and modernization and progress. See Janet R. Jakobsen and Ann Pellegrini, "Introduction: Times Like These," in *Secularisms*, ed. Janet R. Jakobsen and Ann Pellegrini (Durham, NC: Duke University Press, 2008), 1–35. Ingolf Dalferth identifies differentiation, transformation, transfer of authority, transition, and decline in religiosity as secularization's five salient features. Ingolf U. Dalferth, "Post-Secular Society: Christianity and the Dialectics of the Secular," *Journal of the American Academy of Religion* 78, no. 2 (2010): 317–45.

27. Molly McGarry, *Ghosts of Futures Past: Spiritualism and the Cultural Politics of Nineteenth-Century America* (Berkeley: University of California Press, 2008), 13.

28. Bryce Traister, *Female Piety and the Invention of American Puritanism* (Columbus: Ohio State University Press, 2016), 5.

29. In the 2012 General Social Survey (GSS), a record number of Americans—20 percent—reported that they belonged to "no religion." But only 3 percent of survey respondents said that they did not believe in God. While the former number has risen steadily over the last two decades, the latter has barely budged since the GSS began tracking religious affiliation in 1972. I discuss these trends in some detail in the conclusion to this book. Michael Hout, Claude S. Fischer, and Mark A. Chaves, "More Americans Have No Religious Preference: Key Finding from the 2012 General Social Survey," Institute for the Study of Societal Issues, March 7, 2013, https://sociology.berkeley.edu/sites/default/files/faculty/fischer/Hout%20et%20al_No%20Relig%20Pref%202012_Release%20Mar%202013.pdf. See also Kevin M.

Schultz and Paul Harvey, "Everywhere and Nowhere: Recent Trends in American Religious History and Historiography," *Journal of the American Academy of Religion* 78, no. 1 (2010): 129–30, http://dx.doi.org/10.1093/jaarel/lfp087.

30. Traister, *Female Piety*, 5.

31. Modern, *Secularism in Antebellum America*, 283.

32. Robert Orsi, "On Not Talking to the Press," *Religious Studies News* 19, no. 3 (2004): 15.

33. Ibid., 15.

34. Modern, *Secularism in Antebellum America*, 7–8. For discussions of secularism across a variety of disciplines, see Asad, *Genealogies of Religion* and *Formations of the Secular: Christianity, Islam, Modernity* (Stanford, CA: Stanford University Press, 2003); José Casanova, *Public Religions in the Modern World* (Chicago: University of Chicago Press, 1994); Dipesh Chakrabarty, *Provincializing Europe: Postcolonial Thought and Historical Difference* (Princeton, NJ: Princeton University Press, 2000); C. Taylor, *Secular Age*; Janet R. Jakobsen and Ann Pellegrini, eds., *Secularisms* (Durham, NC: Duke University Press, 2008); Michael Warner, Jonathan VanAntwerpen, and Craig Calhoun, eds., *Varieties of Secularism in a Secular Age* (Cambridge, MA: Harvard University Press, 2010); Linell E. Cady and Tracy Fessenden, eds., *Religion, the Secular, and the Politics of Sexual Difference* (New York: Columbia University Press, 2013); Saba Mahmood, *Religious Difference in a Secular Age: A Minority Report* (Princeton, NJ: Princeton University Press, 2016); and Joan Wallach Scott, *Sex and Secularism* (Princeton, NJ: Princeton University Press, 2017).

35. Amy Hungerford, *Postmodern Belief: American Literature and Religion since 1960* (Princeton, NJ: Princeton University Press, 2010), xiv. Critics of Charles Taylor's work often point out that his model of secularity is highly rationalized: the modern secular subject makes a conscious choice to believe or not to believe. But this is not the way most people experience their religion. For discussions of the Taylorian choice model's faults, see John Modern, "My God, David Brooks," Religion Dispatches, July 28, 2013, http://religiondispatches.org/my-god-david-brooks/; and Dawn Coleman, "The Spiritual Authority of Literature in a Secular Age," *Christianity and Literature* 67, no. 3 (2018): 519–30, http://dx.doi.org/10.1177/0148333117734161 526.

36. As Michael Warner has explained, this definition of secularity ("the conditions that structure even the religious once religiosity has become one option among others") must be carefully distinguished from "political secularism," which is a "project for regulating religion" by, for instance, outlawing the public display of religious symbols. Michael Warner, "Was Antebellum America Secular?" *Immanent Frame*, October 2, 2012, para. 23, http://tif.ssrc.org/2012/10/02/was-antebellum-america-secular/.

37. Coleman, "Spiritual Authority of Literature," 528.

38. Peter Coviello and Jared Hickman, "Introduction: After the Postsecular," *American Literature* 86, no. 4 (2014): 646, http://doi.org/10.1215/00029831-2811622.

39. Michael W. Kaufmann, "The Religious, the Secular, and Literary Studies: Rethinking the Secularization Narrative in Histories of the Profession," *New Literary History* 38, no. 4 (2007): 614, http://www.jstor.org/stable/20058029. This belief long bolstered the mode of criticism that Bruno Latour calls "iconoclastic"—a word revealingly borrowed from the Protestant Reformation—or "antifetishist," in which the critic replaces a hermeneutic regime she or he does not believe in with one she or he does believe in. See Bruno Latour, "Why Has Critique Run Out of Steam? From Matters

of Fact to Matters of Concern," *Critical Inquiry* 30, no. 2 (2004): 225–48, http://doi .org/10.1086/421123. Latour warned that the iconoclastic mode could be too easily adopted by proponents of reactionary causes. Twelve years later, Tracy Fessenden lamented the "wrenching irony" that "the affect some of us nursed and cultivated for decades—skeptical, wary, arch, adversarial, darkly pessimistic—should so nearly match the national mood that gave us our implausible 45th president." Fessenden, "A Hermeneutics of Resilience and Repair," *Religion and Literature* 48, no. 2 (2016): 167.

40. Anne Goodwyn Jones, *Tomorrow Is Another Day: The Woman Writer in the South, 1859–1936* (Baton Rouge: Louisiana State University Press, 1981), 28.

41. Jenny Franchot, "Invisible Domain: Religion and American Literary Studies," *American Literature* 67, no. 4 (1995): 836, 837, 840, http://doi.org/10.2307/2927901.

42. Susan Mizruchi, *Religion and Cultural Studies* (Princeton, NJ: Princeton University Press, 2001), x.

43. Jonathan Ebel and Justine S. Murison, "American Literatures / American Religions," *American Literary History* 26, no. 1 (2014): 2–3, http://doi.org/10.1093/alh /ajt062. Ebel and Murison note that this demotion was much more pronounced among scholars of nineteenth- and twentieth-century literature; the field of early American studies has always been attuned to the importance of religion. See also Jordan Alexander Stein and Justine S. Murison, "Introduction: Religion and Method," *Early American Literature* 45, no. 1 (2010): 1–29, http://www.jstor.org/stable/27856602; and Brooks, "From Edwards to Baldwin."

44. Kaufmann, "Religious, the Secular," 607.

45. For Bercovitch, see Michael P. Kramer and Nan Goodman, eds., *The Turn around Religion in America: Literature, Culture, and the Work of Sacvan Bercovitch* (London: Routledge, 2016). For special issues: "Methods for the Study of Religion in Early American Literature," special issue, *Early American Literature* 45, no. 1 (Winter 2010); "After the Postsecular," special issue, *American Literature* 86, no. 4 (Dec. 2014); "American Literatures / American Religions," special issue, *American Literary History* 26, no. 1 (2014). For edited collections: Harold K. Bush and Brian Yothers, eds., *Above the American Renaissance: David S. Reynolds and the Spiritual Imagination in American Literary Studies* (Amherst: University of Massachusetts Press, 2018); Mary McCartin Wearn, ed., *Nineteenth-Century American Women Write Religion: Lived Theologies and Literature* (Surrey, UK: Ashgate, 2014). For monographs: Dawn Coleman, *Preaching and the Rise of the American Novel* (Columbus: Ohio State University Press, 2013); Stokes, *Altar at Home*; Kevin Pelletier, *Apocalyptic Sentimentalism: Love and Fear in U.S. Antebellum Literature* (Athens: University of Georgia Press, 2015); Jared Winston Hickman, *Black Prometheus: Race and Radicalism in the Age of Atlantic Slavery* (New York: Oxford University Press, 2016).

While much of this scholarship has approached nineteenth-century religious life by examining the various forms of Protestantism that dominated both public discourse and private worship, many scholars have turned their attention to Catholicism—and anti-Catholicism—in the nineteenth-century United States. I discuss this work in my fourth chapter. Other important scholarship has brought greater critical attention to non-Christian religions in the nineteenth-century United States. Timothy Marr's *The Cultural Roots of American Islamicism* (New York: Cambridge University Press, 2006) examines figurations of Islam in the United States between the Revolution and the Civil War. Toni Wall Jaudon and Kelly Wisecup have brought obeah into view as a New World religion in Jaudon, "Obeah's Sensations: Rethinking Religion at the Transnational Turn," *American Literature* 84, no. 4 (2012): 715–41, http://dx.doi.org/10.1215/00029831-1901418; and in "Obeah: Knowledge, Power, and Writing in the Early Atlantic World," special issue, *Atlantic Studies* 12, no. 2 (2015). And Elizabeth Fenton, Jared Hickman, and Peter Coviello have dedicated serious attention to the Book of Mormon as a work of American literature. See Elizabeth Fenton, "Open Canons: Sacred History and American History in the Book of Mormon," *J19: The Journal of Nineteenth-Century Americanists* 1, no. 2 (2013): 339–61, http://doi.org/10.1353/jnc.2013.0036; Jared Hickman, "The Book of Mormon as Amerindian Apocalypse," *American Literature* 86, no. 3 (2014): 429–61, http://dx.doi.org/10.1215/00029831-2717371; and Peter M. Coviello, *Tomorrow's Parties: Sex and the Untimely in Nineteenth-Century America* (New York: New York University Press, 2013).

46. Coviello and Hickman, "Introduction," 647.

47. Nancy Glazener, *Reading for Realism: The History of a US Literary Institution, 1850–1910* (Durham, NC: Duke University Press, 1997), 18.

48. Jaudon, "Obeah's Sensations," 731.

49. Amy Hollywood, "Gender, Agency, and the Divine in Religious Historiography," *Journal of Religion* 84, no. 4 (2004): 523, http://doi.org/10.1086/422478.

50. Edward W. Said, *The World, the Text, and the Critic* (Cambridge, MA: Harvard University Press, 1983), 290, 5. Gil Anidjar has suggested that Said's *Orientalism* (1978), in which he exhaustively traced "the network of agencies, of Christian agencies, that produce and institutionalize the division between religious and secular," was the original work of secularism studies but that by the time Said published *The World, the Text, and the Critic*, he "forgot that he had written the book on" secularism. Gil Anidjar, "Secularism," *Critical Inquiry* 33, no. 1 (2006): 69, 66, http://doi.org/10.1086/509746.

51. See Elizabeth Maddock Dillon, *The Gender of Freedom: Fictions of Liberalism and the Literary Public Sphere* (Stanford, CA: Stanford University Press, 2004), 2.

52. Judith Butler, *Excitable Speech* (New York: Routledge, 1997), 26.

53. Saba Mahmood, "Women's Agency within Feminist Historiography," *Journal of Religion* 84, no. 4 (2004): 575, http://doi.org/10.1086/422481.

54. Saba Mahmood, "Agency, Performativity, and the Feminist Subject," in *Bodily Citations: Religion and Judith Butler*, ed. Ellen T. Armour and Susan M. St. Ville (New York: Columbia University Press, 2006), 180.

55. Jonathan Edwards, *A Careful and Strict Enquiry into the Modern Prevailing Notions of That Freedom of Will, Which is Supposed to Be Essential to Moral Agency, Virtue and Vice, Reward and Punishment, Praise and Blame* (Boston: reprinted for Thomas Field, 1762), 42.

56. 1 Corinthians 14:34; Genesis 9:25. All quotations from the Bible are from the King James Version.

57. Joan Wallach Scott, "Sexularism" (lecture, Robert Schuman Centre for Advanced Studies Distinguished Lectures, Florence, Italy, 2009), http://hdl.handle.net/1814/11553.

58. Linell E. Cady and Tracy Fessenden, "Gendering the Divide: Religion, the Secular, and the Politics of Sexual Difference," in *Religion, the Secular, and the Politics of Sexual Difference*, ed. Cady and Fessenden (New York: Columbia University Press, 2013), 8–9.

59. Scott, *Sex and Secularism*, 13. Also see Carol Pateman, *The Disorder of Women: Democracy, Feminism and Political Theory* (Stanford, CA: Stanford University Press, 1989).

60. Traister, *Female Piety*, 60.

61. Cady and Fessenden, "Gendering the Divide," 11.

62. William Ellery Channing, "On Catholicism," in *The Works of William Ellery Channing, Vol. II* (Boston: American Unitarian Association, 1903), 280.

63. Dillon, *Gender of Freedom*, 19.

64. Jakobsen and Pellegrini, "Introduction: Times Like These," 18.

65. Saba Mahmood, *Politics of Piety: The Islamic Revival and the Feminist Subject* (Princeton, NJ: Princeton University Press, 2005), xi; Cady and Fessenden, "Gendering the Divide," 3.

66. On "the modern," see Bruno Latour, *We Have Never Been Modern*, trans. Catherine Porter (Cambridge, MA: Harvard University Press, 1993); and *On the Modern Cult of the Factish Gods*, trans. Catherine Porter and Heather MacLean (Durham, NC: Duke University Press, 2010). On the "secular agent," see Asad, *Formations of the Secular*.

67. Emily Ogden, *Credulity: A Cultural History of US Mesmerism* (Chicago: University of Chicago Press, 2018), 17.

68. Ibid., 121.

1. "My Resolve Is the Feminine of My Father's Oath"

1. Quoted in Timothy Kenslea, *The Sedgwicks in Love: Courtship, Engagement, and Marriage in the Early Republic* (Boston: Northeastern University Press, 2006), 21.

2. For discussions of Pamela's Sedgwick's life and death, see Mary Kelley, "Introduction," in Catharine Maria Sedgwick, *The Power of Her Sympathy: The Autobiography and Journal of Catharine Maria Sedgwick*, ed. Mary Kelley (Boston: Massachusetts Historical Society, 1993), 12–15; and Kenslea, *Sedgwicks in Love*, 13–36.

3. Quoted in C. Sedgwick, *Power of Her Sympathy*, 66. For quotations from Sedgwick's autobiography, I refer to the definitive print edition found in *Power of Her Sympathy*. Except where noted otherwise, quotations from Sedgwick's letters are drawn from Mary Dewey, ed., *Life and Letters of Catharine M. Sedgwick* (New York: Harper & Brothers, 1871).

4. C. Sedgwick, *Power of Her Sympathy*, 58, 59.

5. Ibid., 63.

6. Stephen West, *The Scripture Doctrine of Atonement, Proposed to Careful Examination; By Stephen West, A.M. Pastor of the Church in Stockbridge* (New Haven, CT: Meigs, Bowen and Dana, 1785), 121–22.

7. William Ellery Channing, *Sermon Delivered at the Ordination of the Rev. Jared Sparks, to the Pastoral Care of the First Independent Church in Baltimore, May 5, 1819* (Boston: Wells and Lilly, 1819), 27.

8. Pateman, *Disorder of Women*, 4.

9. Dillon, *Gender of Freedom*, 11.

10. For comparative studies of Child and Sedgwick as early American authors of historical romance, see Sabina Matter-Seibel, "Native Americans, Women, and the Culture of Nationalism in Lydia Maria Child and Catharine Maria Sedgwick," in *Early America Re-explored: New Readings in Colonial, Early National, and Antebellum Culture*, ed. Klaus H. Schmidt and Fritz Fleischman (New York: Peter Lang, 2000), 411–40; Susanne Opfermann, "Lydia Maria Child, James Fenimore Cooper, and Catharine Maria Sedgwick: A Dialogue on Race, Culture, and Gender," in *Soft Canons: American Women Writers and Masculine Tradition*, ed. Karen L. Kilcup (Iowa City: University of Iowa Press, 1999), 27–47; Nancy F. Sweet, "Dissent and the Daughter in *A New England Tale* and *Hobomok*," *Legacy: A Journal of American Women Writers* 22, no. 2 (2005): 107–25, http://

www.jstor.org/stable/25679547; Ezra F. Tawil, "Domestic Frontier Romance, or How the Sentimental Heroine Became White," *Novel: A Forum on Fiction* 32, no. 1 (1998): 99–124, http://doi.org/10.2307/1346058; and Mark G. Vásquez, "'Your Sister Cannot Speak to You and Understand You as I Do': Native American Culture and Female Subjectivity in Lydia Maria Child and Catharine Maria Sedgwick," *American Transcendental Quarterly* 15, no. 3 (2001): 173–90.

11. Catharine Maria Sedgwick, letter to Theodore Sedgwick, April 1, 1804, reprinted in Dewey, *Life and Letters*, 80.

12. Catharine Maria Sedgwick, letter to Susan Channing, March 12, 1821, reprinted in Dewey, *Life and Letters*, 117.

13. Although Sedgwick's critics and biographers have generally made note of her changing religious commitments, they are more likely to characterize her as a popularizer of liberal Christianity than a perceptive participant in American religious discourse. This attitude marks the work of the Sedgwick biographers Edward Halsey Foster and Jane Giles and of the literary historian Carolyn Karcher. See Jane Giles, "Catharine Maria Sedgwick: An American Literary Biography" (PhD dissertation, City University of New York, 1984); Edward Halsey Foster, *Catharine Maria Sedgwick* (New York: Twayne, 1974); and Carolyn L. Karcher, "Introduction," in Catharine Maria Sedgwick, *Hope Leslie or, Early Times in the Massachusetts* (New York: Penguin Books, 1998), xv.

14. Carolyn L. Karcher, *The First Woman in the Republic: A Cultural Biography of Lydia Maria Child* (Durham, NC: Duke University Press, 1994), 7–8, 14.

15. Milton Meltzer and Patricia G. Holland, eds. *Lydia Maria Child: Selected Letters, 1817–1880* (Amherst: University of Massachusetts Press, 1982), 1–3.

16. On the history of Unitarianism in North America, see Conrad Wright, *The Liberal Christians: Essays on American Unitarian History* (Boston: Beacon, 1970); David Robinson, *The Unitarians and the Universalists* (Westport, CT: Greenwood, 1985); Jonathan S. Carey and Sydney E. Ahlstrom, *An American Reformation: A Documentary History of Unitarian Christianity* (Middletown, CT: Wesleyan University Press, 1985); and Andrea Greenwood and Mark W. Harris, *An Introduction to the Unitarian and Universalist Traditions* (Cambridge: Cambridge University Press, 2011).

17. Robinson, *Unitarians and the Universalists*, 10.

18. William Ellery Channing, "Unitarian Christianity Most Favorable to Piety: Discourse at the Dedication of the Second Congregational Unitarian Church, New York, 1826," in *The Works of William E. Channing, D.D.* (Boston: American Unitarian Association, 1875), 385.

19. Charles Buck, *Definitions of All Religious Terms* (Philadelphia: W. W. Woodward, 1821), 37.

20. West, *Scripture Doctrine of Atonement*, 121–22, emphasis in original.

21. Channing, *Sermon Delivered*, 33.

22. Channing, "Unitarian Christianity Most Favorable," 397.

23. For discussions of the political investments of women's historical novels, see Nina Baym, *American Women Writers and the Work of History, 1790–1860* (New Brunswick, NJ: Rutgers University Press, 1995); and Philip B. Gould, *Covenant and Republic: Historical Romance and the Politics of Puritanism* (New York: Cambridge University Press, 1996).

24. Page numbers for *Hobomok* are cited parenthetically in the text and refer to the following edition: Lydia Maria Child, *Hobomok and Other Writings on Indians*, ed. Carolyn L. Karcher (New Brunswick, NJ: Rutgers University Press, 1986).

25. Georg Lukács, *The Historical Novel*, trans. Hannah Mitchell and Stanley Mitchell (London: Merlin, 1962), 25.

26. Ibid., 33.

27. Ian Dennis, *Nationalism and Desire in Early Historical Fiction* (London: MacMillan, 1997), 17. See also Marta Kvande and Sara Spurgeon, "The Removes of Harriot Stuart: Charlotte Lennox and the Birth of the Western," in *Before the West Was West: Critical Essays on Pre-1800 Literature of the American Frontiers*, ed. Amy T. Hamilton and Tom J. Hillard (Lincoln: University of Nebraska Press, 2014), 213–38.

28. Ernest Erwin Leisy, *The American Historical Novel* (Norman: University of Oklahoma Press, 1950), 4.

29. Nina Baym, "The Women of Cooper's Leatherstocking Tales," *American Quarterly* 23, no. 5 (1971): 697–698, http://doi.org/10.2307/2712252. For discussion of Sedgwick and Cooper's relationship to one another as colleagues and sometime-competitors, see Patricia Larson Kalayjian, "Cooper and Sedgwick: Rivalry or Respect," *James Fenimore Cooper Society Miscellaney* 4 (1993): 9–19.

30. Accusations of cannibalism and human sacrifice, Mario Klarer writes, "originat[ed] in the texts of Columbus and Vespucci" and "serve[d] as a leitmotif in all major subsequent travel narratives, but also function[ed] as a seemingly irreconcilable counterpart to the Utopian setting of the continent." Mario Klarer, "Cannibalism and Carnivalesque: Incorporation as Utopia in the Early Image of America," *New Literary History* 30, no. 2 (1999): 390, http://www.jstor.org/stable/20057543. While there is little physical or ethnohistoric evidence of headhunting or cannibalism in precolonial North America, early European visitors to the continent spread rumors of cannibalism and headhunting to scare off competitors and keep their crews in check. See Joan A. Lovisek, "Human Trophy Taking on the Northwest Coast: An Ethnohistorical Perspective," in *The Taking and Displaying of Human Body Parts as Trophies by Amerindians*, ed. Richard J. Chacon and David H. Dye (New York: Springer, 2007), 49. While there is some evidence of human sacrifice among Mesoamerican tribes, anthropologists debate whether images of human sacrifice and trophy taking "are representations of mythic or actual historic events." Carrie Anne Berryman, "Captive Sacrifice and Trophy Taking among the Ancient Maya: An Evaluation of the Bioarchaeological Evidence and Its Sociopolitical Implications," in Chacon and Dye, *Taking and Displaying*, 377.

31. Quoted in Alexander Du Toit, "Who Are the Barbarians? Scottish Views of Conquest and Indians, and Robertson's 'History of America,'" *Scottish Studies Review* 26, no. 1 (1999): 36.

32. For discussions of the "four stages" model of civilizational development and its role in shaping the American historical novel, see Ronald Meek, *Social Science and the Ignoble Savage* (Cambridge: Cambridge University Press, 1976); and George Dekker, *The American Historical Romance* (Cambridge: Cambridge University Press, 1987).

33. Jean-Luc Nancy, "The Unsacrificeable," *Yale French Studies* 79 (1991): 26, http://doi.org/10.2307/2930245.

34. Ibid., 22–24.

35. "He was wounded for our transgressions, he was bruised for our iniquities: the chastisement of our peace was upon him; and with his stripes we are healed." On the myth of the vanishing Indian in early America, see Philip J. Deloria, *Playing Indian* (New Haven, CT: Yale University Press, 1998); Brian Dippie, *The Vanishing American: White*

Attitudes and U.S. Indian Policy (Middletown, CT: Wesleyan University Press, 1972); Richard Slotkin, *Regeneration through Violence: The Mythology of the American Frontier, 1600–1860* (Middletown, CT: Wesleyan University Press, 1973); and, more recently, Roxanne Dunbar-Ortiz and Dina Gilio-Whitaker, *"All the Real Indians Died Off" and 20 Other Myths about Native Americans* (Boston: Beacon, 2016); and Paul Jentz, *Seven Myths of Native American History* (Indianapolis: Hackett, 2018).

36. For a discussion of *Hobomok*'s intra-Protestant reconciliation and early nineteenth-century religious change, see Grant Shreve, "Fragile Belief: Lydia Maria Child's *Hobomok* and the Scene of American Secularity," *American Literature* 86, no. 4 (2014): 655–82, http://dx.doi.org/10.1215/00029831-2811742.

37. Page numbers for *Hope Leslie* are cited parenthetically in the text and refer to the following edition: Catharine Maria Sedgwick, *Hope Leslie, or Early Times in the Massachusetts*, ed. Carolyn. L. Karcher (New York: Penguin Books, 1998).

38. For discussion of the captivity motif in *Hope Leslie* and of the Sedgwick family's complicated relationship to New England Native Americans, see Karen Woods Weierman, "Reading and Writing *Hope Leslie*: Catharine Maria Sedgwick's Indian 'Connections,'" *New England Quarterly* 75, no. 3 (2002): 415–43, http://doi.org/10.2307/1559786. For an enumeration of the historical sources Sedgwick drew from in writing *Hope Leslie*, see R. D. Madison, "Sedgwick's Memorials: *Hope Leslie* and Colonial Historiography," *Literature in the Early American Republic* 4 (2012): 1–9. For discussions of *Hope Leslie* in the context of early national history writing, including historical fiction, see Amanda Emerson, "History, Memory, and the Echoes of Equivalence in Catharine Maria Sedgwick's *Hope Leslie*," *Legacy: A Journal of American Women Writers* 24, no. 1 (2007): 24–49, http://www.jstor.org/stable/25679590; Laurel V. Hankins, "The Voice of Nature: *Hope Leslie* and Early American Romanticism," *Legacy: A Journal of American Women Writers* 31, no. 2 (2014): 160–82, http://doi.org/10.2307/2927692; Jeffrey Insko, "Anachronistic Imaginings: *Hope Leslie*'s Challenge to Historicism," *American Literary History* 16, no. 2 (2004): 179–207, http://www.jstor.org/stable/3568071; Pratt, *Archives of American Time*, 98–117; and Amy Dunham Strand, "Interpositions: *Hope Leslie*, Women's Petitions, and Historical Fiction in Jacksonian America," *Studies in American Fiction* 32, no. 2 (2004): 131–64.

39. See Christopher Castiglia, *Bound and Determined: Captivity, Culture-Crossing and White Womanhood from Mary Rowlandson to Patty Hearst* (Chicago: University of Chicago Press, 1996), 173. Erica Burleigh likewise overestimates the possibilities for transformation that self-sacrifice entails, tracing in *Hope Leslie* "an ethic of interposition" that enables Sedgwick to "reimagin[e] what it means to be related to a human being." As I demonstrate in this chapter, self-sacrifice may create new relations between people, but these new relations continue to replicate existing structures of power. Erica Burleigh, "Sisters in Arms: Incest, Miscegenation, and Sacrifice in Catharine Maria Sedgwick's *Hope Leslie*," *New England Quarterly* 86, no. 2 (2013): 223, http://doi.org/10.1162/TNEQ_a_00276.

40. Maurice Bloch, *Political Language and Oratory in Traditional Society* (London: Academic, 1975), 15.

41. Webb Keane, "Language and Religion," in *Companion to Linguistic Anthropology*, ed. Alessandro Duranti (Malden, MA: Blackwell, 2004), 434.

42. Bloch, *Political Language*, 15.

43. Shirley Samuels reads the appearance of sacrifice in *Hope Leslie* and *Hobomok* as a substitute for discussions of contract in which women's bodies figure as both

property and the means of property's transmission through inheritance. But this reading imposes a transhistorical understanding of sacrifice onto these novels, overlooking the fact that sacrifice itself—its history, its participants, and its social function—is a primary point of contention in the texts. Shirley Samuels, "Women, Blood, and Contract," *American Literary History* 20, no. 1–2 (2007): 57–75, http://doi.org/10.1093/alh/ajm049. See also Andy Doolen, "Blood, Republicanism, and the Return of George Washington: A Response to Shirley Samuels," *American Literary History* 20, no. 1–2 (2007): 76–82, http://doi.org/10.1093/alh/ajm046.

44. In highlighting *Hope Leslie*'s critique of atonement theology, I am disagreeing with the critic Dan McKanan, who classes Sedgwick among a group of liberal authors who, in his view, affirmed atonement logic rather than undermining it. See Dan McKanan, *Identifying the Image of God: Radical Christians and Nonviolent Power in the Antebellum United States* (Oxford: Oxford University Press, 2002), 11–45.

45. Judith Fetterley, "'My Sister! My Sister!': The Rhetoric of Catharine Sedgwick's *Hope Leslie,*" *American Literature* 70, no. 3 (1998): 501, http://doi.org/10.2307/2902707. On the portrayal of natives in *Hope Leslie*, see Philip Gould, "Catharine Sedgwick's 'Recital' of the Pequot War," *American Literature* 66, no. 4 (1994): 641–62; Dana Luciano, "Voicing Removal: Mourning (as) History in *Hope Leslie,*" *Western Humanities Review* 58, no. 2 (2004): 48–67; Maureen Tuthill, "Land and the Narrative Site in Sedgwick's *Hope Leslie,*" *ATQ: 19th Century American Literature and Culture* 19, no. 2 (2005): 95–114; Gustávus Stadler, "Magawisca's Body of Knowledge: Nation-Building in *Hope Leslie,*" *Yale Journal of Criticism* 12, no. 1 (1999): 41–56, http://doi.org/10.1353/yale.1999.0012; and Sandra Zagarell, "Expanding 'America': Lydia Sigourney's *Sketch of Connecticut,* Catharine Sedgwick's *Hope Leslie,*" *Tulsa Studies in Women's Literature* 6, no. 2 (1987): 225–45, http://doi.org/10.2307/464270.

46. Channing, *Sermon Delivered,* 31.

47. Channing, "Unitarian Christianity Most Favorable," 385; and *Sermon Delivered,* 30–31.

48. William Ware, *Address, Delivered Nov. 24, 1825, on the Occasion of Laying the Foundation Stone of the Second Unitarian Church in New York, By the Rev. Wm. Ware, Pastor of the First Church* (Newcastle upon Tyne, UK: Newcastle Unitarian Tract Society, 1825), 2.

49. Catharine Maria Sedgwick, letter to Susan Channing, September 25, 1821, reprinted in Dewey, *Life and Letters,* 144.

50. Henry Ware Jr., *Discourses on the Offices and Character of Jesus Christ* (Boston: David Reed, 1826), 86.

51. Channing, *Sermon Delivered,* 33–34.

52. Page numbers for *The Linwoods* are cited parenthetically in the text and refer to the following edition: Catharine Maria Sedgwick, *The Linwoods, or "Sixty Years Since" in America,* ed. Maria Karafilis (Hanover, NH: University Press of New England, 2002).

53. Esther 3–9.

54. Keane, "Language and Religion," 431.

55. Bruno Latour, "'Thou Shall Not Freeze-Frame,' or How Not to Misunderstand the Science and Religion Debate," in *Science, Religion and the Human Experience,* ed. James D. Proctor (Oxford: Oxford University Press, 2005), 29–30.

56. Catharine Maria Sedgwick, "Slavery in New England," *Bentley's Miscellany* 34 (1853): 421–22.

57. For a discussion of the legal history of this and other cases that led to the abolition of slavery in Massachusetts, see Emily Blanck, "Seventeen Eighty-Three: The Turning Point in the Law of Slavery and Freedom in Massachusetts," *New England Quarterly* 75, no. 1 (2002): 24–51, http://doi.org/10.2307/1559880; and Arthur Zilversmit, "Quok Walker, Mumbet, and the Abolition of Slavery in Massachusetts," *Third Series* 25, no. 4 (1968): 614–24, http://doi.org/10.2307/1916801. Modern legal scholars generally agree that Freeman's case, while representing an important step in the eventual abolition of slavery in Massachusetts, was not immediately responsible for it.

58. Richard S. Briggs, *Words in Action: Speech Act Theory and Biblical Interpretation* (Edinburgh: T & T Clark, 2001), 150. Evans's concept of self-involvement is similar to Latour's concept of religious language in "'Thou Shall Not Freeze-Frame'": Latour's paradigmatic piece of religious language, "I love you," is a highly self-involving statement.

59. Michelle Z. Rosaldo, "Toward an Anthropology of Self and Feeling," in *Culture Theory: Essays on Mind, Self, and Emotion*, ed. Robert A. LeVine and Richard A. Shweder (New York: Cambridge University Press, 1984), 143.

60. In emphasizing the rejection of ritual forms in *The Linwoods*, I am obviously in conversation with the recent work of Michelle Sizemore, who has argued convincingly that the eruptions of popular sovereignty seen in the wake of the American Revolution are best categorized not as the working out of the people's rational deliberative will but as "ritual acts [that] invest participants and objects with sacred aura, . . . conjurings of the people as a transcendent principle or force." See Sizemore, *American Enchantment: Rituals of the People in the Post-Revolutionary World* (New York: Oxford University Press, 2018), 11. In historicizing the meaning of ritual within the particular context of theological debates between Trinitarians and Unitarians in the early nineteenth century, I am not contradicting Sizemore's argument so much as clarifying how the rejection of a particularly violent ritual—vicarious sacrifice for salvational means—could make way for the broader participation of women and people of color in the enchanted public sphere that she eloquently describes.

61. C. Sedgwick, "Slavery in New England," 421.

62. Scott, "Sexularism," 4.

63. Karen Woods Weierman, "'A Slave Story I Began and Abandoned': Sedgwick's Antislavery Manuscript," in *Catharine Maria Sedgwick: Critical Perspectives*, ed. Victoria Clements and Lucinda L. Damon-Bach (Boston: Northeastern University Press, 2003), 122–38; Catharine Maria Sedgwick, letter to James Parton, February 28, 1865[?], James Parton Correspondence and Other Papers, Houghton Library, Harvard University.

64. See H[enry] D. Sedgwick, *The Practicability of the Abolition of Slavery: A Lecture Delivered at the Lyceum in Stockbridge, Massachusetts February, 1831* (New York: J. Seymour, 1831), 16–18.

65. C. Sedgwick, "Slavery in New England," 421.

66. See Charlene Avallone, "Catharine Sedgwick's White Nation-Making: Historical Fiction and *The Linwoods*," *ESQ: A Journal of the American Renaissance* 55, no. 2 (2009): 97–133, http://doi.org/10.1353/esq.0.0028. For more discussion of *The Linwoods* as historical fiction, see Philip Gould, "Catharine Sedgwick's Cosmopolitan Nation," *New England Quarterly* 78, no. 2 (2005): 232–58, http://www.jstor.org/stable/30045525; and

Jeffrey Insko, "Passing Current: Electricity, Magnetism, and Historical Transmission in *The Linwoods*," *ESQ: A Journal of the American Renaissance* 56, no. 3 (2010): 293–326, http://muse.jhu.edu/article/409451.

67. Jenny Franchot, "Unseemly Commemoration: Religion, Fragments, and the Icon," in *Religion and Cultural Studies*, ed. Susan L. Mizruchi (Princeton, NJ: Princeton University Press, 2001), 44.

68. C. Sedgwick, *Power of Her Sympathy*, 69.

69. H. Sedgwick, *Practicability of the Abolition*, 18.

70. Joanna Brooks, *American Lazarus: Religion and the Rise of African-American and Native American Literatures* (Oxford: Oxford University Press, 2003), 46.

2. "Unsheathe the Sword of a Strong, Unbending Will"

1. Catharine Maria Sedgwick, *A New-England Tale; or, Sketches of New-England Character and Manners*, ed. Susan K. Harris (New York: Penguin Books, 2003), 4.

2. Catharine Maria Sedgwick, letter to Susan Channing, 1822, reprinted in Dewey, *Life and Letters*, 153–54.

3. C. Sedgwick, *New-England Tale*, 2.

4. George Willis Cooke, *Unitarianism in America: A History of its Origin and Development* (Boston American Unitarian Association, 1910), 107–8. For a detailed history of Christian publishing activities in the nineteenth century, see Candy Gunther Brown, *The Word in the World: Evangelical Writing, Publishing, and Reading in America, 1789–1880* (Chapel Hill: University of North Carolina Press, 2004).

5. Catharine Maria Sedgwick, *Mary Hollis. An Original Tale* (Concord, NH: Mead and Butters, 1834).

6. Henry Sedgwick, letter to Catharine Maria Sedgwick, May 25, 1822, reprinted in Dewey, *Life and Letters*, 153.

7. I am grateful to Melissa Homestead for her extensive scholarship on Sedgwick and for kindly providing me with copies of two unpublished conference papers on the relationship between *Mary Hollis* and *A New-England Tale* that helped guide my thinking as I wrote this chapter.

8. Nina Baym, *Woman's Fiction: A Guide to Novels by and about Women in America, 1820–1870* (Ithaca, NY: Cornell University Press, 1978), 11.

9. Sherry B. Ortner, "Theory in Anthropology since the Sixties," *Comparative Studies in Society and History* 26, no. 1 (1984): 152, http://www.jstor.org/stable/178524. I have found Ortner's discussion of practice orientations in anthropological studies to be beneficial for thinking about historical subjects, including women authors, as well.

10. Sentimental texts, to use June Howard's succinct formulation, concern themselves with "moment[s] when the discursive processes that construct emotion become visible." June Howard, "What Is Sentimentality?" *American Literary History* 11, no. 1 (1999): 76, http://dx.doi.org/10.1093/alh/11.1.63.

11. Marianne Noble, *The Masochistic Pleasures of Sentimental Literature* (Princeton, NJ: Princeton University Press, 2000), 6.

12. For discussions of nineteenth-century sentimental culture, see Philip Fisher, *Hard Facts: Setting and Form in the American Novel* (New York: Oxford University Press, 1985); Gillian Brown, *Domestic Individualism: Imagining Self in Nineteenth-Century America* (Berkeley: University of California Press, 1990); Shirley Samuels, ed., *The Culture*

of Sentiment: Race, Gender, and Sentimentality in Nineteenth-Century America (New York: Oxford University Press, 1992); Karen Sánchez-Eppler, *Touching Liberty: Abolition, Feminism, and the Politics of the Body* (Berkeley: University of California Press, 1993); Michelle Burnham, *Captivity and Sentiment: Cultural Exchange in American Literature, 1682–1861* (Hanover, NH: University Press of New England, 1997); Elizabeth Barnes, *States of Sympathy: Seduction and Democracy in the American Novel* (New York: Columbia University Press, 1997); Julie Ellison, *Cato's Tears and the Making of Anglo-American Emotion* (Chicago: University of Chicago Press, 1999); Mary Louise Kete, *Sentimental Collaborations: Mourning and Middle-Class Identity in Nineteenth-Century America* (Durham, NC: Duke University Press, 1999); Mary Chapman and Glenn Hendler, eds., *Sentimental Men: Masculinity and the Politics of Affect in American Culture* (Berkeley: University of California Press, 1999); Noble, *Masochistic Pleasures*; Lori Merish, *Sentimental Materialism: Gender, Commodity Culture, and Nineteenth-Century American Literature* (Durham, NC: Duke University Press, 2000); Glenn Hendler, *Public Sentiments: Structures of Feeling in Nineteenth-Century American Literature* (Chapel Hill: University of North Carolina Press, 2001); McKanan, *Identifying the Image*; Cindy Weinstein, *Family, Kinship, and Sympathy in Nineteenth-Century American Literature* (New York: Cambridge University Press, 2004); Berlant, *Female Complaint*; Elizabeth Barnes, *Love's Whipping Boy: Violence and Sentimentality in the American Imagination* (Chapel Hill: University of North Carolina Press, 2014); Stokes, *Altar at Home*; Pelletier, *Apocalyptic Sentimentalism*; Abram Van Engen, *Sympathetic Puritans: Calvinist Fellow Feeling in Early New England* (New York: Oxford University Press, 2015); and Harold K. Bush, *Continuing Bonds with the Dead: Parental Grief and Nineteenth-Century American Authors* (Tuscaloosa: University of Alabama Press, 2016). Given the immense critical literature devoted to sentimentalism and its cultural effects, this list is by no means comprehensive.

13. Sullivan, *Impossibility of Religious Freedom*, 7. For a discussion of "small-p protestantism," see the introduction to this book.

14. Noble, *Masochistic Pleasures*, 23.

15. Philip F. Gura, *Jonathan Edwards: America's Evangelical* (New York: Hill & Wang, 2005).

16. Stokes, *Altar at Home*, 3, 48–53.

17. Mary McCartin Wearn, "Introduction," in *Nineteenth-Century American Women Write Religion: Lived Theologies and Literature*, ed. Mary McCartin Wearn (Surrey, UK: Ashgate, 2014), 14.

18. Abram C. Van Engen, "Three Questions for American Literature and Religion," *Journal of American Studies* 51, no. 1 (2017): 218, http://doi.org/10.1017/S002187581600178X.

19. Mahmood, "Agency, Performativity," 184.

20. First published in 1678, *The Pilgrim's Progress*, as Gregory Jackson has noted, was the most significant homiletic text in circulation in the eighteenth- and nineteenth-century United States and "the most influential heuristic for helping readers not simply to profess but to live their faith." Jackson, *Word and Its Witness*, 104–5. See also Stokes, *Altar at Home*, 14–15.

21. Calvinism traces its roots to the early Reformed theologian John Calvin of Geneva; Arminianism is named for its first expounder, Calvin's sixteenth-century contemporary Jacobus Arminius (the Latinized name of Jakob Hermanszoon) of Leiden. The two theologies arose in opposition to one another; the Synod of Dort, called in

1618–1619 by the Dutch Reformed Church, affirmed predestinarian theology and specifically condemned the Arminian assertion that "God decreed to save all believers and that Christ died for all people, so that grace sufficient for faith was given to all." Holifield, *Theology in America*, 37.

22. Robert J. Wilson III, *The Benevolent Deity: Ebenezer Gay and the Rise of Rational Religion in New England, 1696–1787* (Philadelphia: University of Pennsylvania Press, 2015), xi–xii; John H. Wigger, *Taking Heaven by Storm: Methodism and the Rise of Popular Christianity in America* (New York: Oxford University Press, 1998), 3.

23. Page numbers for *The Wide, Wide World* and *Beulah* are cited parenthetically in the text and refer to the following editions: Susan Warner, *The Wide, Wide World*, ed. Jane Tompkins (New York: Feminist Press, 1987); Augusta Jane Evans, *Beulah*, ed. Elizabeth Fox-Genovese (Baton Rouge: Louisiana State University Press, 1992).

24. Proverbs 8:17; Genesis 17:7.

25. Baym, *Woman's Fiction*, xxiv.

26. Sharon Kim, "Puritan Realism: *The Wide, Wide World* and *Robinson Crusoe*," *American Literature* 75, no. 4 (2003): 256–88, http://dx.doi.org/10.1215/00029831-75-4-783. See also Sharon Kim, "Beyond the Men in Black: Jonathan Edwards and Nineteenth-Century Woman's Fiction," in *Jonathan Edwards at Home and Abroad: Historical Memories, Cultural Movements, Global Horizons*, ed. David William Kling and Douglas A. Sweeney (Columbia: University of South Carolina Press, 2003), 137–53.

27. Stokes, *Altar at Home*, 49–50.

28. For an example of a strong and intellectually gifted nineteenth-century woman struggling with Calvinist conversion theology for years before finally receiving evidence of election, see Kathryn Kish Sklar, *Catharine Beecher: A Study in American Domesticity* (New Haven, CT: Yale University Press, 1973), esp. 28–58.

29. Cynthia L. Lyerly, *Methodism and the Southern Mind, 1770–1810* (New York: Oxford University Press, 1998), 28.

30. Wigger, *Taking Heaven by Storm*, 16.

31. Ibid., 16; Lyerly, *Methodism*, 32. For a discussion of the struggle for Christian perfection as a sentimental theological trope, see Stokes, *Altar at Home*, 52–55.

32. Anna B. Warner, *Susan Warner ("Elizabeth Wetherell")* (New York: G. P. Putnam's Sons, 1909), 202. Further biographical information on Warner can be found in Edward Halsey Foster, *Susan and Anna Warner* (Boston: Twayne, 1978), and in Jane Tompkins's afterword to the Feminist Press edition of *The Wide, Wide World*.

33. On the differences between Old School and New School Presbyterians, see Sydney E. Ahlstrom, *A Religious History of the American People* (New Haven, CT: Yale University Press, 1972), 464.

34. Augusta Jane Evans, letter to Rachel Lyons, October 3, 1861, reprinted in Rebecca Grant Sexton, ed., *A Southern Woman of Letters: The Correspondence of Augusta Jane Evans Wilson* (Columbia: University of South Carolina Press, 2002), 37.

35. According to Sara Frear, Evans joined St. Francis Street Methodist Church in Mobile, Alabama, in 1848 along with her mother and father and remained a member there until her death in 1909. In a series of letters written (probably in 1858 and 1859) to her friend Walter Clopton Harriss, a Methodist minister, Evans described religious struggles that would inform her depiction of Beulah Benton. See Sarah S. Frear, "'You My Brother Will Be Glad with Me': The Letters of Augusta Jane Evans to Walter Clop-

ton Harriss, January 29, 1856, to October 29, 185[8?]," *Alabama Review* 60, no. 2 (2007): 111–41, http://doi.org/10.1353/ala.2007.0048.

36. "Art. II.—Arminianism and Grace," *Biblical Repertory and Princeton Review* (January 1856): 21, 44.

37. "Art. V.—The *Princeton Review* on Arminianism and Grace," *Methodist Quarterly Review* (April 1856): 8.

38. "English Wesleyanism," *Puritan Recorder* (September 5, 1850): 35–36.

39. Fideliter, "Calvinism versus Arminianism," *Zion's Herald and Wesleyan Journal* (October 30, 1850): 21.

40. William B. Sprague, *Letters on Practical Subjects to a Daughter*, 2nd ed (New York: John P. Haven, 1831), 142.

41. Holifield, *Theology in America*, 9–10.

42. "Art. II.," 28.

43. "Art. V.," 8.

44. Holifield, *Theology in America*, 9.

45. On the importance of adoption to nineteenth-century sentimental fiction, see Weinstein, *Family, Kinship, and Sympathy*; and Carol J. Singley, *Adopting America: Childhood, Kinship and National Identity in Literature* (Oxford: Oxford University Press, 2011).

46. Edwards, *Careful and Strict Enquiry*.

47. Gura, *Jonathan Edwards*, 193–194, emphasis in original.

48. Holifield, *Theology in America*, 348. For discussions of Edwards's doctrine of religious affections and its influence on nineteenth-century sentimentalism, see Douglas A. Sweeney, *Nathaniel Taylor, New Haven Theology, and the Legacy of Jonathan Edwards* (Oxford: Oxford University Press, 2003), 142; and Gura, *Jonathan Edwards*, 235.

49. *An Essay on the Freedom of Will in God and in Creatures* (London: Printed for J. Roberts, 1732), 8–9. This book was widely attributed to Isaac Watts, a respected English Puritan minister, hymnodist, and theologian. Edwards's preface to his *Careful and Strict Enquiry* expresses disbelief at this attribution, since he had trouble ascribing the Arminian doctrines outlined in the *Essay* to such an eminent Calvinist divine.

50. John Wesley, *The Question, What Is An Arminian? Answered. By a Lover of Free Grace* (London: G. Whitfield, City-Road, 1798), 6.

51. Francis Asbury was an itinerant English preacher who arrived in the colonies in 1771 after John Wesley called for missionaries to spread the gospel in North America. When American Methodism officially split from British Methodism at the "Christmas Conference" of 1784, Asbury became the first bishop of the new Methodist Episcopal Church. Ahlstrom, *Religious History*, 371–73.

52. A. Warner, *Susan Warner*, 249–50.

53. Quoted in Frear, "'You My Brother,'" 129, 131, 136.

54. Baym, *Woman's Fiction*, 180.

55. Stokes, *Altar at Home*, 132.

56. Nineteenth-century editions of *The Wide, Wide World* only hinted at John and Ellen's eventual marriage; Warner's final chapter, in which John and Ellen return to America as a married couple, arrived at the publishers too late to be included. I discuss it here because Warner's original ending reflects the novel's doctrinal intentions. See the "Note on the Text" in the Feminist Press edition of *The Wide, Wide World*, 8.

57. Noble, *Masochistic Pleasures*, 94–125.

58. Howard, "What Is Sentimentality?" 72.

59. Jones, *Tomorrow Is Another Day*, 90.

60. Isaiah 62:4.

61. Tracy Fessenden has described the literary-historical processes "by which religion disappears from critical inquiry by being dismissed as epiphenomenal." Fessenden, *Culture and Redemption*, 12.

62. Douglas, *Feminization of American Culture*. David Reynolds has noted that since many nineteenth-century writers subscribed to the liberal Protestant belief that "Calvinism [was] a repressive system which not only thwarted human effort but created a timid languor and listlessness," the effort to liberalize Calvinism through fiction could be considered heroic and full of masculine interest. David S. Reynolds, *Faith in Fiction: The Emergence of Religious Literature in America* (Cambridge, MA: Harvard University Press, 1981), 109.

63. Jane P. Tompkins, *Sensational Designs: The Cultural Work of American Fiction, 1790–1860* (New York: Oxford University Press, 1985), 151.

64. One reason the doctrinal diversity of woman's fiction has been difficult to recognize is that many of the most influential critical works on sentimental fiction have studied only women writers who were raised in Calvinist traditions (including Harriet Beecher Stowe, Emily Dickinson, and Elizabeth Stuart Phelps) so that what critics have termed a generally "Christian," "Protestant," or "evangelical" sentimental mode is more accurately labeled a specifically Calvinist form of the sentimental. See, as examples, Tompkins, *Sensational Designs*; Noble, *Masochistic Pleasures*; and Kete, *Sentimental Collaborations*.

65. *Religion in America* included among the "evangelicals" Episcopalians, Presbyterians, Congregationalists, Methodists, Baptists, Moravians, and Quakers. Among the "unevangelicals" it listed Unitarians, Universalists, Shakers, Mormons, Swedenborgians, Tunkers, and Rappists but also Deists, Atheists, Fourierists, Catholics, and Jews. See Robert Baird, *Religion in America; or, An Account of the Origin, Progress, Relation to the State, and Present Condition of the Evangelical Churches in the United States. With Notices of the Unevangelical Denominations*, American ed. (New York: Harper & Brothers, 1844). As Toni Wall Jaudon has noted in her work on Schaff and Baird's predecessor Hannah Adams, Adams's *Alphabetical Compendium of the Various Sects Which Have Appeared from the Beginning of the Christian Era to the Present Day* (1784) eschewed such value judgments and attempted, sometimes unsuccessfully, to treat all sects equally. See Jaudon, "The Compiler's Art: Hannah Adams, the *Dictionary of All Religions*, and the Religious World," *American Literary History* 26, no. 1 (2014): 28–41, http://doi.org/10.1093/alh/ajt061.

66. Linford D. Fisher, "Evangelicals and Unevangelicals: The Contested History of a Word, 1500–1950," *Religion and American Culture: A Journal of Interpretation* 26, no. 2 (2016): 187, https://doi.org/10.1525/rac.2016.26.2.184.

67. R. Laurence Moore, *Religious Outsiders and the Making of Americans* (New York: Oxford University Press, 1986), 5.

68. Randall Balmer, *Mine Eyes Have Seen the Glory: A Journey into the Evangelical Subculture in America* (Oxford: Oxford University Press, 1993).

69. Martin Marty, *Protestantism in the United States: Righteous Empire*, 2nd ed. (New York: Charles Scribner's Sons, 1986), vii. Despite increasing awareness among religious historians that it is difficult to define evangelicalism "transhistorically," media accounts

and popular histories continue to read backward from the current use of the term, projecting it anachronistically onto earlier eras. Frances FitzGerald's *The Evangelicals: The Struggle to Shape America* (New York: Simon & Schuster, 2017) is a recent example. See L. Fisher, "Evangelicals and Unevangelicals," 186.

70. Douglas, *Feminization of American Culture*, 28.

71. Tompkins, *Sensational Designs*, 156.

72. Douglas, *Feminization of American Culture*, 24.

73. Two examples will suffice. In an article about *Beulah* and *The Wide, Wide World*, Nina Baym classifies Warner's text as an antisentimental novel because the heroine strives to "perfor[m] herself to others as an intellectual, even a scholarly, being." Assuming the Douglas-Tompkins position that emotion and intellect are opposites, Baym posits that any text displaying clear intellectual ambitions must be "antisentimental." Nina Baym, "Women's Novels and Women's Minds: An Unsentimental View of Nineteenth-Century American Women's Fiction," *Novel: A Forum on Fiction* 31, no. 3 (1998): 337, 336, https://doi.org/10.2307/1346104. More recently, Dawn Coleman's work on *Uncle Tom's Cabin* accepts the Douglas-Tompkins association of the sentimental with a feminized evangelicalism and demonstrates how a text can become "unsentimental" by taking up theological problems. When the narrator of *Uncle Tom's Cabin* employs a sympathetic, feminine voice, Coleman identifies it as "evangelical"; when it assumes an intellectual, masculine voice, this new voice is "Calvinist." Coleman, *Preaching and the Rise*, 156–73.

74. Van Engen, *Sympathetic Puritans*; Van Engen, "Advertising the Domestic: Anne Bradstreet's Sentimental Poetics," *Legacy: A Journal of American Women Writers* 28, no. 1 (2011): 47–68, http://doi.org/10.5250/legacy.28.1.0047; and Van Engen, "Eliza's Disposition: Freedom, Pleasure, and Sentimental Fiction," *Early American Literature* 51, no. 2 (2016): 297–331, http://www.jstor.org/stable/43946749. Coleman, *Preaching and the Rise*; see also Coleman, "Spiritual Authority of Literature." Susanna Compton Underland, "Sacred Spaces, Secular Fictions: Nineteenth-Century American Domestic Literature" (PhD diss., University of Maryland, 2018); and Underland, "Sentimentalism and Secularism in *Pierre*," *Leviathan* 19, no. 3 (2017): 59–78, http://dx.doi.org/10.1353/lvn.2017.0035. Pelletier, *Apocalyptic Sentimentalism*. Fessenden, *Culture and Redemption*, esp. chaps. 5 and 7; see also Fessenden, "Gendering Religion," *Journal of Women's History* 14, no. 1 (2002): 163–69, http://doi.org/10.1353/jowh.2002.0017; and Fessenden, "Disappearances: Race, Religion, and the Progress Narrative of U.S. Feminism," in Jakobsen and Pellegrini, *Secularisms*, 139–61. Molly K. Robey, "Sacred Geographies: Religion and Race in Women's Holy Land Writings," *American Literature* 80, no. 3 (2008): 471–500, http://dx.doi.org/10.1215/00029831-2008-019; Robey, "Domesticating Palestine: Elizabeth Champney's *Three Vassar Girls in the Holy Land*," *Tulsa Studies in Women's Literature* 35, no. 2 (2016): 365–94, http://doi.org/10.1353/tsw.2016.0030; and Robey, "Excavating Ethiopia: Biblical Archaeology in Pauline Hopkins's *Of One Blood*," *Studies in American Fiction* 43, no. 2 (2016): 183–206, http://doi.org/10.1353/saf.2016.0009. Ashley C. Barnes, "The Word Made Exhibition: Protestant Reading Meets Catholic Worship in *Uncle Tom's Cabin* and *The Gates Ajar*," *Legacy: A Journal of American Women Writers* 29, no. 2 (2012): 179–200, http://doi.org/10.5250/legacy.29.2.0179. Randi Lynn Tanglen, "Reconfiguring Religion, Race, and the Female Body Politic in American Fiction by Women, 1859–1911" (PhD diss., University of Arizona, 2008). Claudia Stokes, "'Sinful Creature, Full of Weakness':

The Theology of Disability in Cummins's *The Lamplighter*," *Studies in American Fiction* 43, no. 2 (2016): 139–59, http://muse.jhu.edu/article/640076. Other important work on women's writing has centered on Catholicism's role in nineteenth-century literary culture. I address this scholarship in chapter 4.

75. Fessenden, *Culture and Redemption*, 94.

76. Mahmood, *Politics of Piety*, xi.

77. Leti Volpp, "Framing Cultural Difference: Immigrant Women and Discourses of Tradition," *differences: A Journal of Feminist Cultural Studies* 22, no. 1 (2011): 106, http://doi.org/10.1215/10407391-1218256.

78. Sara R. Farris, *In the Name of Women's Rights: The Rise of Femonationalism* (Durham, NC: Duke University Press, 2017). For discussions of Farris's work alongside Joan Scott's *Sex and Secularism*, see the *Immanent Frame* forum, "Sex, Secularism, and Femonationalism," https://tif.ssrc.org/category/exchanges/sex-secularism-femonationalism/.

79. Taylor, James E, "The New Atheists," *The Internet Encyclopedia of Philosophy*, accessed August 22, 2019, https://www.iep.utm.edu/n-atheis/#H8.

3. "I Have Sinned against God and Myself"

1. S. Warner, *Wide, Wide World*, 441.

2. Evans, *Beulah*, 318; *Essay on the Freedom of Will*, 8.

3. Page numbers for *Incidents* are cited parenthetically in the text and refer to the following edition: Harriet Jacobs, *Incidents in the Life of a Slave Girl, Written by Herself*, ed. Nell Irvin Painter (New York: Penguin Books, 2000).

4. On seduction, criminality, and slave personhood, see Saidiya V. Hartman, *Scenes of Subjection: Terror, Slavery, and Self-Making in Nineteenth-Century America* (New York: Oxford University Press, 1997), 79–112.

5. For a detailed analysis of theodicy as an aspect of African American Christian theology, see Christopher Z. Hobson, *The Mount of Vision: African-American Prophetic Tradition, 1800–1950* (Oxford: Oxford University Press, 2012), 45–76.

6. See Winifred Morgan, "Gender-Related Difference in the Slave Narratives of Harriet Jacobs and Frederick Douglass," *American Studies* 35, no. 2 (1994): 73–94, http://www.jstor.org/stable/40642688; and Hazel V. Carby, "'Hear My Voice, Ye Careless Daughters': Narratives of Slave and Free Women before Emancipation," in *Black Women's Intellectual Traditions: Speaking Their Minds*, ed. Kristin Waters and Carol B. Conaway (Hanover, NH: University Press of New England, 2007), 91–112.

7. For a discussion of the generic similarities between Jacobs's *Incidents* and a work of woman's fiction like *The Wide, Wide World*, see Weinstein, *Family, Kinship, and Sympathy*, 130–58. For analyses of Brown's *Clotel* as a work of woman's fiction, see Ann duCille, *The Coupling Convention: Sex, Text, and Tradition in Black Women's Fiction* (New York: Oxford University Press, 1993); and duCille, "Where in the World Is William Wells Brown? Thomas Jefferson, Sally Hemings, and the DNA of African-American Literary History," *American Literary History* 12, no. 3 (2000): 443–62, http://dx.doi.org/10.1093/alh/12.3.443.

8. William L. Andrews, *To Tell a Free Story: The First Century of Afro-American Autobiography, 1760–1865* (Urbana: University of Illinois Press, 1986), 7. See also Andrews, *Sisters of the Spirit: Three Black Women's Autobiographies of the Nineteenth Century* (Bloom-

ington: Indiana University Press, 1986); Kerry Sinanan, "The Slave Narrative and the Literature of Abolition," in *The Cambridge Companion to the African American Slave Narrative*, ed. Audrey A. Fisch (Cambridge: Cambridge University Press, 2007), 61–80; Yolanda Pierce, "Redeeming Bondage: The Captivity Narrative and the Spiritual Autobiography in the African American Slave Narrative Tradition," in Fisch, *Cambridge Companion*, 83–98; and Rosetta R. Haynes, *Radical Spiritual Motherhood: Autobiography and Empowerment in Nineteenth-Century African American Women* (Baton Rouge: Louisiana State University Press, 2011).

9. A few critics have noted Jacobs's debt to the spiritual autobiography; Margaret Lindgren, for instance, remarks that *Incidents* owes "some of [its] voice[e] to the sentimental novel, some to the slave narrative, some to the spiritual autobiography and some to the demands of the abolitionist movement." Lindgren, "Harriet Jacobs, Harriet Wilson, and the Redoubled Voice," *Obsidian II* 8, no. 1 (1993): 24, http://www.jstor.org/stable/44485362.

10. Ibid., 23; see also Elizabeth Fox-Genovese, "My Statue, My Self: Autobiographical Writings of Afro-American Women," in *The Private Self: Theory and Practice of Women's Autobiographical Writings*, ed. Shari Benstock (Chapel Hill: University of North Carolina Press, 1988), 63–89.

11. Nell Irvin Painter, "Introduction," in Harriet Jacobs, *Incidents in the Life of a Slave Girl, Written by Herself*, ed. Nell Irvin Painter (New York: Penguin, 2000), xi; Ann Taves, "Spiritual Purity and Sexual Shame: Religious Themes in the Writings of Harriet Jacobs," *Church History* 56, no. 1 (1987): 67, http://doi.org/10.2307/3165304.

12. Hartman, *Scenes of Subjection*, 53, 54.

13. Jean F. Yellin, "Text and Contexts of Harriet Jacobs' *Incidents in the Life of a Slave Girl: Written By Herself*," in *The Slave's Narrative*, ed. Charles T. Davis and Henry L. Gates Jr. (New York: Oxford University Press, 1985), 273.

14. Geoff Hamilton, *The Life and Undeath of Autonomy in American Literature* (Charlottesville: University of Virginia Press, 2013), 8–10.

15. Hartman, *Scenes of Subjection*, 112.

16. "And if it seem evil unto you to serve the Lord, choose you this day whom ye will serve; . . . but as for me and my house, we will serve the Lord." Joshua 24:15.

17. Mississippi Supreme Court ruling in *George v. State*, cited in Hartman, *Scenes of Subjection*, 96.

18. For the story of Paul's conversion on the road to Damascus, see Acts 26.

19. Virginia Lieson Brereton, *From Sin to Salvation: Stories of Women's Conversions, 1800 to the Present* (Bloomington: Indiana University Press, 1991), xii.

20. Andrews, *Sisters of the Spirit*, 11. In her study of nineteenth- and twentieth-century conversion narratives, Virginia Lieson Brereton lists a number of published "guides for would-be converts" that provided models and instruction for the Christian life and that came to shape the generic conventions of the spiritual autobiography. See Brereton, *From Sin to Salvation*, 10–11.

21. For the Calvinist, as I discussed in my last chapter, this realizing sense of grace would arrive as conviction of one's divine election. For the Arminian, it would be experienced as the acceptance of God's gift of forgiveness.

22. Brereton, *From Sin to Salvation*, 9, 4.

23. Jean Fagan Yellin's biography of Jacobs describes how Harriet spent the spring and summer of 1849 "read[ing] her way through the abolitionists' library" while her

brother, the reading room's official manager, was away lecturing for the antislavery cause. Though the advertisement that John S. Jacobs ran in the *North Star* in 1849 listed only ten works available at the reading room, there were likely many more options for visitors. See Jean Fagan Yellin, *Harriet Jacobs: A Life* (New York: Basic Civitas Books, 2004), 102–3; and Yellin, ed., *The Harriet Jacobs Family Papers* (Chapel Hill: University of North Carolina Press, 2008), 1:141. While I have been unable to locate any source listing texts available at the Rochester Anti-Slavery Office, Elizabeth McHenry asserts that African American literary societies and reading rooms often offered white-authored classical and literary texts in addition to abolitionist literature and that they usually subscribed to such periodicals as the *Colored American Magazine*, the *Liberator*, the *National Anti-Slavery Standard*, and, of course, Frederick Douglass's *North Star*. See Elizabeth McHenry, *Forgotten Readers: Recovering the Lost History of African American Literary Societies* (Durham, NC: Duke University Press, 2002).

My sense that Jacobs may have had access to spiritual autobiographies by Truth and Lee is an extrapolation from the fact that, of the few texts published by African American women before the Civil War, these had relatively large print runs. Jarena Lee published two editions of her narrative, one in 1836 and another in 1846 with additional material added. Sojourner Truth's narrative, dictated to Olive Gilbert, sold well enough that she was able to purchase a home for herself. Because I cannot positively state that Jacobs read these texts, I can make no claims for direct influence, but the form of the spiritual autobiography was pervasive in nineteenth-century Protestant culture, both black and white.

24. Page numbers for Lee's *Life and Religious Experience of Jarena Lee* are from the edition included in Andrews, *Sisters of the Spirit*, 25–48, and are cited parenthetically in the text.

25. John Wesley, *A Plain Account of Christian Perfection, as Believed and Taught by the Rev. Mr. John Wesley, from the Year 1725, to the Year 1777*, 5th ed. (London: printed by J. Paramore, at the Foundry, Moorfields, 1785), 28.

26. Sojourner Truth and Olive Gilbert, *Narrative of Sojourner Truth, a Northern Slave, Emancipated from Bodily Servitude by the State of New York, in 1828* (Boston: J. B. Yerrinton and Son, 1850), North American Slave Narratives Collection, https://docsouth.unc.edu/neh/truth50/truth50.html. Page numbers are cited parenthetically in the text.

27. Andrews, *Sisters of the Spirit*, 11.

28. Brereton, *From Sin to Salvation*, 9.

29. Jackson, *Word and Its Witness*, 122.

30. Erik Nielson, "'Go in De Wilderness': Evading the 'Eyes of Others' in the Slave Songs," *Western Journal of Black Studies* 35, no. 2 (2011): 110.

31. For a discussion of demonic imagery as a tool for encoding sexual abuse in *Incidents*, see Anne B. Dalton, "The Devil and the Virgin: Writing Sexual Abuse in *Incidents in the Life of a Slave Girl*," in *Violence, Silence, and Anger: Women's Writing as Transgression*, ed. Deirdre Lashgari (Charlottesville: University Press of Virginia, 1995), 38–61.

32. In 1667 the Virginia General Assembly, after witnessing several cases in which a slave's conversion had been used as an argument for manumission, enacted a law declaring that the "conferring of baptisme doth not alter the condition of the person as to his bondage or Freedome." For discussions of the law's passage, see Warren M. Billings, "The Cases of Fernando and Elizabeth Key: A Note on the Status of Blacks

in Seventeenth-Century Virginia," *William and Mary Quarterly* 30, no. 3 (1973): 467–74, http://doi.org/10.2307/1918485; and Billings, "The Law of Servants and Slaves in Seventeenth-Century Virginia," *Virginia Magazine of History and Biography* 99, no. 1 (1991): 45–62, http://www.jstor.org/stable/4249198. The full text of the law can be found at https://www.encyclopediavirginia.org/_An_act_declaring_that_baptisme_of_slaves_doth_not_exempt_them_from_bondage_1667.

33. As Jared Hickman has shown, the idea that slavery was antithetical to Christianity was not self-evident to most slaveholders, and defining slaveholding as antichristian was in fact an immense undertaking accomplished by black and white abolitionists over hundreds of years. Jared Hickman, "Globalization and the Gods, or the Political Theology of 'Race,'" *Early American Literature* 45, no. 1 (2010): 163, http://dx.doi.org/10.1353/eal.0.0090.

34. "Be sober, be vigilant; because your adversary the devil, as a roaring lion, walketh about, seeking whom he may devour." 1 Peter 5:8.

35. "God is no respecter of persons: But in every nation one who fears him, and works righteousness, is accepted with him" (Acts 10:34–35); "For He has made of one blood all the nations of the world to dwell on the face of the earth" (Acts 17:26); and "There is neither Jew nor Greek, neither slave nor free, male or female: for you are all one in Christ Jesus" (Galatians 3:28). See Denise Kimber Buell, *Why This New Race: Ethnic Reasoning in Early Christianity* (New York: Columbia University Press, 2005), 11.

36. George M. Fredrickson, *Racism: A Short History* (Princeton, NJ: Princeton University Press, 2002), 11.

37. Ibid., 17, 27.

38. The doctrine of Christian universalism—that Christ died for all people and that all souls are *eligible* for salvation—is not to be confused with the belief held by the Protestant denomination known as Universalists, which is the doctrine of universal salvation: that all souls eventually *will be* saved. On the Universalists, see Ahlstrom, *Religious History*, 481–83.

39. Galatians 3:28.

40. Genesis 9:20–27.

41. For a discussion of this process in the earliest years of the Virginia Colony, see George M. Fredrickson, *White Supremacy: A Comparative Study in American and South African History* (New York: Oxford University Press, 1981), 76–80.

42. For discussions of the theological valences of race and racism, see Fredrickson, *Racism: A Short History*; J. Kameron Carter, *Race: A Theological Account* (Oxford: Oxford University Press, 2008); Hickman, *Black Prometheus*; Hickman, "Globalization and the Gods"; Willie James Jennings, *The Christian Imagination: Theology and the Origins of Race* (New Haven, CT: Yale University Press, 2010); and Colin Kidd, *The Forging of Races: Race and Scripture in the Protestant-Atlantic World, 1600–2000* (New York: Cambridge University Press, 2006).

43. Denise Buell and Jared Hickman have warned that placing too much emphasis on the doctrine of Christian universalism when discussing race and racism can lead to simplistic assertions that Christianity, properly practiced, provides an easy antidote to racist oppression and violence. See D. Buell, *Why This New Race*, 10–13; and Hickman, "Globalization and the Gods," 162–63. Such assertions can then be used to diminish or dismiss what Jon Butler has called the "African spiritual holocaust"—the decimation of African religions that accompanied enslavement. See Jon Butler, *Awash in a Sea*,

129–63; and Albert J. Raboteau, *African American Religion* (New York: Oxford University Press, 1999). While I acknowledge these concerns, I discuss the doctrine of Christian universalism in this chapter because it provided the theological warrant for much nineteenth-century antislavery activism and writing, including Jacobs's *Incidents*.

44. Peter P. Hinks, ed., *David Walker's Appeal to the Coloured Citizens of the World* (University Park: Pennsylvania State University Press, 2000), 7.

45. Henry Brown and Charles Stearns, *Narrative of Henry Box Brown, Who Escaped from Slavery, Enclosed in a Box 3 Feet Long and 2 Wide* (Boston: Brown and Stearns, 1849), 16, North American Slave Narratives Collection, https://docsouth.unc.edu/neh/boxbrown/boxbrown.html. For a detailed discussion of the religious valences of Henry Brown's escaped-slave narrative, see Edward Blum, "Slaves, Slavery, and the Secular Age," in *Race and Secularism in America*, ed. Jonathon S. Kahn and Vincent W. Lloyd (New York: Columbia University Press, 2016), 77–98.

46. William Wells Brown, *Clotel, or The President's Daughter* (New York: Penguin, 2004), 112.

47. Harriet Beecher Stowe, *Uncle Tom's Cabin, or Life among the Lowly* (New York: W. W. Norton, 1994), 210.

48. *The New England Primer: To Which is Added, the Shorter Catechism of the Westminster Assembly of Divines* (Concord, NH: Rufus Merrill, 1850), 27, 28.

49. Hobson, *Mount of Vision*, 8.

50. Romans 3:23.

51. Morgan, "Gender-Related Difference," 75. When *Incidents* was recovered and authenticated in the 1970s, the text's early critics asserted that it was unique in its exposure of slavery's sexual horrors. See Hazel V. Carby, *Reconstructing Womanhood: The Emergence of the Afro-American Woman Novelist* (New York: Oxford University Press, 1987); and Jean Fagan Yellin, *Women and Sisters: The Antislavery Feminists in American Culture* (New Haven, CT: Yale University Press, 1989). But Franny Nudelman has argued that by the time Jacobs published *Incidents* "the sexual abuse of slave women . . . had been extensively publicized by the abolitionist writing of white women." See Nudelman, "Harriet Jacobs and the Sentimental Politics of Female Suffering," *ELH* 59, no. 4 (1992): 941, http://doi.org/10.2307/2873301; and Sánchez-Eppler, *Touching Liberty*. Black abolitionist men, too, decried slavery not only for its violence against themselves but for the horrors it perpetrated against their mothers, sisters, and wives; see Xiomara Santamarina, "Black Womanhood in North American Women's Slave Narratives," in Fisch, *Cambridge Companion*, 237.

52. Cindy Weinstein, "The Slave Narrative and Sentimental Literature," in Fisch, *Cambridge Companion*, 123.

53. Brereton, *From Sin to Salvation*, 29.

54. Thomas C. Parramore, "Covenant in Jerusalem," in *Nat Turner: A Slave Rebellion in History and Memory*, ed. Kenneth Greenberg (Oxford: Oxford University Press, 2003), 262n1.

55. Herbert Aptheker, "The Event," in Greenberg, *Nat Turner: A Slave Rebellion in History and Memory*, 47.

56. Andrews, *Sisters of the Spirit*, 14.

57. Philip F. Gura, *The Life of William Apess, Pequot* (Chapel Hill: University of North Carolina Press, 2015), 31–43.

58. Andrews, *Sisters of the Spirit*, 6–7.

59. Hobson, *Mount of Vision*, 31.

60. Painter, "Introduction," xii.

61. Frederick Douglass, *Narrative of the Life of Frederick Douglass, an American Slave, Written by Himself*, in *Frederick Douglass, Autobiographies*, ed. Henry Louis Gates Jr. (New York: Library of America, 1994), 17–18.

62. Ibid., 97.

63. Stephanie Li remarks that "the acclaim accorded to Douglass's 1845 *Narrative* has caused a troubling conflation between freedom and flight" that "reflects a significant male bias in discussions of slave resistance." See Stephanie Li, *Something Akin to Freedom: The Choice of Bondage in Narratives by African American Women* (Albany: State University of New York Press, 2010), 11. Harryette Mullen argues that Jacobs's narrative eschews the "rhetorical conflation of literacy, freedom, and manhood, which reinforces rather than challenges the symbolic emasculation of the male slave and the silencing of the female slave." Mullen, "Runaway Tongue: Resistant Orality in *Uncle Tom's Cabin, Our Nig, Incidents in the Life of a Slave Girl*, and *Beloved*," in Samuels, *Culture of Sentiment*, 250.

64. "For I was an hungred, and ye gave me meat: I was thirsty, and ye gave me drink: I was a stranger, and ye took me in: Naked, and ye clothed me: I was sick, and ye visited me: I was in prison, and ye came unto me." Douglass, *Narrative of the Life*, 40.

65. Ibid.

66. Douglass's second autobiography, *My Bondage and My Freedom* (1855), grants more narrative space and personal agency to the women who populated his early life. Douglass's mother, whose absence is conspicuous in the *Narrative*, appears in *Bondage* in a famous scene in which she defends her small son from a fellow servant and then gifts him a "sweet cake." Whereas the *Narrative* emphasizes the horror of Aunt Hester's beating, in *Bondage* the renamed Esther is beaten by her lecherous master for, like Jacobs, refusing to renounce an honest and virtuous sentiment. And in the story of Sophia Auld, *Bondage* again details the powerful effect that slaveholding had on her originally benign temperament but also dwells on her innate resistance and on the difficulty of her conversion to slaveholding. Though the facts of each anecdote are roughly the same, *Bondage* acknowledges these women's agency in their own lives. Frederick Douglass, *My Bondage and My Freedom*, in *Frederick Douglass, Autobiographies*, ed. Henry Louis Gates Jr. (New York: Library of America, 1996), 175, 222.

67. John Ernest, "Beyond Douglass and Jacobs," in Fisch, *Cambridge Companion*, 218–31.

68. Nat Turner and Thomas R. Gray, *The Confessions of Nat Turner, the Leader of the Late Insurrection in Southampton, VA* (Baltimore: Thomas R. Gray, 1831), 20, North American Slave Narratives Collection, https://docsouth.unc.edu/neh/turner/turner.html.

69. Ibid., 9.

70. Lydia Maria Child to Harriet Jacobs, August 13, 1860, reprinted in Yellin, *Harriet Jacobs Family Papers*, 277–78.

71. Walter Johnson, "On Agency," *Journal of Social History* 37, no. 1 (2003): 119, http://www.jstor.org/stable/3790316, emphasis in original.

72. Quoted in Parramore, "Covenant in Jerusalem," 74.

73. Haynes, *Radical Spiritual Motherhood*, 5.

74. Hartman, *Scenes of Subjection*, 66, 67.

75. Laura Donaldson, "The Breasts of Columbus: A Political Anatomy of Postcolonialism and Feminist Religious Discourse," in *Postcolonialism, Feminism, and Religious Discourse*, ed. Laura E. Donaldson and Kwok Pui-lan (New York: Routledge, 2002), 51.

76. Carla Kaplan, "Narrative Contracts and Emancipatory Readers: *Incidents in the Life of a Slave Girl*," *Yale Journal of Criticism* 6, no. 1 (1993): 104, 100.

77. Johnson, "On Agency," 115.

78. Isaiah 32:6, 9–11, 13.

79. Caleb Smith, "Harriet Jacobs among the Militants: Transformations in Abolition's Public Sphere, 1859–61," *American Literature* 84, no. 4 (2012): 748, http://dx.doi.org/10.1215/00029831-1901427.

4. "The Human Soul . . . Makes All Things Sacred"

1. Charles Beecher, *The Incarnation; or Pictures of the Virgin and Her Son* (New York: Harper & Brothers, 1849). Page numbers are cited parenthetically in the text.

2. Harriet Beecher Stowe, *The Minister's Wooing*, ed. Susan K. Harris (New York: Penguin Books, 1999). Page numbers are cited parenthetically in the text, in some cases with the abbreviation *MW* to avoid confusion with other primary sources.

3. Christopher Wilson has also argued for Stowe's "theological rationale for romance." But because Wilson reads romance as secular and theology as religious, he finds their juxtaposition in *The Minister's Wooing* to be "paradoxical." I demonstrate in this chapter that that "paradox" is an artifact produced by our secularized misreadings of Stowe's theological and social project. See Christopher P. Wilson, "Tempests and Teapots: Harriet Beecher Stowe's *The Minister's Wooing*," *New England Quarterly* 58, no. 4 (1985): 559, http://doi.org/10.2307/365561.

4. Jenny Franchot, *Roads to Rome: The Antebellum Protestant Encounter with Catholicism* (Berkeley: University of California Press, 1994), 251.

5. Jackson notes that literary critics who have failed to differentiate homiletic realism from high realism "have tended to dismiss the homiletic novel as romance or, worse, sentimentalism." By claiming an antisentimental genealogy for homiletic realism, Jackson works to cleanse authors like Stead and Sheldon of the taint of feminization. Jackson, *Word and Its Witness*, 6–10.

6. See Karen Halttunen, "Gothic Imagination and Social Reform: The Haunted Houses of Lyman Beecher, Henry Ward Beecher, and Harriet Beecher Stowe," in *New Essays on "Uncle Tom's Cabin,"* ed. Eric J. Sundquist (Cambridge: Cambridge University Press, 1986), 107–34.

7. Coleman, *Preaching and the Rise*, 156–73. As Coleman has noted, it is something of a critical truism to assert that writing novels was Stowe's form of preaching—one that goes back to the earliest reviews of *Uncle Tom's Cabin*. For discussions of Stowe's aspirations to the ministerial calling and the effect of those aspirations on her writing career, see John Gatta, "Calvinism Feminized: Divine Matriarchy in Harriet Beecher Stowe," *Connotations: A Journal for Critical Debate* 5 (1995): 147–66; Jacob Stratman, "Harriet Beecher Stowe's Preachers of the Swamp: *Dred* and the Jeremiad," *Christianity and Literature* 57, no. 3 (2008): 379–400, http://dx.doi.org/10.1177/014833310805700302; Joan Hedrick, "'Peaceable Fruits': The Ministry of Harriet Beecher Stowe," *American Quarterly* 40, no. 3 (1988): 307–32, http://doi.org/10.2307/2712953; Hedrick, *Harriet*

Beecher Stowe: A Life (New York: Oxford University Press, 1994); Anne Nichols, "Harriet Beecher Stowe's 'Woman in Sacred History': Biblical Criticism, Evolution, and the Maternal Ethic," *Religion and Literature* 47, no. 3 (2015): 57–75, http://www.jstor.org/stable/26377442; and Carla Rineer, "Stowe and Religious Iconography," in *Transatlantic Stowe: Harriet Beecher Stowe and European Culture*, ed. Denise Kohn, Sarah Meer, Emily B. Todd, and Joan D. Hedrick (Iowa City: University of Iowa Press, 2006), 187–207.

8. Charles Howell Foster, *The Rungless Ladder: Harriet Beecher Stowe and New England Puritanism* (Durham, NC: Duke University Press, 1954); Lawrence Buell, "Rival Romantic Interpretations of New England Puritanism: Hawthorne versus Stowe," *Texas Studies in Literature and Language* 25, no. 1 (1983): 77, http://www.jstor.org/stable/40754704. See also Lawrence Buell, *New England Literary Culture: From Revolution through Renaissance* (Cambridge: Cambridge University Press, 1986); and Lawrence Buell, "Calvinism Romanticized: Harriet Beecher Stowe, Samuel Hopkins, and *The Minister's Wooing*," *ESQ: A Journal of the American Renaissance* 24 (1978): 119–32.

9. Helen Petter Westra, "Confronting Antichrist: The Influence of Jonathan Edwards's Millennial Vision," in *The Stowe Debate: Rhetorical Strategies in "Uncle Tom's Cabin,"* ed. Mason I. Lowance Jr., Ellen E. Westbrook, and R. C. De Prospo (Amherst: University of Massachusetts Press, 1994), 141–58.

10. Mason I. Lowance Jr., "Biblical Typology and the Allegorical Mode: The Prophetic Strain," in Lowance, Westbrook, and De Prospo, *Stowe Debate*, 159; and Rineer, "Stowe and Religious Iconography," 199.

11. Halttunen, "Gothic Imagination"; Jeffrey Cass, "Harriet Beecher Stowe's Acts of Theological Terror: Conservatism in *Uncle Tom's Cabin*," *Selected Essays from the International Conference on Word and World of Discovery*, ed. Gerald Garmon (Carrollton: West Georgia College, 1992), 21–30; and Pelletier, *Apocalyptic Sentimentalism*, 23. I discuss the branch of Stowe criticism that addresses the theology of "salvific domesticity" later in this chapter; see the section titled "Stowe's Enchanted Materialities."

12. C. Wilson, "Tempests and Teapots," 558.

13. For examples see Gatta, "Calvinism Feminized"; and Susan K. Harris, "The Female Imaginary in Harriet Beecher Stowe's *The Minister's Wooing*," *New England Quarterly* 66, no. 2 (1993): 179–98, http://doi.org/10.2307/365843. For these critics, men's religion is articulate and intellectual, while women's religion is wordless and intuitive.

14. See, as examples, C. Foster, *Rungless Ladder*; and L. Buell, "Calvinism Romanticized." These and other scholars reduce Stowe's theology to a version of the Halfway Covenant agreed to by her Puritan ancestors, with the slight alteration that salvation is passed down matrilineally rather than patrilineally.

15. Wearn, "Introduction," 11.

16. Harriet Beecher Stowe, "New England Ministers," in *Stories, Sketches, and Studies* (Boston: Houghton, Mifflin, 1896), 218–33. Page numbers are cited parenthetically in the text.

17. Dorothy Z. Baker's scholarship suggests the possibility that Stowe may have found Sprague wanting because his work paled in comparison to the *Magnalia Christi Americana*. See Baker, "Puritan Providences in Stowe's *The Pearl of Orr's Island*: The Legacy of Cotton Mather," *Studies in American Fiction* 22, no. 1 (1994): 61–79, http://doi.org/10.1353/saf.1994.0002.

18. Holifield, *Theology in America*, 9.

19. John Locke, *A Letter concerning Toleration* (New York: Liberal Arts, 1950), 45, 46.

20. Peter Jauhiainen, "Samuel Hopkins and Hopkinsianism," in *After Jonathan Edwards: The Courses of the New England Theology*, ed. Oliver D. Crisp and Douglas A. Sweeney (New York: Oxford University Press, 2012), 114–15.

21. Holifield, *Theology in America*, 140.

22. Harriet Beecher Stowe, letter to Henry Ward Beecher and Eunice White Beecher, August 30, 1859, Beecher Family Papers (MS 71), Manuscripts and Archives, Yale University Library. Transcription courtesy of the E. Bruce Kirkham Collection, Harriet Beecher Stowe Center, Hartford, CT.

23. Harriet Beecher Stowe, letter to Martha Wetherill, December 13, 1860, Harriet Beecher Stowe Center, Hartford, CT. Transcription courtesy of the E. Bruce Kirkham Collection, Harriet Beecher Stowe Center, Hartford, CT.

24. Park, like Stowe herself, had grown up under the direct influence of the "New England Ministers" they both admired, but he was "by birth and training a Hopkinsian." Charles Phillips, "Edwards Amasa Park: The Last Edwardsian," in Crisp and Sweeney, *After Jonathan Edwards*, 153.

25. Harriet Beecher Stowe, letter to Henry Ward Beecher and Eunice White Beecher, August 30, 1859, Beecher Family Papers (MS 71), Manuscripts and Archives, Yale University Library. Transcription courtesy of the E. Bruce Kirkham Collection, Harriet Beecher Stowe Center, Hartford, CT. For an excellent and succinct discussion of the path of Edwardsean theology in the late eighteenth and early nineteenth centuries and of theological and gender politics at Andover Seminary in the 1850s, see Kimberly VanEsveld Adams, "Family Influences on *The Minister's Wooing* and *Oldtown Folks*: Henry Ward Beecher and Calvin Stowe," *Religion and Literature* 38, no. 4 (2006): 28–36, http://www.jstor.org/stable/40060037.

26. Harriet Beecher Stowe, letter to Martha Wetherill, December 13, 1860, Harriet Beecher Stowe Center, Hartford, CT. Transcription courtesy of the E. Bruce Kirkham Collection, Harriet Beecher Stowe Center, Hartford, CT. That Edwards Park should be the bugbear of *The Minister's Wooing* is somewhat surprising, since the novel is arguably the best exemplar of the "theology of the feelings" that Park had approvingly described in a famous 1850 sermon. See Edwards A. Park, *The Theology of the Intellect and of the Feelings: A Discourse Delivered Before the Convention of the Congregational Ministers of Massachusetts, in Brattle Street Meeting House, Boston, May 30, 1850* (Andover, MA: W. F. Draper, 1850).

27. Excerpts from Roxana's letter can be found in Charles Beecher, ed., *Autobiography, Correspondence, Etc. of Lyman Beecher, D.D.* (New York: Harper & Brothers, 1866), 83–86. For discussions of the letter in criticism of Stowe, see C. Foster, *Rungless Ladder*; and L. Buell, "Calvinism Romanticized."

28. Matthew 9:20.

29. Kaufmann, "Religious, the Secular," 612.

30. Derek R. Peterson and Darren R. Walhof, "Rethinking Religion," in *The Invention of Religion: Rethinking Belief in Politics and History*, ed. Derek R. Peterson and Darren R. Walhof (New Brunswick, NJ: Rutgers University Press, 2002), 2.

31. Hedrick, "'Peaceable Fruits,'" 320.

32. Tompkins, *Sensational Designs*, 125.

33. Hedrick, "'Peaceable Fruits,'" 317.

34. See Mary Kelley, "At War With Herself: Harriet Beecher Stowe as Woman in Conflict within the Home," *American Studies* 19, no. 2 (1978): 23–40, http://www.jstor

.org/stable/40641357; and Elizabeth Ammons, "Stowe's Dream of the Mother-Savior: *Uncle Tom's Cabin* and American Women Writers Before the 1920s," in Sundquist, *New Essays*, 155–95. Amy Kaplan, "Manifest Domesticity," *American Literature* 70, no. 3 (1998): 582, http://doi.org/10.2307/2902710. Molly Farrell has argued along similar lines in "Dying Instruction: Puritan Pedagogy in *Uncle Tom's Cabin*," *American Literature* 82, no. 2 (2010): 246, http://dx.doi.org/10.1215/00029831-2010-001.

35. Allison S. Curseen, "'Never Was Born [Again]': Grace, Blackness, and Harriet Beecher Stowe's Domestic Evangelicalism," in *Saving the World: Girlhood and Evangelicalism in Nineteenth-Century Literature*, ed. Allison Giffen and Robin L. Cadwallader (New York: Routledge, 2018), 75.

36. Rosemarie Thomson, "Benevolent Maternalism and Physically Disabled Figures: Dilemmas of Female Embodiment in Stowe, Davis, and Phelps," *American Literature* 68, no. 3 (1996): 555–61, http://doi.org/10.2307/2928244.

37. Merish, *Sentimental Materialism*, 5, 11, emphasis in original.

38. C. Wilson, "Tempests and Teapots," 577.

39. Lynn Wardley, "Relic, Fetish, Femmage: The Aesthetics of Sentiment in the Work of Stowe," *Yale Journal of Criticism* 5, no. 3 (1992): 170. Tracy Fessenden likewise traces Stowe's theology of the afterlife to both Catholic and West African (and later Afro-Christian) cosmologies. See Fessenden, *Culture and Redemption*, 132.

40. G. Brown, *Domestic Individualism*, 24.

41. C. Taylor, *Secular Age*, 28.

42. As I noted in the introduction, this is Molly McGarry's literal translation of Max Weber's term *Entzauberung*, usually translated as "disenchantment." See McGarry, *Ghosts of Futures Past*, 13.

43. Michael Gilmore has argued convincingly for Stowe's "sacramental aesthetic," as in *Uncle Tom's Cabin* she sought "to create a text of 'real presence' that would, as an *imitatio Dei*, bring to life the letters on the page." See Gilmore, "*Uncle Tom's Cabin* and the American Renaissance: The Sacramental Aesthetic of Harriet Beecher Stowe," in *The Cambridge Companion to Harriet Beecher Stowe*, ed. Cindy Weinstein (Cambridge: Cambridge University Press, 2004), 64. Also writing of *Uncle Tom's Cabin*, Ashley Barnes has argued that material objects—both those that appear in the novel, like Little Eva's lock of hair, and those the novel inspired, such as postcards and even "Tom shows"—are the signs of Stowe's "exhibitional style," which sought to "balanc[e] the appeals of Catholic and Protestant faith." A. Barnes, "Word Made Exhibition," 179.

44. Maura E. Shea has argued that the true preachers in Stowe's New England novels are her numerous spinsters who, "although marginalized and comical, effectively embody a successful ministry." See Shea, "Spinning toward Salvation: The Ministry of Spinsters in Harriet Beecher Stowe," *American Transcendental Quarterly* 10, no. 4 (1996): 293.

45. For discussions of Miss Prissy as an artist and agent of narrative propulsion, see Christiane E. Farnan, "The 'Least Drop of Oil': Locating Narrative Authority in Harriet Beecher Stowe's *The Minister's Wooing*," in *Beyond "Uncle Tom's Cabin": Essays on the Writing of Harriet Beecher Stowe*, ed. Sylvia Mayer and Monika Mueller (Madison, WI: Fairleigh Dickinson, 2011), 95–107; and Nancy Lusignan Schultz, "The Artist's Craftiness: Miss Prissy in *The Minister's Wooing*," *Studies in American Fiction* 20, no. 1 (1992): 33–44, http://dx.doi.org/10.1353/saf.1992.0022.

46. See John 17:14–16; John 15:19.

47. Stokes, *Altar at Home*, 125.

48. Wendy Gamber, *The Female Economy: The Millinery and Dressmaking Trades, 1860–1930* (Urbana: University of Illinois Press, 1997), 10.

49. Ibid., 14.

50. These scenes have frequently been read as Stowe's conservative retreat from debates about "wage slavery" and factory conditions that by 1859 were deeply entwined with antislavery agitation. See, most recently, Gretchen Murphy, "States of Innocence: Stowe, London Needlewomen, and the New England Novel," *Legacy: A Journal of American Women Writers* 34, no. 2 (2017): 278–300, http://muse.jhu.edu/article/679781.

51. Modern, *Secularism in Antebellum America*, 18.

52. Asad, *Genealogies of Religion*, 49.

53. C. Taylor, *Secular Age*, 28.

54. Harriet Beecher Stowe, letter to Calvin Stowe, January 16, 1860, reprinted in Charles Edward Stowe, ed., *The Life of Harriet Beecher Stowe, Compiled from Her Letters and Journals* (Boston: Houghton, Mifflin, 1889), 351.

55. Harriet Beecher Stowe, *Agnes of Sorrento* (New York: AMS, 1967). Page numbers are cited parenthetically in the text.

56. Susan M. Griffin, *Anti-Catholicism and Nineteenth-Century Fiction* (Cambridge: Cambridge University Press, 2004); Elizabeth Fenton, *Religious Liberties: Anti-Catholicism and Liberal Democracy in Nineteenth-Century U.S. Literature and Culture* (Oxford: Oxford University Press, 2011); Marie Anne Pagliarini, "The Pure American Woman and the Wicked Catholic Priest: An Analysis of Anti-Catholic Literature in Antebellum America," *Religion and American Culture: A Journal of Interpretation* 9, no. 1 (1999): 97–128, http://doi.org/10.2307/1123928.

57. Franchot, *Roads to Rome*, 248. For discussions of Stowe's relationship with Roman Catholicism and its appearances in her fiction, see Gilmore, "American Renaissance"; A. Barnes, "Word Made Exhibition"; Kimberly VanEsveld Adams, "From Stabat Pater to Prophetic Virgin: Harriet Beecher Stowe's Recovery of the Madonna-Figure," *Religion and the Arts* 13, no. 1 (2009): 81–121, http://doi.org/10.1163/156852908X388340; John Gatta, "The Anglican Aspect of Harriet Beecher Stowe," *New England Quarterly* 73, no. 3 (2000): 412–33, http://doi.org/10.2307/366685; Gatta, "Calvinism Feminized"; Anthony E. Szczesiul, "The Canonization of Tom and Eva: Catholic Hagiography and *Uncle Tom's Cabin*," *American Transcendental Quarterly* 10, no. 1 (1996): 59–72; Nichols, "'Woman in Sacred History'"; Rineer, "Stowe and Religious Iconography"; Brigitte Bailey, "Religious Icons, National Iconography, and Female Bodies in Hawthorne and Stowe," in *Religion in America: European and American Perspectives*, ed. Derek Rubin and Hans Krabbendam (Amsterdam: VU University Press, 2004), 69–79; and Gail K. Smith, "Art and the Body in *Agnes of Sorrento*," in Kohn et al., *Transatlantic Stowe*, 167–86.

58. This bond also transcends the earthly schism of the Protestant Reformation, as *Agnes of Sorrento* rewrites Roman Catholic history as a proto-Protestant genealogy for the American church. See Franchot, *Roads to Rome*, 247–55; and Bailey, "Religious Icons, National Iconography."

59. For a discussion of other texts in which Stowe invokes the Catholic doctrine of saintly intercession, see Szczesiul, "Canonization of Tom and Eva."

60. Tracy Fessenden, "The Convent, the Brothel, and the Protestant Woman's Sphere," *Signs* 25, no. 2 (2000): 460–61, http://dx.doi.org/10.1086/495447.

61. Nancy Lusignan Schultz, "Introduction: A Veil of Fear," in *Veil of Fear: Nineteenth-Century Convent Tales by Rebecca Reed and Maria Monk* (West Lafayette, IN: Purdue University Press, 1999), xix.

62. Pagliarini, "Pure American Woman," 99.

63. In addition to Fessenden, Pagliarini, and Schultz, further discussion of the convent captivity narrative can be found in Ray Allen Billington, *The Protestant Crusade, 1800–1860: A Study of the Origins of American Nativism* (Chicago: Quadrangle Books, 1938), 99–108; Franchot, *Roads to Rome*, 135–61; Griffin, *Anti-Catholicism*; Griffin, "Women, Anti-Catholicism"; James Lewis, "'Mind-Forged Manacles': Anti-Catholic Convent Narratives in the Context of the American Captivity Tradition," *Mid-America Review* 72, no. 3 (1990): 149–67; and Reynolds, *Faith in Fiction*, 181–87.

64. As Nancy F. Sweet has elaborated, there are exceptions to this rule, including Josephine Bunkley's first-person narrative of leaving a Catholic convent, *Miss Bunkley's Book* (1855). See Sweet, "Renegade Religious: Performativity, Female Identity, and the Antebellum Convent-Escape Narrative," in Wearn, *Nineteenth-Century American Women Write Religion*, 15–32.

65. Joseph Helminski, Neil Meyer, and Peter Gardella find similar hints of the convent captivity narrative—and its inversion—in *The Minister's Wooing*. See Helminski, "Harriet Beecher Stowe's Marianettes: Reconstruction of Womanhood in *The Minister's Wooing* and *Agnes of Sorrento*," in Mayer and Mueller, *Beyond "Uncle Tom's Cabin,"* 169–88; Meyer, "One Language in Prayer: Evangelicalism, Anti-Catholicism, and Harriet Beecher Stowe's *The Minister's Wooing*," *New England Quarterly* 85, no. 3 (2012): 468–90, http://www.jstor.org/stable/23251388; and Gardella, *Innocent Ecstasy: How Christianity Gave America an Ethic of Sexual Pleasure* (New York: Oxford University Press, 2016), 29–30.

66. Matthew 4:1–11; Luke 4:1–13.

67. Franchot, *Roads to Rome*, 252.

68. According to staff at the Harriet Beecher Stowe Center in Hartford, Connecticut, Stowe owned at least six paintings depicting the Madonna and child or the Holy Family, two of which were copies of paintings by Raphael.

69. Adams, "From Stabat Pater," 82, 81.

70. Gatta, "Calvinism Feminized," 148. See also Gatta, *American Madonna: Images of the Divine Woman in Literary Culture* (New York: Oxford University Press, 1997); and Gatta, "Anglican Aspect."

71. Elizabeth Hayes Alvarez, *The Valiant Woman: The Virgin Mary in Nineteenth Century American Culture* (Chapel Hill: University of North Carolina Press, 2016), 5.

72. Jackson, *Word and Its Witness*, 27–30.

73. David Morgan, *Protestants and Pictures: Religion, Visual Culture, and the Age of American Mass Production* (New York: Oxford University Press, 1999), 6.

74. Thomas Weld, *A Short Story of the Rise, Reign, and Ruin of the Antinomians* (London, 1644), [8–9]. See Jonathan Edwards, *Some Thoughts Concerning the Present Revival of Religion in New-England* (Boston, 1742). For discussions of Sarah Pierrepont as a model for *The Minister's Wooing*'s fictional Mary Scudder, see Gatta, "Calvinism Feminized"; and Hedrick, "'Peaceable Fruits.'"

75. John Bunyan, *The Pilgrim's Progress* (Mineola, NY: Dover, 2003), 206. For a discussion of the early Protestant rejection of both visual iconography and the divine feminine, see Rineer, "Stowe and Religious Iconography."

76. Scott, "Sexularism," 2.

77. G. Smith, "Art and the Body," 169.

78. Luke 1:35, 38.

79. Luke 2:19.

80. Howard, "What Is Sentimentality?" 77.

81. John Donne, "Of the Progress of the Soule. The Second Anniversary," in *John Donne: The Major Works* (Oxford: Oxford University Press, 1990), 218–31.

82. Jenny Franchot reads Mary's pondering of the shipwrecked painting as an act of cultural and ethnic appropriation. See Franchot, "Unseemly Commemoration."

5. "I Have No Disbelief"

1. Harriet Beecher Stowe, letter to Elizabeth Barrett Browning, November 20, 1860, Harry Ransom Center, University of Texas at Austin. Transcription courtesy of the E. Bruce Kirkham Collection, Harriet Beecher Stowe Center, Hartford, CT.

2. Harriet Beecher Stowe, letter to Calvin Stowe, January 16, 1860, reprinted in C. E. Stowe, *Life of Harriet Beecher Stowe*, 349–51.

3. McGarry, *Ghosts of Futures Past*, 2.

4. For thorough treatments of Spiritualism in the nineteenth-century United States, see Ann Braude, *Radical Spirits: Spiritualism and Women's Rights in Nineteenth-Century America* (Boston: Beacon, 1989); Bret E. Carroll, *Spiritualism in Antebellum America* (Bloomington: Indiana University Press, 1997); Robert S. Cox, *Body and Soul: A Sympathetic History of American Spiritualism* (Charlottesville: University of Virginia Press, 2003); McGarry, *Ghosts of Futures Past*; and Cathy Gutierrez, *Plato's Ghost: Spiritualism in the American Renaissance* (New York: Oxford University Press, 2009). For primary source documents related to Spiritualism and other occult movements in Europe and the United States during the long nineteenth century, see Shane McCorristine, ed., *Spiritualism, Mesmerism, and the Occult, 1800–1920* (London: Pickering & Chatto, 2012).

5. McCorristine, *Spiritualism, Mesmerism*, xvii.

6. Howard Kerr, *Mediums, and Spirit-Rappers, and Roaring Radicals: Spiritualism and American Literature, 1850–1900* (Urbana: University of Illinois Press, 1972), 4.

7. Recent treatments of Spiritualist fiction have begun to remedy Kerr's oversight. See Bridget Bennett, *Transatlantic Spiritualism and Nineteenth-Century American Literature* (New York: Palgrave Macmillan, 2007); John Kucich, *Ghostly Communion: Cross-Cultural Spiritualism in Nineteenth-Century American Literature* (Hanover, NH: Dartmouth College Press, 2004); and Mitzi Schrag, "Rei(g)ning Mediums: Spiritualism and Social Controls in Nineteenth-Century American Literature" (PhD diss., University of Washington, 2006). While these texts complicate Kerr's work, to my knowledge there has been no comprehensive revision of his claims about American Spiritualist fiction.

8. See Braude, *Radical Spirits*, for a thorough treatment of the relationship between abolitionism, Spiritualism, and the women's rights movement in antebellum America.

9. C. Taylor, *Secular Age*, 299.

10. Modern, *Secularism in Antebellum America*, xxix.

11. Elizabeth Stoddard, *The Morgesons* (New York: Carleton, 1862). The authoritative scholarly edition of *The Morgesons*, edited by Lawrence Buell and Sandra Zagarell, reprints the revised text of the novel that Stoddard's publishers issued in 1889. See Elizabeth Stoddard, *The Morgesons and Other Writings, Published and Unpublished*, ed. Lawrence Buell and Sandra Zagarell (Philadelphia: University of Pennsylvania Press, 1984). Because I seek to demonstrate how *The Morgesons* reflects the changing religious atmosphere of midcentury New England—particularly the rise of Spiritualist practice—I draw on the 1862 Carleton edition. All quotations from the novel refer to that edition and are cited parenthetically in the text.

12. For examples of these secularized readings, see Lawrence Buell, *New England Literary Culture: From Revolution through Renaissance* (Cambridge: Cambridge University Press, 1986), 364–65; and Sandra Zagarell, "The Repossession of a Heritage: Elizabeth Stoddard's *The Morgesons*," *Studies in American Fiction* 13, no. 1 (1985): 45–56, http://doi.org/10.1353/saf.1985.0014.

13. Ann Braude, "Women's History *Is* American Religious History," in *Retelling U.S. Religious History*, ed. Thomas A. Tweed (Berkeley: University of California Press, 1997), 93.

14. Fessenden, *Culture and Redemption*, 3.

15. Very few critics have examined the intimations of Spiritualist and other occult religiosity that permeate *The Morgesons*, but for discussions of witchcraft in the novel, see Christopher Felker, *Reinventing Cotton Mather in the American Renaissance: Magnalia Christi Americana in Hawthorne, Stowe, and Stoddard* (Boston: Northeastern University Press, 1994), 202–27; and Michelle Ann Abate, "The 'Possessed' Reassessed: Elizabeth Stoddard's *The Morgesons*, the Salem Witchcraft Hysteria and Literary (Anti)nationalism," *American Transcendental Quarterly* 21, no. 1 (2007): 47–65.

16. The question of literary genre has perplexed Stoddard's critics since her novel's recovery in the 1970s. Ellen Weinauer and Robert McClure Smith remark that Stoddard has been "variously identified as a domestic novelist, an antisentimentalist, a local-color precursor of realism, a Brontë-inspired gothicist, a provincial gothicist, and a proto-modernist." Ellen Weinauer and Robert McClure Smith, "Introduction: Crossing Can(n)on Street," in *American Culture, Canons, and the Case of Elizabeth Stoddard*, ed. Robert McClure Smith and Ellen Weinauer (Tuscaloosa: University of Alabama Press, 2003), 6–7. For critical discussions of the perplexing generic properties of *The Morgesons*, see Julia Stern, "'I Am Cruel Hungry': Dramas of Twisted Appetite and Rejected Identification in Elizabeth Stoddard's *The Morgesons*," in Smith and Weinauer, *American Culture*, 107–27; Elizabeth Stockton, "'A Crusade against Duty': Property, Self-Possession, and the Law in the Novels of Elizabeth Stoddard," *New England Quarterly* 79, no. 3 (2006): 413–38, http://www.jstor.org/stable/20474465; and Christopher Hager, "Hunger for the Literal: Writing and Industrial Change in Elizabeth Stoddard's *The Morgesons*," *American Literature* 77, no. 4 (2005): 699–728, http://dx.doi.org/10.1215/00029831-77-4-699.

17. See Kerr (who reports this as fact), *Mediums, and Spirit-Rappers*, 66. Quoted in Cox, *Body and Soul*, 3.

18. See Bayard Taylor, "Confessions of a Medium," *Atlantic Monthly* 6, no. 38 (1860), 699–715; B. Taylor, "The Haunted Shanty," *Atlantic Monthly* 8, no. 45 (1861), 57–72; and B. Taylor, "The Experiences of the A.C." *Atlantic Monthly* 9, no. 52 (1862), 170–88.

19. Richard Baxter, *The Saints' Everlasting Rest*, ed. Benjamin Fawcett (1658; repr., Boston: Lincoln and Edmands, 1828); "Uncle Richard," *Northern Regions, Or, Uncle Richard's Relation of Captain Parry's Voyages for the Discovery of a North-west Passage: And Franklin's and Cochrane's Overland Journeys to Other Parts of the World* (New York: O. A. Roorbach, 1827).

20. The Spiritualist medium and trance lecturer Cora Hatch was particularly famous for her clairvoyant conversations with Franklin, including her ability to accurately describe Arctic landscapes she had never visited. See Amy Lehman, *Victorian Women and the Theatre of Trance: Mediums, Spiritualists and Mesmerists in Performance* (Jefferson, NC: McFarland, 2009), 104–5.

21. Laurence Sterne, *A Sentimental Journey and Other Writings* (New York: Oxford University Press, 2003).

22. For a discussion of the legal and social implications of the term *possession* in Stoddard's novel, see Stockton, "'Crusade against Duty.'"

23. Cox, *Body and Soul*, 17–19.

24. Felker, *Reinventing Cotton Mather*, 216.

25. Jennifer Putzi recognizes Cassandra's scars as a sign of her sexual agency; see Putzi, "'Tattooed Still': The Inscription of Female Agency in Elizabeth Stoddard's *The Morgesons*," *Legacy: A Journal of American Women Writers* 17, no. 2 (2000), 168, http://www.jstor.org/stable/25679335.

26. Until the mid-nineteenth century many Protestant churches charged pew rental fees that supported the activities of the church. Wealthy families got the best seats in the house, in front near the pulpit, while those who could not afford the fees sat at the back or in the balcony, in the "poor seats."

27. See Jennifer Putzi and Elizabeth Stockton, eds., *Selected Letters of Elizabeth Stoddard* (Iowa City: University of Iowa Press, 2012), 21n3, 109n6, 236.

28. The planchette is a "piece of wood, heart-shaped and mounted on two castors, with a pencil fixed point downwards in place of a third castor. When a hand is placed on the wood, the pencil moves, and is alleged to write messages from spirits." *The Hutchinson Dictionary of World Religions* (Abingdon, UK: Helicon Publishing and RM Education, 2005), 443.

29. Elizabeth Stoddard, "Preface to the 1901 Edition," in *The Morgesons*, ed. Sandra Zagarell and Lawrence Buell (New York: Penguin Books, 1997), 262–64.

30. Like Stoddard, Stowe made this statement late in life; the earliest occurrences of it in print appear in the 1880s, and the story was widely circulated after her death. See Florine Thayer McCray, *The Life-Work of the Author of Uncle Tom's Cabin* (New York: Funk & Wagnalls, 1889).

31. Emma Hardinge Britten, *Modern American Spiritualism: A Twenty Years' Record of the Communion Between Earth and the World of Spirits*, 2nd ed. (New York: New-York Print, 1870).

32. [A. T. Tracy], "Spiritual Materialism," *Putnam's Monthly Magazine of American Literature, Science, and Art*, August 1854, 160. Like most pieces in *Putnam's*, "Spiritual Materialism" was printed without attribution, but according to *Poole's Index of Periodicals* it was written by "A. T. Tracy."

33. Ibid., 159.

34. Ibid., 160.

35. Ibid., 160. Self-appointed debunkers of Spiritualism often distinguished the unusual physical phenomena of the séance from Spiritualists' claims to communicate directly with the dead. Accepting table turning while scoffing at spirit communication removed the dangerous power of the medium's (often female) body from consideration, since table turning could be performed by any group of people without a medium present. See, for instance, Count Agénor Étienne de Gasparin, *Science vs. Modern Spiritualism. A Treatise on Turning Tables, the Supernatural in General and Spirits*, trans. E. W. Robert (New York: Kiggins & Kellogg, 1857), xviii.

36. Judith Butler, *Excitable Speech*, 16.

37. Elizabeth Oakes Smith is best known among scholars today as the author of *The Western Captive* (1842) and *The Sinless Child* (1843). In her own time, she was a widely published poet, a member of Edgar Allan Poe's inner circle, an outspoken women's rights advocate and lecturer, and an author of fiction. See Timothy H. Scherman, "Elizabeth Oakes (Prince) Smith," in *American Women Prose Writers: 1820–1870*, ed. Amy E. Hudock and Katharine Rodier (Detroit: Gale, 2001).

38. Elizabeth Oakes Smith, *Shadow Land; or, The Seer* (New York: Fowlers and Wells, 1852).

39. Elizabeth Oakes Smith, *Bertha and Lily; or, The Parsonage of Beech Glen* (New York: J. C. Derby, 1854). Quotations are cited parenthetically in the text.

40. Elizabeth Stoddard, "From Our Lady Correspondent. [For the Alta California]— New York, Sept. 20, 1854," *Daily Alta California*, October 22, 1854.

41. See Gail K. Smith, "From the Seminary to the Parlor: The Popularization of Hermeneutics in *The Gates Ajar*," *Arizona Quarterly: A Journal of American Literature, Culture, and Theory* 54, no. 2 (1998): 99–133, http://doi.org/10.1353/arq.1998.0000.

42. Kate Field, *Planchette's Diary* (New York: J. S. Redfield, 1868). Quotations are cited parenthetically in the text.

43. Eliza Richards, *Gender and the Poetics of Reception in Poe's Circle* (Cambridge: Cambridge University Press, 2004), 111.

44. Cox, *Body and Soul*, 20.

45. Gutierrez, *Plato's Ghost*, 141.

46. McGarry, *Ghosts of Futures Past*, 126–27.

47. Sabina Matter-Seibel, "Subverting the Sentimental: Elizabeth Barstow Stoddard's *The Morgesons*," in *Flip Sides: New Critical Essays in American Literature*, ed. Klaus H. Schmidt (Frankfurt: Peter Lang, 1995), 31.

48. For diagnostic readings of Veronica's character, see Matter-Seibel, "Subverting the Sentimental"; Hager, "Hunger for the Literal"; Stern, "'I Am Cruel Hungry'"; Putzi, "'Tattooed Still'"; Zagarell, "Repossession of a Heritage"; and Ayse Çelikkol, "*The Morgesons*, Aesthetic Predicaments, and the Competitive Logic of the Market Economy," *American Literature* 78, no. 1 (2006): 29–57, http://dx.doi.org/10.1215/00029 831-78-1-29.

49. Franchot, "Invisible Domain," 837.

50. Jennifer L. Fleissner, "Is Feminism a Historicism?" *Tulsa Studies in Women's Literature* 21, no. 1 (2002): 55, http://doi.org/10.2307/4149215.

51. McGarry, *Ghosts of Futures Past*, 126.

52. Emma Hardinge Britten, *Nineteenth Century Miracles, or Spirits and Their Work in Every Country of the Earth* (1884; repr., New York: Arno, 1976), 192.

53. William James, *The Varieties of Religious Experience: A Study in Human Nature* (London: Routledge, 2008), 14–15.

54. Daniel Cottom, "On the Dignity of Tables," *Critical Inquiry* 14, no. 4 (1988): 774, http://dx.doi.org/10.1086/448465.

Conclusion

1. Pew Research Center, *"Nones" on the Rise*, Pew Research Center: Religion and Public Life, October 9, 2012, http://pewrsr.ch/14gdLju.

2. Kimberly Winston, "Losing Our Religion: One in Five Americans Are Now 'Nones,'" *Washington Post*, October 9, 2012, https://www.washingtonpost.com/national/on-faith/losing-our-religion-one-in-five-americans-are-now-nones/2012/10/09/60dfc2e4-1218-11e2-9a39-1f5a7f6fe945_story.html?tid=ss_tw.

3. Heidi Glenn, "Losing Our Religion: The Growth of the 'Nones,'" NPR, January 13, 2013, https://n.pr/11nB2g6. Danielle Kurtzleben, "Religious Nones Are Growing Quickly: Should Republicans Worry?" NPR, June 12, 2015, https://n.pr/1I3IiP1

4. Cathy Lynn Grossman, "The Emerging Social, Political Force: 'Nones,'" *USA Today*, October 9, 2012, http://usat.ly/PkzMGk.

5. For comparison, Europeans report much lower levels of religious affiliation and practice than Americans do. According to Pew Research Center results reported in 2018, 53 percent of U.S. adults say that religion is "very important in their lives," while only 10 percent of Brits and Germans do; 36 percent of U.S. adults attend worship services at least weekly, while 8 percent of Brits and 10 percent of Germans do. See Pew Research Center, *The Age Gap in Religion around the World*, Pew Research Center: Religion and Public Life, June 13, 2018, https://pewrsr.ch/2t5iqE7.

6. Pew Research Center, *"Nones" on the Rise*.

7. Pew Research Center, *The Gender Gap in Religion around the World*, Pew Research Center: Religion and Public Life, March 22, 2016, http://pewrsr.ch/1U5n4Lz. The gender gap is smaller among Muslims than among Christians; Muslim and Orthodox Jewish men are much more likely to attend worship services than women in these traditions (for reasons related to gender norms around worship); and in sub-Saharan Africa the gender gap is almost nonexistent, regardless of religious tradition.

8. Ana Swanson, "Why Women Are More Religious Than Men," *Washington Post*, March 30, 2016, http://wapo.st/1SmxSPK?tid=ss_tw.

9. Harriet Sherwood, "Women More Religiously Devout Than Men, New Study Finds," *The Guardian*, March 22, 2016, https://www.theguardian.com/world/2016/mar/22/women-more-religiously-devout-than-men-new-study-finds.

10. Deborah Orr, "It's Not Surprising That Women Are More Religious Than Men: What Else Do They Have to Believe In?" *The Guardian*, January 23, 2015, https://www.theguardian.com/commentisfree/2015/jan/23/its-not-surprising-women-are-more-religious-than-men.

11. Mahmood, *Politics of Piety*.

12. See Fessenden, *Culture and Redemption*, 2–3.

13. Pew's analysts offered charts showing the voting behavior of the following religious groups: "Protestant/other Christian," "Catholic," "Jewish," "other faiths," "religiously non-affiliated," and "white, born-again/evangelical Christian." It is this last

group, the "white, born-again/evangelical Christians," who voted for Trump by a 65-percentage-point margin. But a footnote to the figure reports that "'Protestant' refers to people who described themselves as 'Protestant,' 'Mormon,' or 'other Christian' in exit polls" and that "the 'white, born-again/evangelical Christian' row includes both Protestants and non-Protestants (e.g., Catholics, Mormons) who self-identify as born-again/evangelical Christians." Pew Research Center, *How the Faithful Voted: A Preliminary 2016 Analysis*, Pew Research Center, November 9, 2016, http://pewrsr .ch/2fSNWBY.

14. In exit polls, half of voters (52 percent) identified themselves as "Protestant/ other Christian" (as opposed to "evangelical") and another quarter (23 percent) identified as "Catholic." See Pew Research Center, *How the Faithful Voted*. In July 2019 the *New York Times* reported that evangelical Christians made up 15 percent of the U.S. population but 26 percent of the national electorate. See Thomas B. Edsall, "Trump Needs His Base to Burn with Anger," *New York Times*, July 3, 2019, https://www .nytimes.com/2019/07/03/opinion/trump-republican-base.html. Marty, *Protestantism*, vii. It is in this most recent sense that I am employing the term in this conclusion.

15. Pew Research Center, "Racial and Ethnic Composition," *Religious Landscape Study*, Pew Research Center: Religion and Public Life, 2014, http://pewrsr. ch/1cpBNNW. Indeed, in the Pew Center's exit poll analysis, only Catholics (who are separated into "white" and "Hispanic" categories) and "born-again/evangelical Christians" are distinguished by race or ethnicity.

16. Pew Research Center, *How the Faithful Voted*.

17. Daniel Cox and Robert P. Jones, "The 2016 Religion Vote," Public Religion Research Institute (website), October 27, 2016, https://www.prri.org/spotlight/religion -vote-2016/.

18. For studies that debunk the theory that Trump voters were primarily motivated by economic anxiety, see Tyler T. Reny, Loren Collingwood, and Ali A. Valenzuela, "Vote Switching in the 2016 Election: How Racial and Immigration Attitudes, Not Economics, Explain Shifts in White Voting," *Public Opinion Quarterly* 83, no. 1 (Spring 2019), 91–113, https://doi.org/10.1093/poq/nfz011; and Marc Hooghe and Ruth Dassonneville, "Explaining the Trump Vote: The Effect of Racist Resentment and Anti-Immigrant Sentiments," *PS: Political Science and Politics* 51, no. 3 (2018), 528–34, doi:10.1017/S1049096518000367.

19. Sarah Pulliam Bailey, "Evangelicals Helped Get Trump into the White House: Pete Buttigieg Believes the Religious Left Will Get Him Out," *Washington Post*, March 29, 2019, https://www.washingtonpost.com/religion/2019/03/29/evangelicals -helped-get-trump-into-white-house-pete-buttigieg-believes-religious-left-will-get -him-out/.

20. For a discussion of Buttigieg's comments and of the Christian Left, see Elizabeth Bruenig, "The Religious Left Is Always Just about to Happen: Will it Ever Arrive?" *Washington Post*, April 11, 2019, https://www.washingtonpost.com/opinions /the-religious-left-is-always-just-about-to-happen-will-it-ever-arrive/2019/04/11 /f4500bc6-5c83-11e9-9625-01d48d50ef75_story.html.

21. For a detailed breakdown of the political affiliations of religious groups in the United States (Christian and non), see Michael Lipka, "U.S. Religious Groups and Their Political Leanings," Pew Research Center, Facttank: News in the Numbers, February 23, 2016, http://pewrsr.ch/1p0ZNNT.

22. Emily Suzanne Johnson, "How Prominent Women Built and Sustained the Religious Right," *Religion and Politics*, April 19, 2019, https://religionandpolitics.org /2019/04/16/how-prominent-women-built-and-sustained-the-religious-right/; and E. Johnson, *This Is Our Message: Women's Leadership in the New Christian Right* (New York: Oxford University Press, 2019).

23. Azza Karam, "Must It Be Either Secular or Religious? Reflections on the Contemporary Journeys of Women's Rights Activists in Egypt," in Cady and Fessenden, *Religion, the Secular, and the Politics of Sexual Difference*, 60.

24. Ann Braude, "A Religious Feminist—Who Can Find Her? Historiographical Challenges from the National Organization for Women," *Journal of Religion* 84, no. 4 (2004): 559–60, 556.

25. Sarah Pulliam Bailey, "How Rachel Held Evans Became the Most Polarizing Woman in Evangelicalism," *Washington Post*, April 16, 2015, http://wapo.st/1CPeOT1 ?tid=ss_tw.

26. Rachel Held Evans, "I'm a Pro-Life Christian: Here's Why I'm Voting for Hillary Clinton," *Vox*, August 4, 2016, https://www.vox.com/2016/8/4/12369912/hillary -clinton-pro-life.

27. Bailey, "How Rachel Held Evans."

28. Rachel Held Evans, "Is Abolition 'Biblical'?" *Rachel Held Evans* (blog), February 28, 2013, https://rachelheldevans.com/blog/is-abolition-biblical.

29. Rachel Held Evans, "'All Right, Then, I'll Go to Hell,'" *Rachel Held Evans* (blog), May 23, 2012, https://rachelheldevans.com/blog/huck-finn-hell.

30. Evans, "Is Abolition 'Biblical'?"

31. Maggie Haberman, "Trump Assails Ilhan Omar with Video of 9/11 Attacks," *New York Times*, April 13, 2019, https://www.nytimes.com/2019/04/13/us/politics /trump-ilhan-omar-sept-11.html.

32. This required a change to House rules; see Tara Law, "Congressional Rule Change Allows Head Scarves, Religious Headwear on House Floor," *Time*, January 6, 2019, http://time.com/5494964/muslim-omar-rule-change-head/.

33. Masha Gessen, "The Dangerous Bullying of Ilhan Omar," *New Yorker*, April 15, 2019, https://www.newyorker.com/news/our-columnists/the-dangerous-bullying-of -ilhan-omar.

34. Ben Weingarten, "Why Is Ilhan Omar's Collusion with Islamists Acceptable?" *The Federalist*, April 30, 2019, https://thefederalist.com/2019/04/30/ilhan-omars -collusion-islamists-acceptable/.

35. "Meet Our Khateebas," Women's Mosque of America, accessed May 29, 2019, https://womensmosque.com/about-2/meet-our-khateebahs/. The Women's Mosque of America (WMA) was brought to my attention by Tazeen Ali, who has performed ethnographic research at the mosque and whose dissertation addresses American Muslim women's cultural authority as exercised at the WMA. I am immensely grateful to Ali for sharing with me the text of an unpublished talk she delivered at Virginia Tech on December 6, 2018.

36. "FAQ," Women's Mosque of America, accessed May 29, 2019, https:// womensmosque.com/faq/.

37. "Description of Our Services," Women's Mosque of America, accessed May 29, 2019, https://womensmosque.com/about-2/description-of-our-services/.

38. "Meet Our Khateebas," Women's Mosque of America, accessed May 25, 2019, https://womensmosque.com/about-2/meet-our-khateebahs/.

39. Tazeen Ali, "Rethinking Interpretative Authority: Gender, Race, and Scripture at the Women's Mosque of America" (presentation delivered at Virginia Tech, Blacksburg, VA, December 6, 2018).

40. "About," Women's Mosque of America, accessed May 29, 2019, https://womensmosque.com/about-2/.

41. "FAQ," Women's Mosque of America, accessed May 29, 2019, https://womensmosque.com/faq/.

BIBLIOGRAPHY

Abate, Michelle Ann. "The 'Possessed' Reassessed: Elizabeth Stoddard's *The Morgesons*, the Salem Witchcraft Hysteria and Literary Anti-Nationalism." *American Transcendental Quarterly* 21, no. 1 (2007): 47–65.

Adams, Kimberly VanEsveld. "Family Influences on *The Minister's Wooing* and *Oldtown Folks*: Henry Ward Beecher and Calvin Stowe." *Religion and Literature* 38, no. 4 (2006): 27–61. http://www.jstor.org/stable/40060037.

——. "From Stabat Pater to Prophetic Virgin: Harriet Beecher Stowe's Recovery of the Madonna-Figure." *Religion and the Arts* 13, no. 1 (2009): 81–121. http://doi.org/10.1163/156852908X388340.

Ahlstrom, Sydney E. *A Religious History of the American People*. New Haven, CT: Yale University Press, 1972.

Ali, Tazeen. "Rethinking Interpretative Authority: Gender, Race, and Scripture at the Women's Mosque of America." Presentation delivered at Virginia Tech, Blacksburg, VA, December 6, 2018.

Alvarez, Elizabeth Hayes. *The Valiant Woman: The Virgin Mary in Nineteenth Century American Culture*. Chapel Hill: University of North Carolina Press, 2016.

Ammons, Elizabeth. "Stowe's Dream of the Mother-Savior: *Uncle Tom's Cabin* and American Women Writers before the 1920s." In Sundquist, *New Essays*, 155–95.

Andrews, William L. *Sisters of the Spirit: Three Black Women's Autobiographies of the Nineteenth Century*. Bloomington: Indiana University Press, 1986.

——. *To Tell a Free Story: The First Century of Afro-American Autobiography, 1760–1865*. Urbana: University of Illinois Press, 1986.

Anidjar, Gil. "Secularism." *Critical Inquiry* 33, no. 1 (2006): 52–77. http://doi.org/10.1086/509746.

Aptheker, Herbert. "The Event." In *Nat Turner: A Slave Rebellion in History and Memory*, edited by Kenneth S. Greenberg, 45–57. New York: Oxford University Press, 2003.

"Art. II.—Arminianism and Grace." *Biblical Repertory and Princeton Review* 28, no. 1 (January 1856): 28–59.

"Art. V.—the *Princeton Review* on Arminianism and Grace." *Methodist Quarterly Review* 8 (April 1856): 257–69.

Asad, Talal. *Genealogies of Religion: Discipline and Reasons of Power in Islam and Christianity*. Baltimore: Johns Hopkins University Press, 1993.

——. *Formations of the Secular: Christianity, Islam, Modernity*. Stanford, CA: Stanford University Press, 2003.

Avallone, Charlene. "Catharine Sedgwick's White Nation-Making: Historical Fiction and *The Linwoods.*" *ESQ: A Journal of the American Renaissance* 55, no. 2 (2009): 97–133. http://doi.org/10.1353/esq.0.0028.

Bailey, Brigitte. "Religious Icons, National Iconography, and Female Bodies in Hawthorne and Stowe." In *Religion in America: European and American Perspectives*, edited by Derek Rubin and Hans Krabbendam, 69–79. Amsterdam: VU University Press, 2004.

Baird, Robert. *Religion in America; or, An Account of the Origin, Progress, Relation to the State, and Present Condition of the Evangelical Churches in the United States. With Notices of the Unevangelical Denominations.* American ed. New York: Harper & Brothers, 1844.

Baker, Dorothy Z. "Puritan Providences in Stowe's *The Pearl of Orr's Island*: The Legacy of Cotton Mather." *Studies in American Fiction* 22, no. 1 (1994): 61–79. http://doi.org/10.1353/saf.1994.0002.

Balmer, Randall. *Mine Eyes Have Seen the Glory: A Journey into the Evangelical Subculture in America.* Oxford: Oxford University Press, 1993.

Barnes, Ashley C. "The Word Made Exhibition: Protestant Reading Meets Catholic Worship in *Uncle Tom's Cabin* and *The Gates Ajar.*" *Legacy: A Journal of American Women Writers* 29, no. 2 (2012): 179–200. http://doi.org/10.5250/legacy.29.2.0179.

Barnes, Elizabeth. *States of Sympathy: Seduction and Democracy in the American Novel.* New York: Columbia University Press, 1997.

——. *Love's Whipping Boy: Violence and Sentimentality in the American Imagination.* Chapel Hill: University of North Carolina Press, 2014.

Baxter, Richard. *The Saints' Everlasting Rest.* Edited by Benjamin Fawcett. First published in 1658. Boston: Lincoln and Edmands, 1828.

Baym, Nina. "The Women of Cooper's Leatherstocking Tales." *American Quarterly* 23, no. 5 (1971): 696–709. http://doi.org/10.2307/2712252.

——. *Woman's Fiction: A Guide to Novels by and about Women in America, 1820–1870.* Ithaca, NY: Cornell University Press, 1978.

——. *American Women Writers and the Work of History, 1790–1860.* New Brunswick, NJ: Rutgers University Press, 1995.

——. "Women's Novels and Women's Minds: An Unsentimental View of Nineteenth-Century American Women's Fiction." *Novel: A Forum on Fiction* 31, no. 3 (1998): 335–50. https://doi.org/10.2307/1346104.

Bednarowski, Mary Farrell. *The Religious Imagination of American Women.* Bloomington: Indiana University Press, 1999.

Beecher, Charles. *The Incarnation; or Pictures of the Virgin and Her Son.* New York: Harper & Brothers, 1849.

——, ed. *Autobiography, Correspondence, Etc. of Lyman Beecher, D.D.* New York: Harper & Brothers, 1866.

Bennett, Bridget. *Transatlantic Spiritualism and Nineteenth-Century American Literature.* New York: Palgrave Macmillan, 2007.

Berlant, Lauren. *The Female Complaint: The Unfinished Business of Sentimentality in American Culture.* Durham, NC: Duke University Press, 2008.

Berryman, Carrie Anne. "Captive Sacrifice and Trophy Taking among the Ancient Maya: An Evaluation of the Bioarchaeological Evidence and Its Sociopolitical Implications." In Chacon and Dye, *Taking and Displaying*, 377–99.

Billings, Warren M. "The Cases of Fernando and Elizabeth Key: A Note on the Status of Blacks in Seventeenth-Century Virginia." *William and Mary Quarterly* 30, no. 3 (1973): 467–74. http://doi.org/10.2307/1918485.

——. "The Law of Servants and Slaves in Seventeenth-Century Virginia." *Virginia Magazine of History and Biography* 99, no. 1 (1991): 45–62. http://www.jstor.org /stable/4249198.

Billington, Ray Allen. *The Protestant Crusade, 1800–1860: A Study of the Origins of American Nativism.* Chicago: Quadrangle Books, 1938.

Blanck, Emily. "Seventeen Eighty-Three: The Turning Point in the Law of Slavery and Freedom in Massachusetts." *New England Quarterly* 75, no. 1 (2002): 24–51. http://doi.org/10.2307/1559880.

Bloch, Maurice. *Political Language and Oratory in Traditional Society.* London: Academic, 1975.

Blum, Edward. "Slaves, Slavery, and the Secular Age." In *Race and Secularism in America,* edited by Jonathon S. Kahn and Vincent W. Lloyd, 77–98. New York: Columbia University Press, 2016.

Braude, Ann. *Radical Spirits: Spiritualism and Women's Rights in Nineteenth-Century America.* Boston: Beacon, 1989.

——. "Women's History *Is* American Religious History." In *Retelling U.S. Religious History,* edited by Thomas A. Tweed, 87–107. Berkeley: University of California Press, 1997.

——. "A Religious Feminist—Who Can Find Her? Historiographical Challenges from the National Organization for Women." *Journal of Religion* 84, no. 4 (2004): 555–72.

Brereton, Virginia Lieson. *From Sin to Salvation: Stories of Women's Conversions, 1800 to the Present.* Bloomington: Indiana University Press, 1991.

Briggs, Richard S. *Words in Action: Speech Act Theory and Biblical Interpretation.* Edinburgh: T & T Clark, 2001.

Britten, Emma Hardinge. *Modern American Spiritualism: A Twenty Years' Record of the Communion Between Earth and the World of Spirits.* 2nd ed. New York: New-York Print, 1870.

——. *Nineteenth Century Miracles, or Spirits and Their Work in Every Country of the Earth.* First published in 1884. New York: Arno, 1976.

Brooks, Joanna. *American Lazarus: Religion and the Rise of African-American and Native American Literatures.* Oxford: Oxford University Press, 2003.

——. "From Edwards to Baldwin: Heterodoxy, Discontinuity, and New Narratives of American Religious-Literary History." *American Literary History* 22, no. 2 (2010): 439–53. http://doi.org/10.1093/alh/ajq001.

Brown, Candy Gunther. *The Word in the World: Evangelical Writing, Publishing, and Reading in America, 1789–1880.* Chapel Hill: University of North Carolina Press, 2004.

Brown, Gillian. *Domestic Individualism: Imagining Self in Nineteenth-Century America.* Berkeley: University of California Press, 1990.

Brown, Henry, and Charles Stearns. *Narrative of Henry Box Brown, Who Escaped from Slavery, Enclosed in a Box 3 Feet Long and 2 Wide.* Boston: Brown and Stearns, 1849. North American Slave Narratives Collection. https://docsouth.unc.edu /neh/boxbrown/boxbrown.html.

Brown, William Wells. *Clotel, or The President's Daughter*. New York: Penguin, 2004.

Buck, Charles. *Definitions of All Religious Terms*. Philadelphia: W. W. Woodward, 1821.

Buell, Denise Kimber. *Why This New Race: Ethnic Reasoning in Early Christianity*. New York: Columbia University Press, 2005.

Buell, Lawrence. "Calvinism Romanticized: Harriet Beecher Stowe, Samuel Hopkins, and *The Minister's Wooing*." *ESQ: A Journal of the American Renaissance* 24 (1978): 119–32.

——. "Rival Romantic Interpretations of New England Puritanism: Hawthorne versus Stowe." *Texas Studies in Literature and Language* 25, no. 1 (1983): 77–99. http://www.jstor.org/stable/40754704.

——. *New England Literary Culture: From Revolution through Renaissance*. Cambridge: Cambridge University Press, 1986.

Bunyan, John. *The Pilgrim's Progress*. Mineola, NY: Dover, 2003.

Burleigh, Erica. "Sisters in Arms: Incest, Miscegenation, and Sacrifice in Catharine Maria Sedgwick's *Hope Leslie*." *New England Quarterly* 86, no. 2 (2013): 196–231. http://doi.org/10.1162/TNEQ_a_00276.

Burnham, Michelle. *Captivity and Sentiment: Cultural Exchange in American Literature, 1682–1861*. Hanover, NH: University Press of New England, 1997.

Bush, Harold K. *Continuing Bonds with the Dead: Parental Grief and Nineteenth-Century American Authors*. Tuscaloosa: University of Alabama Press, 2016.

Bush, Harold K., and Brian Yothers, eds. *Above the American Renaissance: David S. Reynolds and the Spiritual Imagination in American Literary Studies*. Amherst: University of Massachusetts Press, 2018.

Butler, Jon. *Awash in a Sea of Faith: Christianizing the American People*. Cambridge, MA: Harvard University Press, 1990.

Butler, Judith. *Excitable Speech*. New York: Routledge, 1997.

Cady, Linell E., and Tracy Fessenden. "Gendering the Divide: Religion, the Secular, and the Politics of Sexual Difference." In Cady and Fessenden, *Religion, the Secular, and the Politics of Sexual Difference*, 3–24.

——, eds. *Religion, the Secular, and the Politics of Sexual Difference*. New York: Columbia University Press, 2013.

Carby, Hazel V. *Reconstructing Womanhood: The Emergence of the Afro-American Woman Novelist*. New York: Oxford University Press, 1987.

——. "'Hear My Voice, Ye Careless Daughters': Narratives of Slave and Free Women before Emancipation." In *Black Women's Intellectual Traditions: Speaking Their Minds*, edited by Kristin Waters and Carol B. Conaway, 91–112. Hanover, NH: University Press of New England, 2007.

Carey, Jonathan S., and Sydney E. Ahlstrom. *An American Reformation: A Documentary History of Unitarian Christianity*. Middletown, CT: Wesleyan University Press, 1985.

Carroll, Bret E. *Spiritualism in Antebellum America*. Bloomington: Indiana University Press, 1997.

Carter, J. Kameron. *Race: A Theological Account*. Oxford: Oxford University Press, 2008.

Casanova, José. *Public Religions in the Modern World*. Chicago: University of Chicago Press, 1994.

Cass, Jeffrey. "Harriet Beecher Stowe's Acts of Theological Terror: Conservatism in *Uncle Tom's Cabin*." *Selected Essays from the International Conference on Word and World of Discovery*, edited by Gerald Garmon, 21–30. Carrollton: West Georgia College, 1992.

Castiglia, Christopher. *Bound and Determined: Captivity, Culture-Crossing and White Womanhood from Mary Rowlandson to Patty Hearst*. Chicago: University of Chicago Press, 1996.

Çelikkol, Ayse. "*The Morgesons*, Aesthetic Predicaments, and the Competitive Logic of the Market Economy." *American Literature* 78, no. 1 (2006): 29–57. http://dx.doi.org/10.1215/00029831-78-1-29.

Chacon, Richard J., and David H. Dye, eds. *The Taking and Displaying of Human Body Parts as Trophies by Amerindians*. New York: Springer, 2007.

Chakrabarty, Dipesh. *Provincializing Europe: Postcolonial Thought and Historical Difference*. Princeton, NJ: Princeton University Press, 2000.

Channing, William Ellery. *Sermon Delivered at the Ordination of the Rev. Jared Sparks, to the Pastoral Care of the First Independent Church in Baltimore, May 5, 1819*. Boston: Wells and Lilly, 1819.

——. "Unitarian Christianity Most Favorable to Piety: Discourse at the Dedication of the Second Congregational Unitarian Church, New York, 1826." In *The Works of William E. Channing, D.D.*, 384–400. Boston: American Unitarian Association, 1875.

——. "On Catholicism." In *The Works of William Ellery Channing, D.D., Vol. II*, 261–288. Boston: American Unitarian Association, 1903.

Chapman, Mary, and Glenn Hendler, eds. *Sentimental Men: Masculinity and the Politics of Affect in American Culture*. Berkeley: University of California Press, 1999.

Child, Lydia Maria. *Hobomok and Other Writings on Indians*. Edited by Carolyn L. Karcher. New Brunswick, NJ: Rutgers University Press, 1986.

Coleman, Dawn. *Preaching and the Rise of the American Novel*. Columbus: Ohio State University Press, 2013.

——. "The Spiritual Authority of Literature in a Secular Age." *Christianity and Literature* 67, no. 3 (2018): 519–30. http://dx.doi.org/10.1177/0148333117734161.

Cooke, George Willis. *Unitarianism in America: A History of Its Origin and Development*. Boston: American Unitarian Association, 1910.

Cottom, Daniel. "On the Dignity of Tables." *Critical Inquiry* 14, no. 4 (1988): 765–83. http://dx.doi.org/10.1086/448465.

Coviello, Peter M. *Tomorrow's Parties: Sex and the Untimely in Nineteenth-Century America*. New York: New York University Press, 2013.

Coviello, Peter, and Jared Hickman. "Introduction: After the Postsecular." *American Literature* 86, no. 4 (2014): 645–54. http://doi.org/10.1215/00029831-2811622.

Cox, Daniel, and Robert P. Jones. "The 2016 Religion Vote." Public Religion Research Institute (website), October 27, 2016. https://www.prri.org/spotlight/religion-vote-2016/.

Cox, Robert S. *Body and Soul: A Sympathetic History of American Spiritualism*. Charlottesville: University of Virginia Press, 2003.

Curseen, Allison S. "'Never Was Born [Again]': Grace, Blackness, and Harriet Beecher Stowe's Domestic Evangelicalism." In *Saving the World: Girlhood and*

Evangelicalism in Nineteenth-Century Literature, edited by Allison Giffen and Robin L. Cadwallader, 73–92. New York: Routledge, 2018.

Dalferth, Ingolf U. "Post-Secular Society: Christianity and the Dialectics of the Secular." *Journal of the American Academy of Religion* 78, no. 2 (2010): 317–45. http://dx.doi.org/10.1093/jaarel/lfp053.

Dalton, Anne B. "The Devil and the Virgin: Writing Sexual Abuse in *Incidents in the Life of a Slave Girl*." In *Violence, Silence, and Anger: Women's Writing as Transgression*, edited by Deirdre Lashgari, 38–61. Charlottesville: University Press of Virginia, 1995.

Davidson, Cathy N. *Revolution and the Word: The Rise of the Novel in America*. Oxford: Oxford University Press, 2004.

de Gasparin, Count Agénor Étienne. *Science vs. Modern Spiritualism. A Treatise on Turning Tables, the Supernatural in General and Spirits*. Translated by E. W. Robert. New York: Kiggins & Kellogg, 1857.

Dekker, George. *The American Historical Romance*. Cambridge: Cambridge University Press, 1987.

Deloria, Philip J. *Playing Indian*. New Haven, CT: Yale University Press, 1998.

Dennis, Ian. *Nationalism and Desire in Early Historical Fiction*. London: MacMillan, 1997.

Dewey, Mary, ed. *Life and Letters of Catharine M. Sedgwick*. New York: Harper & Brothers, 1871.

Dillon, Elizabeth Maddock. *The Gender of Freedom: Fictions of Liberalism and the Literary Public Sphere*. Stanford, CA: Stanford University Press, 2004.

Dippie, Brian. *The Vanishing American: White Attitudes and U.S. Indian Policy*. Middletown, CT: Wesleyan University Press, 1972.

Donaldson, Laura. "The Breasts of Columbus: A Political Anatomy of Postcolonialism and Feminist Religious Discourse." In *Postcolonialism, Feminism, and Religious Discourse*, edited by Laura E. Donaldson and Kwok Pui-lan, 41–61. New York: Routledge, 2002.

Donne, John. "Of the Progress of the Soule. The Second Anniversary." In *John Donne: The Major Works*, 218–31. Oxford: Oxford University Press, 1990.

Doolen, Andy. "Blood, Republicanism, and the Return of George Washington: A Response to Shirley Samuels." *American Literary History* 20, no. 1–2 (2007): 76–82. http://doi.org/10.1093/alh/ajm046.

Douglas, Ann. *The Feminization of American Culture*. New York: Knopf, 1977.

Douglass, Frederick. *My Bondage and My Freedom*. In *Frederick Douglass, Autobiographies*, edited by Henry Louis Gates Jr., 103–452. New York: Library of America, 1996.

——. *Narrative of the Life of Frederick Douglass, an American Slave, Written by Himself.* In *Frederick Douglass, Autobiographies*, edited by Henry Louis Gates Jr., 1–102. New York: Library of America, 1996.

duCille, Ann. *The Coupling Convention: Sex, Text, and Tradition in Black Women's Fiction*. New York: Oxford University Press, 1993.

——. "Where in the World Is William Wells Brown? Thomas Jefferson, Sally Hemings, and the DNA of African-American Literary History." *American Literary History* 12, no. 3 (2000): 443–62. http://dx.doi.org/10.1093/alh/12.3.443.

Dunbar-Ortiz, Roxanne, and Dina Gilio-Whitaker. *"All the Real Indians Died Off" and 20 Other Myths about Native Americans*. Boston: Beacon, 2016.

Du Toit, Alexander. "Who Are the Barbarians? Scottish Views of Conquest and Indians, and Robertson's 'History of America.'" *Scottish Studies Review* 26, no. 1 (1999): 29–47.

Ebel, Jonathan, and Justine S. Murison. "American Literatures / American Religions." *American Literary History* 26, no. 1 (2014): 1–5. http://doi.org/10.1093/alh/ajt062.

Edwards, Jonathan. *Some Thoughts Concerning the Present Revival of Religion in New-England*. Boston, 1742.

——. *A Careful and Strict Enquiry into the Modern Prevailing Notions of That Freedom of Will, Which is Supposed to Be Essential to Moral Agency, Vertue and Vice, Reward and Punishment, Praise and Blame*. Boston: Reprinted for Thomas Field, 1762.

Ellison, Julie. *Cato's Tears and the Making of Anglo-American Emotion*. Chicago: University of Chicago Press, 1999.

Emerson, Amanda. "History, Memory, and the Echoes of Equivalence in Catharine Maria Sedgwick's *Hope Leslie*." *Legacy: A Journal of American Women Writers* 24, no. 1 (2007): 24–49. http://www.jstor.org/stable/25679590.

"English Wesleyanism." *Puritan Recorder*, September 5, 1850, 35–36.

Ernest, John. "Beyond Douglass and Jacobs." In Fisch, *Cambridge Companion*, 218–31.

An Essay on the Freedom of Will in God and in Creatures. London: Printed for J. Roberts, 1732.

Evans, Augusta Jane. *Beulah*. Edited by Elizabeth Fox-Genovese. Baton Rouge: Louisiana State University Press, 1992.

Farnan, Christiane E. "The 'Least Drop of Oil': Locating Narrative Authority in Harriet Beecher Stowe's *The Minister's Wooing*." In Mayer and Mueller, *Beyond "Uncle Tom's Cabin,"* 95–107.

Farrell, Molly. "Dying Instruction: Puritan Pedagogy in *Uncle Tom's Cabin*." *American Literature* 82, no. 2 (2010): 243–69. http://dx.doi.org/10.1215/00029831-2010-001.

Farris, Sara R. *In the Name of Women's Rights: The Rise of Femonationalism*. Durham, NC: Duke University Press, 2017.

Felker, Christopher. *Reinventing Cotton Mather in the American Renaissance: Magnalia Christi Americana in Hawthorne, Stowe, and Stoddard*. Boston: Northeastern University Press, 1994.

Fenton, Elizabeth. *Religious Liberties: Anti-Catholicism and Liberal Democracy in Nineteenth-Century U.S. Literature and Culture*. Oxford: Oxford University Press, 2011.

——. "Open Canons: Sacred History and American History in the Book of Mormon." *J19: The Journal of Nineteenth-Century Americanists* 1, no. 2 (2013): 339–61. http://doi.org/10.1353/jnc.2013.0036.

Fessenden, Tracy. "The Convent, the Brothel, and the Protestant Woman's Sphere." *Signs* 25, no. 2 (2000): 451–78. http://dx.doi.org/10.1086/495447.

——. "Gendering Religion." *Journal of Women's History* 14, no. 1 (2002): 163–69. http://doi.org/10.1353/jowh.2002.0017.

——. *Culture and Redemption: Religion, the Secular, and American Literature*. Princeton, NJ: Princeton University Press, 2007.

——. "Disappearances: Race, Religion, and the Progress Narrative of U.S. Feminism." In Jacobsen and Pellegrini, *Secularisms*, 139–61.

———. "A Hermeneutics of Resilience and Repair." *Religion and Literature* 48, no. 2 (2016): 167–73.

Fetterley, Judith. "'My Sister! My Sister!': The Rhetoric of Catharine Sedgwick's *Hope Leslie*." *American Literature* 70, no. 3 (1998): 491–516. http://doi.org/10.2307/2902707.

Fideliter. "Calvinism versus Arminianism." *Zion's Herald and Wesleyan Journal*, October 30, 1850, 21.

Field, Kate. *Planchette's Diary*. New York: J. S. Redfield, 1868.

Fisch, Audrey A., ed. *The Cambridge Companion to the African American Slave Narrative*. Cambridge: Cambridge University Press, 2007.

Fisher, Linford D. "Evangelicals and Unevangelicals: The Contested History of a Word, 1500–1950." *Religion and American Culture: A Journal of Interpretation* 26, no. 2 (2016): 184–226. https://doi.org/10.1525/rac.2016.26.2.184.

Fisher, Philip. *Hard Facts: Setting and Form in the American Novel*. New York: Oxford University Press, 1985.

FitzGerald, Frances. *The Evangelicals: The Struggle to Shape America*. New York: Simon & Schuster, 2017.

Fleissner, Jennifer L. "Is Feminism a Historicism?" *Tulsa Studies in Women's Literature* 21, no. 1 (2002): 45–66. http://doi.org/10.2307/4149215.

Foster, Charles Howell. *The Rungless Ladder: Harriet Beecher Stowe and New England Puritanism*. Durham, NC: Duke University Press, 1954.

Foster, Edward Halsey. *Catharine Maria Sedgwick*. New York: Twayne, 1974.

———. *Susan and Anna Warner*. Boston: Twayne, 1978.

Fox-Genovese, Elizabeth. "My Statue, My Self: Autobiographical Writings of Afro-American Women." In *The Private Self: Theory and Practice of Women's Autobiographical Writings*, edited by Shari Benstock, 63–89. Chapel Hill: University of North Carolina Press, 1988.

Franchot, Jenny. *Roads to Rome: The Antebellum Protestant Encounter with Catholicism*. Berkeley: University of California Press, 1994.

———. "Invisible Domain: Religion and American Literary Studies." *American Literature* 67, no. 4 (1995): 833–42. http://doi.org/10.2307/2927901.

———. "Unseemly Commemoration: Religion, Fragments, and the Icon." In *Religion and Cultural Studies*, edited by Susan L. Mizruchi, 38–55. Princeton, NJ: Princeton University Press, 2001.

Frear, Sarah S. "'You My Brother Will Be Glad with Me': The Letters of Augusta Jane Evans to Walter Clopton Harriss, January 29, 1856, to October 29, 185[8?]." *Alabama Review* 60, no. 2 (2007): 111–41. http://doi.org/10.1353/ala.2007.0048.

Fredrickson, George M. *White Supremacy: A Comparative Study in American and South African History*. New York: Oxford University Press, 1981.

———. *Racism: A Short History*. Princeton, NJ: Princeton University Press, 2002.

Gamber, Wendy. *The Female Economy: The Millinery and Dressmaking Trades, 1860–1930*. Urbana: University of Illinois Press, 1997.

Gardella, Peter. *Innocent Ecstasy: How Christianity Gave America an Ethic of Sexual Pleasure*. New York: Oxford University Press, 2016.

Gatta, John. "Calvinism Feminized: Divine Matriarchy in Harriet Beecher Stowe." *Connotations: A Journal for Critical Debate* 5 (1995): 147–66.

——. *American Madonna: Images of the Divine Woman in Literary Culture*. New York: Oxford University Press, 1997.

——. "The Anglican Aspect of Harriet Beecher Stowe." *New England Quarterly* 73, no. 3 (2000): 412–33. http://doi.org/10.2307/366685.

Giles, Jane. "Catharine Maria Sedgwick: An American Literary Biography." PhD diss., City University of New York, 1984.

Gilmore, Michael T. "*Uncle Tom's Cabin* and the American Renaissance: The Sacramental Aesthetic of Harriet Beecher Stowe." In *The Cambridge Companion to Harriet Beecher Stowe*, edited by Cindy Weinstein, 58–76. Cambridge: Cambridge University Press, 2004.

Glazener, Nancy. *Reading for Realism: The History of a US Literary Institution, 1850–1910*. Durham, NC: Duke University Press, 1997.

Gould, Philip B. "Catharine Sedgwick's 'Recital' of the Pequot War." *American Literature* 66, no. 4 (1994): 641–62.

——. *Covenant and Republic: Historical Romance and the Politics of Puritanism*. New York: Cambridge University Press, 1996.

——. "Catharine Sedgwick's Cosmopolitan Nation." *New England Quarterly* 78, no. 2 (2005): 232–58. http://www.jstor.org/stable/30045525.

Greenwood, Andrea, and Mark W. Harris. *An Introduction to the Unitarian and Universalist Traditions*. Cambridge: Cambridge University Press, 2011.

Griffin, Susan M. "Women, Anti-Catholicism, and Narrative in Nineteenth-Century America." In *The Cambridge Companion to Nineteenth-Century American Women's Writing*, edited by Dale M. Bauer and Philip Gould, 157–75. Cambridge: Cambridge University Press, 2001.

——. *Anti-Catholicism and Nineteenth-Century Fiction*. Cambridge: Cambridge University Press, 2004.

Gubar, Susan. "What Ails Feminist Criticism?" *Critical Inquiry* 24, no. 4 (1998): 878–902. http://dx.doi.org/10.1086/448900.

Gura, Philip F. *Jonathan Edwards: America's Evangelical*. New York: Hill & Wang, 2005.

——. *The Life of William Apess, Pequot*. Chapel Hill: University of North Carolina Press, 2015.

Gutierrez, Cathy. *Plato's Ghost: Spiritualism in the American Renaissance*. New York: Oxford University Press, 2009.

Hager, Christopher. "Hunger for the Literal: Writing and Industrial Change in Elizabeth Stoddard's *The Morgesons*." *American Literature* 77, no. 4 (2005): 699–728. http://dx.doi.org/10.1215/00029831-77-4-699.

Halttunen, Karen. "Gothic Imagination and Social Reform: The Haunted Houses of Lyman Beecher, Henry Ward Beecher, and Harriet Beecher Stowe." In Sundquist, *New Essays*, 107–34.

Hamilton, Geoff. *The Life and Undeath of Autonomy in American Literature*. Charlottesville: University of Virginia Press, 2013.

Hankins, Laurel V. "The Voice of Nature: *Hope Leslie* and Early American Romanticism." *Legacy: A Journal of American Women Writers* 31, no. 2 (2014): 160–82. http://doi.org/10.2307/2927692.

Harris, Susan K. "The Female Imaginary in Harriet Beecher Stowe's *The Minister's Wooing*." *New England Quarterly* 66, no. 2 (1993): 179–98. http://doi.org/10.2307/365843.

Hartman, Saidiya V. *Scenes of Subjection: Terror, Slavery, and Self-Making in Nineteenth-Century America*. New York: Oxford University Press, 1997.

Hatch, Nathan O. *The Democratization of American Christianity*. New Haven, CT: Yale University Press, 1989.

Haynes, Rosetta R. *Radical Spiritual Motherhood: Autobiography and Empowerment in Nineteenth-Century African American Women*. Baton Rouge: Louisiana State University Press, 2011.

Hedrick, Joan D. "'Peaceable Fruits': The Ministry of Harriet Beecher Stowe." *American Quarterly* 40, no. 3 (1988): 307–32. http://doi.org/10.2307/2712953.

——. *Harriet Beecher Stowe: A Life*. New York: Oxford University Press, 1994.

Helminski, Joseph. "Harriet Beecher Stowe's Marianettes: Reconstruction of Womanhood in *The Minister's Wooing* and *Agnes of Sorrento*." In Mayer and Mueller, *Beyond "Uncle Tom's Cabin,"* 169–88.

Hendler, Glenn. *Public Sentiments: Structures of Feeling in Nineteenth-Century American Literature*. Chapel Hill: University of North Carolina Press, 2001.

Hickman, Jared Winston. "Globalization and the Gods, or the Political Theology of 'Race.'" *Early American Literature* 45, no. 1 (2010): 145–82. http://dx.doi.org/10.1353/eal.0.0090.

——. "The Book of Mormon as Amerindian Apocalypse." *American Literature* 86, no. 3 (2014): 429–61. http://dx.doi.org/10.1215/00029831-2717371.

——. *Black Prometheus: Race and Radicalism in the Age of Atlantic Slavery*. New York: Oxford University Press, 2016.

Hinks, Peter P., ed. *David Walker's Appeal to the Coloured Citizens of the World*. University Park: Pennsylvania State University Press, 2000.

Hobson, Christopher Z. *The Mount of Vision: African-American Prophetic Tradition, 1800–1950*. Oxford: Oxford University Press, 2012.

Holifield, E. Brooks. *Theology in America: Christian Thought from the Age of the Puritans to the Civil War*. New Haven, CT: Yale University Press, 2003.

Hollywood, Amy. "Gender, Agency, and the Divine in Religious Historiography." *Journal of Religion* 84, no. 4 (2004): 514–28. http://doi.org/10.1086/422478.

Hooghe, Marc, and Ruth Dassonneville. "Explaining the Trump Vote: The Effect of Racist Resentment and Anti-Immigrant Sentiments." *PS: Political Science and Politics* 51, no. 3 (2018): 528–34. http://doi.org/10.1017/S1049096518000367.

Hout, Michael, Claude S. Fischer, and Mark A. Chaves. "More Americans Have No Religious Preference: Key Finding from the 2012 General Social Survey." Institute for the Study of Societal Issues, March 7, 2013. https://sociology.berkeley.edu/sites/default/files/faculty/fischer/Hout%20et%20al_No%20Relig%20Pref%202012_Release%20Mar%202013.pdf.

Howard, June. "What Is Sentimentality?" *American Literary History* 11, no. 1 (1999): 63–81. http://dx.doi.org/10.1093/alh/11.1.63.

Hungerford, Amy. *Postmodern Belief: American Literature and Religion since 1960*. Princeton, NJ: Princeton University Press, 2010.

The Hutchinson Dictionary of World Religions. Abingdon, UK: Helicon Publishing and RM Education, 2005.

Insko, Jeffrey. "Anachronistic Imaginings: *Hope Leslie*'s Challenge to Historicism." *American Literary History* 16, no. 2 (2004): 179–207. http://www.jstor.org/stable/3568071.

———. "Passing Current: Electricity, Magnetism, and Historical Transmission in *The Linwoods.*" *ESQ: A Journal of the American Renaissance* 56, no. 3 (2010): 293–326. http://muse.jhu.edu/article/409451.

Jackson, Gregory S. *The Word and Its Witness: The Spiritualization of American Realism.* Chicago: University of Chicago Press, 2009.

Jacobs, Harriet. *Incidents in the Life of a Slave Girl, Written by Herself.* Edited by Nell Irvin Painter. New York: Penguin Books, 2000.

Jakobsen, Janet R., and Ann Pellegrini. "Introduction: Times Like These." In Jakobsen and Pellegrini, *Secularisms*, 1–35.

———, eds. *Secularisms.* Durham, NC: Duke University Press, 2008.

James, William. "The Will to Believe." In *The Will to Believe and Other Essays in Popular Philosophy.* Cambridge, MA: Harvard University Press, 1979.

———. *The Varieties of Religious Experience: A Study in Human Nature.* London: Routledge, 2008.

Jaudon, Toni Wall. "Obeah's Sensations: Rethinking Religion at the Transnational Turn." *American Literature* 84, no. 4 (2012): 715–41. http://dx.doi.org/10.1215/00029831-1901418.

———. "The Compiler's Art: Hannah Adams, the *Dictionary of All Religions*, and the Religious World." *American Literary History* 26, no. 1 (2014): 28–41. http://doi.org/10.1093/alh/ajt061.

Jauhiainen, Peter. "Samuel Hopkins and Hopkinsianism." In *After Jonathan Edwards: The Courses of the New England Theology*, edited by Oliver D. Crisp and Douglas A. Sweeney, 107–17. New York: Oxford University Press, 2012.

Jennings, Willie James. *The Christian Imagination: Theology and the Origins of Race.* New Haven, CT: Yale University Press, 2010.

Jentz, Paul. *Seven Myths of Native American History.* Indianapolis: Hackett, 2018.

Johnson, Emily Suzanne. "How Prominent Women Built and Sustained the Religious Right." *Religion and Politics*, April 19, 2019. https://religionand politics.org/2019/04/16/how-prominent-women-built-and-sustained-the -religious-right/.

———. *This Is Our Message: Women's Leadership in the New Christian Right.* New York: Oxford University Press, 2019.

Johnson, Walter. "On Agency." *Journal of Social History* 37, no. 1 (2003): 113–24. http://www.jstor.org/stable/3790316.

Jones, Anne Goodwyn. *Tomorrow Is Another Day: The Woman Writer in the South, 1859–1936.* Baton Rouge: Louisiana State University Press, 1981.

Kalayjian, Patricia Larson. "Cooper and Sedgwick: Rivalry or Respect." *James Fenimore Cooper Society Miscellany* 4 (1993): 9–19.

Kaplan, Amy. "Manifest Domesticity." *American Literature* 70, no. 3 (1998): 581–606. http://doi.org/10.2307/2902710.

Kaplan, Carla. "Narrative Contracts and Emancipatory Readers: *Incidents in the Life of a Slave Girl.*" *Yale Journal of Criticism* 6, no. 1 (1993): 93–120.

Karam, Azza. "Must It Be Either Secular or Religious? Reflections on the Contemporary Journeys of Women's Rights Activists in Egypt." In Cady and Fessenden, *Religion, the Secular, and the Politics of Sexual Difference*, 59–67.

Karcher, Carolyn L. *The First Woman in the Republic: A Cultural Biography of Lydia Maria Child.* Durham, NC: Duke University Press, 1994.

——. "Introduction." In Catharine Maria Sedgwick, *Hope Leslie; or, Early Times in the Massachusetts,* ix–xxxiii. New York: Penguin Books, 1998.

Kaufmann, Michael W. "The Religious, the Secular, and Literary Studies: Rethinking the Secularization Narrative in Histories of the Profession." *New Literary History* 38, no. 4 (2007): 607–27. http://www.jstor.org/stable/20058029.

Keane, Webb. "Language and Religion." In *Companion to Linguistic Anthropology,* edited by Alessandro Duranti, 431–38. Malden, MA: Blackwell, 2004.

Kelley, Mary. "At War with Herself: Harriet Beecher Stowe as Woman in Conflict within the Home." *American Studies* 19, no. 2 (1978): 23–40. http://www.jstor.org/stable/40641357.

——. "Introduction." In Catharine Maria Sedgwick, *The Power of Her Sympathy: The Autobiography and Journal of Catharine Maria Sedgwick,* edited by Mary Kelley, 1–41. Boston: Massachusetts Historical Society, 1993.

Kenslea, Timothy. *The Sedgwicks in Love: Courtship, Engagement, and Marriage in the Early Republic.* Boston: Northeastern University Press, 2006.

Kerr, Howard. *Mediums, and Spirit-Rappers, and Roaring Radicals: Spiritualism and American Literature, 1850–1900.* Urbana: University of Illinois Press, 1972.

Kete, Mary Louise. *Sentimental Collaborations: Mourning and Middle-Class Identity in Nineteenth-Century America.* Durham, NC: Duke University Press, 1999.

Kidd, Colin. *The Forging of Races: Race and Scripture in the Protestant-Atlantic World, 1600–2000.* New York: Cambridge University Press, 2006.

Kim, Sharon. "Beyond the Men in Black: Jonathan Edwards and Nineteenth-Century Woman's Fiction." In *Jonathan Edwards at Home and Abroad: Historical Memories, Cultural Movements, Global Horizons,* edited by David William Kling and Douglas A. Sweeney, 137–53. Columbia: University of South Carolina Press, 2003.

——. "Puritan Realism: *The Wide, Wide World* and *Robinson Crusoe.*" *American Literature* 75, no. 4 (2003): 256–88. http://dx.doi.org/10.1215/00029831-75-4-783.

Klarer, Mario. "Cannibalism and Carnivalesque: Incorporation as Utopia in the Early Image of America." *New Literary History* 30, no. 2 (1999): 389–410. http://www.jstor.org/stable/20057543.

Kohn, Denise, Sarah Meer, Emily B. Todd, and Joan D. Hedrick, eds. *Transatlantic Stowe: Harriet Beecher Stowe and European Culture.* Iowa City: University of Iowa Press, 2006.

Kramer, Michael P., and Nan Goodman, eds. *The Turn around Religion in America: Literature, Culture, and the Work of Sacvan Bercovitch.* London: Routledge, 2016.

Kucich, John. *Ghostly Communion: Cross-Cultural Spiritualism in Nineteenth-Century American Literature.* Hanover, NH: Dartmouth College Press, 2004.

Kvande, Marta, and Sara Spurgeon. "The Removes of Harriot Stuart: Charlotte Lennox and the Birth of the Western." In *Before the West Was West: Critical Essays on Pre-1800 Literature of the American Frontiers,* edited by Amy T. Hamilton and Tom J. Hillard, 213–38. Lincoln: University of Nebraska Press, 2014.

Latour, Bruno. *We Have Never Been Modern*. Translated by Catherine Porter. Cambridge, MA: Harvard University Press, 1993.

——. "Why Has Critique Run Out of Steam? From Matters of Fact to Matters of Concern." *Critical Inquiry* 30, no. 2 (2004): 225–48. http://doi.org/10.1086/421123.

——. "'Thou Shall Not Freeze-Frame,' or How Not to Misunderstand the Science and Religion Debate." In *Science, Religion and the Human Experience*, edited by James D. Proctor, 27–48. Oxford: Oxford University Press, 2005.

——. *On the Modern Cult of the Factish Gods*. Translated by Catherine Porter and Heather MacLean. Durham, NC: Duke University Press, 2010.

Lee, Jarena. *Life and Religious Experience of Jarena Lee*. In *Sisters of the Spirit: Three Black Women's Autobiographies of the Nineteenth Century*, edited by William L. Andrews, 25–48. Bloomington: Indiana University Press, 1986.

Lehman, Amy. *Victorian Women and the Theatre of Trance: Mediums, Spiritualists and Mesmerists in Performance*. Jefferson, NC: McFarland, 2009.

Leisy, Ernest Erwin. *The American Historical Novel*. Norman: University of Oklahoma Press, 1950.

Lewis, James. "'Mind-Forged Manacles': Anti-Catholic Convent Narratives in the Context of the American Captivity Tradition." *Mid-America Review* 72, no. 3 (1990): 149–67.

Li, Stephanie. *Something Akin to Freedom: The Choice of Bondage in Narratives by African American Women*. Albany: State University of New York Press, 2010.

Lindgren, Margaret. "Harriet Jacobs, Harriet Wilson, and the Redoubled Voice." *Obsidian II* 8, no. 1 (1993): 18–38. http://www.jstor.org/stable/44485362.

Lipka, Michael. "U.S. Religious Groups and Their Political Leanings." Pew Research Center, Facttank: News in the Numbers, February 23, 2016. http://pewrsr.ch/1p0ZNNT.

Locke, John. *A Letter concerning Toleration*. New York: Liberal Arts, 1950.

Lovisek, Joan A. "Human Trophy Taking on the Northwest Coast: An Ethnohistorical Perspective." In Chacon and Dye, *Taking and Displaying*, 45–64.

Lowance, Mason I., Jr. "Biblical Typology and the Allegorical Mode: The Prophetic Strain." In Lowance, Westbrook, and De Prospo, *The Stowe Debate*, 159–84.

Lowance, Mason I., Jr., Ellen E. Westbrook, and R. C. De Prospo, eds. *The Stowe Debate: Rhetorical Strategies in "Uncle Tom's Cabin."* Amherst: University of Massachusetts Press, 1994.

Luciano, Dana. "Voicing Removal: Mourning (as) History in *Hope Leslie*." *Western Humanities Review* 58, no. 2 (2004): 48–67.

Lukács, Georg. *The Historical Novel*. Translated by Hannah Mitchell and Stanley Mitchell. London: Merlin, 1962.

Lyerly, Cynthia L. *Methodism and the Southern Mind, 1770–1810*. New York: Oxford University Press, 1998.

Madison, R. D. "Sedgwick's Memorials: *Hope Leslie* and Colonial Historiography." *Literature in the Early American Republic* 4 (2012): 1–9.

Mahmood, Saba. "Women's Agency within Feminist Historiography." *Journal of Religion* 84, no. 4 (2004): 573–79. http://doi.org/10.1086/422481.

——. *Politics of Piety: The Islamic Revival and the Feminist Subject*. Princeton, NJ: Princeton University Press, 2005.

——. "Agency, Performativity, and the Feminist Subject." In *Bodily Citations: Religion and Judith Butler*, edited by Ellen T. Armour and Susan M. St. Ville, 177–224. New York: Columbia University Press, 2006.

——. *Religious Difference in a Secular Age: A Minority Report*. Princeton, NJ: Princeton University Press, 2016.

Marr, Timothy. *The Cultural Roots of American Islamicism*. New York: Cambridge University Press, 2006.

Marty, Martin. *Protestantism in the United States: Righteous Empire*. 2nd ed. New York: Charles Scribner's Sons, 1986.

Matter-Seibel, Sabina. "Subverting the Sentimental: Elizabeth Barstow Stoddard's *The Morgesons*." In *Flip Sides: New Critical Essays in American Literature*, edited by Klaus H. Schmidt, 15–41. Frankfurt: Peter Lang, 1995.

——. "Native Americans, Women, and the Culture of Nationalism in Lydia Maria Child and Catharine Maria Sedgwick." In *Early America Re-explored: New Readings in Colonial, Early National, and Antebellum Culture*, edited by Klaus H. Schmidt and Fritz Fleischman, 411–40. New York: Peter Lang, 2000.

Mayer, Sylvia, and Monika Mueller, eds. *Beyond "Uncle Tom's Cabin": Essays on the Writing of Harriet Beecher Stowe*. Madison, WI: Fairleigh Dickinson, 2011.

McCorristine, Shane, ed. *Spiritualism, Mesmerism, and the Occult, 1800–1920*. London: Pickering & Chatto, 2012.

McCray, Florine Thayer. *The Life-Work of the Author of "Uncle Tom's Cabin."* New York: Funk & Wagnalls, 1889.

McGarry, Molly. *Ghosts of Futures Past: Spiritualism and the Cultural Politics of Nineteenth-Century America*. Berkeley: University of California Press, 2008.

McHenry, Elizabeth. *Forgotten Readers: Recovering the Lost History of African American Literary Societies*. Durham, NC: Duke University Press, 2002.

McKanan, Dan. *Identifying the Image of God: Radical Christians and Nonviolent Power in the Antebellum United States*. Oxford: Oxford University Press, 2002.

Meek, Ronald. *Social Science and the Ignoble Savage*. Cambridge: Cambridge University Press, 1976.

Meltzer, Milton, and Patricia G. Holland, eds. *Lydia Maria Child: Selected Letters, 1817–1880*. Amherst: University of Massachusetts Press, 1982.

Merish, Lori. *Sentimental Materialism: Gender, Commodity Culture, and Nineteenth-Century American Literature*. Durham, NC: Duke University Press, 2000.

Meyer, Neil. "One Language in Prayer: Evangelicalism, Anti-Catholicism, and Harriet Beecher Stowe's *The Minister's Wooing*." *New England Quarterly* 85, no. 3 (2012): 468–90. http://www.jstor.org/stable/23251388.

Mizruchi, Susan L. *Religion and Cultural Studies*. Princeton, NJ: Princeton University Press, 2001.

Modern, John Lardas. *Secularism in Antebellum America*. Chicago: University of Chicago Press, 2011.

——. "My God, David Brooks." Religion Dispatches, July 28, 2013. http://religiondispatches.org/my-god-david-brooks/.

Moore, R. Laurence. *Religious Outsiders and the Making of Americans*. New York: Oxford University Press, 1986.

Morgan, David. *Protestants and Pictures: Religion, Visual Culture, and the Age of American Mass Production*. New York: Oxford University Press, 1999.

Morgan, Winifred. "Gender-Related Difference in the Slave Narratives of Harriet Jacobs and Frederick Douglass." *American Studies* 35, no. 2 (1994): 73–94. http://www.jstor.org/stable/40642688.

Mullen, Harryette. "Runaway Tongue: Resistant Orality in *Uncle Tom's Cabin, Our Nig, Incidents in the Life of a Slave Girl*, and *Beloved*." In Samuels, *The Culture of Sentiment*, 244–64.

Murphy, Gretchen. "States of Innocence: Stowe, London Needlewomen, and the New England Novel." *Legacy: A Journal of American Women Writers* 34, no. 2 (2017): 278–300. http://muse.jhu.edu/article/679781.

Nancy, Jean-Luc. "The Unsacrificeable." *Yale French Studies* 79 (1991): 20–38. http://doi.org/10.2307/2930245.

The New England Primer: To Which is Added, the Shorter Catechism of the Westminster Assembly of Divines. Concord, NH: Rufus Merrill, 1850. Sabin Americana, 1500–1926.

Nichols, Anne. "Harriet Beecher Stowe's 'Woman in Sacred History': Biblical Criticism, Evolution, and the Maternal Ethic." *Religion and Literature* 47, no. 3 (2015): 57–75. http://www.jstor.org/stable/26377442.

Nielson, Erik. "'Go in De Wilderness': Evading the 'Eyes of Others' in the Slave Songs." *Western Journal of Black Studies* 35, no. 2 (2011): 106–17.

Noble, Marianne. *The Masochistic Pleasures of Sentimental Literature.* Princeton, NJ: Princeton University Press, 2000.

Nudelman, Franny. "Harriet Jacobs and the Sentimental Politics of Female Suffering." *ELH* 59, no. 4 (1992): 939–64. http://doi.org/10.2307/2873301.

Ogden, Emily. *Credulity: A Cultural History of US Mesmerism.* Chicago: University of Chicago Press, 2018.

Opfermann, Susanne. "Lydia Maria Child, James Fenimore Cooper, and Catharine Maria Sedgwick: A Dialogue on Race, Culture, and Gender." In *Soft Canons: American Women Writers and Masculine Tradition*, edited by Karen L. Kilcup, 27–47. Iowa City: University of Iowa Press, 1999.

Orsi, Robert A. "On Not Talking to the Press." *Religious Studies News* 19, no. 3 (2004): 15.

——. *History and Presence.* Cambridge, MA: Harvard University Press, 2016.

Ortner, Sherry B. "Theory in Anthropology since the Sixties." *Comparative Studies in Society and History* 26, no. 1 (1984): 126–66. http://www.jstor.org/stable/178524.

Pagliarini, Marie Anne. "The Pure American Woman and the Wicked Catholic Priest: An Analysis of Anti-Catholic Literature in Antebellum America." *Religion and American Culture: A Journal of Interpretation* 9, no. 1 (1999): 97–128. http://doi.org/10.2307/1123928.

Painter, Nell Irvin. "Introduction." In Harriet Jacobs, *Incidents in the Life of a Slave Girl, Written by Herself*, edited by Nell Irvin Painter, ix–xxxiii. New York: Penguin Books, 2000.

Park, Edwards A. *The Theology of the Intellect and of the Feelings: A Discourse Delivered Before the Convention of the Congregational Ministers of Massachusetts, in Brattle Street Meeting House, Boston, May 30, 1850.* Andover, MA: W. F. Draper, 1850.

Parramore, Thomas C. "Covenant in Jerusalem." In *Nat Turner: A Slave Rebellion in History and Memory*, edited by Kenneth Greenberg, 58–77. Oxford: Oxford University Press, 2003.

Pateman, Carol. *The Disorder of Women: Democracy, Feminism and Political Theory.* Stanford, CA: Stanford University Press, 1989.

Pelletier, Kevin. *Apocalyptic Sentimentalism: Love and Fear in U.S. Antebellum Literature.* Athens: University of Georgia Press, 2015.

Peterson, Derek R., and Darren R. Walhof. "Rethinking Religion." In *The Invention of Religion: Rethinking Belief in Politics and History*, edited by Derek R. Peterson and Darren R. Walhof, 1–18. New Brunswick, NJ: Rutgers University Press, 2002.

Pew Research Center. *"Nones" on the Rise.* Pew Research Center: Religion and Public Life, October 9, 2012. http://pewrsr.ch/14gdLju.

——. "Racial and Ethnic Composition," *Religious Landscape Study*, Pew Research Center: Religion and Public Life, 2014, http://pewrsr.ch/1cpBNNW.

——. *Exit Polls and the Evangelical Vote: A Closer Look.* Pew Research Center, March 14, 2016. http://pewrsr.ch/1pGQG5o.

——. *The Gender Gap in Religion around the World.* Pew Research Center: Religion and Public Life, March 22, 2016. http://pewrsr.ch/1U5n4Lz.

——. *How the Faithful Voted: A Preliminary 2016 Analysis.* Pew Research Center, November 9, 2016. http://pewrsr.ch/2fSNWBY.

——. *The Age Gap in Religion around the World.* Pew Research Center: Religion and Public Life, June 13, 2018. https://pewrsr.ch/2t5iqE7.

Phillips, Charles. "Edwards Amasa Park: The Last Edwardsian." In *After Jonathan Edwards: The Courses of the New England Theology*, edited by Oliver D. Crisp and Douglas A. Sweeney, 151–62. New York: Oxford University Press, 2012.

Pierce, Yolanda. "Redeeming Bondage: The Captivity Narrative and the Spiritual Autobiography in the African American Slave Narrative Tradition." In Fisch, *Cambridge Companion*, 83–98.

Pratt, Lloyd. *Archives of American Time.* Philadelphia: University of Pennsylvania Press, 2010.

Putzi, Jennifer. "'Tattooed Still': The Inscription of Female Agency in Elizabeth Stoddard's *The Morgesons.*" *Legacy: A Journal of American Women Writers* 17, no. 2 (2000): 165–73. http://www.jstor.org/stable/25679335.

Putzi, Jennifer, and Elizabeth Stockton, eds. *Selected Letters of Elizabeth Stoddard.* Iowa City: University of Iowa Press, 2012.

Raboteau, Albert J. *African American Religion.* New York: Oxford University Press, 1999.

Reny, Tyler T., Loren Collingwood, and Ali A. Valenzuela. "Vote Switching in the 2016 Election: How Racial and Immigration Attitudes, Not Economics, Explain Shifts in White Voting." *Public Opinion Quarterly* 83, no. 1 (Spring 2019): 91–113. http://doi.org/10.1093/poq/nfz011.

Reynolds, David S. "From Doctrine to Narrative: The Rise of Pulpit Storytelling in America." *American Quarterly* 32, no. 5 (1980): 479–98. http://doi.org/10.2307/2712409.

——. *Faith in Fiction: The Emergence of Religious Literature in America.* Cambridge, MA: Harvard University Press, 1981.

Richards, Eliza. *Gender and the Poetics of Reception in Poe's Circle.* Cambridge: Cambridge University Press, 2004.

Rineer, Carla. "Stowe and Religious Iconography." In Kohn et al., *Transatlantic Stowe*, 187–207.

Robertson-Lorant, Laurie. "Mr. Omoo and the Hawthornes: The Biographical Background." In *Hawthorne and Melville: Writing a Relationship*, edited by Jana L. Argersinger and Leland S. Person, 27–49. Athens: University of Georgia Press, 2008.

Robey, Molly K. "Sacred Geographies: Religion and Race in Women's Holy Land Writings." *American Literature* 80, no. 3 (2008): 471–500. http://dx.doi/10.1215/00029831-2008-019.

——. "Domesticating Palestine: Elizabeth Champney's *Three Vassar Girls in the Holy Land*." *Tulsa Studies in Women's Literature* 35, no. 2 (2016): 365–94. http://doi.org/10.1353/tsw.2016.0030.

——. "Excavating Ethiopia: Biblical Archaeology in Pauline Hopkins's *Of One Blood*." *Studies in American Fiction* 43, no. 2 (2016): 183–206. http://doi.org/10.1353/saf.2016.0009.

Robinson, David. *The Unitarians and the Universalists*. Westport, CT: Greenwood, 1985.

Rosaldo, Michelle Z. "Toward an Anthropology of Self and Feeling." In *Culture Theory: Essays on Mind, Self, and Emotion*, edited by Robert A. LeVine and Richard A. Shweder, 137–57. New York: Cambridge University Press, 1984.

Ryan, Susan M. "Charity Begins at Home: Stowe's Antislavery Novels and the Forms of Benevolent Citizenship." *American Literature* 72, no. 4 (2000): 751–82. http://doi.org/10.1215/00029831-72-4-751.

Said, Edward W. *The World, the Text, and the Critic*. Cambridge, MA: Harvard University Press, 1983.

Samuels, Shirley, ed. *The Culture of Sentiment: Race, Gender, and Sentimentality in Nineteenth-Century America*. New York: Oxford University Press, 1992.

——. "Women, Blood, and Contract." *American Literary History* 20, no. 1–2 (2007): 57–75. http://doi.org/10.1093/alh/ajm049.

Sánchez-Eppler, Karen. *Touching Liberty: Abolition, Feminism, and the Politics of the Body*. Berkeley: University of California Press, 1993.

Santamarina, Xiomara. "Black Womanhood in North American Women's Slave Narratives." In Fisch, *Cambridge Companion*, 232–45.

Scherman, Timothy H. "Elizabeth Oakes Prince Smith." In *American Women Prose Writers: 1820–1870*, edited by Amy E. Hudock and Katharine Rodier. Detroit: Gale, 2001.

Schrag, Mitzi. "Rei(g)ning Mediums: Spiritualism and Social Controls in Nineteenth-Century American Literature." PhD diss, University of Washington, 2006.

Schultz, Kevin M., and Paul Harvey. "Everywhere and Nowhere: Recent Trends in American Religious History and Historiography." *Journal of the American Academy of Religion* 78, no. 1 (2010): 129–62. http://dx.doi.org/10.1093/jaarel/lfp087.

Schultz, Nancy Lusignan. "The Artist's Craftiness: Miss Prissy in *The Minister's Wooing*." *Studies in American Fiction* 20, no. 1 (1992): 33–44. http://dx.doi.org/10.1353/saf.1992.0022.

——. "Introduction: A Veil of Fear." In *Veil of Fear: Nineteenth-Century Convent Tales by Rebecca Reed and Maria Monk*, vii–xxxiii. West Lafayette, IN: Purdue University Press, 1999.

Scott, Joan Wallach. "Sexularism." Lecture presented at the Robert Schuman Centre for Advanced Studies Distinguished Lectures, Florence, Italy, 2009. http://hdl.handle.net/1814/11553.

——. *Sex and Secularism*. Princeton, NJ: Princeton University Press, 2017.

Sedgwick, Catharine Maria. *Mary Hollis. An Original Tale*. Concord, NH: Mead and Butters, 1834.

——. "Slavery in New England." *Bentley's Miscellany* 34 (1853): 417–424.

——. *The Power of Her Sympathy: The Autobiography and Journal of Catharine Maria Sedgwick*. Edited by Mary Kelley. Boston: Massachusetts Historical Society, 1993.

——. *Hope Leslie, or Early Times in the Massachusetts*. Edited by Carolyn L. Karcher. New York: Penguin Books, 1998.

——. *The Linwoods, or "Sixty Years Since" in America*. Edited by Maria Karafilis. Hanover, NH: University Press of New England, 2002.

——. *A New-England Tale; or, Sketches of New-England Character and Manners*. Edited by Susan K. Harris. New York: Penguin Books, 2003.

Sedgwick, H[enry] D. *The Practicability of the Abolition of Slavery: A Lecture Delivered at the Lyceum in Stockbridge, Massachusetts February, 1831*. New York: J. Seymour, 1831.

Sexton, Rebecca Grant, ed. *A Southern Woman of Letters: The Correspondence of Augusta Jane Evans Wilson*. Columbia: University of South Carolina Press, 2002.

Shea, Maura E. "Spinning toward Salvation: The Ministry of Spinsters in Harriet Beecher Stowe." *American Transcendental Quarterly* 10, no. 4 (1996): 293–310.

Shreve, Grant. "Fragile Belief: Lydia Maria Child's *Hobomok* and the Scene of American Secularity." *American Literature* 86, no. 4 (2014): 655–82. http://dx.doi.org/10.1215/00029831-2811742.

Sinanan, Kerry. "The Slave Narrative and the Literature of Abolition." In Fisch, *Cambridge Companion*, 61–80.

Singley, Carol J. *Adopting America: Childhood, Kinship and National Identity in Literature*. Oxford: Oxford University Press, 2011.

Sizemore, Michelle. *American Enchantment: Rituals of the People in the Post-Revolutionary World*. New York: Oxford University Press, 2018.

Sklar, Kathryn Kish. *Catharine Beecher: A Study in American Domesticity*. New Haven, CT: Yale University Press, 1973.

Slotkin, Richard. *Regeneration through Violence: The Mythology of the American Frontier, 1600–1860*. Middletown, CT: Wesleyan University Press, 1973.

Smith, Caleb. "Harriet Jacobs among the Militants: Transformations in Abolition's Public Sphere, 1859–61." *American Literature* 84, no. 4 (2012): 743–68. http://dx.doi.org/10.1215/00029831-1901427.

Smith, Elizabeth Oakes. *Shadow Land; or, The Seer*. New York: Fowlers and Wells, 1852.

——. *Bertha and Lily; or, The Parsonage of Beech Glen*. New York: J. C. Derby, 1854.

Smith, Gail K. "From the Seminary to the Parlor: The Popularization of Hermeneutics in *The Gates Ajar*." *Arizona Quarterly: A Journal of American Literature, Culture, and Theory* 54, no. 2 (1998): 99–133. http://doi.org/10.1353/arq.1998.0000.

——. "Art and the Body in *Agnes of Sorrento*." In Kohn et al., *Transatlantic Stowe*, 167–86.

Smith, Robert McClure, and Ellen Weinauer. *American Culture, Canons, and the Case of Elizabeth Stoddard*. Tuscaloosa: University of Alabama Press, 2003.

Sprague, William B. *Letters on Practical Subjects to a Daughter*. 2nd ed. New York: John P. Haven, 1831.

Stadler, Gustavus. "Magawisca's Body of Knowledge: Nation-Building in *Hope Leslie*." *Yale Journal of Criticism* 12, no. 1 (1999): 41–56. http://doi.org/10.1353/yale.1999.0012.

Stein, Jordan Alexander, and Justine S. Murison. "Introduction: Religion and Method." *Early American Literature* 45, no. 1 (2010): 1–29. http://www.jstor.org/stable/27856602.

Stern, Julia. "'I Am Cruel Hungry': Dramas of Twisted Appetite and Rejected Identification in Elizabeth Stoddard's *The Morgesons*." In Smith and Weinauer, *American Culture*, 107–27.

Sterne, Laurence. *A Sentimental Journey and Other Writings*. New York: Oxford University Press, 2003.

Stockton, Elizabeth. "'A Crusade against Duty': Property, Self-Possession, and the Law in the Novels of Elizabeth Stoddard." *New England Quarterly* 79, no. 3 (2006): 413–38. http://www.jstor.org/stable/20474465.

Stoddard, Elizabeth. "From Our Lady Correspondent. [For the Alta California]— New York, Sept. 20, 1854." *Daily Alta California*, October 22, 1854.

——. *The Morgesons*. New York: Carleton, 1862.

——. *The Morgesons and Other Writings, Published and Unpublished*. Edited by Lawrence Buell and Sandra Zagarell. Philadelphia: University of Pennsylvania Press, 1984.

——. "Preface to the 1901 Edition." In Elizabeth Stoddard, *The Morgesons*, edited by Lawrence Buell and Sandra A. Zagarell, 261–64. New York: Penguin Books, 1997.

Stokes, Claudia. *The Altar at Home: Sentimental Literature and Nineteenth-Century American Religion*. Philadelphia: University of Pennsylvania Press, 2014.

——. "'Sinful Creature, Full of Weakness': The Theology of Disability in Cummins's *The Lamplighter*." *Studies in American Fiction* 43, no. 2 (2016): 139–59. http://muse.jhu.edu/article/640076.

Stowe, Charles Edward, ed. *The Life of Harriet Beecher Stowe, Compiled from Her Letters and Journals*. Boston: Houghton, Mifflin, 1889.

Stowe, Harriet Beecher. "Introduction." In Charles Beecher, *The Incarnation; or Pictures of the Virgin and Her Son*, iii–ix. New York: Harper & Brothers, 1849.

——. "New England Ministers." In *Stories, Sketches, and Studies*, 218–33. Boston: Houghton, Mifflin, 1896.

——. *Agnes of Sorrento*. New York: AMS, 1967.

——. *Uncle Tom's Cabin, or Life among the Lowly*. New York: W. W. Norton, 1994.

——. *The Minister's Wooing*. Edited by Susan K. Harris. New York: Penguin Books, 1999.

Strand, Amy Dunham. "Interpositions: *Hope Leslie*, Women's Petitions, and Historical Fiction in Jacksonian America." *Studies in American Fiction* 32, no. 2 (2004): 131–64.

Stratman, Jacob. "Harriet Beecher Stowe's Preachers of the Swamp: *Dred* and the Jeremiad." *Christianity and Literature* 57, no. 3 (2008): 379–400. http://dx.doi.org/10.1177/014833310805700302.

Sullivan, Winnifred Fallers. *The Impossibility of Religious Freedom*. Princeton, NJ: Princeton University Press, 2005.

Sundquist, Eric J., ed. *New Essays on "Uncle Tom's Cabin."* Cambridge: Cambridge University Press, 1986.

Sweeney, Douglas A. *Nathaniel Taylor, New Haven Theology, and the Legacy of Jonathan Edwards.* Oxford: Oxford University Press, 2003.

Sweet, Nancy F. "Dissent and the Daughter in *A New England Tale* and *Hobomok.*" *Legacy: A Journal of American Women Writers* 22, no. 2 (2005): 107–25. http://www.jstor.org/stable/25679547.

——. "Renegade Religious: Performativity, Female Identity, and the Antebellum Convent-Escape Narrative." In Wearn, *Nineteenth-Century American Women Write Religion,* 15–32.

Szczesiul, Anthony E. "The Canonization of Tom and Eva: Catholic Hagiography and *Uncle Tom's Cabin.*" *American Transcendental Quarterly* 10, no. 1 (1996): 59–72.

Tanglen, Randi Lynn. "Reconfiguring Religion, Race, and the Female Body Politic in American Fiction by Women, 1859–1911." PhD diss., University of Arizona, 2008.

Taves, Ann. "Spiritual Purity and Sexual Shame: Religious Themes in the Writings of Harriet Jacobs." *Church History* 56, no. 1 (1987): 59–72. http://doi.org/10.2307/3165304.

Tawil, Ezra F. "Domestic Frontier Romance, or How the Sentimental Heroine Became White." *Novel: A Forum on Fiction* 32, no. 1 (1998): 99–124. http://doi.org/10.2307/1346058.

Taylor, Bayard. "Confessions of a Medium." *Atlantic Monthly* 6, no. 38 (1860): 699–715.

——. "The Haunted Shanty." *Atlantic Monthly* 8, no. 45 (1861): 57–72.

——. "The Experiences of the A.C." *Atlantic Monthly* 9, no. 52 (1862): 170–88.

Taylor, Charles. *A Secular Age.* Cambridge, MA: Belknap Press of Harvard University Press, 2007.

Thomson, Rosemarie. "Benevolent Maternalism and Physically Disabled Figures: Dilemmas of Female Embodiment in Stowe, Davis, and Phelps." *American Literature* 68, no. 3 (1996): 555–61. http://doi.org/10.2307/2928244.

Tischleder, Bärbel. "Literary Interiors, Cherished Things, and Feminine Subjectivity in the Gilded Age." *English Studies in Canada* 31, no. 1 (2005): 96–117. http://doi.org/10.1353/esc.2007.0007.

Tompkins, Jane P. *Sensational Designs: The Cultural Work of American Fiction, 1790–1860.* New York: Oxford University Press, 1985.

Tracy, A. T. "Spiritual Materialism." *Putnam's Monthly Magazine of American Literature, Science, and Art,* August 1854, 158–72.

Traister, Bryce. *Female Piety and the Invention of American Puritanism.* Columbus: Ohio State University Press, 2016.

Truth, Sojourner, and Olive Gilbert. *Narrative of Sojourner Truth, a Northern Slave, Emancipated from Bodily Servitude by the State of New York, in 1828.* Boston: J. B. Yerrinton and Son, 1850. North American Slave Narratives Collection. https://docsouth.unc.edu/neh/truth50/truth50.html.

Turner, Nat, and Thomas R. Gray. *The Confessions of Nat Turner, the Leader of the Late Insurrection in Southampton, VA.* Baltimore: Thomas R. Gray, 1831. North American Slave Narratives Collection. https://docsouth.unc.edu/neh/turner/turner.html.

Tuthill, Maureen. "Land and the Narrative Site in Sedgwick's *Hope Leslie*." *ATQ: 19th Century American Literature and Culture* 19, no. 2 (2005): 95–114.

"Uncle Richard." *Northern Regions, Or, Uncle Richard's Relation of Captain Parry's Voyages for the Discovery of a North-west Passage: And Franklin's and Cochrane's Overland Journeys to Other Parts of the World.* New York: O. A. Roorbach, 1827.

Underland, Susanna Compton. "Sentimentalism and Secularism in *Pierre*." *Leviathan* 19, no. 3 (2017): 59–78. http://dx.doi.org/10.1353/lvn.2017.0035.

——. "Sacred Spaces, Secular Fictions: Nineteenth-Century American Domestic Literature." PhD diss., University of Maryland, 2018.

Van Engen, Abram C. "Advertising the Domestic: Anne Bradstreet's Sentimental Poetics." *Legacy: A Journal of American Women Writers* 28, no. 1 (2011): 47–68. http://doi.org/10.5250/legacy.28.1.0047.

——. *Sympathetic Puritans: Calvinist Fellow Feeling in Early New England.* New York: Oxford University Press, 2015.

——. "Eliza's Disposition: Freedom, Pleasure, and Sentimental Fiction." *Early American Literature* 51, no. 2 (2016): 297–331. http://www.jstor.org/stable/43946749.

——. "Three Questions for American Literature and Religion." *Journal of American Studies* 51, no. 1 (2017): 214–20. http://doi.org/10.1017/S002187581600178X.

Vásquez, Mark G. "'Your Sister Cannot Speak to You and Understand You as I Do': Native American Culture and Female Subjectivity in Lydia Maria Child and Catharine Maria Sedgwick." *American Transcendental Quarterly* 15, no. 3 (2001): 173–90.

Volpp, Leti. "Framing Cultural Difference: Immigrant Women and Discourses of Tradition." *differences: A Journal of Feminist Cultural Studies* 22, no. 1 (2011): 90–110. http://doi.org/10.1215/10407391-1218256.

Wardley, Lynn. "Relic, Fetish, Femmage: The Aesthetics of Sentiment in the Work of Stowe." *Yale Journal of Criticism* 5, no. 3 (1992): 165–91.

Ware, Henry, Jr. *Discourses on the Offices and Character of Jesus Christ.* Boston: David Reed, 1826.

Ware, William. *Address, Delivered Nov. 24, 1825, on the Occasion of Laying the Foundation Stone of the Second Unitarian Church in New York, By the Rev. Wm. Ware, Pastor of the First Church.* Newcastle upon Tyne, UK: Newcastle Unitarian Tract Society, 1825.

Warner, Anna B. *Susan Warner ("Elizabeth Wetherell").* New York: G. P. Putnam's Sons, 1909.

Warner, Michael. *Publics and Counterpublics.* New York: Zone Books, 2002.

——. "Between Freethought and Evangelicalism: Jonathan Edwards and Benjamin Franklin." Lecture presented at the Evangelical Public Sphere lecture series, University of Pennsylvania, Philadelphia, PA, March 23, 2009. http://repository.upenn.edu/rosenbach/2/.

——. "Was Antebellum America Secular?" *Immanent Frame*, October 2, 2012. http://tif.ssrc.org/2012/10/02/was-antebellum-america-secular/.

Warner, Michael, Jonathan VanAntwerpen, and Craig Calhoun, eds. *Varieties of Secularism in a Secular Age.* Cambridge, MA: Harvard University Press, 2010.

Warner, Susan. *The Wide, Wide World.* Edited by Jane Tompkins. New York: Feminist Press, 1987.

Wearn, Mary McCartin. "Introduction." In Wearn, *Nineteenth-Century American Women Write Religion*, 1–14.

——, ed. *Nineteenth-Century American Women Write Religion: Lived Theologies and Literature*. Surrey, UK: Ashgate, 2014.

Weierman, Karen Woods. "Reading and Writing *Hope Leslie*: Catharine Maria Sedgwick's Indian 'Connections.'" *New England Quarterly* 75, no. 3 (2002): 415–43. http://doi.org/10.2307/1559786.

——. "'A Slave Story I Began and Abandoned': Sedgwick's Antislavery Manuscript." In *Catharine Maria Sedgwick: Critical Perspectives*, edited by Victoria Clements and Lucinda L. Damon-Bach, 122–38. Boston: Northeastern University Press, 2003.

Weinauer, Ellen, and Robert McClure Smith. "Introduction: Crossing Can(n)on Street." In Smith and Weinauer, *American Culture*, 1–20.

Weinstein, Cindy. *Family, Kinship, and Sympathy in Nineteenth-Century American Literature*. New York: Cambridge University Press, 2004.

——. "The Slave Narrative and Sentimental Literature." In Fisch, *Cambridge Companion*, 115–34.

Weld, Thomas. *A Short Story of the Rise, Reign, and Ruin of the Antinomians*. London, 1644.

Wesley, John. *A Plain Account of Christian Perfection, as Believed and Taught by the Rev. Mr. John Wesley, from the Year 1725, to the Year 1777*. 5th ed. London: printed by J. Paramore, at the Foundry, Moorfields, 1785.

——. *The Question, What Is an Arminian? Answered. By a Lover of Free Grace*. London: G. Whitfield, City-Road, 1798.

West, Stephen. *The Scripture Doctrine of Atonement, Proposed to Careful Examination; By Stephen West, A.M. Pastor of the Church in Stockbridge*. New Haven, CT: Meigs, Bowen and Dana, 1785.

Westra, Helen Petter. "Confronting Antichrist: The Influence of Jonathan Edwards's Millennial Vision." In Lowance, Westbrook, and De Prospo, *The Stowe Debate*, 141–58.

Wigger, John H. *Taking Heaven by Storm: Methodism and the Rise of Popular Christianity in America*. New York: Oxford University Press, 1998.

Wilson, Christopher P. "Tempests and Teapots: Harriet Beecher Stowe's *The Minister's Wooing*." *New England Quarterly* 58, no. 4 (1985): 554–77. http://doi.org/10.2307/365561.

Wilson, Robert J., III. *The Benevolent Deity: Ebenezer Gay and the Rise of Rational Religion in New England, 1696–1787*. Philadelphia: University of Pennsylvania Press, 2015.

Wright, Conrad. *The Liberal Christians: Essays on American Unitarian History*. Boston: Beacon Press, 1970.

Yellin, Jean Fagan. "Text and Contexts of Harriet Jacobs' *Incidents in the Life of a Slave Girl: Written By Herself*." In *The Slave's Narrative*, edited by Charles T. Davis and Henry L. Gates Jr., 262–82. New York: Oxford University Press, 1985.

——. *Women and Sisters: The Antislavery Feminists in American Culture*. New Haven, CT: Yale University Press, 1989.

——. *Harriet Jacobs: A Life*. New York: Basic Civitas Books, 2004.

——, ed. *The Harriet Jacobs Family Papers*. 2 vols. Chapel Hill: University of North Carolina Press, 2008.

Zagarell, Sandra. "Biographical and Critical Introduction." In Elizabeth Stoddard, *The Morgesons and Other Writings, Published and Unpublished*, xi–xxvi. Philadelphia: University of Pennsylvania Press, 1984.

——. "The Repossession of a Heritage: Elizabeth Stoddard's *The Morgesons*." *Studies in American Fiction* 13, no. 1 (1985): 45–56. http://doi.org/10.1353/saf.1985.0014.

——. "Expanding 'America': Lydia Sigourney's *Sketch of Connecticut*, Catharine Sedgwick's *Hope Leslie*." *Tulsa Studies in Women's Literature* 6, no. 2 (1987): 225–45. http://doi.org/10.2307/464270.

Zilversmit, Arthur. "Quok Walker, Mumbet, and the Abolition of Slavery in Massachusetts." *Third Series* 25, no. 4 (1968): 614–24. http://doi.org/10.2307/1916801.

INDEX

abolitionism: history of, 203n57; in *Incidents*, 91–93, 98–104, 107–11, 114; Quakers and, 21; Sedgwick, Henry and, 27; Spiritualism and, 152

Acts, book of, 100, 213n35

adoption, 68–69, 72, 79

African Americans: as characters, 51–52, 87, 126–28. *See also* Allen, Richard; Brent, Linda; Freeman, Elizabeth; Jacobs, Harriet; Lee, Jarena; Truth, Sojourner; Turner, Nat

African Methodist Episcopal (AME) Church, 96, 105

African Methodist Episcopal (AME) Church, Zion, 111

agency: definition of, 19, 154; discourse about, 78; in Douglas-Tompkins debate, 83; of enslaved persons, 92–95, 112; in ritual, 39; in women's writing, 78, 153, 156, 171–72. *See also* circulating agency; collaborative agency; communal agency; doctrinal agency; intercessory agency; religious agency; sovereign agency

Agnes (*Agnes of Sorrento*): agency of, 117, 134, 136–37, 143; as icon, 120; as Marian, 11, 118, 144, 147–49; story of, 139–142

Agnes of Sorrento (Stowe): agency in, 117, 135, 137, 143–44; as convent captivity narrative, 139–42; enchanted materiality in, 118, 130, 134; homiletic realism and, 118; incarnational theology of, 146–49; secular modernity and, 120; setting of, 135–36; as theological romance, 10, 117, 138

Allen, Richard, 96, 105, 114

Altar at Home, The (Stokes), 56, 84

Alvarez, Elizabeth Hayes, 144

American Revolution, as setting, 28, 42, 45, 50–51, 123

American Woman's Home, The (Stowe), 129

Andrews, William, 92

Annals of the American Pulpit (Sprague), 120–21

Annunciation to Mary, 144, 147–48

anti-Catholicism, 66, 136, 144, 188

anti-Muslim ideology, 87, 187–88

antislavery efforts. *See* abolitionism

Apess, William, 105

apocalypticism, 84, 119, 133

Aquinas, Thomas, 121

Arminianism: in *Beulah*, 10, 57, 60, 63, 69, 86; critique of, 66–68; definition of, 59–60; Evans, Augusta Jane and, 75, 87; free grace in, 56, 63, 66–68, 100; human will in, 70–72, 89; Christian universalism in, 100–101; in *Wide, Wide World*, 63. *See also* Calvinist-Arminian debate

Asad, Talal, 22–23, 135

Atlantic Monthly, 117, 120, 122, 156

atonement: in Arminianism, 59, 64, 101; in Calvinism, 59; Child, Lydia Maria and, 27–31; in *Hobomok*, 35–36; in *Hope Leslie*, 37–41; in *Linwoods*, 49; of nation, 27–28; Sedgwick, Catharine Maria and, 14, 25–28, 31; in spiritual autobiography, 95; theologies of, 30–31; Unitarians and, 26–31, 42–43; in *Wide, Wide World*, 61

Augustine, Saint, 95, 118

Auld, Sophia, 107, 215n66

autonomy: agency versus, 19, 112, 143; enslaved persons and, 92–94, 112–13; evangelicals and, 186; impossibility of, 23–24; modern liberal understandings of, 18, 58, 86, 112

backsliding, 60, 64

Baird, Robert, 82

baptism and enslavement, 99, 101

Baptists, 7, 105, 181, 186

Barnes, Ashley, 84, 136

Baxter, Richard, 157

Baym, Nina, 10, 33–34, 54, 63, 75

Lightning Source UK Ltd.
Milton Keynes UK
UKHW012259090820
367846UK00015B/225